Recent Advances in Parsing Technology

Text, Speech and Language Technology

VOLUME 1

Recent Advances in Parsing Technology

Edited by

Harry Bunt

Center for Language, Information and Artificial Intelligence,
Tilburg University, Tilburg, The Netherlands

and

Masaru Tomita

Institute for Environmental Sciences,
Keio University, Fujisawa, Japan

KLUWER ACADEMIC PUBLISHERS

DORDRECHT / BOSTON / LONDON

Library of Congress Cataloging-in-Publication Data

Recent advances in parsing technology / edited by Harry Bunt, Masaru Tomita.
p. cm. -- (Text, speech, and language technology ; v. 1)
Includes bibliographical references and index.
ISBN 0-7923-4152-X (hb : alk. paper)
1. Parsing (Computer grammar) I. Bunt, Harry C. II. Tomita, Masaru. III. Series.
P98.5.P38R43 1996 96-25047
CIP

ISBN 0-7923-4152-X

Published by Kluwer Academic Publishers,
P.O. Box 17, 3300 AA Dordrecht, The Netherlands.

Kluwer Academic Publishers incorporates
the publishing programmes of
D. Reidel, Martinus Nijhoff, Dr W. Junk and MTP Press.

Sold and distributed in the U.S.A. and Canada
by Kluwer Academic Publishers,
101 Philip Drive, Norwell, MA 02061, U.S.A.

In all other countries, sold and distributed
by Kluwer Academic Publishers Group,
P.O. Box 322, 3300 AH Dordrecht, The Netherlands.

Printed on acid-free paper

02-0998-150 ts

Printed in the Netherlands

Contents

CONTRIBUTING AUTHORS

Michio Aizawa, Canon Inc., Media Technology Laboratory, 890-12 Kasimada Saiwai, Kawasaki, Kanagawa 211, Japan
aizawa@cis.canon.co.jp

Rieks op den Akker, Department of Computer Science, University of Twente, P.O. Box 217, 7500 AE Enschede, The Netherlands
infrieks@cs.utwente.nl

Rens Bod, Institute for Logic, Language and Computation, Spuistraat 134, NL-1012 VB Amsterdam, The Netherlands
Rens.Bod@let.uva.nl

Eric Brill, Department of Computer Science, Johns Hopkins University, Baltimore, 21218-2694 Maryland, USA
brill@cs.jhu.edu

Harry Bunt, Center for Language, Information and Artificial Intelligence, Tilburg University, P.O. Box 90153, 5000 LE Tilburg, The Netherlands
bunt@kub.nl

Bob Carpenter, Computational Linguistics Program, Philosophy Department, Carnegie Mellon University, Pittsburgh, PA 15213, USA
carp@lcl.cmu.edu

David A. Evans, Department of Philosophy, Carnegie Mellon University, Pittsburgh, PA 15213-3890, USA

Ted Gibson, Department of Brain and Cognitive Sciences, E10-034C, Massachusetts Institute of Technology, Cambridge MA 02139, USA
gibson@psyche.mit.edu

Sadao Kurohashi, Department of Electrical Engineering, Kyoto University, Yoshida-honmachi Sakyo, Kyoto 606, Japan
kurohashi@kuee.kyoto-univ.ac.jp

Alon Lavie, School of Computer Science, Carnegie Mellon University, 5000 Forbes Avenue, Pittsburgh, PA 15213, USA
lavie@cs.cmu.edu

Rudi Lutz, School of Cognitive and Computing Sciences, University of Sussex, Falmer, Brighton BN1 9QH, East Sussex, England
rudil@cogs.susx.ac.uk

David D. McDonald, Department of Computer Science, Brandeis University, 14 Brantwood Road, Arlington MA 02174-8004, USA
mcdonald@cs.brandeis.edu

Makoto Nagao, Department of Electronics and Communication, Kyoto University, Yoshida-honmachi Sakyo, Kyoto 606, Japan
nagao@kuee.kyoto-u.ac.jp

Mark-Jan Nederhof, Faculty of Arts, University of Groningen, 9700 AS Groningen, The Netherlands
markjan@cs.kun.nl

Gerald Penn, Computational Linguistics Program, Philosophy Department, Carnegie Mellon University, Pittsburgh, PA 15213, USA
penn@lcl.cmu.edu

Stephan Raaijmakers, Institute for Dutch Lexicology INL, P.O. Box 9515, 2300 RA Leiden, The Netherlands.
raaijmakers@rulxho.leidenuniv.nl

James Rogers, Department of Computer and Information Sciences, University of Pennsylvania, Suite 400C, 3401 Walnut Street, Philadelphia, PA 19104-6228, USA
jrogers@linc.cis.upenn.edu

Ralph Rönnquist, Australian Artificial Intelligence Institute (AAII), Level 6, 171 La Trobe Street, Melbourne, Victoria 3000, Australia
ralph@aaii.oz.au

Janos J. Sarbo, Department of Computer Science, University of Nijmegen, Toernooiveld, 6525 ED Nijmegen, The Netherlands
janos@cs.kun.nl

Yves Schabes, Mitsubishi Electric Research Laboratories, 201 Broadway, Cambridge, MA 02139 USA
schabes@merl.com

Peter G. N. Scheyen, Department of Computer Science, The University of Western Ontario, Middlesex College 341B, London, Ontario N6A 5B7, Canada
pete@csd.uwo.ca

Klaas Sikkel, GMD – Forschungszentrum Informationstechnik, FIT.CSCW, Schloß Birlinghoven, D-53757 Sankt Augustin, Germany
sikkel@gmd.de

Ko van der Sloot, Center for Language, Information and Artificial Intelligence, Tilburg University, P.O. Box 90153, 5000 LE Tilburg, The Netherlands sloot@kub.nl

Tomek Strzalkowski, GE Corporate Research & Development P.O. Box 8, Schenectady, NY 12301 USA
tomek@thuban.crd.ge.com

Hozumi Tanaka, Department of Computer Science, Tokyo Institute of Technology, 2-12-1 Ookayama, Meguro-ku, Tokyo 152, Japan
tanaka@titech.ac.jp

Takenobu Tokunaga, Department of Computer Science, Tokyo Institute of Technology, Ookayama, Meguro-ku, Tokyo 152, Japan
take@cs.titech.ac.jp

Masaru Tomita, Institute for Environmental Sciences, Keio University, 5322 Endo, Fujisawa, 252 Tokyo, Japan
mt@sfc.keio.ac.jp

Akira Ushioda, Fujitsu Laboratories Ltd., 1-1, Kamikodanaka 4-chome, Nakahara-ku, Kawasaki 211-88, Japan
ushioda@flab.fujitsu.co.jp

K. Vijay-Shanker, Department of Computer and Information Sciences, University of Delaware, Newark, DE 19716 USA
vijay@cis.udel.edu

Alex Waibel, Computational Linguistics Program, Carnegie Mellon University, Pittsburgh, PA 15213-3890, USA
waibel@cs.cmu.edu

Richard C. Waters,
Mitsubishi Electric Research Laboratories, 201 Broadway, Cambridge, MA 02139 USA
dick@merl.com

Mats Wirén, Swedish Institute of Computer Science, Box 1263, S-164 28 KISTA, Sweden
wiren@sics.se

Kent Wittenburg, Bellcore, 445 South Street, MCC 1A-332R, Morristown, NJ 07962-1910, USA
kentw@bellcore.com

Note: author's affiliations as mentioned in chapter headings are those at the time of writing the original versions of the chapters. In some cases, these affiliations differ from the most recent ones mentioned in the above list.

ACKNOWLEDGEMENTS

Earlier versions of the chapters in this book were originally presented at the *Third International Workshop on Parsing Technologies – IWPT'93*, held at Tilburg University, the Netherlands, and in the 'Sanglier des Ardennes' conference hotel in Durbuy, Belgium, on August 10-13, 1994. The workshop was organized by Masaru Tomita (general chair) and Harry Bunt (workshop chair), together with the programme committee for reviewing the submitted papers. At the workshop, 29 accepted papers were presented plus an invited paper by Makoto Nagao. Of these 30 papers, 19 have been selected and revised for publication in this volume, based on recommendations by the programme committee.

The members of the programme committee were: Robert Berwick, Harry Bunt, Ken Church, Aravind Joshi, Ronald Kaplan, Martin Kay, Bernard Lang, Makoto Nagao, Anton Nijholt, Mark Steedman, Henry Thompson, Masaru Tomita (chair), K. Vijay-Shanker, Yorick Wilks, and Kent Wittenburg. We gratefully acknowledge their efforts in reviewing the workshop contributions.

We also wish to express our thanks to Arthur van Horck and Gerrit Rentier for their help in preparing the final manuscript of this book.

Harry Bunt and Masaru Tomita

1. PARSING TECHNOLOGIES AND WHY WE NEED THEM

HARRY BUNT
Institute for Language Technology and Artificial Intelligence
Tilburg University

1. PARSING TECHNOLOGIES

Parsing technologies are concerned with the automatic decomposition of complex structures into their constituent parts, with structures in formal or natural languages as their main, but certainly not their only domain of application. The development of parsing technologies raises a wide variety of computational, linguistic, and mathematical issues, as well as technical issues relating to advanced software engineering and systems design. Some of the most important of these issues are the following:

- *Scope:* To what kinds of structure does a given technology apply? Given a particular class of structures, which technologies can be used to parse them?
- *Effectiveness:* Given a parsing technology and a class of structures within its scope, in what application domains can the technology be effectively used?
- *Efficiency:* How fast does the technology work? How much memory and other computational resources does it require? What is its worst case performance, and what is its performance on a representative sample of data?
- *Robustness:* Does the technology behave well when applied to corrupted or unexpected input? Can it deliver partial results? Does it produce useful results if it cannot fully process a given input?
- *Learnability:* Does the technology involve algorithms that can effectively be learned, by machine and/or by humans?
- *Integration:* Is the technology suitable for integration with other processing, for instance with semantic interpretation, with signal processing, or with text editing?

H. Bunt and M. Tomita (eds.), Recent Advances in Parsing Technology, 1–10.

Parsing is usually not a goal in itself, but is intended to be instrumental to the recognition, interpretation, or transformation of complex structures. The relative importance of the issues relating to parsing technology therefore depends very much on the intended application.

In computer science, where parsing technologies emerged for the interpretation of computer programs, the most important issues are efficiency and robustness. Efficiency is important because of the obvious desire for rapid compilation and interpretation of program code during software development; robustness is important because syntactically incorrect expressions should not result in a breakdown, but should be detected, diagnosed, and reported.

The application of computers to natural language parsing raised the issue of scope for existing parsing technologies. A large volume of research on the (non-)context-freeness of natural languages has been conducted, inspired by the question whether parsing technologies developed for context-free formal languages would be applicable in natural language processing. This has played in role in the emergence of a variety of formalisms for representing grammatical knowledge which enrich traditional context-free descriptions in various ways, such as Augmented Phrase Structure Grammar (APSG), Generalized Phrase Structure Grammar (GPSG), Head Grammar, and Discontinuous Phrase-Structure Grammar (DPSG). In the domain of parsing research, Tomita's work on generalizing LR parsing to ambiguous languages (Tomita, 1986) is a famous example directly concerned with enlarging the scope of an existing technology (as well as with optimizing its efficiency).

Parsing techniques that have been developed especially for natural languages tend to depend very much on the kind of grammatical description they are intended to take into account, as Nagao argues in chapter 5 of this book. One reason why we need new parsing technologies is that, as new grammar formalisms develop from studies into the syntactic structure of natural languages, existing technologies have to be adapted or entirely new technologies must be developed.

When natural language parsing is intended to be instrumental for speech recognition, or for language processing in a multimodal context, the issue of integration becomes very important and often puts parsing technologies in a new light. A successful parser for written text, for instance, may be entirely inadequate in a speech recognition context, as a result of the uncertainty of input signal recognition; similarly, if spoken language is to be interpreted in a context where visual or gestural information is available, a parsing technology which depends on the linear structure of purely linguistic inputs may be inappropriate. The rapid advances in speech technology and multimedia applications cause an increasing demand for parsing technologies where language, speech, and other modalities are integrated. In applications of parsing in text or spoken discourse *understanding*, integration is also an issue of central importance. For instance, a parsing method that cleverly 'packs' alternative parses in a compact data structure may be an unfortunate choice from the point of view of on-line semantic interpretation, where each alternative parse has to be considered separately.

The effectiveness and robustness of natural language parsing technologies closely relate to the integration issue. Effectiveness is the success of a technology in meeting the requirements of an application. Applications, as we noted, typically require parsing to be useful for further processing, which mostly entails demands on integration. Applications typically require robustness: appropriate behaviour for imperfect inputs. Natural language parsers always have to deal with 'imperfect' sentences, due to deviant linguistic behaviour, to typing and speaking errors, and to the occurrence of inputs which are outside the coverage of the parser's grammar. Inputs that cause problems for purely syntactic parsing can often be processed successfully by taking other information into account; use of semantic and pragmatic information is probably the key to achieving robustness, rather than the use of special syntax-based devices or syntactic probabilities.

Natural language parsing also raises the issue of learnability, because humans are able to parse natural language expressions extremely effectively, robustly, and efficiently, and fully integrated with other perceptual and cognitive processing. This suggests that designers of parsing algorithms would do well to take their inspiration from what we know about human parsing. This appears not to happen very much, perhaps because the processing power of computers is believed to enable parsing behaviour superior to what can be achieved by modelling human processing, just like brute-force techniques have produced chess playing programs that outperform programs modelled after human chess playing, and in fact outperform most human chess players. Also, some researchers believe that the traditional approach of describing linguistic competence in a rule-based fashion is fundamentally wrong, and that language should be characterized stochastically, in terms of the probabilities of linguistic patterns to occur in certain contexts; this naturally leads to conceiving of natural language parsing as a stochastic process, a view which is taken in several of the chapters in this book.

Efficiency, finally, or rather *speed*, very much remains the name of the game in the end, also in the case of natural language parsing. Parsing technologies can be compared on all the dimensions corresponding to the issues listed above, and it depends on the situation and on one's goals how these dimensions should be weighed; in any case, for many practical applications the time the parser needs to produce useful results is of crucial importance.

Parsing is not restricted to computer programs and natural language texts. With the growing importance of multimedia, other input structures are rapidly gaining importance. This is yet another reason why we need new parsing technologies. Powerful parsing technologies of two- as well as threedimensional structures are needed to make full use of the potential of graphical interfaces and of the graphical elements in multimodal interfaces. The last two chapters in this book are devoted to this area.

2. ABOUT THIS BOOK

The chapters in this book all address one or more of the issues related to parsing, mentioned above. The first 7 chapters are all concerned in one way or another with the scope of an existing parsing technology, or with developing new approaches intended to apply to relatively new formalisms for representing linguistic knowledge.

In chapter 2, entitled *Fully Incremental Parsing*, Mats Wirén and Ralph Rönnquist generalize the parsing-as-deduction technology to a form of non-cumulative text production where changes can be made to already parsed material, for example by a person using a grammar-checking text editor. The basic approach is to exploit the properties of a chart to determine which parts of the string need to be reanalysed in response to a change, thereby obtaining an incremental solution. The approach has the advantage of a very low overhead of keeping and using the chart information. The proposed technology has been implemented for on-line processing under a simple text editor, thus providing a system which parses a text simultaneously as it is entered and edited.

In chapter 3, *Increasing the Applicability of LR Parsing*, Mark-Jan Nederhof and Janos Sarbo discuss a phenomenon present in some context-free grammars, called *hidden left recursion*, which forms an obstacle to standard LR parsing. They indicate a range of solutions to this problem. One solution is a variant of (generalized) LR parsing, which yields smaller parsers than other solutions, measured in the number of states. They show that this new parsing technique can be used both with and without lookahead, and that nondeterminism can be realized using backtracking or using a graph-structured stack.

James Rogers and K. Vijay-Shanker examine in chapter 4, *Towards a Formal Understanding of the Determinism Hypothesis in D-Theory*, the meaning of Marcus' determinism hypothesis within the context of D-theory parsing, and propose a definition based on the notion of the 'standard referent' (Marcus et al., 1983). With this definition, D-theory parsers can be understood as a means of accommodating, through the use of *descriptions of trees* rather than trees, a degree of ambiguity which is strictly limited by the definition of the standard referent. The authors develop a formal framework in which various notions of standard referent can be defined, and which allows a formal characterization of the circumstances under which a parser meets the determinism hypothesis.

In chapter 5, *Varieties of Heuristics in Sentence Parsing*, Makoto Nagao makes a brief comparison between phrase structure grammar, dependency grammar, case grammar and some other kinds of grammar, and argues that a combination of dependency analysis and case frame analysis is the best approach for parsing word-order-free languages such as Japanese. He indicates how methods of ambiguity resolution, anaphora and ellipsis estimation, and classification of referential property and number fit into this approach.

Chapter 6, *Parsing as Dynamic Interpretation of Feature Structures* by Harry Bunt and Ko van der Sloot, develops an approach to parsing based on the dynamic semantic interpretation of a formal language in which grammatical knowledge is expressed. For the formal language they use EL, which has been defined and implemented independently for computational semantic applications, and enrich it with the basic constructions and operations of typed feature structures. The semantics of the resulting language 'Generalized EL' (GEL) is defined model-theoretically, with the unusual feature that GEL models contain both the familiar kinds of 'semantic' objects, relations, etc. but also syntactic concepts. In GEL one can express dominance and precedence structures as well as grammar rules. A grammar rule in GEL can be viewed as a proposition in dynamic semantics: it can be evaluated recursively, resulting in the minimal changes in the model, needed to make the proposition true. For a syntactic rule, this may correspond to creating an object in the model that corresponds to a phrasal node. The viability of this idea is demonstrated by an implementation of chart parsing of DPSG (see Bunt, 1996) and an emulation of HPSG parsing.

In chapter 7, *Proof Theory for HPSG Parsing*, Stephan Raaijmakers, reinterprets HPSG in a proof-theoretic context. He describes a decision procedure to establish whether a given string is generated by a given HPSG grammar. This eploits the insight that HPSG can be viewed as a fragment of linear logic, subject to partiality and side conditions on inference rules. He shows how HPSG signs can be mapped onto quantified formulae, which can be interpreted as second-order types, according to the Curry-Howard isomorphism. The type inferencing is based on a partial logic for the undirected implication connective, plus the usual quantifier introduction and elimination rules. The author shows how this logical perspective can be turned into a parsing perspective.

The next group of chapters is devoted to the efficiency and robustness of parsing techniques. In chapter 8, *Efficient Parsing of Compiled Typed*

Attribute-Value Logic Grammars, Bob Carpenter and Gerald Penn propose an alternative to the standard unification-based approach to processing attribute-value logic grammars, which is similar to Prolog interpretation. The alternative, embodied in the Attribute-Logic Engine, is based on the Warren Abstract Machine (WAM) approach to *compiling* Prolog. The WAM has proven to be the most efficient architecture yet developed for implementing parsers for unification-based grammars. The authors show how grammars, based on attribute-value logic, can be efficiently compiled into low-level Prolog instructions which exploit the inherent efficiency of the WAM. Just as for Prolog programs themselves, the compilation of grammars leads to a boost in efficiency of at least an order of magnitude over interpreted code.

The next chapter, *Predictive Head-Corner Chart Parsing* by Klaas Sikkel and Rieks Op den Akker (chapter 9), gives a formal presentation of a head-corner chart parser enhanced with prediction, and analyses its time- and space-complexity. The head-corner approach, which is motivated by linguistic arguments, cannot be claimed to be more efficient in general then other technologies, such as (generalized) left-corner parsing. It is a heuristic approach, that can be expected to be efficient when most of the feature information of a constituent is located in the head. It is therefore important to consider what happens when the heuristic doesn't pay off. The authors prove that the worst-case behaviour has cubic time complexity in the length of the input.

Chapter 10, *GLR* - An Efficient Noise-Skipping Parsing Algorithm for Context-Free Grammars* by Alon Lavie and Masaru Tomita, describes GLR*, an enhanced version of the standard Generalized LR parser that can parse any input string by ignoring unrecognizable parts. Given a grammar G and an input string S, GLR* finds and parses S', the maximal subset of words of S such that $S' \in L(G)$. Skipping of words is accommodated by allowing shift operations from inactive state nodes of the graph-structured stack. The algorithm is coupled with a beam-search-like heuristic, that controls the shifting from inactive states to a limited beam, and maintains computational tractability. GLR* has been implemented and integrated with the latest version of the Generalized LR Parser/Compiler. The authors report experiments on the effectiveness of GLR* parsing, indicating that the approach can successfully handle two major problems of parsing spontaneous speech: noise contamination and limited grammar coverage.

Chapter 11 by Tomek Strzalkowski and Peter Scheyen presents an evaluation of the Tagged Text Parser (TTP), a fast and robust natural language parser designed to process vast quantities of unrestricted text. A novel feature of TTP is that it has a skip-and-fit recovery mechanism that allows for fast closing of difficult sub-constituents after a preset amount of time has elapsed without producing a parse. Though a complete analysis is attempted for each sentence, the parser may ignore fragments of input, which are later analyzed separately and attached as incomplete constituents to the main parse tree. At present, TTP is a part of a natural language information retrieval system. Along with a stochastic part-of-speech tagger, morpho-lexical stemmer and phrase extractor, it constitutes the linguistic pre-processor built on top of a statistical information retrieval system. In various experiments a significant increase of retrieval precision was noted over the purely statistical base system; therefore, at least in applications such as document retrieval or information extraction, TTP-level parsing appears very useful.

The four chapters to follow are concerned with stochastic approaches to language processing. In the first chapter of this group, *Learning to Parse with Transformations* (chapter 12), Eric Brill describes a new technique for parsing free text: a grammar is automatically learned, capable of parsing text into binary-branching syntactic trees. Experiments have shown that these parses conform with high accuracy to the structural descriptions specified in a manually annotated corpus. Starting from a very naive state of knowledge about phrase structure, the algorithm repeatedly compares the results of bracketing in the current state to proper bracketing provided in a training corpus. In this way, the system learns a set of simple structural transformations that can be applied to reduce the number of errors. The chapter presents results and comparisons to other recent achievements in automatic grammar induction.

In chapter 13, Akira Ushioda, David Evans, Ted Gibson, and Alex Waibel describe a mechanism for automatically estimating frequencies of verb subcategorization frames in a large corpus. A tagged corpus is first partially parsed to identify noun phrases and then a regular grammar is used to estimate the appropriate subcategorization frame for each verb token in the corpus. In an experiment involving the identification of six fixed subcategorization frames the system showed more than 80% accuracy. In addition, a new statistical method enables the system to learn patterns of errors based on a set of training samples, and substantially improves the accuracy of the frequency estimation.

Chapter 14 by Rens Bod, *Monte Carlo Parsing*, focuses on a central problem in stochastic language processing, that of finding the most probable parse. The Viterbi algorithm is a well-known tool to calculate the most probable derivation of a string generated by a stochastic context-free grammar. In language models that use different derivations, however, like Data Oriented Parsing or Stochastic Lexicalized Tree-Adjoining Grammar, the most probable derivation does not necessarily produce the most probable parse. Bod shows that by applying Monte Carlo techniques the maximum probability parse can be estimated as accurately as desired in polynomial time. For stochastic grammars that are parsable in cubic time, the time complexity of estimating the most probable parse with Monte Carlo techniques turns out to be $O(n^3\varepsilon^{-2})$, where n is the length of the input string and ε the estimation error. Experiments on a set of manually corrected trees from the Penn Treebank showed 96% parse accuracy.

In Chapter 15, *Stochastic Tree-Insertion Grammar*, Yves Schabes and Richard Waters argue that the formalism they call 'Stochastic Lexicalized Tree-Insertion Grammar' (SLTIG) is an attractive compromise between the parsing efficiency of stochastic context-free grammar (SCFG) and the lexical sensitivity of Stochastic Lexicalized Tree-Adjoining Grammar (SLTAG). SLTIG is a restricted form of SLTAG, not allowing wrapping auxiliary trees, which can only generate context-free languages and can be parsed in cubic time. SLTIG combines the processing speed of SCFG with the greater ability of SLTAG to capture distributional information about words. As such, SLTIG has the potential of being a very useful tool for natural language processing tasks where statistical assessment/prediction is required.

The next group of chapters is concerned with the issue of integration in natural language parsing. In chapter 16, *The Interplay of Syntactic and Semantic Node Labels in Parsing*, David McDonald presents extensions to the theory of semantic grammars. These extensions make semantic grammars linguistically disciplined and more systematic to develop, while retaining the strength that comes from linking the categories used by the parser with the semantic categories of the domain model. He describes how the domain-specific labels on the productions of a semantic grammar can be complemented by labels from standard syntactic vocabulary, and how these syntactic labels can extend the capacity of the grammar by providing default interpretations of standard constructions. The author also describes how to systematically instantiate the semantic grammar rules for relational object types in the domain model, by assigning them to families of phrase structure trees in a Tree Adjoining Grammar. These techniques are fully implemented and run as part of the Sparser text understanding system.

Chapter 18, *Integration of Morphological and Syntactic Analysis Based on GLR Parsing* by Hozumi Tanaka, Takenobu Tokunaga and Michio Aizawa, addresses the problems of morphosyntactic analysis of Japanese and other languages which are written without spaces between words, and thus present a segmentation problem. Segmentation, i.e. the identification of word boundaries, is a very important process, since the wrong segmentation may cause fatal errors in later stages such as syntactic, semantic and contextual analysis. Correct segmentation is not always possible with morphological information only; syntactic, semantic and contextual information are also necessary to resolve the ambiguities in segmentation. The authors propose a method to integrate morphological and syntactic parsing, representing morphological constraints in connection matrices and syntactic constraints in CFGs, and compiling both kinds of constraints into an LR table. The compiled LR table makes it possible to use the existing, efficient generalized LR parsing technology. The proposed method has been implemented using the EDR dictionary with 300,000 words. The method proposed in this chapter is also applicable to the integration of phonological and syntactic analysis.

Sadao Kurohashi and Makoto Nagao in chapter 18, *Structural Disambiguation in Japanese by Case Structure Evaluation based on Examples in a Case Frame Dictionary*, propose a method to integrate certain semantic information into parsing for the purpose of structural disambiguation. They use case frame structures to represent the semantic information, and electronic resources such as a verb dictionary and a thesaurus to find the relevant information. Both word sense ambiguity and structural ambiguity present difficulties for the consultation of verb dictionaries. A conventional method for solving these problems is to use selectional restrictions, but this method has a drawback in the semantic marker system — the trade-off between descriptive power and construction cost. To overcome this, the authors propose a method where a proper case frame for an input is selected using a measure of the similarity between the input and typical example sentences of each case frame. The authors report an experiment testing the effectiveness of this method for resolving structural ambiguity in comparison with commercial machine translation systems, based on the use of semantic markers, and shows that their method is far superior.

The last two chapters of this book are devoted to the parsing of two- or moredimensional structures.

Chapter 19, *Flowgraph Parsing*, by Rudi Lutz, is concerned with the analysis of diagrams. Many computer applications make use of diagrams to represent complex objects, where it is often necessary to recognize how a diagram has been pieced together from other diagrams. Examples are electrical circuit analysis, and program understanding in the plan calculus. In these applications the recognition process can be formalized as flowgraph parsing, where a flowgraph is defined as a particular kind of graph. Nodes in a flowgraph are connected to each other via intermediate points known as 'tie-points'. In earlier work, the author generalized chart parsing of context-free string languages to context-free flowgraph languages, enabling bottom-up and top-down recognition of flowgraphs. However, there are various features of the plan calculus that complicate this - in particular attributes, structure sharing, and relationships between tie-points. This chapter presents a chart parsing algorithm for analysing graphs with all these features, suitable for both program understanding and digital circuit analysis. For a fixed grammar, the algorithm runs in time polynomial in the number of tie-points in the input graph.

The final chapter by Kent Wittenburg, *Predictive Parsing for Unordered Relational Languages*, is concerned with predictive parsing of multidimensional structures. More specifically, the author discusses motivations and methods for predictive, Earley-style parsing of multidimensional languages when the relations involved do not necessarily yield an ordering, e.g., when the relations in the input are symmetric or nontransitive, as is the case in some real-world application domains. The solution which is offered involves guaranteeing that a single start position for parsing can be associated with any member of an input set of relations. Wittenburg presents the first known predictive, Early-style parsing algorithm for the full class of Atomic Relational Grammars, a class of grammars that appears to be widely useful. An implementation of the proposed algorithm has been applied to incremental parsing in user interfaces and off-line verification of multidimensional data.

References

Bunt, H.C. (1996) Formal tools for modelling and processing discontinuous constituency. In H.C. Bunt & A. van Horck (eds.) *Discontinuous Constituency*. De Gruyter, Berlin.

Marcus, M.P., Hindle, D., and Fleck, M.M. (1983) D-theory: Talking about talking about trees. *Proceedings of the 21st Annual Meeting of the Association for Computational Linguistics.*

Tomita, M. (1986) *Efficient Parsing for Natural Language.* Kluwer Academic Publishers, Boston/Dordrecht.

2. FULLY INCREMENTAL PARSING

MATS WIRÉN
Fachrichtung Computerlinguistik, Universität des Saarlandes, Saarbrücken

AND

RALPH RÖNNQUIST
Department of Computer and Information Science
Linköping University

Abstract.
This chapter generalizes the notion of parsing as deduction to non-cumulative text production, in which changes can be made to already parsed material, for example, by a person using a grammar-checking text editor. The basic approach is to exploit the properties of a chart to determine which parts of the string need to be reanalysed in response to a change, thereby obtaining an incremental solution. An implementation of the proposed technique exists, which has been adapted to on-line processing under a simple text editor, thus providing a system which parses a text simultaneously as it is entered and edited.

1. INTRODUCTION

1.1. THE PROBLEM

Incremental parsing of written language can be performed in two ways: either in a piecemeal, cumulative fashion as a text is extended from left to right,[1] or in such a way that arbitrary changes are handled, for example, as the text is modified with an editor. We refer to these notions as *left-to-right* (*LR*) *incrementality* and *full incrementality*, respectively.

LR-incremental parsing can be handled by a monotonic algorithm: as the text grows from left to right, new lemmas are added to the analysis, but

[1]Strictly speaking front to back, that is, in the conventional direction of writing.

H. Bunt and M. Tomita (eds.), Recent Advances in Parsing Technology, 11–34.

none are removed. Chart parsing and its deductive analogue (Pereira and Warren, 1983) are necessarily monotonic and often LR incremental, and constitute a commonly used technique for this task. In contrast, fully incremental parsing is non-monotonic: if, for instance, a new word is inserted in the midst of the text, then some lemmas become invalid.

Several approaches to LR-incremental parsing exist, for example, Marcus (Marcus, 1980; Marcus, 1987) (based on deterministic parsing), Pareschi (Pareschi, 1987) (chart parsing with combinatory categorial grammar), and Tomita (Tomita, 1985) (chart-based, pseudo-parallel LR parsing). Furthermore, Tomita's system and several others are able to unparse deletions from right to left.

Fully incremental parsing has long been studied in interactive language-based programming environments, and it was in this area that the problem was first stated (Lindstrom, 1970; Earley and Caizergues, 1972; Ghezzi and Mandrioli, 1979; Ghezzi and Mandrioli, 1980). Incremental parsing and compilation have here been used to perform syntactic analysis and type checking, to report errors, and to generate code while a program is being edited (see, for example, (Reps and Teitelbaum, 1987; Reps and Teitelbaum, 1989) and (Shilling, 1991)). However, as for natural-language approaches, we are only aware of (Wirén, 1989; Wirén, 1992). Rekers and Koorn's (Rekers and Koorn, 1991) adaptation of Tomita's algorithm to substring parsing is indeed relevant, but the extent to which it is useful for incremental parsing is not yet clear. Vilares Ferro's (Vilares Ferro, 1990) preliminary work on adapting Earley's algorithm to incremental parsing is also relevant, but its applicability to the problem studied here is not clear to us.

The aim of this chapter is to further develop our approach to fully incremental parsing, particularly its formal basis. Most of the material of the chapter can be found in (Wirén, 1992). A first treatment of the same basic problem was reported by (Wirén, 1989).

1.2. MOTIVATIONS

From an engineering point of view, the main motivation for exploring fully incremental parsing is that it can be used to support highly interactive text-processing tasks, for example, checking of grammar, spelling and style immediately and in real time within a text-editing environment. Currently, several systems exist that attempt to deal with aspects of this task (Dale, 1989), but none of those that parse a text make use of incremental parsing.

By furthermore combining incremental parsing with incremental generation, and by adopting a bidirectional grammar (thereby allowing the same linguistic structures to be used in both directions), one could begin to explore highly interactive text-processing facilities such as the following:

- Structure-editing operations, for instance, changing the number of a noun phrase from singular to plural.[2]
- Propagation of minimal grammatical changes triggered by a text-editing operation, as in the following German example, which presupposes that "Editor" is changed from singular to plural form:

  "Der neue Editor erkennt Inkonsistenzen" $\leadsto$

  "Die neuen Editoren erkennen Inkonsistenzen"

- On-line translation, in which the target-language text is generated in parallel with the source-language text (Somers *et al.*, 1990; Somers, 1991).

An appealing way of thinking about a system of this kind is as a *linguistic spreadsheet*, in which the effects of small changes of a text immediately ripple through the analysis and (possibly) back to the text. The fact that word processing is among the largest applications of personal computing provides additional motivation for attempts at exploring such systems.

From a psycholinguistic point of view, fully incremental parsing (and interpretation) might be useful for modelling re-reading of written text following an erroneous encoding of a word or constituent. It might also be useful for handling repair moves in spoken language, since, in effect, these change parts of previously produced utterances from the point of view of both the speaker and hearer (Levelt, 1989; Neumann and van Noord, 92, page 478ff.).

1.3. OUTLINE OF THE CHAPTER

The rest of this chapter is organized as follows: In section 2, we begin by outlining the overall incremental process. Section 3 then specifies the algorithm for reparsing. To obtain a measure of the minimal amount of work needed to handle a change, section 4 introduces the notions of affected and regenerated edge sets. Section 5 then defines a dependency relation on the set of chart edges and describes how the affected set can be approximated based on this relation. Section 6 goes on to describing the primitive changes used. Section 7 considers formal properties of the system. Section 8 briefly describes the experiences of an implementation. Finally, section 9 provides the conclusions.

[2] Similar operations, such as transforming a Pascal *while* statement to the corresponding *repeat* statement, are available in syntax-directed program editors (Reps and Teitelbaum, 1987, page 30).

2. THE CHANGE–UPDATE LOOP

In ordinary, batch-mode parsing, an input text x is mapped once and for all to an output $f(x)$, representing an analysis of the text. In contrast, the purpose of incremental parsing is to efficiently handle a sequence of small changes to a text. To achieve this, the old output $f(x)$ is re-used as much as possible in the new output. Thus, if the text is changed from x to $x + \Delta x$, then the old output $f(x)$, the old input x and the change Δx are mapped to the new output $f(x + \Delta x)$. The process that realizes a sequence of such mappings can be seen as a change–update loop: as a user makes small changes to the text, the task of the incremental parser is to update the analysis in such a way that it remains consistent with the text.

The incremental parser presented here is grounded in a chart-parsing algorithm, each step of which corresponds to an inference rule in the deductive view (Kay, 1980; Thompson, 1981; Thompson, 1983; Pereira and Warren, 1983). The analysis of a text is thus represented by a chart, C (see section 3.1). Because of the monotonicity of chart parsing, new input cannot invalidate old analyses, given that the linear order of the old input is respected. However, in the fully incremental case this is no longer true, because material can then be deleted from or inserted *within* a text. To keep track of the part of the previous analysis that is (potentially) affected by such 'decremental' changes, we shall make use of a dependency relation $\mathcal{D}$ on the set of chart edges. To allow for flexible scheduling of parsing tasks, changes will be handled via an agenda, $Agda$. The process state will thus be determined by a triple $\langle C, \mathcal{D}, Agda \rangle$.

We shall assume that the textual input to the parsing system consists of *tokens*; that is, contiguous sequences of characters — words, punctuation symbols, etc. — which have been grouped together by a tokenizer (scanner).[3]For the purpose of simplicity, we shall restrict our attention to *unit changes*, that is, insertion and deletion of a single token. More complex (user-oriented) editing operations can then be defined on the basis of these.

Briefly put, the change–update loop consists of the following two steps:

1. One or several editing operations, each of which consists in insertion or deletion of a token, followed by removal of edges that are (potentially) affected by the change.
2. Reparsing, which, as we shall see, consists in ordinary chart parsing.

We assume that these steps are realized by two processes, which we refer to as the editing process and the parsing process, respectively.

[3]It is possible to extend incrementality to this level by means of similar techniques (Wirén, 1992, page 80f.).

3. REPARSING

3.1. THE CHART

We take a chart to be a graph $\langle V, E, T\rangle$ consisting of vertices and edges. The vertices $v_1, \ldots, v_{n+1} \in V$ correspond to the linear positions between the tokens of an n-token text $\tau_1 \cdots \tau_n$. An edge $e \in E$ between vertices v_i and v_j carries information about a (partially) analysed constituent between the corresponding positions. A token edge $t_k \in T$ represents a token, and is here assumed to extend between two adjacent vertices, v_k and v_{k+1}. These edges are added and removed by the editing process and serve as the basic input to the parsing process. It is therefore convenient to keep them on the chart.

The linguistic information represented by a chart edge is determined by the grammar and lexicon. For the purpose of the parsing algorithm, we shall restrict our attention to a standard context-free grammar without cyclic or empty productions.

In order to define the chart, we first introduce three sets: R is the set of dotted context-free rules obtained from the grammar. A dotted rule $X \rightarrow \alpha . \beta$ corresponds to an X edge containing an analysis of constituents α, seeking constituents β. Q is the set of (partial) analyses according to the grammar and lexicon, for example, the set of feature structures under a unification grammar. S is the set of tokens, each of which we take to correspond to a lexical entry.

Definition 1 (Chart) A *chart* is a directed graph $C = \langle V, E, T\rangle$ such that V is a finite, non-empty set of vertices, $E \subseteq V \times V \times R \times Q$ is a finite set of 'ordinary' edges, and $T \subseteq V \times V \times S$ is a finite set of token edges.

We shall sometimes omit the Q component, writing an edge as a triple $\langle v_i, v_j, X \rightarrow \alpha . \beta\rangle$.

We shall also need the following notion:

Definition 2 (Width) We define the *width* of an edge $e = \langle v_i, v_j, X \rightarrow \alpha . \beta\rangle$ by the function $\mathit{Width}(e) = j - i$. A zero-width edge is called a *looping* edge.

3.2. THE CHART PARSER

Since the non-monotonicity of the system is handled by making use of edge dependencies, it is possible to retain monotonic inference, and reparsing can actually be realized as ordinary chart parsing. Each round of the parsing algorithm consists in taking one task off the agenda and executing the appropriate chart-parsing step. We here specify the basic bottom-up (strictly speaking, left-corner) and top-down (Earley-style) strategies, assuming that the one or the other is chosen throughout a session of the change–update loop. To achieve a high degree of incrementality, we have chosen a formulation which is 'focused' in the sense that the algorithm works locally off the change (using the agenda), rather than going through the entire chart to check for possible new edges.

Algorithm 1 (Chart parsing with CFG)

Input: A process state $\langle C_{in}, \mathcal{D}_{in}, Agda_{in}\rangle$.
Output: A process state $\langle C_{out}, \mathcal{D}_{out}, Agda_{out}\rangle$.
Initialization:[4] If the top-down strategy is used, then add an initial top-down prediction $\langle v_1, v_1, S \rightarrow .\alpha\rangle$ for each rule $S \rightarrow \alpha$, where S is the start category of the grammar. Add resulting new tasks to the agenda. Install new dependencies.
Method: Take the next task from the agenda. Select and execute the appropriate step below:

Scan: If the token edge is of the form $\langle v_j, v_{j+1}, \tau\rangle$, then, for each lexical entry of the form $X \rightarrow \tau$, add an edge $\langle v_j, v_{j+1}, X \rightarrow \tau.\rangle$. Add resulting new tasks to the agenda. Install new dependencies.
Informally, this means adding an inactive edge for each sense of the token. We refer to the new edges as *lexical* edges.

Predict 1 (Bottom-up): If the edge is of the form $\langle v_j, v_k, X \rightarrow \alpha.\rangle$, then, for each rule of the form $Y \rightarrow X\gamma$, add an edge $\langle v_j, v_j, Y \rightarrow .X\beta\rangle$ unless it already exists. Add resulting new tasks to the agenda. Install new dependencies.
Informally, this means adding an edge according to each rule whose right-hand-side category matches the category of the triggering inactive edge, provided that an equivalent edge does not already exist in the chart. We refer to the new edges as *predicted* edges.

Predict 2 (Top-down): If the edge is of the form $\langle v_i, v_j, X \rightarrow \alpha.Y\beta\rangle$, then, for each rule of the form $Y \rightarrow \gamma$, add an edge $\langle v_j, v_j, Y \rightarrow .\gamma\rangle$ unless it already exists. Add resulting new tasks to the agenda. Install new dependencies.
Informally, this means adding an edge according to each rule whose first left-hand-side category matches the needed category of the triggering active edge, provided that an equivalent edge does not already exist in the chart. Again, we call the new edges *predicted* edges.

Combine:[5] If the first edge is of the form $\langle v_i, v_j, X \rightarrow \alpha.Y\beta\rangle$ and the second is of the form $\langle v_j, v_k, Y \rightarrow \gamma.\rangle$, then add an edge $\langle v_i, v_k, X \rightarrow$

[4]To be made prior to invoking the change–update loop. Addition of tasks to the agenda is described in section 3.3; installation of dependencies is described in section 5.1.
[5]This step is called the *completer* operation by Earley (Earley, 1970) and the *fundamental rule* by Thompson (Thompson, 1981).

$\alpha Y \cdot \beta\rangle$. Add resulting new tasks to the agenda. Install new dependencies.
Informally, this means adding an edge whenever the category of the first needed constituent of the active edge matches the category of the inactive edge. We refer to the new edge as a *combined* edge.

3.3. THE AGENDA

The agenda contains a set of tasks, which are created in response to edges being added to or removed from the chart, and which may be ordered according to their priorities (compare Thompson, 1983). There are three types of task, namely, scanning, prediction and combination tasks. Prediction tasks can be further subdivided according to the rule-invocation (inference) strategy used. Each type of task is thus executed by one step of the algorithm specified above (in section 3.2).

Whenever an edge (of any type) is added to the chart, new tasks are created as follows: If the new edge is a token edge, then a scanning task represented by this edge is created. If the new edge is an ordinary edge, then a prediction task represented by this edge is created. Furthermore, for each active–inactive pair in which the new edge is an element, a combination task represented by the two edges is created. Finally, whenever a *token* edge is removed from the chart, a combination task is created for each pair of active–inactive edges that result from 'joining' the two endpoint vertices of the token edge.

To define the agenda, we make use of the set of possible token edges *Tkns* and the set of possible (ordinary) edges *Edgs*.

Definition 3 (Agenda) We define the *agenda* as

$$Agda \subseteq Tkns \cup Edgs \cup (Edgs \times Edgs)$$

4. THE AFFECTED AND REGENERATED SETS

Assume that token τ_i, represented by a token edge between v_i and v_{i+1}, is deleted from a text. A measure of the minimal amount of work needed to handle this change can be established by comparing the charts $C = \langle V, E, T\rangle$ and $C' = \langle V', E', T'\rangle$ that are obtained by batch-mode parsing of the texts before and after the change, respectively: only the edges that are in C but not in C' must be removed, and only the edges that are in C' but not in C must be generated anew.

However, to enable a fair comparison of the edges in the two charts, we must first establish a one-to-one correspondence between their vertices. The problem is that, because of the deleted token, the two vertices v_i and v_{i+1} would seem to correspond to a single vertex in V'. However, we can regard this single vertex as consisting of a 'left half' and a 'right half', which we assign different indices. The left half is then associated with the incoming non-predicted edges as well as (looping) top-down predictions, and the right half is associated with the outgoing non-predicted edges as well as (looping) bottom-up predictions.[6] The reason for dividing the predicted edges in this way is that a top-down prediction is made at the ending vertex of the triggering edge (that is, from the left), whereas a bottom-up prediction is made at the starting vertex of the triggering edge (that is, from the right).

We then obtain the following mapping between vertices in C and C':

- Vertices $v_1, \ldots, v_{i-1} \in V$ correspond to $v'_1, \ldots, v'_{i-1} \in V'$.
- Vertex v_i corresponds to the 'left half' of vertex v'_i.
- Vertex v_{i+1} corresponds to the 'right half' of vertex v'_i.
- Vertices $v_{i+2}, \ldots, v_{n+1}$ correspond to $v'_{i+1}, \ldots, v'_n$.

The same mapping, but in the opposite direction, can be used in the case when token τ_i is inserted. The above correspondences can thus be established with respect to both of the unit changes. We can then make the following definitions:

Definition 4 (Affected and regenerated sets) Assume that E and E' are the sets of edges of the charts C and C' obtained by batch-mode parsing of a text before and after a change, respectively. We then define the *set of affected edges* as the set difference $A = E \setminus E'$ and the *set of regenerated edges* as the set difference $G = E' \setminus E$.

Definition 5. We define the *set of changed edges* as $\Delta = A \cup G$ and the *set of unchanged edges* as $U = E \cap E'$.

As an illustration, the chart in figure 2 is obtained under bottom-up parsing, given the grammar in figure 1 and the sentence "The old man the tall ships". If the token "tall" is removed, the chart in figure 3 is obtained. Vertex v_5 in figure 2 then corresponds to the left half of vertex v'_5 in figure 3, and vertex v_6 corresponds to the right half of vertex v'_5. Furthermore, v_7 corresponds to v'_6. The affected edge set then contains the three ordinary edges A_{26}, NP_{27} and NP_{34} plus the token edge "tall" in figure 2, and the regenerated edge set contains the single edge NP_{32} in figure 3. (We are assuming that also the Q components of two edges can be compared with respect to equality.) If instead "tall" is inserted before the last word in the sentence in figure 3, then the affected set contains the same edges as the regenerated set above and vice versa.

[6] As mentioned above, we assume that only the one *or* the other strategy is used, so that it is known beforehand which kind of predictions the chart contains.

S	$\rightarrow$	$NP\ VP$	the	$\leftarrow$	Det
NP	$\rightarrow$	$Det\ N$	old	$\leftarrow$	$N,\ A$
NP	$\rightarrow$	$Det\ A\ N$	man	$\leftarrow$	$N,\ V$
VP	$\rightarrow$	V	ships	$\leftarrow$	$N,\ V$
VP	$\rightarrow$	$V\ NP$			

Figure 1. Example grammar and lexicon.

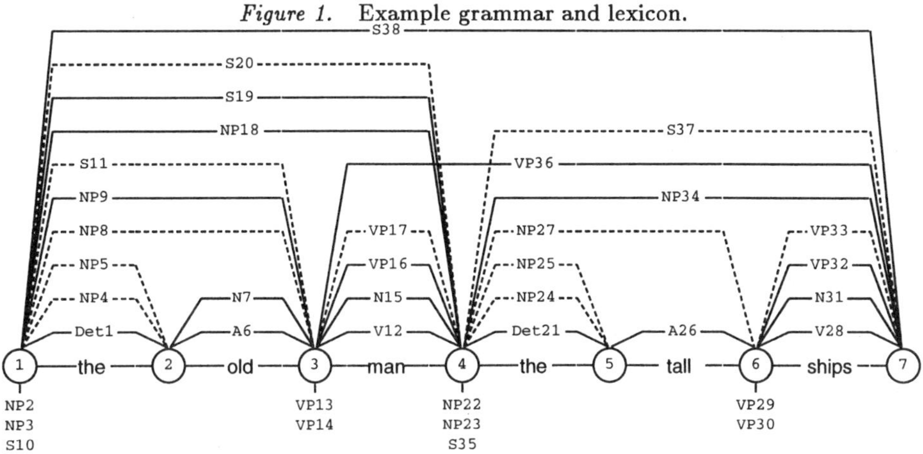

Figure 2. Chart of the sentence "The old man the tall ships" under bottom-up parsing. Inactive edges are drawn using continuous lines, active edges using dashed lines, and predicted (looping) edges are depicted below the vertices. Token edges are labelled only with the tokens that they represent.

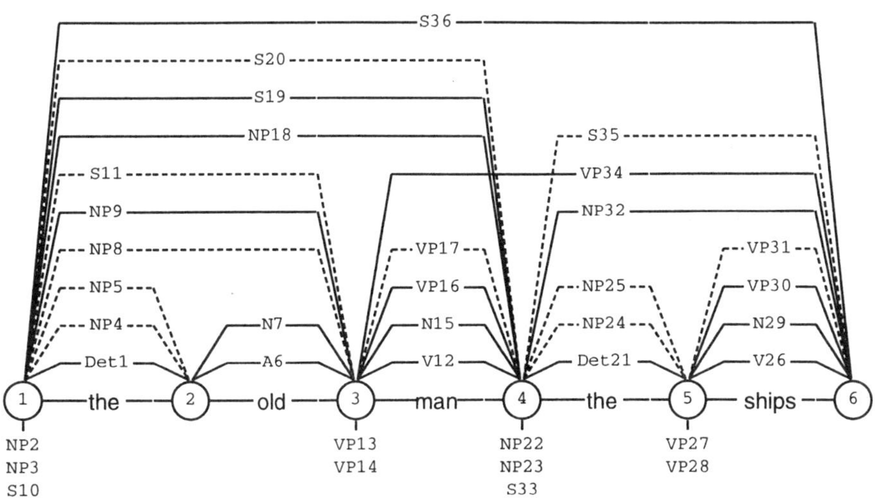

Figure 3. Chart of the sentence "The old man the ships" under bottom-up parsing.

5. THE DISTURBANCE SET

5.1. EDGE DEPENDENCIES

The key idea of the incremental-parsing algorithm is to make use of dependencies between chart edges in order to limit the number of edges that have to be removed in response to a change. In what ways can chart edges be taken to depend on each other? Intuitively, an edge e' depends upon another edge e if it is formed (derived) directly on the basis of e (where e is an ordinary edge or a token edge). Furthermore, if e' is redundantly proposed by an edge f, then e' can be said to depend (also) on f. By e' being 'redundantly proposed', we mean that the parser attempts to add an edge that is equivalent to e' to the chart, but that that edge is rejected by the standard redundancy test in chart parsing. In effect, f provides an additional 'justification' for e'.

Given a chart $C = \langle V, E, T \rangle$, these conditions correspond to the following dependency relation on E and T:

Definition 5 (Edge dependencies) We define $\mathcal{D}$ as a binary relation on the set of chart edges $E \cup T$ such that $\mathcal{D}(s, d)$ holds if and only if $d \in E$ is formed, or is redundantly proposed, directly using $s \in E \cup T$ according to the chart-parsing algorithm in section 3.2. We say that d is a *dependent* (or *derivative*) edge of s, and that s is a *source* edge of d.

Under a context-free grammar, only predicted edges can be redundantly proposed, whereas under a unification grammar such as PATR, both predicted and combined edges can be redundantly proposed. In the former case, the following dependencies are thus induced by the three chart-parsing steps:

- A *predicted* edge depends upon the edge that has formed it and the edges that have proposed it, unless it is an initial top-down prediction, which does not depend on any edge.
- A *combined* edge depends upon the active and inactive edge that have formed it according to the fundamental rule.
- A *lexical* edge depends upon the token edge that triggered it.

$\mathcal{D}$ can be illustrated by the corresponding graph. Given the grammar in figure 1 and the sentence "The old man the ships", the chart in figure 3 is obtained under bottom-up parsing. The resulting dependency graph is then shown in figure 4.

At this point, it is interesting to compare the dependency set and the affected set. For example, the set of edges that depend on the token edge "tall" also includes, in addition to A_{26}, NP_{27}, NP_{34} and the token edge "tall" in figure 2, the four edges S_{35}, VP_{36}, S_{37} and S_{38}. The latter four edges are unchanged, because each one of them exist in the new analysis in figure 3, namely, S_{33}, VP_{34}, S_{35} and S_{36}, respectively. For example, VP_{36} in figure 2 and VP_{34} in figure 3 both represent the partial analysis $VP \rightarrow V\ NP\ ..$

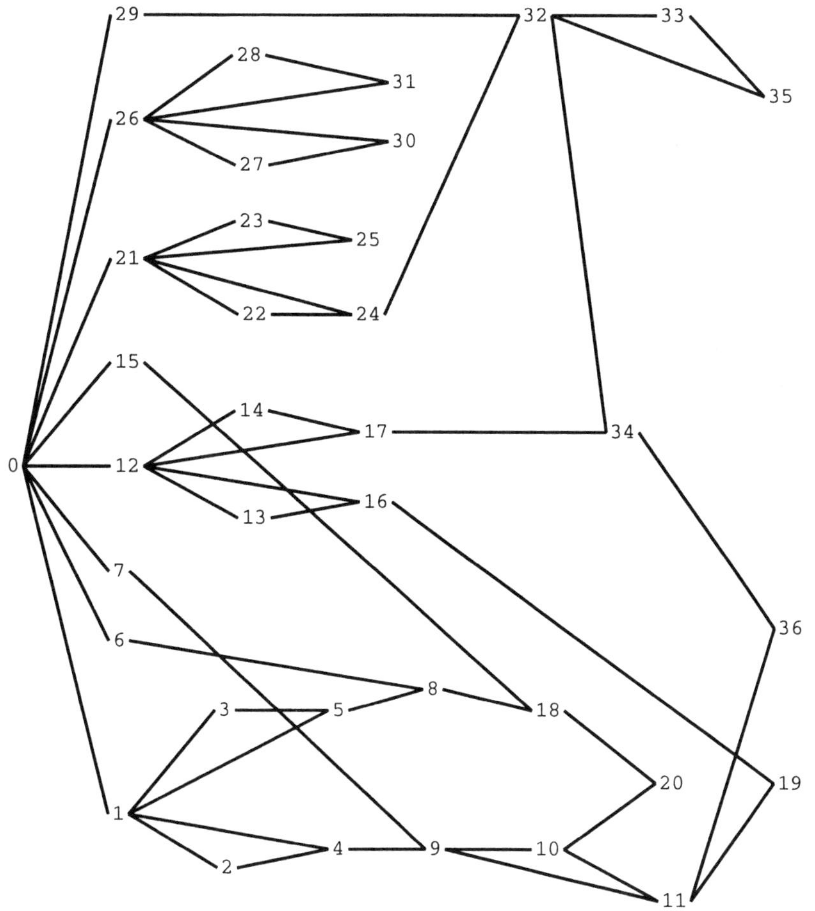

Figure 4. Edge-dependency graph induced by $\mathcal{D}$. The nodes of the graph correspond to the chart edges in figure 3, whereas a dummy root node 0 is shown instead of nodes corresponding to the token edges. Furthermore, the dependency between the only redundantly proposed edge S_{10} and the source NP_{18} is not shown in the figure.

5.2. MOTIVATION

Ideally, an incremental algorithm should remove only those edges that are affected when processing a change. However, in practice this may be too costly because of the overhead involved in determining this set exactly. The strategy here is therefore to approximate the affected set by making use of edge dependencies.[7] More specifically, we shall make use of $\mathcal{D}^*$, the transitive closure of $\mathcal{D}$. A formal argument for this will be given in section 7.2 by showing that $\mathcal{D}^*$ is complete with respect to the set of affected edges.

However, completeness in this sense is a weak condition; for instance, one complete set is the set of all edges, corresponding to exhaustive recomputation. Furthermore, it is easy to see that $\mathcal{D}^*$ includes also unaffected edges. Hence, $\mathcal{D}^*$ is not sound — in other words, it is not always the case that if an edge is in the dependency set, then it is affected.

In order to save work, we are therefore interested in finding restrictions of $\mathcal{D}^*$ that still include the affected set. In addition, such restrictions may be needed from the point of view of retaining completeness of the reparsing process. In other words, if too many edges are removed in response to a change, then the 'focused' reparsing algorithm specified in section 3.2 may not suffice. Instead, it might be necessary to check the entire chart in order to find all legal analyses, something which is at odds with incrementality.

To be able to talk about such a restricted set, we begin by introducing the notion of a disturbance:

Definition 7. We define a *disturbance* as a function *Disturbed*: $E \cup T \mapsto 2^E$. We call the set given by the function the *disturbance set* of an edge e.

In an actual text-editing application, we shall use the disturbance set to determine the edges that need to be removed from the chart in response to a change.

5.3. ELIMINATING UNWANTED SOURCES OF PREDICTIONS

Assume that the disturbance set is obtained directly from $\mathcal{D}$. In the example shown in figure 3, edge S_{10} depends on both NP_9 and NP_{18}, as indicated in figure 4. To handle a change, the dependency from NP_{18} to S_{10} is then superfluous, because NP_{18}, due to its greater width, depends on all the tokens on which NP_9 depends. If something is changed within the interval of NP_9 (the tokens "the" or "old"), then S_{10} is in the disturbance sets of both NP_9 and NP_{18}. If something is changed outside of the interval of NP_9 but within the interval of NP_{18} (the token "man"), then S_{10} need not be in the disturbance set, because S_{10} still depends on NP_9. (A dual case exists in top-down parsing.)

Actually, S_{10} *should not* be in the disturbance set, because by updating "man", S_{10} is disturbed via NP_{18}, although it is still 'justified' by NP_9. Furthermore, S_{10} disturbs S_{11}, which means that the parsing process will

[7] A strategy for avoiding spurious update altogether is described by Wirén (Wirén, 1994). Essentially, the idea is to initially retain the disturbance set, to compare new and old edges during reparsing, and to discontinue the reparsing process whenever a certain equivalence (quiescence) condition holds between a new and an old edge.

be incomplete, since no S predictions from the first vertex are available anymore. In principle, this problem could be avoided by reinstalling the disturbed S edges from NP_9, but such an approach is at odds with incrementality, since it involves checking vertices outside of the change interval.[8]

As an aside, this example also illustrates why the dependency relation needs to be based on both formed and redundantly proposed edges: Imagine that it is based on formed edges only, and that, in the above example, search is carried out in such a way that NP_{18} is generated before NP_9. Then if "man" is removed, completeness of the reparsing process is again lost for the same reasons as above.

If a predicted edge has several source edges that are combined, we thus want to include in the disturbance set only those that have the least width — put differently, the 'least committing' combined source edges. By doing this, we obtain a set which corresponds to the graph in figure 4 in that there is no dependency from NP_{18} to S_{10}. We define the set as follows:

Definition 6 (Primary disturbance set) Given an edge e, a disturbance *Disturbed*(e) is called *primary* only if it satisfies the following condition for all edges $e' \in \mathit{Disturbed}(e)$:

$$\mathcal{D}(e,e') \wedge \neg(\mathit{Width}(e') = 0 \wedge \exists e''[\mathcal{D}(e'',e') \wedge \mathit{Width}(e'') < \mathit{Width}(e)])$$

For a given dependency structure, there is a unique maximal primary disturbance. We refer to this as *the* primary disturbance.

The following disturbances are induced by the primary condition:

- A *lexical* edge can be disturbed by the token edge that triggered it.
- A *predicted* edge can be disturbed by the least-width edges that have formed or proposed it, unless it is an initial top-down prediction, which cannot be disturbed by any edge.
- A *combined* edge can be disturbed by the active–inactive edges that have formed it.

The disturbances induced with respect to combined and lexical edges coincide with the dependencies contained in $\mathcal{D}$.

5.4. ELIMINATING TOP-DOWN PREDICTIONS

We now turn to restrictions of $\mathcal{D}$ that are relevant under top-down parsing. Consider again the sentence "The old man the ships", whose top-down analysis is shown in figure 5. From the corresponding dependency graph,

[8] An alternative approach would be to keep track of independent justifications as in reason maintenance. Because of circularity, a current-support update algorithm is then needed (see, for example, Nebel (1990), p. 178).

shown in figure 6, it is clear that the primary disturbance set is inadequate for incremental top-down parsing: removal of token edge t_i actually disturbs *all* predicted and combined edges to the right of the change. For example, the disturbance set of the first token in the sentence, "the", represented by the lexical edge Det_4, is a subtree which includes most edges of the chart. The source of this problem is that a top-down prediction is made at the *ending* vertex of the triggering (active) edge. This prediction may then generate new dependants, some of which are active edges that in turn generate predictions at their ending vertices, and so on. In contrast, a bottom-up prediction is made at the *starting* vertex of the tr is made at the *starting* vertex of the triggering, inactive edge, which means that the disturbance set remains localized.

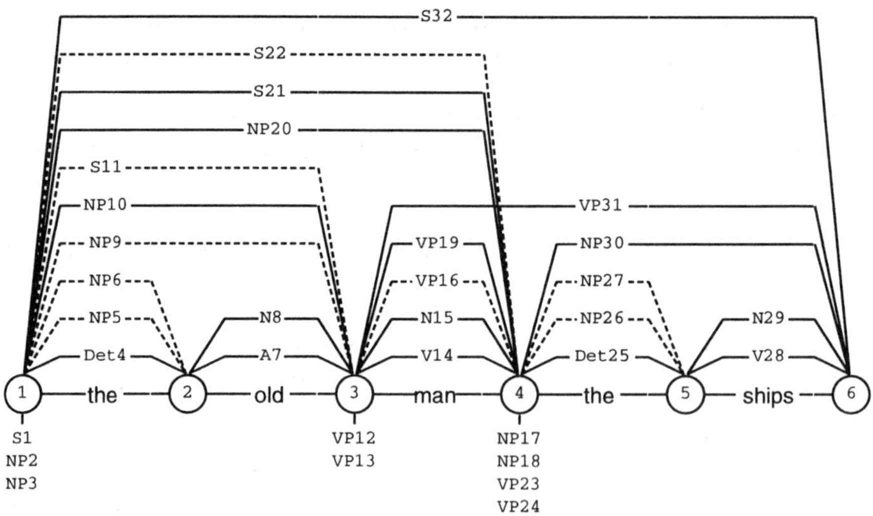

Figure 5. Chart of the sentence "The old man the ships" under top-down parsing.

This problem can be dealt with in different ways. Clearly, some dependencies in which top-down predictions participate should be eliminated from the disturbance set — the question is which dependencies to choose. One option is to exclude top-down predictions altogether by eliminating the dependency links both to and from every such edge. A graph showing the possible disturbances according to this condition, and with respect to the previous example, is shown in figure 7. As can be seen from the figure, the disturbance graph is then pruned before every top-down prediction. The condition thereby effectively prevents disturbances from chaining to the right. It is also easy to see that the *integrity* of the disturbance graph is preserved in the sense that no dangling links or subtrees are left in the graph. The price to be paid for adopting this condition is that a predicted

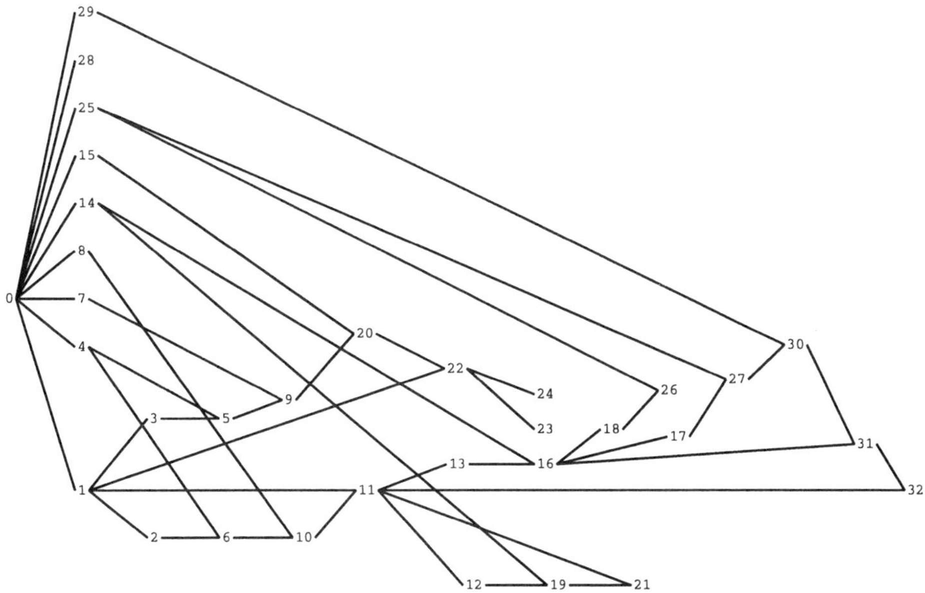

Figure 6. Edge-dependency graph whose nodes correspond to the chart edges in figure 5. The graph corresponds to $\mathcal{D}$ such that it is both primary and non-primary (since there are no redundantly proposed edges). Note that, as before, a dummy root node 0 is shown instead of nodes corresponding to the token edges.

edge remains on the chart indefinitely, independently of all changes. In particular, since an *affected* top-down prediction is never removed, completeness is lost. However, the correctness of the overall parsing process is retained, because an obsolete prediction can only generate structure according to the grammar that otherwise would not have been generated (superfluous edges). Thus, in practice the major disadvantage of adopting the condition is that it increases the workload of the parser.

Another option is to exclude only dependency links *from* top-down predictions to combined edges; that is, links to structure that it has generated to the right. In contrast to the previous condition, dependency links to top-down predictions, as well as links between top-down predictions, are then retained. Also, the primary condition can be retained. Since a prediction is disturbed by its sources, this option comes closer to completeness, and the integrity of the disturbance graph is again preserved. However, completeness is still lost, because the dependants to the right of the top-down prediction might be affected, but cannot be disturbed. For example, assume that "man" is removed from the sentence in figure 5 (page 24). Then the edges NP_{17} and NP_{18} are disturbed, but their (affected) dependants NP_{26},

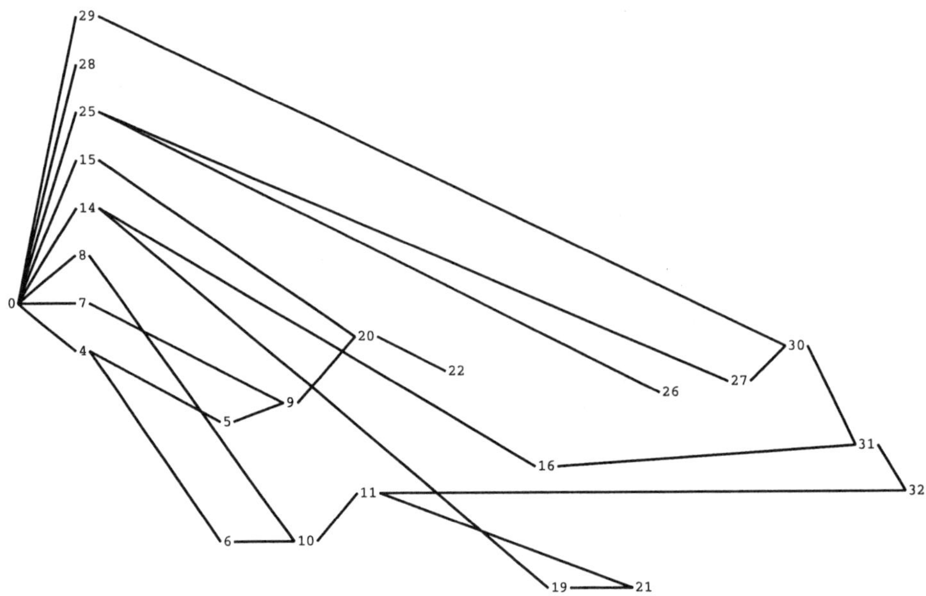

Figure 7. Edge-dependency graph whose nodes correspond to the chart edges in figure 5. Compared to the graph in figure 6, all (looping) top-down predictions are excluded.

NP_{27} and NP_{30} are not. In other words, the latter edges would not have been generated if the changed sentence was reparsed.

A third option is to exclude dependency links from combined edges *to* top-down predictions. This means that a prediction can disturb its dependants, but that it can itself only be disturbed by another prediction. However, if a token is removed, then disturbances will percolate only from tokens and lexical edges via *combined* edges to other (combined and predicted) edges. Hence, no prediction will ever be disturbed in this case. This is reflected in the disturbance graph, which loses its integrity. For example, if NP_{16} is disturbed, then NP_{17} and NP_{18} are left 'dangling'.

One way of preventing obsolete top-down predictions from being accumulated on the chart in the first and last cases above is to introduce a process of garbage collection. In order to remove superfluous top-down predictions, we would then want to remove only predictions for which no dependants and no sources remain. It is essential that both conditions hold: If no source but a dependant exists, the prediction has generated some (possibly useful) structure and should therefore be kept. If no dependant but a source exists, the prediction has not yet generated any structure, but could do so as a result of subsequent changes, and should therefore be kept. However, an additional complication is that, since garbage collection makes use of the dependency graph, the integrity of this must be preserved by reinstantiating incoming and outgoing dependency links with respect to top-down predictions.

In conclusion, the first approach above — excluding top-down predictions altogether from the disturbance set, possibly combined with garbage collection — seems preferable. This condition is simple and does not destroy possibly useful structure. The other two conditions seem less intuitive in the sense that they presuppose that either predictions are in the disturbance set and their (combined) dependants are not, or vice versa.

6. PRIMITIVE CHANGES

As previously mentioned, we restrict our attention to unit changes — insertion or deletion of a single token. To modularize these operations, we shall divide each of them into two primitive ones and introduce an intermediary state, in which the chart may contain *empty* token edges of the form $\langle v_i, v_{i+1}, \epsilon\rangle$. (Henceforth, we refer to these as just 'empty edges'.) We call vertex v_i, at which the changed token edge starts, the *change vertex*. For simplicity, we assume that the agenda is emptied before executing a sequence of the primitive operations. Thereby, the edge manipulations below only affect the first two components of $\langle C, \mathcal{D}, Agda\rangle$.

Insertion of a token is then handled by the two operations below.

Add empty edge: Renumber edges as follows: First, replace each edge $\langle v_j, v_k, \rho\rangle$ where $j \geq i$ and $k \neq i$ with an edge $\langle v_{j+1}, v_k, \rho\rangle$. Secondly, replace each edge $\langle v_j, v_k, \rho\rangle$ where $k > i$ with an edge $\langle v_j, v_{k+1}, \rho\rangle$. Then add the empty edge $\langle v_i, v_{i+1}, \epsilon\rangle$ to the chart. Looping edges at the change vertex, which have the form $\langle v_i, v_i, \rho\rangle$, are dealt with differently depending on whether their sources are to the left or right, which in turn depends on the rule-invocation strategy:

1. Bottom-up case: If the looping edge depends on an edge $\langle v_i, v_j, \rho\rangle$ that is outgoing to the right ($j > i$), then it is replaced with an edge $\langle v_{i+1}, v_{i+1}, \epsilon\rangle$ (in effect, it is moved).
2. Top-down case: If the looping edge depends on an edge $\langle v_j, v_k, \rho\rangle$ that is incoming from the left or looping ($k \leq i$), then do nothing.

Finally, update the dependency relation $\mathcal{D}$ so that any edge $\langle v_j, v_k, \rho\rangle$ such that $j \leq i$ and $k > i$ is made dependent on the empty edge.

Raise empty edge to token edge: Remove the disturbance set of the empty edge $\langle v_i, v_{i+1}, \epsilon\rangle$. Replace the empty edge with the token edge $\langle v_i, v_{i+1}, \tau\rangle$. Add resulting new tasks to the agenda.

Note that insertion of a token at the end of a text reduces to ordinary (LR-incremental) chart parsing, in which case the disturbance set is empty.

Deletion of a token is handled by the following two operations:

Reduce token edge to empty edge: Remove the disturbance set of the token edge. Replace the token edge $\langle v_i, v_{i+1}, \tau \rangle$ with the empty edge $\langle v_i, v_{i+1}, \epsilon \rangle$.

Remove empty edge: Renumber edges as follows: First, replace each edge $\langle v_j, v_k, \rho \rangle$ where $j \geq i$ with an edge $\langle v_{j-1}, v_k, \rho \rangle$. Then replace each edge $\langle v_j, v_k, \rho \rangle$ where $k \geq i$ with an edge $\langle v_j, v_{k-1}, \rho \rangle$. Then remove the empty edge $\langle v_i, v_{i+1}, \epsilon \rangle$. Finally, add resulting new tasks to the agenda.

Replacement of one token with another one can be handled by first reducing a token edge and then raising it with the new token.

Addition and removal of empty edges can be seen as virtual changes: although empty edges enter into the dependency relation, adding or removing them does not generate disturbances or new agenda tasks. We can think of two charts with the same non-empty but different empty edges as belonging to the same equivalence class.

7. FORMAL PROPERTIES

7.1. TERMINATION

To show termination of the system, we must show that if the editing process finishes, then the parsing process terminates. That the editing process finishes means that no new token edges are put on the chart. That the parsing process then terminates follows from the way in which edges are put on the agenda, which ensures that any scanning, prediction and combination task is carried out only once. Whenever the same edge is proposed for the second or more time, it gives rise to a dependency, but no new task is put on the agenda. Hence, any task appears on the agenda only once. Furthermore, each parsing step removes one task from the agenda. There is a finite number of potential agenda tasks, namely, $|\mathit{Tkns}| + |\mathit{Edgs}| + |\mathit{Edgs}|^2$. It can then be shown by induction that the parsing process terminates.

7.2. COMPLETENESS OF THE DEPENDENCY RELATION

In order to make sure that the dependency relation $\mathcal{D}$ is useful as a basis for approximating the affected set, we must show that it is complete with respect to the affected set. In other words, given a unit change (insertion or deletion of a token), we must show that $\mathcal{D}^*$, (the transitive closure of $\mathcal{D}$) with respect to the token contains the affected set. To this end, we begin with two lemmas:

Lemma 1 An initial top-down prediction cannot be affected by a change.

Proof In the reparsing algorithm, initial top-down predictions are only made at vertex v_1, which is guaranteed to exist, since by definition 1 the set of vertices V is non-empty. Furthermore, by the division of vertices described in section 4, top-down predictions are associated with the left half of a vertex, which in this case means that they can never be affected. ■

Lemma 2 For every non-lexical edge e affected by a change of token edge t_i, there is an edge e' such that $\mathcal{D}^*(e',e) \wedge \neg\mathcal{D}^*(e,e')$ and e' is affected by a change of t_i.

Proof Let e be a non-lexical edge affected by a change of token edge t_i. Since such non-lexical edges are either predicted or combined, we obtain the following cases:

1. If e is formed by prediction from edge e', then $\mathcal{D}^*(e',e)$ must hold, and edge e' must also be affected by a change of t_i.
2. If e is formed by combination of edges e' and e'', then $\mathcal{D}^*(e',e)$ and $\mathcal{D}^*(e'',e)$ must hold, and at least one of e' and e'' must be affected by a change of t_i. Assume then that e' is affected by a change of t_i, and assume furthermore $\mathcal{D}^*(e,e')$; that is, e and e' belong to a dependency cycle. However, the formation of an edge relies on a prior formation (or existence) of the source edges, and therefore there must be some edge f in the cycle that is formed prior to the other edges in the cycle.
   (a) If f is formed by prediction from edge f', then case 1 above applies for edge f, which also implies that (in this case) there is an edge f' affected by a change of t_i such that $\mathcal{D}^*(f',e) \wedge \neg\mathcal{D}^*(e,f')$.
   (b) If f is formed by combination of edges f' and f'', then f' and f'' must both be outside of the dependency cycle involving e, and $\mathcal{D}^*(f',e)$ and $\mathcal{D}^*(f'',e)$ must hold, and at least one of f' and f'' must be affected by a change of t_i.

Since edge e cannot be formed in any other way, the lemma follows. ■

The completeness of $\mathcal{D}^*$ is then captured by the following theorem:

Theorem 1 Given a change of token edge t_i, the dependency set $\mathcal{D}^*$ is complete; that is, it contains the set of affected edges.

Proof Follows from lemmas 1 and 2, since each affected edge e is either acyclically dependent on some other affected edge e', or is immediately dependent on one of the lexical edges representing token edge t_i. ■

7.3. COMPLETENESS OF THE DISTURBANCE SET

Next, we must show that the primary condition retains completeness. The following theorem captures this.

Theorem 2 The closure of the primary disturbance set $\mathit{Disturbed}(t_i)$ of token edge t_i is complete; that is, it contains the affected set.

Proof As shown by theorem 1, the dependency set $\mathcal{D}^*$ is complete. The primary condition eliminates certain sources of predicted edges from this set. Since a prediction can be made bottom-up or top-down, we obtain two cases:

1. *Bottom-up case:* Assume that a predicted edge e' immediately depends (only) on the edges e and f, and that $\mathit{Width}(e) < \mathit{Width}(f)$. Then e is either a combined or a lexical edge and f is a combined edge. Since a combined or lexical edge depends on all tokens extending within its vertex interval, it follows that e' will also be disturbed by all tokens extending within the vertex intervals of e and f. Since there are no other combined edges that can affect the prediction, the theorem follows in this case.
2. *Top-down case:* Assume that a top-down-predicted edge e' immediately depends (only) on the edges e and f, and that $\mathit{Width}(e) < \mathit{Width}(f)$. Then e is either another top-down prediction or a combined edge and f is a combined edge. If e is combined the case above applies. If e is a top-down prediction, then it must depend on a combined edge that is incoming to the same vertex. Since all incoming combined edges depend on the token that is incoming to the vertex, there are no other edges that can affect the prediction. Hence, the theorem follows in this case.

■

7.4. FURTHER ASPECTS

By proving that the primary disturbance set is complete, we have taken a step towards showing soundness for the overall process. It remains to be shown that the overall process, and hence reparsing, is sound and complete. Since the disturbance set is bigger than the affected set, soundness and completeness of reparsing must be shown with respect to the set of edges that are regenerated *or* disturbed and non-affected. Also, the complexity of the process as a function of the size of the change remains to be worked out (Ramalingam and Reps, 1991). Here the notion of the changed edge set should be useful.

8. IMPLEMENTATION

An implementation exists, which has been adapted to on-line processing under a simple text editor, thus providing a system which parses a text simultaneously as it is entered and edited (Dahlén, 1991).[9] No systematic empirical assessments have been made, but when using small sentence grammars, it appears that typically about 25 % of the edges are disturbed by deleting a token in the middle of a text. If the change preserves the grammatical well-formedness of the text, and if a context-free grammar is used, typically less than half of these edges are affected. Although this is a bit coarse-grained, it is compensated by the low overhead of the algorithm. If a unification grammar is used, a larger fraction of the disturbance set is likely to be affected, and thus the algorithm comes closer to the ideal of not removing useful edges. An interesting property of the algorithm is that the cost of LR-incremental parsing hardly exceeds the cost of an algorithm that *only* handles this problem, since the cost of just maintaining dependencies is marginal.

9. CONCLUSIONS

Highly interactive natural-language applications require incremental parsing: although exhaustive reanalysis of the input can be fast enough for small problems, incremental algorithms are ultimately necessary in order to cope with larger problems. Fully incremental parsing is required to handle non-cumulative changes of a text. The approach to this problem described here is based on maintaining dependencies between chart edges. The advantage of this is that the overhead of keeping, and using, this information is very low. A disadvantage is that many unaffected edges may be removed. Another disadvantage is that in top-down parsing, some additional overhead, such as garbage collection, is needed. It is desirable to find out whether there are more exact characterizations of the affected set that are practically useful, especially in top-down parsing. For example, it might be possible to reparse while initially retaining the disturbance set. By propagating new information along the dependency links, and by comparing old and new edges in each step, reparsing can be discontinued when changes die out. A related question is whether full incrementality can be usefully translated to the level of feature structures.

[9] However, the schemes for eliminating top-down predictions in section 5.4 have not been implemented.

Acknowledgements

First, we would like to thank the anonymous referees for their very useful comments. Secondly, we would like to thank many colleagues (too numerous to mention) in Linköping, Saarbrücken and elsewhere for feedback and discussions on the material presented here. The first author has been supported by the German Science Foundation (DFG) through the Sonderforschungsbereich 314, project N3 (BiLD), and, previously, by the Swedish National Board for Industrial and Technical Development (NUTEK) and the Board of Research in the Humanistic and Social Sciences (HSFR).

References

Dahlén, Ulf (1991) LIPS. Ett system för interaktiv och inkrementell parsning av naturligt språk [LIPS. A System for Interactive and Incremental Parsing of Natural Language]. Master's Thesis LiTH-IDA-Ex-9136, Department of Computer and Information Science, Linköping University, Linköping, Sweden. In Swedish.

Dale, Robert (1989) Computer-based Editorial Aids. In Jeremy Peckham, editor, *Recent Developments and Applications of Natural Language Processing.* UNICOM Applied Information Technology Reports, Kogan Page Limited, London, England, 8–22.

Earley, Jay (1970) An Efficient Context-Free Parsing Algorithm. *Communications of the ACM*, 13(2):94–102.

Earley, Jay and Caizergues, Paul (1972) A Method for Incrementally Compiling Languages with Nested Statement Structure. *Communications of the ACM*, 15(12):1040–1044.

Ghezzi, Carlo and Mandrioli, Dino (1979) Incremental Parsing. *ACM Transactions on Programming Languages and Systems*, 1(1):58–70.

Ghezzi, Carlo and Mandrioli, Dino (1980) Augmenting Parsers to Support Incrementality. *Journal of the Association for Computing Machinery*, 27(3):564–579.

Kay, Martin (1980) Algorithm Schemata and Data Structures in Syntactic Processing. In Barbara Grosz, Karen Sparck Jones, and Bonnie Lynn Webber, editors, *Readings in Natural Language Processing.* Morgan Kaufmann Publishers, Inc., Los Altos, California, USA, 1986, 35–70. Also Report CSL-80-12, Xerox PARC, Palo Alto, California, USA.

Levelt, Willem J. M. (1989) *Speaking. From Intention to Articulation.* MIT Press, Cambridge, Massachusetts, USA.

Lindstrom, Gary (1970) The Design of Parsers for Incremental Language Processors. In *Proc. 2nd ACM Symposium on Theory of Computing.* Northampton, Massachusetts, USA, 81–91.

Marcus, Mitchell P. (1980) *A Theory of Syntactic Recognition for Natural Language.* MIT Press, Cambridge, Massachusetts, USA.

Marcus, Mitchell P. (1987) Deterministic Parsing and Description Theory. In Peter Whitelock, Mary McGee Wood, Harold Somers, Rod Johnson, and Paul Bennett, editors, *Linguistic Theory and Computer Applications.* Academic Press, London, England, 69–112.

Nebel, Bernhard (1990) *Reasoning and Revision in Hybrid Representation Systems.* Number 422 in Lecture Notes in Artificial Intelligence. Springer, Heidelberg, Germany.

Neumann, Günter and van Noord, Gertjan (1992) Self-Monitoring with Reversible Grammars. In *Proc. 14th International Conference on Computational Linguistics*, Nantes, France, 700–706.

Pareschi, Remo (1987) Combinatory Grammar, Logic Programming, and Natural Language Processing. In Nicholas Haddock, Ewan Klein, and Glyn Morrill, editors, *Categorial Grammar, Unification Grammar and Parsing*, volume 1. Centre for Cognitive Science, University of Edinburgh, Scotland, 85–114.

Pereira, Fernando C. N. and Warren, David H. D. (1983) Parsing as Deduction. In *Proc. 21st Annual Meeting of the Association for Computational Linguistics*, Cambridge, Massachusetts, USA, 137–144.

Ramalingam, G. and Reps, Thomas W. (1991) On the Computational Complexity of Incremental Algorithms. Technical Report 1033, Computer Sciences Department, University of Wisconsin, Madison, Wisconsin, USA.

Rekers, Jan and Koorn, Wilco (1991) Substring Parsing for Arbitrary Context-Free Grammars. In *Proc. Second International Workshop on Parsing Technologies*, Cancun, Mexico, 218–224.

Reps, Thomas W. and Teitelbaum, Tim (1987) Language Processing in Program Editors. *Computer*, 20(11):29–40.

Reps, Thomas W. and Teitelbaum, Tim (1989) *The Synthesizer Generator. A System for Constructing Language-based Editors*. Springer-Verlag, New York, New York, USA.

Shilling, John J. (1991) Incremental LL(1) Parsing in Language-based Editors. In *Proc. Second International Workshop on Parsing Technologies*, Cancun, Mexico, 41–51.

Somers, Harold L. (1991) Example-based MT and Dialogue. In Harold L. Somers, editor, *Working Papers in Computational Semantics, Dialogue and Discourse*. Papers from DANDI workshop/COSMOS report number 19, Department of Mathematics, University of Oslo, Oslo, Norway, 23–32.

Somers, Harold L., Tsujii, Jun-ichi, and Jones, Danny (1990) Machine Translation Without a Source Text. In *Proc. 13th International Conference on Computational Linguistics*, volume 3, Helsinki, Finland, 271–276.

Thompson, Henry S. (1981) Chart Parsing and Rule Schemata in GPSG. In *Proc. 19th Annual Meeting of the Association for Computational Linguistics*, Stanford, California, USA, 167–172.

Thompson, Henry S. (1983) MCHART: A Flexible, Modular Chart Parsing System. In *Proc. Third National Conference on Artificial Intelligence*, Washington, DC, USA, 408–410.

Tomita, Masaru (1985) An Efficient Context-Free Parsing Algorithm for Natural Languages. In *Proc. Ninth International Joint Conference on Artificial Intelligence*, Los Angeles, California, USA, 756–764.

Vilares Ferro, Manuel (1989) Interactive Incremental Chart Parsing. In *Proc. Fourth Conference of the European Chapter of the Association for Computational Linguistics*, Manchester, England, 241–248.

Wirén, Mats (1989) Interactive Incremental Chart Parsing. In *Proceedings Fourth Conference of the European Chapter of the Association for Computational Linguistics*, 461–467.

Wirén, Mats (1992) Studies in Incremental Natural-Language Analysis. Linköping Studies in Science and Technology, Dissertation 292, Department of Computer and Information Science, Linköping University, Linköping, Sweden.

Wirén, Mats (1994) Minimal Change and Bounded Incremental Parsing. In *Proc. 15th International Conference on Computational Linguistics*, volume 1, Kyoto, Japan, 461–467.

3. INCREASING THE APPLICABILITY OF LR PARSING

MARK-JAN NEDERHOF AND JANOS J. SARBO
Department of Computer Science, University of Nijmegen

Abstract.

In this chapter we discuss a phenomenon present in some context-free grammars, called *hidden left recursion*. We show that ordinary LR parsing according to hidden left-recursive grammars is not possible and we indicate a range of solutions to this problem. One of these solutions is a new parsing technique, which is a variant of traditional LR parsing. This new parsing technique can be used both with and without lookahead and the nondeterminism can be realized using backtracking or using a graph-structured stack.

1. INTRODUCTION

The class of LR parsing strategies constitutes one of the strongest and most efficient classes of parsing strategies for context-free grammars. LR parsing is commonly used in compilers as well as in systems for the processing of natural language.

Deterministic LR parsing with lookahead of k symbols is possible for LR(k) grammars. Deterministic parsing according to grammars which are not LR(k) can in some cases be achieved with some disambiguating techniques. (Important progress in this field has been reported by Thorup (1994).) However, these techniques are not powerful enough to handle practical grammars for e.g. natural languages.

If we consider LR parsing tables in which an entry may contain multiple actions, then we obtain nondeterministic LR parsing. We will refer to realizations of nondeterministic LR parsing as *generalized* LR parsing. The most straightforward way to obtain generalized LR parsing is by using backtracking (Nilsson, 1986).

H. Bunt and M. Tomita (eds.), Recent Advances in Parsing Technology, 35–57.

A more efficient kind of generalized LR parsing has been proposed by Tomita (1986). The essence of this approach is that multiple parses are processed simultaneously. Where possible, the computation processing two or more parses is shared. This is accomplished by using a *graph-structured stack.*

Although generalized LR parsing can handle a large class of grammars, there is one phenomenon which it cannot deal with, viz. *hidden left recursion.* Hidden left recursion, defined at the end of this section, occurs very often in grammars for natural languages.

A solution for handling hidden left-recursive grammars using Tomita's algorithm was proposed by Nozohoor-Farshi (1989). In that paper, the ordinary acyclic graph-structured stack is generalized to allow cycles. The resulting parsing technique is largely equivalent to a parsing technique which follows from a construction defined earlier by Lang (1974), which makes use of a parse matrix. As a consequence, termination of the parsing process is always guaranteed. This means that hidden left-recursive grammars and even cyclic grammars can be handled.

However, cyclic graph-structured stacks may complicate garbage collection and cannot be realized using memo-functions (Leermakers *et al.*, 1992). Tomita's algorithm furthermore becomes very complicated in the case of augmented context-free grammars (e.g. attribute grammar, affix grammar, definite clause grammar, etc.). In this case, different subparses almost always have different attribute values (or affix values, variable instantiations, etc.) and therefore sharing of the computation of context-free parsing would obstruct the correct computation of these values (Nederhof and Sarbo, 1993).

In this chapter we discuss an alternative approach to adapting the (generalized) LR parsing technique to hidden left-recursive grammars.

Our approach can be roughly described as follows. Reductions with epsilon rules are no longer performed. Instead, a reduction with some non-epsilon rule does not have to pop all the members in the right-hand side off the stack; only those which do not derive the empty string must be popped, for others it is optional. The definition of the closure function for sets of items is changed accordingly. Our approach requires the inspection of the parse stack upon each reduction in order to avoid incorrect parses.

The structure of this chapter is as follows. In the next section we give an introduction to the problem of LR parsing according to hidden left-recursive grammars. We give two naive ways of solving this problem by first transforming the grammar before constructing the (nondeterministic) LR automaton. (These methods are naive because the transformations lead to larger grammars and therefore to much larger LR automata.) We then show how the first of these transformations can be incorporated into the construction of LR automata, which results in parsers with a fewer number of states. We also outline an approach of adapting the LR technique to cyclic grammars.

In Section 3 we prove the correctness of our new parsing technique, called ϵ-LR parsing. Efficient generation of ϵ-LR parsers is discussed in Section 4. We conclude in Section 5 by giving some results on the comparison between the number of states of various LR and ϵ-LR parsers.

We would like to stress beforehand that grammars with nontrivial hidden left recursion can never be handled using deterministic LR parsing (Section 2.5), so that most of the discussion in this chapter is not applicable to deterministic LR parsing. We therefore, contrary to custom, use the term "LR parsing" for *generalized* LR parsing, which can at will be realized using backtracking (possibly in combination with memo-functions) or using *acyclic* graph-structured stacks. Wherever we deal with *deterministic* LR parsing, this will be indicated explicitly.

The notation used in the sequel is for the most part standard and is summarized below.

A context-free grammar $G = (T, N, P, S)$ consists of two finite disjoint sets N and T of nonterminals and terminals, respectively, a start symbol $S \in N$, and a finite set of rules P. Every rule has the form $A \rightarrow \alpha$, where the left-hand side (lhs) A is an element from N and the right-hand side (rhs) α is an element from V^*, where V denotes $(N \cup T)$. P can also be seen as a relation on $N \times V^*$.

We use symbols $A, B, C, \ldots$ to range over N, symbols X, Y, Z to range over V, symbols $\alpha, \beta, \gamma, \ldots$ to range over V^*, and $v, w, x, \ldots$ to range over T^*. We let ϵ denote the empty string. A rule of the form $A \rightarrow \epsilon$ is called an *epsilon rule*.

The relation P is extended to a relation $\stackrel{G}{\rightarrow}$ on $V^* \times V^*$ as usual. We write $\rightarrow$ for $\stackrel{G}{\rightarrow}$ when G is obvious. The transitive closure of $\rightarrow$ is denoted by $\rightarrow^+$ and the reflexive and transitive closure is denoted by $\rightarrow^*$.

We define: $B \angle A$ if and only if $A \rightarrow B\alpha$ for some α. The transitive closure of $\angle$ is denoted by $\angle^+$.

We distinguish between two cases of left recursion. The most simple case, which we call *plain left recursion*, occurs if there is a nonterminal A such that $A \angle^+ A$. The other case, which we call *hidden left recursion*, occurs if $A \rightarrow B\alpha$, $B \rightarrow^* \epsilon$, and $\alpha \rightarrow^* A\beta$, for some A, B, α, and β; the left recursion is "hidden" by the empty-generating nonterminal. (An equivalent definition of hidden left recursion is due to Leermakers *et al.* (1992).)

A grammar is said to be *cyclic* if $A \rightarrow^+ A$ for some nonterminal A.

A nonterminal A is said to be *nullable* if $A \rightarrow^* \epsilon$. A nonterminal A is called a *predicate* if it is nullable and $A \rightarrow^* v$ only for $v = \epsilon$.[1]

We call a nonterminal A *reachable* if $S \rightarrow^* \alpha A \beta$ for some α and β. We call a grammar *reduced* if every nonterminal is reachable and derives some terminal string. Where we give a transformation between context-free grammars, we tacitly assume that the input grammars are reduced and for these grammars the output grammars are guaranteed also to be reduced.

2. HIDDEN LEFT RECURSION AND LR PARSING

The simplest nontrivial case of hidden left recursion is the grammar G_1 given by the following rules.

$$\begin{array}{lcl} A & \rightarrow & BAc \\ A & \rightarrow & a \\ B & \rightarrow & b \\ B & \rightarrow & \epsilon \end{array}$$

In this grammar, nonterminal A is left-recursive. This fact is hidden by the presence of a nullable nonterminal B in the rule $A \rightarrow BAc$. Note that this grammar is ambiguous, as illustrated in Figure 1. This is typically so in the case where the one or more nullable nonterminals which hide the left recursion are not all predicates.

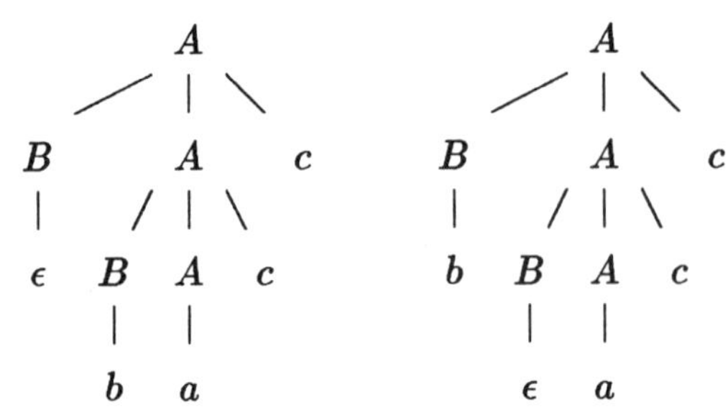

Figure 1. Two parse trees with the same yield, showing ambiguity of G_1.

2.1. GENERALIZED LR PARSING AND HIDDEN LEFT RECURSION

We now discuss informally how (generalized) LR parsing fails to terminate for the above grammar. We assume that the reader is familiar with the construction of (nondeterministic) LR(0) automata. Our terminology is taken from Aho *et al.* (1986).

[1]The term "predicate" seems to have been used in this sense for the first time by Koster (1971).

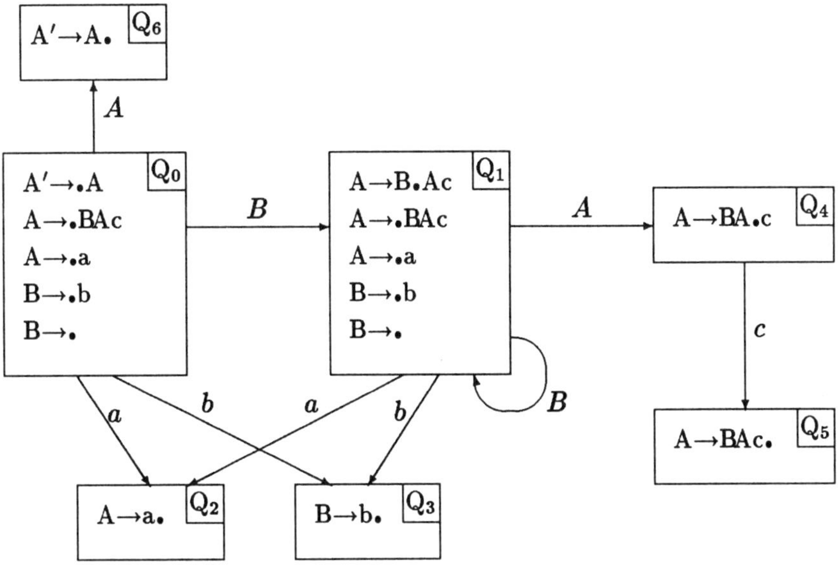

Figure 2. The LR(0) automaton for G_1.

A pictorial representation of the LR(0) parsing table for G_1 is given in Figure 2.

LR parsing of any input w may result in many sequences of parsing steps, one of which is illustrated by the following sequence of configurations.

Stack contents	Inp.	Action
Q_0	w	red$(B \to \epsilon)$
$Q_0\ B\ Q_1$	w	red$(B \to \epsilon)$
$Q_0\ B\ Q_1\ B\ Q_1$	w	red$(B \to \epsilon)$
$Q_0\ B\ Q_1\ B\ Q_1\ B\ Q_1$	w	red$(B \to \epsilon)$
⋮	⋮	⋮

The sequence of parsing steps illustrated above does not terminate. We can find a non-terminating sequence of parsing steps for the LR(0) automaton for every hidden left-recursive grammar. In fact, this is even so for the LR(k), LALR(k), and SLR(k) automata, for any k. Hidden left recursion has been identified by Soisalon-Soininen and Tarhio (1988) as one of two sources, together with cyclicity, of the looping of LR parsers. Various other parsing techniques, such as left-corner parsing (Nederhof, 1993a) and cancellation parsing (Nederhof, 1993b), also suffer from this deficiency.

2.2. ELIMINATING EPSILON RULES

We first discuss a method to allow LR parsing for hidden left-recursive grammars by simply performing a source to source transformation on grammars to eliminate the rules of which the right-hand sides only derive the empty string. To preserve the language, for each rule containing an occurrence of a nullable nonterminal a copy must be added without that occurrence. Following Aho and Ullman (1972), this transformation, called ϵ-*elim*, is described below. The input grammar is called G.

1. Let G_0 be G.
2. Remove from G_0 all rules defining predicates in G and remove all occurrences of these predicates from the rules in G_0.
3. Replace every rule of the form $A \rightarrow \alpha_0 B_1 \alpha_1 B_2 \ldots B_m \alpha_m$ in G_0, $m \geq 0$, where the members which are nullable in G are exactly $B_1, \ldots, B_m$, by the set of rules of the form $A \rightarrow \alpha_0 \beta_1 \alpha_1 \beta_2 \ldots \beta_m \alpha_m$, where β_i is either B_i or ϵ and $\alpha_0 \beta_1 \alpha_1 \beta_2 \ldots \beta_m \alpha_m \neq \epsilon$. Note that this set of rules is empty if $m = 0$ and $\alpha_0 = \epsilon$, in which case the original rule is just eliminated from G_0.
4. If S is nullable in G, then add the rules $S^\dagger \rightarrow S$ and $S^\dagger \rightarrow \epsilon$ to G_0 and make $S^\dagger$ the new start symbol of G_0. (In the pathological case that S is a predicate in G, $S^\dagger \rightarrow S$ should of course not be added to G_0.)
5. Let ϵ-*elim*(G) be G_0.

Note that for every rule $A \rightarrow \alpha$ such that α contains k occurrences of nullable non-predicates, the transformed grammar may contain 2^k rules.

In this chapter, an expression of the form $[B]$ in a rhs indicates that the member B has been eliminated by the transformation. It is for reasons of clarity that we write this expression instead of just leaving B out.

An item of the form $A \rightarrow [\alpha_0] X_1 [\alpha_1] \ldots [\alpha_{i-1}] \bullet X_i \ldots X_m [\alpha_m]$ is said to be *derived* from the *basic* item $A \rightarrow \alpha_0 X_1 \alpha_1 \ldots \alpha_{i-1} \bullet X_i \ldots X_m \alpha_m$.[2] According to the convention mentioned above, $A \rightarrow \alpha_0 X_1 \alpha_1 \ldots X_m \alpha_m$ is a rule in G, and $A \rightarrow X_1 \ldots X_m$ is a rule in ϵ-*elim*(G). The item of the form $S^\dagger \rightarrow \bullet$ which may be introduced by ϵ-*elim* will be regarded as the derived item $S^\dagger \rightarrow [S] \bullet$.

Example 2.1 Let the grammar G_2 be defined by the rules

$$
\begin{array}{lcl}
A & \rightarrow & BCD \\
B & \rightarrow & \epsilon \\
B & \rightarrow & b \\
C & \rightarrow & \epsilon \\
D & \rightarrow & \epsilon \\
D & \rightarrow & d
\end{array}
$$

[2] We avoid writing dots in dotted items immediately to the left of eliminated members.

Step 2 of ϵ-*elim* removes the rule $C \rightarrow \epsilon$ defining the only predicate C. Also the occurrence of C in $A \rightarrow BCD$ is removed, i.e. this rule is replaced by $A \rightarrow B[C]D$.

Step 3 removes all rules with an empty rhs, viz. $B \rightarrow \epsilon$ and $D \rightarrow \epsilon$, and replaces $A \rightarrow B[C]D$ by the set of all rules which result from either eliminating or retaining the nullable members, viz. B and D (C is not a member anymore!), such that the rhs of the resulting rule is not empty. This yields the set of rules

$$\begin{array}{lcl} A & \rightarrow & B[C]D \\ A & \rightarrow & B[CD] \\ A & \rightarrow & [BC]D \end{array}$$

Step 4 adds the rules $A^\dagger \rightarrow A$ and $A^\dagger \rightarrow \epsilon$. The new start symbol is $A^\dagger$.

We have now obtained ϵ-*elim*(G_2), which is defined by

$$\begin{array}{lcl} A^\dagger & \rightarrow & A \\ A^\dagger & \rightarrow & \epsilon \\ A & \rightarrow & B[C]D \\ A & \rightarrow & B[CD] \\ A & \rightarrow & [BC]D \\ B & \rightarrow & b \\ D & \rightarrow & d \end{array}$$

□

Note that in the case that ϵ-*elim* introduces a new start symbol $S^\dagger$, there is no need to augment the grammar (i.e. add the rule $S' \rightarrow S^\dagger$ and make S' the new start symbol) for the purpose of constructing the LR automaton. Augmentation is in this case superfluous because the start symbol $S^\dagger$ is not recursive.

In the case of G_1, the transformation yields the following grammar.

$$\begin{array}{lcl} A & \rightarrow & BAc \\ A & \rightarrow & [B]Ac \\ A & \rightarrow & a \\ B & \rightarrow & b \end{array}$$

The LR(0) table for this grammar is represented in Figure 3.

Together with the growing number of rules, the above transformation may also give rise to a growing number of states in the LR(0) automaton. In the above case, the number of states increases from 7 to 8, as indicated by Figures 2 and 3. As G_1 is only a trivial grammar, we may expect that the increase of the number of states for practical grammars is much larger. Tangible results are discussed in Section 5.

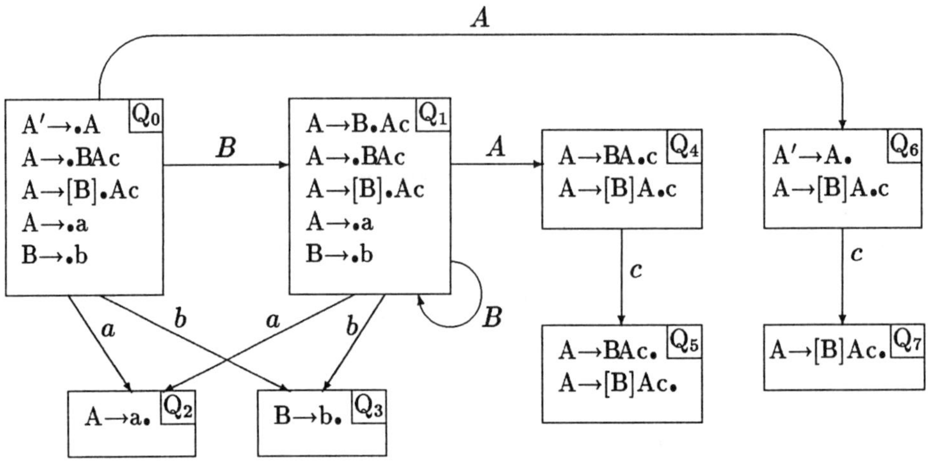

Figure 3. The LR(0) automaton for ϵ-$elim(G_1)$.

2.3. A NEW PARSING ALGORITHM

To reduce the number of states needed for an LR automaton for ϵ-$elim(G)$, we incorporate the transformation in the closure function. This requires changing the behaviour of the LR automaton upon reduction.

This approach can in a different way be explained as follows. Items derived from the same basic item by ϵ-$elim$ are considered the same. For instance, the items $A \to BAc\bullet$ and $A \to [B]Ac\bullet$ in Figure 3 are considered the same because they are derived from the same basic item $A \to BAc\bullet$.

All items are now represented by the basic item from which they are derived. For instance, both items in Q_5 in Figure 3 are henceforth represented by the single basic item $A \to BAc\bullet$. The item $A \to [B]Ac\bullet$ in state Q_7 is now represented by $A \to BAc\bullet$.

As a result, some pairs of states now consist of identical sets of items and may therefore be merged. For the example in Figure 3, the new collection of states is given in Figure 4. It can be seen that states Q_5 and Q_7 are merged into state $Q_{5/7}$.

In the resulting LR table, it is no longer indicated which derived items are actually represented. Correspondingly, the behaviour of the new automaton is such that upon reduction all possibilities of derived items are to be tried nondeterministically.

For instance, consider the parsing of *bacc* using the LR(0) automaton in Figure 4. The first sequence of parsing steps is without complications:

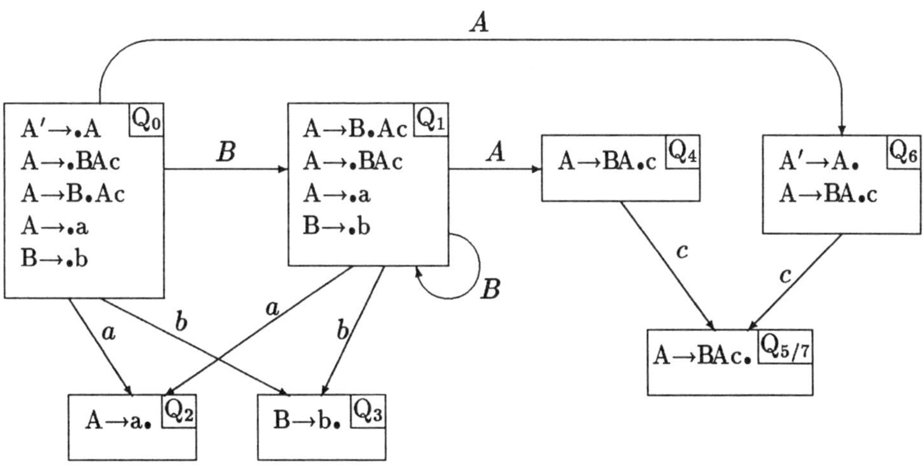

Figure 4. The optimised LR(0) automaton for ϵ-*elim*(G_1) with merged states.

Stack contents	Inp.	Action
Q_0	$bacc$	shift
$Q_0\ b\ Q_3$	acc	red$(B \rightarrow b)$
$Q_0\ B\ Q_1$	acc	shift
$Q_0\ B\ Q_1\ a\ Q_2$	cc	red$(A \rightarrow a)$
$Q_0\ B\ Q_1\ A\ Q_4$	cc	shift
$Q_0\ B\ Q_1\ A\ Q_4\ c\ Q_{5/7}$	c	red(?)

Now there are two ways to perform a reduction with the item $A \rightarrow BAc\bullet$. One way is to assume that B has been eliminated from this rule. In other words, we are dealing with the derived item $A \rightarrow [B]Ac\bullet$. In this case we remove two states and grammar symbols from the stack. The sequence of configurations from here on now begins with

$Q_0\ B\ Q_1\ A\ Q_4\ c\ Q_{5/7}$	c	red$(A \rightarrow [B]Ac)$
$Q_0\ B\ Q_1\ A\ Q_4$	c	
⋮	⋮	⋮

The other way to perform reduction is by taking off the stack all the members in the rule $A \rightarrow BAc$ and the same number of states, and we obtain

$Q_0\ B\ Q_1\ A\ Q_4\ c\ Q_{5/7}$	c	red$(A \rightarrow BAc)$
$Q_0\ A\ Q_6$	c	shift
$Q_0\ A\ Q_6\ c\ Q_{5/7}$		red(?)

We are now at an interesting configuration. We have again the choice between reducing with $A \rightarrow [B]Ac$ or with the unaffected rule $A \rightarrow BAc$.

However, it can be established that reduction with $A \rightarrow BAc$ is not possible, because there is no B on the stack to be popped.

At this point, the main difference between traditional LR parsing and the new parsing technique we are developing becomes clear. Whereas for traditional LR parsing, the grammar symbols on the stack have no other purpose except an explanatory one, for our new parsing technique, the investigation of the grammar symbols on the stack is essential for guiding correct parsing steps.

In general, what happens upon reduction is this. Suppose the state on top of the stack contains an item of the form $A \rightarrow \alpha\bullet$, then reduction with this item is performed in the following steps.

1. The parser nondeterministically looks for some sequence of grammar symbols $X_1, \ldots, X_m$ such that there are $\alpha_0, \ldots, \alpha_m$ with
   - $\alpha = \alpha_0 X_1 \alpha_1 \ldots X_m \alpha_m$
   - $\alpha_0 \rightarrow^* \epsilon \wedge \ldots \wedge \alpha_m \rightarrow^* \epsilon$
   - The top-most m grammar symbols on the stack are $X_1, \ldots, X_m$ in that order, i.e. X_1 is deepest in the stack and X_m is on top of the stack.
   - $m = 0 \Rightarrow A = S'$

   In words, α is divided into a part which is on the stack and a part which consists only of nullable nonterminals. The part on the stack should not be empty with the exception of the case where $A \rightarrow \alpha$ is the rule $S' \rightarrow S$.
2. The top-most m symbols and states are popped off the stack.
3. Suppose that the state on top of the stack is Q, then
   - if $A = S'$, then the input is accepted, provided Q is the initial state and the end of the input has been reached; and
   - if $A \neq S'$, then A and subsequently $goto(Q, A)$ are pushed onto the stack, provided $goto(Q, A)$ is defined (otherwise this step fails).

The way the reduction is handled above corresponds with the reduction with the rule $A \rightarrow [\alpha_0]X_1[\alpha_1] \ldots X_m[\alpha_m]$ in the original LR(0) parser for ϵ-$elim(G)$.

Incorporating the transformation ϵ-$elim$ into the construction of the LR table can be seen as a restatement of the usual closure function, as follows.

$$\begin{aligned} closure(q) \; = \; & \{B \rightarrow \delta\bullet\theta \mid A \rightarrow \alpha\bullet\beta \in q \;\wedge\; \beta \rightarrow^* B\gamma \;\wedge\; B \rightarrow \delta\theta \;\wedge \\ & \qquad \exists v[v \neq \epsilon \;\wedge\; \delta\theta \rightarrow^* v] \;\wedge\; \delta \rightarrow^* \epsilon\} \\ & \cup \\ & \{A \rightarrow \alpha\delta\bullet\beta \mid A \rightarrow \alpha\bullet\delta\beta \in q \;\wedge\; \delta \rightarrow^* \epsilon\} \end{aligned}$$

Note that the expression $\beta \rightarrow^* B\gamma$ allows nonterminals to be rewritten to the empty string. Also note that $\exists v[v \neq \epsilon \wedge \delta\theta \rightarrow^* v]$ excludes rules of which the rhs can only derive ϵ. Efficient implementation of the closure function is investigated in Section 4.1.

Leermakers (1992) proposes similar changes to some functions in the recursive ascent Earley parser in order to allow hidden left recursion. Similar changes were made by Graham *et al.* (1980) and Leiss (1990) in order to improve the efficiency of Earley parsing. A parsing technique very similar to ours is suggested by Leermakers (1993). A similar idea is also suggested by Sikkel (1990), but without details.

The investigation of the grammar symbols on the stack for the purpose of guiding correct parsing steps is reminiscent of Pager (1970), who proposed a general method for the compression of parsing tables by merging states. If the full stack may be investigated at each step, then the need for states in the traditional sense is even completely removed, as shown by Fortes Gálves (1992).[3]

In Section 3 we prove the correctness of the new parsing technique, which we call ϵ-LR parsing.

2.4. DEALING WITH CYCLIC GRAMMARS

If needed, ϵ-LR parsing can be further refined to handle cyclic grammars.

The starting-point is again a transformation on grammars, called *C-elim*, which eliminates all *unit rules*, i.e. all rules of the form $A \rightarrow B$. This transformation consists of the following steps.

1. Let G_0 be G.
2. Replace every non-unit rule $A \rightarrow \alpha$ in G_0 by the set of rules of the form $B \rightarrow \alpha$ such that $B \overset{G}{\rightarrow}{}^* A$ and either $B = S$ or B has an occurrence in the rhs of some non-unit rule.
3. Remove all unit rules from G_0.
4. Let *C-elim*(G) be G_0.

Termination of LR parsing according to *C-elim*$(\epsilon$*-elim*$(G))$ is guaranteed for any G.

If we incorporate *C-elim* into our ϵ-LR parsers, then reduction with $A \rightarrow \alpha$ is performed by the following steps.

1. The parser nondeterministically looks for some sequence of grammar symbols $X_1, \ldots, X_m$ such that there are $\alpha_0, \ldots, \alpha_m$ with

[3] It is interesting to note that various degrees of simplification of the collection of sets of items are possible. For example, there is an approach half-way between our approach and the one by Fortes, according to which items consist only of the parts which occur normally after the dots. A different way to look at this is as LR parsing for a grammar transformed by transformation τ_{two} from Nederhof and Satta (1994).

- $\alpha = \alpha_0 X_1 \alpha_1 \ldots X_m \alpha_m$
- $\alpha_0 \rightarrow^* \epsilon \wedge \ldots \wedge \alpha_m \rightarrow^* \epsilon$
- The top-most m grammar symbols on the stack are $X_1, \ldots, X_m$.
- $m = 0 \Rightarrow A = S'$
- $m = 1 \Rightarrow (X_1 \in T \vee A = S')$

2. The top-most m symbols and states are popped off the stack.
3. Suppose that the state on top of the stack is Q, then
   - if $A = S'$, then the input is accepted, provided Q is the initial state and the end of the input has been reached; and
   - if $A \neq S'$, then the parser nondeterministically looks for some nonterminal B such that $B \rightarrow^* A$ and $goto(Q, B)$ is defined, and then B and subsequently $goto(Q, B)$ are pushed onto the stack.

Note that the parser which performs reduction in this way, using the parse tables from the ϵ-LR parser, may go into unnecessary dead alleys of length one. The reason is that the goto function is defined in cases where is it obvious that the next step must be a reduction with a rule with a single non-predicate in its rhs, which is of course blocked by the above formulation of reduction. This may be avoided by reformulating the closure function such that rules containing a single non-predicate in their right-hand sides are left out.

How to avoid reductions with unit rules (*unit reductions*) in the case of deterministic LR parsing has been investigated in a number of papers, e.g. Heilbrunner (1985). Our particular technique of avoiding unit reductions is reminiscent of an optimization of Earley's algorithm (Graham *et al.*, 1980).

In the remaining part of this chapter, the term "ϵ-LR parsing" will not include the extra extension to ϵ-LR parsing described in this section.

2.5. APPLICABILITY OF ϵ-LR PARSING

In the same way as LR(0) parsing can be refined to SLR(k), LALR(k), and LR(k) parsing ($k > 0$) we can also refine ϵ-LR(0) parsing to ϵ-SLR(k), ϵ-LALR(k), and ϵ-LR(k) parsing. The construction of ϵ-LR tables for these parsing strategies can be adopted from the construction of their LR counterparts in a reasonably straightforward way.

We have shown that ϵ-LR parsing can be used for hidden left-recursive grammars, which cannot be handled using ordinary LR parsing. The variants of ϵ-LR parsing which apply lookahead are useful for making the parsing process more deterministic, i.e. to reduce the number of entries in the parsing table that contain multiple actions.

However, adding lookahead cannot yield completely deterministic parsers in the case of hidden left recursion where at least one of the hiding nonterminals is not a predicate. This is because such a grammar is ambiguous, as discussed earlier. (If all hiding nonterminals are predicates, then we are dealing with a trivial form of hidden left recursion, which can easily be eliminated by eliminating the hiding nonterminals.)

Also in the case of grammars without hidden left recursion, ϵ-LR parsing may have an advantage over ordinary (generalized) LR parsing: the parsing actions corresponding with subtrees of the parse tree which have empty yields are avoided. For these grammars, the application of lookahead may serve to construct deterministic ϵ-LR parsers.

Nederhof (1993a) describes how subtrees which have empty yields can be attached to the complete parse tree without actually parsing the empty string.

2.6. SPECIFIC ELIMINATION OF HIDDEN LEFT RECURSION

For the sake of completeness, we describe a way of removing hidden left recursion without using epsilon rule elimination. The idea is that we selectively remove occurrences of nullable nonterminals which hide left recursion. In case of a nullable non-predicate A, we replace the occurrence of A by an occurrence of a new nonterminal A'. This A' is constructed so as to derive the same set of strings as A does, with the exception of ϵ.

The transformation, constructing the grammar *HLR-elim*(G) from grammar G, consists of the following steps.

1. Let G_0 be G.
2. For every rule $A \to B\alpha$ in G_0 which leads to a hidden left-recursive call (i.e. $\alpha \stackrel{G}{\to}^* A\beta$ for some β, and $B \stackrel{G}{\to}^* \epsilon$), replace the rule by $A \to \alpha$, and also add $A \to B'\alpha$ to G_0 provided B is not a predicate in G. Repeat this step until it can no longer be applied.
3. For every new nonterminal A' introduced in G_0 in step 2, or by an earlier iteration of step 3, and for every rule $A \to \alpha$ in G_0, add to G_0 the rule
   - $A' \to \alpha$ if not $\alpha \stackrel{G}{\to}^* \epsilon$, or rules of the form
   - $A' \to X_i' X_{i+1} \ldots X_n$ if $\alpha \stackrel{G}{\to}^* \epsilon$, where $\alpha = X_1 \ldots X_n$, and X_i $(1 \leq i \leq n)$ is not a predicate.
4. Remove from G_0 all rules $A \to \alpha$ such that A was rendered unreachable by the elimination of rules in step 2.
5. Let *HLR-elim*(G) be G_0.

Example 2.2 Let the grammar G_3 be defined by

$$\begin{array}{lll} A & \rightarrow & ABAa \\ A & \rightarrow & AAB \\ A & \rightarrow & \epsilon \\ B & \rightarrow & \epsilon \end{array}$$

The grammar *HLR-elim*(G_3) is given by

$$\begin{array}{lll} A & \rightarrow & Aa \\ A & \rightarrow & A'BAa \\ A & \rightarrow & AB \\ A & \rightarrow & A'AB \\ A & \rightarrow & \epsilon \\ A' & \rightarrow & Aa \\ A' & \rightarrow & A'BAa \\ A' & \rightarrow & A'B \\ A' & \rightarrow & A'AB \\ B & \rightarrow & \epsilon \end{array}$$ □

The transformation *HLR-elim* is very often incorporated in the construction of parsers which can deal with hidden left recursion. An example is the variant of backtrack left-corner parsing as applied in Programmar (Meijer, 1986). See also Nederhof (1993a). A transformation by Graham *et al.* (1980) is related to *HLR-elim*, but also transforms the grammar into an extended Chomsky normal form.

The size of the grammar resulting from the application of this transformation is much smaller than that in the case of ϵ-*elim*. In fact it is only quadratic in the size of the original grammar.

3. CORRECTNESS OF ϵ-LR PARSING

A formal derivation of ϵ-LR(0) parsing is given by Nederhof (1994). In this section we prove the correctness of ϵ-LR parsing by assuming the correctness of (nondeterministic) LR parsing, which has already been established in the literature.

In Section 2.3 we derived the new parsing technique of ϵ-LR parsing. We showed that this kind of parsing is based on traditional LR parsing, with the following differences:

- Instead of using the original grammar G, the transformed grammar ϵ-*elim*(G) is used.
- No distinction is made between items derived from the same basic item. This can be seen as merging states of the LR automaton of ϵ-*elim*(G).
- Because considering derived items as the same leads to a loss of information, a new mechanisms is introduced, which checks upon reduction whether the members of the applied rule are actually on the stack and

whether the goto function is defined for the lhs and the state which is on top of the stack after the members are popped.

Because the transformation ϵ-*elim* preserves the language and because we assume the correctness of LR parsing, the correctness of ϵ-LR parsing can be proved by mentioning two points:

- The symbols on the stack and the remaining input together derive the original input, which can be proved by induction on the length of a sequence of parsing steps. This argument shows that no incorrect derivations can be found.
- For every sequence of parsing steps performed by an LR parser (LR(k), SLR(k), etc.) for ϵ-*elim*(G) there is a corresponding sequence of parsing steps performed by the corresponding type of ϵ-LR parser (ϵ-LR(k), ϵ-SLR(k), etc.) for G.
  This proves that ϵ-LR parsing cannot fail to find correct derivations by the assumption that LR parsing according to ϵ-*elim*(G) does not fail to find correct derivations.

In case of ϵ-LR(0) and ϵ-SLR parsing it can also be shown that the set of sequences of parsing steps is isomorphic with the set of sequences of the LR(0) or SLR parsers for ϵ-*elim*(G), and that the corresponding sequences are equally long. It is sufficient to prove that if a reduction can be successfully performed in an ϵ-LR parser, then it can be performed in an LR parser in the corresponding configuration.

For this purpose, suppose that in an ϵ-LR parser some reduction is possible with the item $A \to \alpha_0 A_1 \alpha_1 \dots A_m \alpha_m \bullet \in Q_m$ such that

- $\alpha_i \to^* \epsilon$ for $0 \le i \le m$,
- the topmost $2m + 1$ elements of the stack are $Q_0 A_1 Q_1 \dots A_m Q_m$,
- the goto function for Q_0 and A is defined,
- in the corresponding configuration in the LR parser, the states corresponding with Q_i are called Q'_i.

From the fact that the goto function is defined for Q_0 and A we know that it is also defined for Q'_0 and A and that the item $A \to [\alpha_0] \bullet A_1 [\alpha_1] \dots A_m [\alpha_m]$ is in Q'_0. This implies that $A \to [\alpha_0] A_1 [\alpha_1] \dots A_i [\alpha_i] \bullet \dots A_m [\alpha_m]$ is in Q'_i because Q'_i is *goto*(Q'_{i-1}, A_i), for $1 \le i \le m$.

Therefore, in the corresponding LR parser a reduction would also take place according to the item $A \to [\alpha_0] A_1 [\alpha_1] \dots A_m [\alpha_m] \bullet$.

Regrettably, an isomorphism between sequences of parsing steps of ϵ-LR parsers and the corresponding LR parsers is not possible for ϵ-LR(k) and ϵ-LALR(k) parsing, where $k > 0$. This is because merging derived items causes loss of information on the lookahead of items. This causes the parser to be sent up blind alleys which are not considered by the corresponding LR parser.

Because ϵ-LR parsing retains the prefix-correctness of traditional LR parsing (that is, upon incorrect input the parser does not move its input pointer across the first invalid symbol), the blind alleys considered by an ϵ-LR parser but not the corresponding LR parser are of limited length, and therefore unimportant in practical cases.

Theoretically however, the extra blind alleys may be avoided by attaching the lookahead information not to the state on top of the stack before reduction but to the state on top after popping m states and grammar symbols off the stack (m as in Section 2.3). This means that we have lookahead (a set of strings, each of which not longer than k symbols) for each state q and nonterminal A for which $goto(q, A)$ is defined.

In the cases we have examined, the number of pairs (q, A) for which $goto(q, A)$ is defined is larger than the total number of items $A \to \alpha\bullet$ in all states (about 4 to 25 times as large), so this idea is not beneficial to the memory requirements of storing lookahead information. In the case of ϵ-LR(k) parsing ($k > 0$), this idea may however lead to a small reduction of the number of states, since some states may become identical after the lookahead information has been moved to other states.

4. CALCULATION OF ITEMS

In this section we investigate the special properties of the closure function for ϵ-LR parsing. First we discuss the closure function for ϵ-LR(k) parsing and then the equivalent notion of kernel items in ϵ-LR parsing.

4.1. THE CLOSURE FUNCTION FOR ϵ-LR(K) PARSING

If w is a string and k a natural number, then $k : w$ denotes w if the length of w is less than k, and otherwise it denotes the prefix of w of length k. We use lookaheads which may be less than k symbols long to indicate that the end of the string has been reached.

The initial state for ϵ-LR(k) parsing ($k > 0$) is

$$Q_0 = closure(\{[S' \to \bullet S, \epsilon]\})$$

The closure function for ϵ-LR(k) parsing is

$$\begin{aligned} closure(q) = \; & \{[B \to \delta\bullet\theta, x] \mid [A \to \alpha\bullet\beta, w] \in q \wedge \beta \to^* B\gamma \wedge B \to \delta\theta \\ & \quad \wedge \exists v[v \neq \epsilon \wedge \delta\theta \to^* v] \wedge \delta \to^* \epsilon \\ & \quad \wedge \exists y[\gamma \to^* y \wedge x = k : yw]\} \\ & \cup \\ & \{[A \to \alpha\delta\bullet\beta, w] \mid [A \to \alpha\bullet\delta\beta, w] \in q \wedge \delta \to^* \epsilon\} \end{aligned}$$

4.2. THE DETERMINATION OF SMALLEST REPRESENTATIVE SETS

In traditional LR parsing, items are divided into *kernel* items and *nonkernel* items. Kernel items are $S' \rightarrow \bullet S$ and all items whose dots are not at the left end. The nonkernel items are all the others. (At this stage we abstain from lookahead.)

As we will only be looking in this section at sets of items which are either Q_0 or of the form $goto(q, X)$, which result after application of the closure function, we have that the kernel items from a set of items q are a *representative subset* of q. This means that we can

- construct the complete set of items q by applying the closure function to the representative subset, and
- determine whether two sets of items are equal by determining the equality of their representative subsets.

Because the set of kernel items from a set q is in general much smaller than q itself, kernel items are very useful for the efficient generation of LR parsers.

Regrettably, in the case that the grammar contains many epsilon rules, the set of kernel items from a set q may not be much smaller than q itself. In this case therefore, kernel items may not be very useful for generation of ϵ-LR parsers.

Another approach to finding representative subsets for traditional LR parsing can be given in terms of the stages in which the goto function is executed. According to this principle, the representative subset of $goto(q, X)$ is

$$K(q, X) = \{A \rightarrow \alpha X \bullet \beta \mid A \rightarrow \alpha \bullet X\beta \in q\}$$

and other items in $goto(q, X)$ are obtained by applying the closure function to $K(q, X)$.

In the case of traditional LR parsing, K computes exactly the kernel items in $goto(q, X)$, and therefore the two methods for finding representative subsets are equivalent. That this does not hold for ϵ-LR parsing can be easily seen by investigating the definition of *closure* in Section 2.3: according to the second part

$$\{A \rightarrow \alpha\delta \bullet \beta \mid A \rightarrow \alpha \bullet \delta\beta \in q \ \wedge \ \delta \rightarrow^* \epsilon\}$$

in this definition, the dot can be shifted over nullable members and therefore new items can be added whose dots are not at the left end. Therefore, some kernel items may not be in $K(q, X)$.

It turns out that we can also not use K for finding representative subsets in the case of ϵ-LR parsing. The reason is that K does not provide a *well-defined* method to find representative subsets. I.e. for some grammars we can find sets of items q_1 and q_2 and symbols X and Y such that $goto(q_1, X) = goto(q_2, Y)$ but $K(q_1, X) \neq K(q_2, Y)$.

The solution that we propose is more refined than the methods in traditional LR parsing.

First, we determine the equivalence relation of mutually left-recursive nonterminals, whose classes are denoted by $[A]$. Thus, $[A] = \{B | A \rightarrow^* B\alpha \wedge B \rightarrow^* A\beta\}$.

A nice property of these classes is that $A \rightarrow \bullet\alpha \in q$ and $B \in [A]$ together imply that $B \rightarrow \bullet\beta \in q$ for every rule $B \rightarrow \beta$. Using this fact, we can replace every item $A \rightarrow \bullet\alpha$ in q by $[A]$ without loss of information.

We define the set Z to be the union of the set of all items and the set of equivalence classes of mutually left-recursive nonterminals. The variables $E, E', \ldots$ in the sequel range over elements from Z.

Our goal is to find a representative set $q' \subseteq Z$ for each set of items q.

First, we define the binary relation *induces* on elements from Z such that

- $induces(I, J)$ for items I and J
  if and only if $I = A \rightarrow \alpha\bullet B\beta$ and $J = A \rightarrow \alpha B\bullet\beta$ and $B \rightarrow^* \epsilon$
- $induces(I, E)$ for item I and class E
  if and only if $I = A \rightarrow \alpha\bullet B\beta$ and $B \in E$
- $induces(E, E')$ for classes E and E'
  if and only if $E \neq E'$ and there are $A \in E$ and $B \in E'$ such that $A \rightarrow \alpha B\beta$ and $\alpha \rightarrow^* \epsilon$
- $induces(E, I)$ for class E and item I
  if and only if there is $A \in E$ such that $I = A \rightarrow \alpha\bullet\beta$ and $\alpha \rightarrow^* \epsilon$

The smallest set $repr(q) \subseteq Z$ representing a set of items q can now be determined by the following steps:

1. Determine $q_1 \subseteq Z$ by replacing in q every item $A \rightarrow \bullet\alpha$ by $[A]$.
2. Let q_2 be the subset of q_1 which results from eliminating all items I such that $induces(E, I)$ for some equivalence class $E \in q_1$.
3. Determine the set $repr(q)$ defined by $\{E \in q_2 | \neg\exists E' \in q_2[induces(E', E)]\}$.

The reason that no information is lost in step 3 is that the relation *induces* restricted to q_2 is not cyclic.

That $repr(q)$ is the smallest set $q' \subseteq Z$ representing q can be formalized by stating that it is the smallest subset q' of Z such that $closure(q') = q$, where the definition of *closure* is redefined to

$$
\begin{aligned}
closure(q) \; = \\
& \{B \rightarrow \delta{\bullet}\theta \mid ((A \rightarrow \alpha{\bullet}\beta \in q \;\wedge\; \beta \rightarrow^{*} B\gamma) \;\vee\; ([A] \in q \;\wedge\; A \rightarrow^{*} B\gamma)) \;\wedge \\
& \qquad B \rightarrow \delta\theta \;\wedge \\
& \qquad \exists v[v \neq \epsilon \;\wedge\; \delta\theta \rightarrow^{*} v] \;\wedge\; \delta \rightarrow^{*} \epsilon\} \\
& \cup \\
& \{A \rightarrow \alpha\delta{\bullet}\beta \mid A \rightarrow \alpha{\bullet}\delta\beta \in q \;\wedge\; \delta \rightarrow^{*} \epsilon\}
\end{aligned}
$$

It is evident that the *repr*(*goto*(q, X)) must be calculated from the $K(q, X)$ rather than from their closures *goto*(q, X) if efficient parser construction is required. The appropriate restatement of the algorithm calculating *repr* is straightforward.

5. MEMORY REQUIREMENTS

In this chapter we have described three methods of making the (generalized) LR parsing technique applicable to hidden left-recursive grammars:

1. Apply ϵ-*elim* to the grammar before constructing the LR automaton.
2. Apply *HLR-elim* to the grammar before constructing the LR automaton.
3. Construct the ϵ-LR automaton as opposed to the LR automaton.

The last method above is derived from the first one in the sense that an ϵ-LR automaton can be seen as a compressed LR automaton for the transformed grammar ϵ-*elim*(G). The second method is independent from the other two methods.

To investigate the static memory requirements of these methods, we have determined the number of states of the resulting automata for various grammars.

We first investigate the number of states for three kinds of characteristic grammars:

For every $k \geq 0$ we have the grammar G_1^k defined by the rules

$$
\begin{array}{lcl}
S & \rightarrow & B_1 \ldots B_k c \\
B_1 & \rightarrow & \epsilon \\
B_1 & \rightarrow & b_1 \\
 & \vdots & \\
B_k & \rightarrow & \epsilon \\
B_k & \rightarrow & b_k
\end{array}
$$

For every $k \geq 1$ we have the grammar G_2^k defined by the rules

Method of construction	G_1^k $(k \geq 0)$	G_2^k $(k \geq 1)$	G_3^k $(k \geq 2)$	G_{Deltra}
LR(0) for G	$2{\cdot}k+3$	$2{\cdot}k+5$	$2{\cdot}k+2$	855
LR(0) for ϵ-$elim(G)$	$2^{k+1}+k+1$	$3{\cdot}2^k+k+1$	$2^{k+1}+2$	1430
LR(0) for HLR-$elim(G)$	$2{\cdot}k+3$	$\frac{1}{2}{\cdot}k^2+4\frac{1}{2}{\cdot}k+3$	$\frac{1}{2}{\cdot}k^2+2\frac{1}{2}{\cdot}k+1$	1477
ϵ-LR(0) for G	$2{\cdot}k+3$	$k+6$	6	709

Figure 5. The numbers of states resulting from four different methods of constructing LR and ϵ-LR automata.

$$
\begin{array}{lcl}
S & \rightarrow & B_1 \ldots B_k S c \\
S & \rightarrow & d \\
B_1 & \rightarrow & \epsilon \\
B_1 & \rightarrow & b_1 \\
 & \vdots & \\
B_k & \rightarrow & \epsilon \\
B_k & \rightarrow & b_k
\end{array}
$$

For every $k \geq 2$ we have the grammar G_3^k defined by the rules

$$
\begin{array}{lcl}
S & \rightarrow & B_1 \ldots B_k c \\
B_1 & \rightarrow & \epsilon \\
B_1 & \rightarrow & S \\
 & \vdots & \\
B_k & \rightarrow & \epsilon \\
B_k & \rightarrow & S
\end{array}
$$

The grammars of the first group contain no left recursion. The grammars of the second group contain one occurrence of hidden left recursion, and there are k nullable nonterminals hiding the left recursion. The grammars of the third group contain $k-1$ occurrences of hidden left recursion, the j-th one of which is hidden by $j-1$ nullable nonterminals.

Figure 5 shows the numbers of states of various automata for these grammars. It also shows the numbers of states of the LR(0) automata for the original grammars. This kind of automaton does of course not terminate in the case of hidden left recursion, except if the nondeterminism is realized using cyclic graph-structured stacks, against which we raised some objections in Section 1.

These results show that the number of states is always smallest for the ϵ-LR(0) automata. A surprising case is the group of grammars G_3^k, where the number of states of ϵ-LR(0) is 6, regardless of k, whereas the numbers of states of the LR(0) automata for ϵ-*elim*(G) and *HLR-elim*(G) are exponential and quadratic in k, respectively.

In the above grammars we have found some features which cause a difference in the number of states of the automata constructed by the mentioned four methods. The results suggest that ϵ-LR parsing is more efficient in the number of states for grammars containing more hidden left recursion.

The number of states of LR and ϵ-LR automata is however rather unpredictable, and therefore the above relations between the number of states for the four methods may deviate dramatically from those in the case of practical grammars.

Practical hidden left-recursive grammars do however not yet occur frequently in natural language research. The reason is that they are often considered "ill-designed" (Nozohoor-Farshi, 1989) as they cannot be handled using most parsing techniques.

Fortunately, we have been able to find a practical grammar which contains enough hidden left recursion to perform a serious comparison. This grammar is the context-free part of the Deltra grammar, developed at the Delft University of Technology (Schoorl and Belder, 1990). After elimination of the occurrences and definitions of all predicates, this grammar contains 846 rules and 281 nonterminals, 120 of which are nullable. Hidden left recursion occurs in the definitions of 62 nonterminals. Rules are up to 7 members long, the average length being about 1.74 members.

The numbers of states of the automata for this grammar are given in Figure 5. These data suggest that for practical grammars containing much hidden left recursion, the relation between the numbers of states of the four different automata is roughly the same as for the three groups of small grammars G_1^k, G_2^k, and G_3^k: the LR(0) automata for ϵ-*elim*(G) and *HLR-elim*(G) both have a large number of states. (Surprisingly enough, the former has a *smaller* number of states than the latter, although ϵ-*elim*(G) is about 50 % larger than *HLR-elim*(G), measured in the number of symbols.) The ϵ-LR(0) automaton for G has the smallest number of states, even smaller than the number of states of the LR(0) automaton for G.

Although these results are favourable to ϵ-LR parsing as a parsing technique requiring small parsers, not for all practical grammars will ϵ-LR automata be smaller than their traditional LR counterparts. Especially for grammars without left recursion, we have found small increases in the number of states. We consider these grammars not characteristic however because they were developed explicitly for top-down parsing.

CONCLUSIONS

We have described a new solution to adapt (generalized) LR parsing to grammars with hidden left recursion. Also LR parsing of cyclic grammars has been discussed. We claim that our solution yields smaller parsers than other solutions, measured in the number of states. This has been corroborated by theoretical data on small grammars and by an empirical test on a practical grammar for a natural language.

Our solution requires the investigation of the parse stack. We feel however that this does not lead to deterioration of the time complexity of parsing: investigation of the stack for each reduction with some rule requires a constant amount of time. This amount of time is linear in the length of that rule, provided investigation of the symbols on the stack is implemented using a finite state automaton.

The results of our research are relevant to realization of generalized LR parsing using backtracking (possibly in combination with memo-functions) or using acyclic graph-structured stacks. Furthermore, various degrees of lookahead may be used.

We hope that our research will convince linguists and computer scientists that hidden left recursion is not an obstacle to efficient LR parsing. This may in the long term simplify the development of grammars, since hidden left recursion does not have to be avoided or eliminated.

Acknowledgements

We received kind help from Job Honig, Theo Vosse, John Carroll, and Hans de Vreught in finding a practical grammar to test our algorithms on. We acknowledge valuable correspondence with Giorgio Satta, René Leermakers and José Fortes.

References

Aho, A.V., Sethi, R. and Ullman, J.D. (1986) *Compilers: Principles, Techniques, and Tools.* Addison-Wesley.

Aho, A.V. and Ullman, J.D. (1972) *Parsing*, The Theory of Parsing, Translation and Compiling, volume 1. Prentice-Hall.

Fortes Gálves, J. (1992) Generating LR(1) parsers of small size. In: *Compiler Construction, 4th International Conference*, LNCS 641, 16–29, Springer-Verlag.

Graham, S.L., Harrison, M.A. and Ruzzo, W.L. (1980) An improved context-free recognizer. *ACM Trans. Prog. Lang. Syst.* 2(3), 415–462.

Heilbrunner, S. (1985) Truly prefix-correct chain-free LR(1) parsers. *Acta Inf.* 22, 499–536.

Koster, C.H.A. (1971) Affix grammars. In: Peck, J.E.L. (ed) *ALGOL68 Implementation*, 95–109. North Holland Publishing Company.

Lang, B. (1974) Deterministic techniques for efficient non-deterministic parsers. In: *Automata, Languages and Programming, 2nd Colloquium*, LNCS 14, 255–269, Springer-Verlag.

Leermakers, R. (1992) A recursive ascent Earley parser. *Inf. Process. Lett.* 41(2), 87–91.

Leermakers, R. (1993) *The Functional Treatment of Parsing.* Kluwer Academic Publishers.

Leermakers, R., Augusteijn, L. and Kruseman Aretz, F.E.J. (1992) A functional LR parser. *Theoretical Comput. Sci.* 104, 313–323.

Leiss, H. (1990) On Kilbury's modification of Earley's algorithm. *ACM Trans. Prog. Lang. Syst.* 12(4), 610–640.

Meijer, H. (1986) *Programmar: A Translator Generator.* PhD thesis, University of Nijmegen.

Nederhof, M.J. (1993a) Generalized left-corner parsing. In: *Sixth Conference of the European Chapter of the Association for Computational Linguistics*, 305–314.

Nederhof, M.J. (1993b) A new top-down parsing algorithm for left-recursive DCGs. In: *Programming Language Implementation and Logic Programming, 5th International Symposium*, LNCS 714, 108–122, Springer-Verlag.

Nederhof, M.J. (1994) *Linguistic Parsing and Program Transformations.* PhD thesis, University of Nijmegen.

Nederhof, M.J. and Sarbo, J.J. (1993) Efficient decoration of parse forests. In: Trost, H. (ed) *Feature Formalisms and Linguistic Ambiguity*, 53–78. Ellis Horwood.

Nederhof, M.J. and Satta, G. (1994) An extended theory of head-driven parsing. In: *32nd Annual Meeting of the Association for Computational Linguistics*, 210–217.

Nilsson, U. (1986) AID: An alternative implementation of DCGs. *New Generation Computing* 4, 383–399.

Nozohoor-Farshi, R. (1989) Handling of ill-designed grammars in Tomita's parsing algorithm. In: *International Workshop on Parsing Technologies*, 182–192.

Pager, D. (1970) A solution to an open problem by Knuth. *Inf. and Contr.* 17, 462–473.

Schoorl, J.J. and Belder, S. (1990) Computational linguistics at Delft: A status report. Report WTM/TT 90–09, Delft University of Technology, Applied Linguistics Unit.

Sikkel, K. (1990) Cross-fertilization of Earley and Tomita. Memoranda Informatica 90-69, University of Twente.

Sippu, S. and Soisalon-Soininen, E. (1990) *Parsing Theory, Vol. II: LR(k) and LL(k) Parsing.* Springer-Verlag.

Soisalon-Soininen, E. and Tarhio, J. (1988) Looping LR parsers. *Inf. Process. Lett.* 26(5), 251–253.

Thorup, M. (1994) Controlled grammatic ambiguity. *ACM Trans. Prog. Lang. Syst.* 16(3), 1024–1050.

Tomita, M. (1986) *Efficient Parsing for Natural Language.* Kluwer Academic Publishers.

4. TOWARDS A FORMAL UNDERSTANDING OF THE DETERMINISM HYPOTHESIS IN D-THEORY

JAMES ROGERS

Department of Computer and Information Sciences
University of Pennsylvania

AND

K. VIJAY-SHANKER

Department of Computer and Information Sciences
University of Delaware

Abstract.

We examine the determinism hypothesis of Marcus (1980), within the context of the D-theory parsers of Marcus et al. (1983), and propose a definition based on the notion of the standard referent (also of Marcus et al. (1983)). This gives us an understanding of D-theory parsers as parsers which can accommodate ambiguity by working with descriptions of trees rather than trees, but in which the degree of that ambiguity is strictly limited by the definition of the standard referent.

We develop a formal framework within which various notions of the standard referent can be defined, and which allows us to formally characterize the circumstances under which a parser meets our version of the determinism hypothesis relative to some definition of the standard referent. We identify a number of properties of these descriptions which are independent of the definition of standard referent and briefly discuss how the problem of showing that some particular class of descriptions meets the conditions of the hypothesis relative to a definition of the standard referent can be approached within our formal framework.

H. Bunt and M. Tomita (eds.), Recent Advances in Parsing Technology, 59–78.

1. INTRODUCTION

In Marcus (1980), deterministic parsers were introduced. These are parsers which satisfy the conditions of Marcus's determinism hypothesis, i.e., they are strongly deterministic in the sense that they do not simulate non-determinism in any way. In later work (Marcus et al. 1983) these parsers were modified to construct descriptions of trees rather than the trees themselves. The resulting D-theory parsers, by working with these descriptions, are capable of capturing a certain amount of ambiguity in the structures they build. In this context, it is not clear what it means for a parser to meet the conditions of the determinism hypothesis.

The object of this work is to clarify this and other issues pertaining to D-theory parsers and to provide a framework within which these issues can be examined formally. Thus we have a very narrow scope. We make no arguments about the linguistic issues D-theory parsers are meant to address, their relation to other parsing formalisms or the notion of determinism in general. Rather we focus on issues internal to D-theory parsers themselves.

While a D-theory parser constructs a description which may be satisfied by a number of trees, it is assumed that the eventual description it produces will define a single tree—the so called standard referent. We argue here that the conditions of the determinism hypothesis must be based partly on the notion of standard referent it uses. We argue further that those criteria provide a means of precisely characterizing the descriptions that can be built by a D-theory parser given a particular definition of standard referent.

We begin by examining the determinism hypothesis in the light of D-theory parsers and propose a definition, based on the notion of the standard referent, which we believe fulfills the intentions of Marcus (1980). We then survey the descriptions which occur in the literature on D-theory and the standard referents expected for those descriptions. From these examples, we can identify the minimal characteristics of the definition of the standard referent as it appears to be used in current practice.

In the core of the chapter we provide the foundations necessary to treat these notions formally. In Section 3 we introduce a formal language for this purpose. We use this to develop a syntactic characterization of those descriptions which uniquely determine a tree. Such a characterization is needed to capture the property of uniqueness of the standard referent. We then turn our attention to a syntactic mechanism in which various notions of the standard referent can be defined. This mechanism allows us to formally characterize the circumstances under which a description meets the conditions of the determinism hypothesis given a particular definition of the standard referent.

In Section 4 we explore the issues involved in showing that the class of descriptions built by a D-theory parser in fact meet the conditions of the determinism hypothesis relative to the definition of standard referent it uses. In considering these issues, we identify a number of properties which, independent of the definition of the standard referent, are necessarily shared by every description which meets the conditions of the determinism hypothesis. We then indicate how these issues can be approached within the framework introduced in Section 3.

Again, since our focus is not how languages may be parsed by D-theory parsers but rather the theory of the parsers themselves, the particulars of the restrictions and default rules we discuss are meant only to be examples, not proposals. On the other hand, we hope that this work will provide a foundation on which the adequacy of such proposals with respect to the determinism hypothesis may be explored.

2. D-THEORY AND THE DETERMINISM HYPOTHESIS

The determinism hypothesis in the context of the original deterministic parsers (Marcus 1980) asserts, in essence, that natural languages can be parsed left-to-right by a mechanism with limited look-ahead which builds 'indelible' structures, that is: a mechanism which never retracts any part of the structure it builds and uses every part of the structure it builds in an essential way in its output. The structure that these parsers build is a phrase-structure tree for the input. They fail when presented with a sufficiently long initial segment that has multiple readings which are incompatible.

The D-theory parsers of Marcus et al. (1983), build only (a description of) that portion of the phrase-structure tree that is common to all of the readings. Thus the problem of ambiguous initial segments is handled by building a structure that is ambiguous in the sense that there are multiple trees meeting the description which are incompatible.

The question arises: what becomes of the determinism hypothesis in this context? We take descriptions to be sets of formulae over predicates like domination, left-of (i.e., precedence), etc. which have been found to be useful in linguistics (Lasnik and Kupin 1977; Marcus 1980). The ambiguity they incorporate is potentially powerful enough to accommodate any degree of non-determinism, at least if arbitrary disjunction is allowed in the formulae. Thus some limitation must be placed on this ambiguity. The requirement that the parser make essential use of every part of the structure it builds provides some restriction. Since the output of the parser is a tree, and trees are completely determined by the literal formulae they satisfy, no disjunctive formula can be essential to the specification of the output. We interpret this as limiting the descriptions to conjunctions of literals. This can be strengthened considerably, however, simply on the grounds that any deterministic process must have a unique result.

The descriptions built by D-theory parsers never describe a single tree. When the analysis of the input is complete, a minimal representative of the set of trees meeting the description, the standard referent, is taken to represent the phrase structure of the input. Thus the mechanism for extracting the standard referent supplies the defaults to disambiguate the final description. Consequently there is a strong connection between this mechanism and the ambiguity admissible in the descriptions built by the parser—the mechanism must be capable of resolving the description into the appropriate phrase-structure tree.

This is the basis of our formulation of the determinism hypothesis for D-theory parsers: in addition to the requirements of the original determinism hypothesis, the descriptions the parser builds must have a unique standard referent. This clearly must be the case whenever that portion of the input that has been processed is potentially a string in the language. One can argue that it should be the case at all positions in well-formed input, but this is inconsequential for our purposes. What we are interested in is the constraints the descriptions and the mechanism place on each other via the hypothesis at those points at which it holds.

Parsing, then, proceeds in stages with the description being refined at each stage. At any stage there will be many trees which satisfy the description, but there must be a unique standard referent. The standard referent at any stage may well be incompatible with what is known at subsequent stages and thus will change from stage to stage. The description, on the other hand, is indelible.

2.1. DESCRIPTIONS AND STANDARD REFERENTS

Linguistic and psychological considerations (that the parser is intended to capture) determine the kinds of ambiguity which the descriptions must be able to accommodate at a minimum. These considerations were the motivation for introducing D-theory parsers to begin with. The mechanism for extracting the standard referent must be able to resolve at least those ambiguities. Since the mechanism supplies defaults, if one is to claim psycholinguistic significance for the parser, one ought to be able to justify those defaults on these grounds. These considerations determine a limit on the strength of the standard referent mechanism, and consequently a limit on the kinds of ambiguity the descriptions may admit at most. That upper bound is not fixed and it is a design issue for D-theory parsers. As the requirements change, standard referent mechanisms posited for prior versions may no longer be sufficient.

Based on Marcus et al. (1983), Marcus (1987), and Marcus and Hindle (1990), we identify three fundamental types of ambiguity which must be handled.

All descriptions can be extended. Consequently, every description is satisfied by an infinite set of trees. The obvious default is to build a standard referent which contains only those individuals named in the description.

Pairs of individuals may be related, in the description, by proper domination without being connected by a chain of individuals related by parent. In other words, the reflexive transitive closure of the parent relation may be a subset of the domination relation.[1] This is the ambiguity that motivated D-theory parsers in Marcus et al. (1983). The default is to interpret immediate proper domination as parent (Marcus et al. 1983).

Constants (names) may refer to the same individual. There are two specific examples of this. The first has to do with coordination structures, e.g., (Marcus et al. 1983)

They sell ripe apples, pears, and cherries from local orchards.
They sell ripe cheese, bread, and cider from local orchards.

Here, it is uncertain whether the object of "sell" is three conjoined NPs, a single NP containing three conjoined nouns, or something in between. Significantly, the ambiguity cannot be resolved without semantic analysis. Since Marcus et al. associate descriptions with the syntactic phase only, they must settle on a fixed tree before they have the benefit of the semantic analysis. Following Goodall (Goodall 1983), they resolve the issue by building a "three dimensional" structure in these cases, which incorporates each of the possible readings (Marcus et al. 1983; Marcus 1987; Marcus and Hindle 1990). ¿From our point of view, this is at least a violation of the spirit of the determinism hypothesis. On the other hand, the situation seems to resolve easily if one does not require a tree to be produced until all of the processing is complete. A natural default is for the NPs to co-refer if they can consistently do so. This provides a standard referent appropriate for the first sentence. The semantic analysis may add negative domination assertions based on the scope of the modifiers. In the case of the second sentence, for example, it would assert that the NP that dominates "ripe"

[1] We take domination to be reflexive, distinct from what we call "proper domination". What is often termed immediate domination we refer to as "parent" to distinguish it from the case of individuals related by proper domination that could *potentially* be related by parent, a case we refer to as "immediate proper domination".

cannot dominate "bread", etc. The consequence of these assertions in this case is that the NPs cannot co-refer.[2]

The second example occurs in both Marcus (1987), and Marcus and Hindle (1990), in

connection with a mechanism for assuring that all components of an utterance share a common root. Here numerous (names for) nodes linking components are introduced into the structure, and a mechanism for attaching them appropriately is provided. A part of the mechanism is a default that any of the names that can consistently co-refer do co-refer (Marcus 1987). For reasons that will be explained in the Section 4.1, we assume that this process takes place independently of the rest of the syntactic analysis. Nonetheless, we take this as evidence that possibly co-referring nodes might occur and that the appropriate default is to assume that they do co-refer.

2.2. THE BASIC MECHANISM

We understand the mechanism for extracting a standard referent as a mechanism for extending the description to one which unambiguously defines a tree. The first type of ambiguity mentioned above, that descriptions can always be extended, is handled by restricting our attention to trees over the nodes named in the description. There are two ways to interpret our version of the determinism hypothesis in light of this restriction: that all trees satisfying the result of applying the mechanism to the description extend some unique tree over the nodes named in the description, or that there is exactly one tree over the nodes named in the description that satisfies that result. In the second case there may be trees involving individuals other than those named in the description which satisfy the result but do not extend the standard referent. We choose the stronger of these interpretations—that all trees satisfying the result extend the standard referent.

The remaining two types of ambiguity are handled by the default rules:

$\triangleleft$-rule If a node t properly dominates a node u and t can consistently be the parent of u, then take t to be the parent of u,

$\approx$-rule If a node t can consistently be equal to a node u, then take t to equal u.

[2] In Marcus (1987), Marcus notes that it is not clear that the semantic analysis can resolve this situation without building a structure which may not be used. Our account resolves it in a manner that is no less deterministic than the syntactic analysis. On the other hand, in Marcus and Hindle (1990), the three dimensional analysis is a part of a more general mechanism which allows any number of constituents of a maximal projection to accumulate on its right-hand side. We make no claims at all about our approach in the general case.

We assume that the rules are applied simultaneously to all instances. This is not actually sufficient, since application of the rules can introduce new instances. We develop a formal treatment of the standard referent mechanism in Section 3.5, which accounts for such complications. For now assume that the rules are somehow applied to any introduced instances as well.

This mechanism can have three possible outcomes. The result may still be ambiguous, it may be inconsistent, or it may unambiguously determine a tree. In a case like

$$\text{prdom}(a,b), \text{prdom}(a,c), \text{not equal}(b,c) \tag{1}$$

(where *prdom* denotes proper domination) the result is ambiguous, being satisfied by both

$$\text{parent}(a,b), \text{parent}(a,c), \text{left-of}(b,c)$$

and

$$\text{parent}(a,b), \text{parent}(a,c), \text{left-of}(c,b).$$

In other cases like

$$\text{dom}(a,b), \text{dom}(b,c), \text{prdom}(a,c) \tag{2}$$

(where *dom* denotes reflexive domination) the result is inconsistent:

$$\text{equal}(a,b), \text{equal}(b,c), \text{parent}(a,c).$$

It is only in the third case that the description satisfies the requirements of the determinism hypothesis.

3. FORMALIZATION

With these informal notions of the descriptions produced by D-theory parsers and the kind of mechanisms required to extract a standard referent from them, we now turn to developing a formal foundation.

3.1. LANGUAGE

Our language is an ordinary first-order language. In general, we think in terms of a family of languages parameterized by the set constant symbols from which the formulae are built. Given a description we will work in the language of the constants occurring in that description.

Definition 1 *For K a countable set of constant symbols, let L_K be the language built up from K, a fixed countably infinite set of variables X, and* *the symbols:*

r — *a distinguished element of* K, *the* root,

$\lhd, \lhd^*, \lhd^+, \prec$ — *two place predicates:* parent, domination, proper domination, *and* left-of *respectively,*

$\approx$ — *equality,*

$\wedge, \vee, \neg, \forall, \exists, (,), [,]$ —
usual logical connectives, quantifiers, etc.

The terms of L_K are just the members of $K \cup X$. *Atomic formulae, literals* and *well-formed-formulae* are generated in the usual fashion. We use t, u, v, etc. to denote terms and ϕ, ψ, etc. to denote wffs. R denotes any of the predicates.

For any set of formulae Φ, $\mathcal{T}(\Phi)$ is the set of constant terms occurring in Φ and the language L_Φ is the language $L_{\mathcal{T}(\Phi)}$.

Definition 2 *A* description *is a finite set of literal formulae.*

Thus descriptions are conjunctive and quantifier-free.

3.2. MODELS

Our semantics are in terms of trees as first-order structures.

Definition 3 *A* model *for a language* L_K *is a tuple* $\langle \mathcal{U}, \mathcal{I}, \mathcal{P}, \mathcal{D}, \mathcal{L} \rangle$, *where:*
$\mathcal{U}$ *is a non-empty universe,*
$\mathcal{I}$ *is a function from* K *to* $\mathcal{U}$
$\mathcal{P}$, $\mathcal{D}$, *and* $\mathcal{L}$ *are binary relations over* $\mathcal{U}$
(interpreting $\lhd$, $\lhd^*$, *and* $\prec$ *respectively).*

Definition 4 *A* tree *is a model satisfying the conditions:*
For all $w, x, y, z \in \mathcal{U}$,

T1 $\langle \mathcal{I}(r), x \rangle \in \mathcal{D}$,
T2 $\langle x, x \rangle \in \mathcal{D}$,
T3 $\langle x, y \rangle, \langle y, x \rangle \in \mathcal{D} \Rightarrow x = y$,
T4 $\langle x, y \rangle, \langle y, z \rangle \in \mathcal{D} \Rightarrow \langle x, z \rangle \in \mathcal{D}$,
T5 $\langle x, y \rangle \in \mathcal{P} \Rightarrow \langle x, y \rangle \in \mathcal{D}$, *and* $\langle y, x \rangle \notin \mathcal{D}$
T6 $\langle x, z \rangle \in \mathcal{P}$ *and* $\langle x, y \rangle, \langle y, z \rangle \in \mathcal{D} \Rightarrow x = y$ *or* $y = z$,
T7 $\langle x, y \rangle \in \mathcal{D} \Rightarrow \langle y, x \rangle \in \mathcal{D}$ *or* $(\exists x', y')[\langle x, x' \rangle, \langle y', y \rangle \in \mathcal{P}$ *and* $\langle x, y' \rangle, \langle x', y \rangle \in \mathcal{D}]$,
T8 $\langle x, y \rangle \in \mathcal{D}$ *or* $\langle y, x \rangle \in \mathcal{D}$ *or* $\langle x, y \rangle \in \mathcal{L}$ *or* $\langle y, x \rangle \in \mathcal{L}$,
T9 $\langle x, y \rangle \in \mathcal{L} \Rightarrow \langle x, y \rangle \notin \mathcal{D}$, $\langle y, x \rangle \notin \mathcal{D}$ *and* $\langle y, x \rangle \notin \mathcal{L}$,
T10 $\langle x, y \rangle \in \mathcal{L}$ *and* $\langle x, w \rangle, \langle y, z \rangle \in \mathcal{D} \Rightarrow \langle w, z \rangle \in \mathcal{L}$,
T11 $\langle x, y \rangle, \langle y, z \rangle \in \mathcal{L} \Rightarrow \langle x, z \rangle \in \mathcal{L}$,

***T*12** *The sets* $\mathbf{L}_x = \{y \mid (\exists z)[\langle z, y\rangle, \langle z, x\rangle \in \mathcal{P}$ *and* $\langle y, x\rangle \in \mathcal{L}]\}$ *and* $\mathbf{B}_x = \{y \mid \langle y, x\rangle \in \mathcal{D}\}$ *are finite.*

The condition ***T*12** requires that the length of path from the root to any node be finite, and that each node have finitely many left siblings. At least one tree (that consisting of only a root node) satisfies all of these conditions simultaneously. Thus they are consistent. It is not hard to exhibit a model for each condition in which that condition fails while all of the others hold. Thus the conditions are independent.

Definition 5 *A model* $T = \langle \mathcal{U}, \mathcal{I}, \mathcal{P}, \mathcal{D}, \mathcal{L}\rangle$ *is* canonical *if* $\mathcal{I}$ *is surjective.*

Canonical models name every individual in their universe. Since we are concerned with models of descriptions, which we assume name every individual necessary for their satisfaction, our primary concern will be canonical models.

We can now make the notion of one tree extending another precise. Formally, T' extends T iff T is a substructure of T'.

Definition 6 *A tree* $T' = \langle \mathcal{U}', \ldots\rangle$ extends *a tree* $T = \langle \mathcal{U}, \ldots\rangle$ *iff there is an injective homomorphism* $h : \mathcal{U} \to \mathcal{U}'$.

Lemma 1 *If* T' *extends* T *then for all quantifier-free formulae* ϕ

$$T' \models \phi \Leftrightarrow T \models \phi.$$

This is just the homomorphism theorem and is easy to verify.

3.3. SATISFACTION

Satisfaction is simply classical first-order satisfaction with $\approx$ interpreted as identity in the universe. In general, models satisfy a formula relative to some interpretation mapping variables in X to the universe of the model. Since we will restrict our attention to sentences, we can regard satisfaction as being independent of the interpretation of variables.

Proper domination is a defined predicate:

$$T \models t \triangleleft^+ u \Leftrightarrow T \models t \triangleleft^* u, \neg u \triangleleft^* t.$$

If T is a tree for a language L_K then $\mathbf{Th}(T)$ is the set of sentences satisfied by T. $\mathbf{Th}(T)$ is necessarily a subset of L_K. If S is a set of trees, then $\mathbf{Th}(S)$ is the set of sentences satisfied by all $T \in S$.

If Φ is a set of sentences, $\mathbf{Mod}(\Phi)$ is the set of *trees* which satisfy Φ. If Φ is satisfiable then $\mathbf{Mod}(\Phi)$ includes trees for every language extending L_Φ. Usually we will only be interested in those trees in $\mathbf{Mod}(\Phi)$ which are trees for L_Φ.

If Φ is a satisfiable set of sentences, then $\mathbf{Cn}(\Phi)$ is $\mathbf{Th}(\mathbf{Mod}(\Phi))$. If $\mathbf{Mod}(\Phi) = \emptyset$ then $\mathbf{Cn}(\Phi) = L_\Phi$. Since $\mathbf{Mod}(\Phi)$ is restricted to trees, $\mathbf{Cn}(\Phi)$ is the set of sentences which are consequences of Φ with respect to trees. If Φ is satisfiable then $\mathbf{Cn}(\Phi) \subseteq L_\Phi$, since $\mathbf{Cn}(\Phi) \subseteq \mathbf{Th}(T)$ for some T for L_Φ.

3.4. TREE MODEL SETS

We presume that the mechanism for extracting the standard referent is syntactic. We would like to characterize the conditions under which a description (after applying that mechanism) defines a *unique* tree. We capture these as syntactic conditions by defining the notion of a *tree model set.* In order to do this, we begin with a (partial) axiomatization of trees.

Definition 7 *Let A_T be the set of formulae:*

A1 $(\forall x)[\boldsymbol{r} \triangleleft^* x]$,
A2 $(\forall x)[x \triangleleft^* x]$,
A3 $(\forall x, y)[\neg x \triangleleft^* y \vee \neg y \triangleleft^* x \vee x \approx y]$,
A4 $(\forall x, y)[x \not\approx y \vee x \triangleleft^* y]$,
A5 $(\forall x, y)[x \not\approx y \vee y \triangleleft^* x]$,
A6 $(\forall x, y, z)[\neg x \triangleleft^* y \vee \neg y \triangleleft^* z \vee x \triangleleft^* z]$,
A7 $(\forall x, y)[\neg x \triangleleft y \vee x \triangleleft^* y]$,
A8 $(\forall x, y)[\neg x \triangleleft y \vee \neg y \triangleleft^* x]$,
A9 $(\forall x, y, z)[\neg x \triangleleft y \vee z \triangleleft^* x \vee \neg z \triangleleft^* y \vee y \triangleleft^* z]$,
A10 $(\forall w, x, y, z)[\neg x \triangleleft y \vee x \not\approx w \vee y \not\approx z \vee w \triangleleft z]$,
A11 $(\forall x, y)(\exists z)[x \triangleleft y \vee \neg x \triangleleft^+ y \vee (x \triangleleft^+ z \wedge z \triangleleft^+ y)]$,
A12 $(\forall x, y)[x \triangleleft^* y \vee y \triangleleft^* x \vee x \prec y \vee y \prec x]$,
A13 $(\forall x, y)[x \not\prec y \vee \neg x \triangleleft^* y]$,
A14 $(\forall x, y)[x \not\prec y \vee \neg y \triangleleft^* x]$,
A15 $(\forall x, y)[x \not\prec y \vee y \not\prec x]$,
A16 $(\forall w, x, y, z)[x \not\prec y \vee \neg x \triangleleft^* z \vee \neg y \triangleleft^* w \vee z \prec w]$,
A17 $(\forall x, y, z)[x \not\prec y \vee y \not\prec z \vee x \prec z]$.

For a finite set of constants K, let $C_K = \{\boldsymbol{C1}, \ldots, \boldsymbol{C17}\}$ be the set of quantifier-free formulae obtained from A_T by replacing universal quantification with conjunction over all constants in K and existential quantification with disjunction over all terms in K, i.e., replacing $(\forall x)$ with $\bigwedge_{t \in K}$ and $(\exists x)$ with $\bigvee_{t \in K}$.

Note that all of the axioms except ***A11*** are purely universally quantified formulae.

The set A_T forms an axiomatization of trees for structures with finite paths and finitely many left-siblings. The set C_K does the same for finite canonical structures for L_K.[3]

Definition 8 *A set of formulae* Σ *is* consistent *iff there is no formula* ϕ *such that both* $\phi, \neg\phi \in \Sigma$.

Definition 9 *A set of formulae* Σ *is* atomically complete *iff for all atomic* $\phi \in L_\Sigma$ *either* $\phi \in \Sigma$ *or* $\neg\phi \in \Sigma$.

Lemma 2 *If* Σ *is atomically complete and* $T \in \mathbf{Mod}(\Sigma)$ *is a canonical tree for* $L_{\mathcal{T}(\Sigma)}$, *then all trees in* $\mathbf{Mod}(\Sigma)$ *extend* T.

Corollary 1 *If* Σ *is atomically complete then all canonical trees for* $L_{\mathcal{T}(\Sigma)}$ *which satisfy* Σ *are isomorphic.*

The notion of a set of formulae which defines a unique tree over the terms occurring in that set is captured formally by *tree model sets.*

Definition 10 *A set of formulae* Σ *is* downward saturated wrt K *iff* $\Sigma \subseteq L_K$ *and*

$$\begin{aligned}
\neg\neg\phi \in \Sigma &\Rightarrow \phi \in \Sigma, \\
\phi \vee \psi \in \Sigma &\Rightarrow \phi \in \Sigma \text{ or } \psi \in \Sigma, \\
\neg(\phi \vee \psi) \in \Sigma &\Rightarrow \neg\phi, \neg\psi \in \Sigma, \\
\phi \wedge \psi \in \Sigma &\Rightarrow \phi, \psi \in \Sigma, \\
\neg(\phi \wedge \psi) \in \Sigma &\Rightarrow \neg\phi \in \Sigma \text{ or } \neg\psi \in \Sigma, \\
(\exists x)[\phi(x)] \in \Sigma &\Rightarrow \phi(t) \in \Sigma, \text{ for some } t \in K, \\
\neg(\exists x)[\phi(x)] \in \Sigma &\Rightarrow \neg\phi(t) \in \Sigma, \text{ for all } t \in K, \\
(\forall x)[\phi(x)] \in \Sigma &\Rightarrow \phi(t) \in \Sigma, \text{ for all } t \in K, \\
\neg(\forall x)[\phi(x)] \in \Sigma &\Rightarrow \neg\phi(t) \in \Sigma, \text{ for some } t \in K.
\end{aligned}$$

Definition 11 *A set of formulae* Σ, *is a* tree model set *iff it is consistent,* $\mathcal{T}(\Sigma)$ *is finite,* $C_{\mathcal{T}(\Sigma)} \subseteq \Sigma$, *and* Σ *is downward saturated with respect to* $\mathcal{T}(\Sigma)$.

Proposition 1 *If* Σ *is a set of literals over a finite set of constants* $\mathcal{T}(\Sigma)$, *there is a unique (up to isomorphism) canonical tree* T *for* L_Σ *such that* $T \in \mathbf{Mod}(\Sigma)$ *and every tree in* $\mathbf{Mod}(\Sigma)$ *extends* T, *iff* $\mathbf{Cn}(\Sigma)$ *is a tree model set.*

Note that the consequences of a set of formulae are always downward saturated for conjunctive and universally quantified formulae. Thus a set of literals over a finite set of constants will fail to determine such a canonical

[3] All proofs may be found in Rogers and Vijay-Shanker (1993).

tree iff its consequences include some disjunction or existential formula which is not downward saturated.

3.5. FORMAL MECHANISM FOR STANDARD REFERENT

In Section 2.2 we introduced an intuitive mechanism for extracting the standard referent. Here we introduce a formal mechanism which allows us to capture that intuitive notion. The main distinction between the two is that the intuitive mechanism is assumed to work simultaneously on all instances of the default rules. Here we define a mechanism in which the default rules are applied sequentially to pairs in some specific order which is a parameter of the mechanism. We can then capture the simultaneous mechanism by considering the results of the sequential mechanism over all possible orderings of the pairs.

Suppose S is any set of formulae.

Let $\pi : \boldsymbol{N} \to \mathcal{T}(S) \times \mathcal{T}(S)$ such that:

$$(\forall t, u \in \mathcal{T}(S))[\mathbf{card}(\{i \mid \pi(i) = \langle t, u\rangle\}) = \infty].$$

Each π defines an infinite sequence of pairs of terms $\langle \langle t_0, u_0\rangle, \langle t_1, u_1\rangle, \ldots\rangle$. We will frequently ignore the distinction between a π and its corresponding sequence. Given a π, we apply the default rules to pairs of terms in the sequence that π determines.

For any such π, define the sequence of sets of formulae $\langle S^0_\pi, \ldots\rangle$, in stages as follows:

Let $S^0_\pi = \mathbf{Cn}(S)$.

Stage i, for $0 \leq i$:

Let $\langle t_i, u_i\rangle = \pi(i)$.

If $t_i \lhd^+ u_i \in S^i_\pi$ and $\neg t_i \lhd u_i \notin S^i_\pi$ then $S^{i+1}_\pi = \mathbf{Cn}(S^i_\pi \cup \{t_i \lhd u_i\})$.

If $t_i \not\approx u_i \notin S^i_\pi$ then $S^{i+1}_\pi = \mathbf{Cn}(S^i_\pi \cup \{t_i \approx u_i\})$.

Otherwise $S^{i+1}_\pi = S^i_\pi$.

End stage i.

We can make several claims about the construction:

- Since the two conditions are mutually exclusive, for every S^i_π there is a unique S^{i+1}_π.
- If S^0_π is consistent then S^i_π is consistent for all i.
- The definition of π assures that if $t \lhd^+ u$ is introduced at some stage i there will be some $j > i$ for which $\pi(j) = \langle t, u\rangle$. Thus the construction will eventually be applied to every introduced instance.
- If $\mathcal{T}(S)$ is finite then there is some $n \in \boldsymbol{N}$ such that $S^m_\pi = S^n_\pi$ for all $m \geq n$. Thus there is an accessible fixpoint for all π and finite S. Let S^ω_π be that fixpoint.

While the sequence $\langle S^0_\pi, \ldots \rangle$ is always infinite, it always converges. Thus there is always some stage n (dependent on both S and π) such that we can ignore all stages following n. The following lemma assures us that we can restrict our attention to finite sequences of pairs in which no pair occurs twice. Thus there is an n dependent only on S such that we can ignore all stages following n.

Lemma 3 *Let $n = \mathbf{card}(\mathcal{T}(S) \times \mathcal{T}(S))$. Then for every π there exists a π' such that $S^\omega_\pi = S^n_{\pi'}$ and $\{\pi'(i) \mid i < n\} = \mathcal{T}(S) \times \mathcal{T}(S)$, that is, the sequence $\langle \pi'(i) \mid 0 \leq i < n \rangle$ is a permutation of $\mathcal{T}(S) \times \mathcal{T}(S)$.*

This follows from the fact that the rules can apply to any pair of terms no more than once.

The consequences of the result of the intuitive mechanism is the set $\mathbf{Cn}(\bigcup_\pi S^\omega_\pi)$. This "simultaneous" mechanism always produces a unique set, although that set may or may not be consistent. The "sequential" mechanism of this section always produces consistent sets, although there may be different sets for different π. In fact, consistency in the simultaneous mechanism exactly corresponds with uniqueness in the sequential mechanism. To establish this, we first develop a formal notion of a *derivation in the set S*.

Lemma 4 *For any formula ϕ and satisfiable set of formulae S, there is some π and n such that $\phi \in S^n_\pi$ iff there exists a sequence $A = \langle \alpha_1, \alpha_2, \ldots \rangle$ where $|A| \leq n$ and $\alpha_i \in \{\neg t \lhd u, t \not\approx u \mid t, u \in \mathcal{T}(S)\}$ such that:*

4.1. $\phi \vee \bigvee_{\alpha \in A} \alpha \in S^0_\pi$, and
4.2. $\bigvee_{\alpha \in A} \alpha \notin S^0_\pi$, and
4.3. for each $\alpha_k \in A$ if $\alpha_k = \neg t \lhd u$ then $t \lhd^+ u \vee \bigvee_{\alpha_i \in A, i<k} \alpha_i \in S^0_\pi$.

Such a sequence exists iff there is such a sequence which is an ordered subset *of $\{\neg t \lhd u, t \not\approx u \mid t, u \in \mathcal{T}(S)\}$, that is: $\alpha_i \neq \alpha_j$ for all $i \neq j$.*

Note that part 4.2 implies that there is no proper subset of A the disjunction of which is in S^0_π. In particular $\alpha_k \vee \bigvee_{\alpha_i \in A, i<k} \alpha_i \notin S^0_\pi$ for all $\alpha_k \in A$.

The sequence A is the sequence of the *negations* of the formulae added to S when the rules are applied to pairs of terms in the order π. Part 4.1 assures that ϕ is a consequence of those formulae. Part 4.2 assures that they can be added to S^0_π consistently, and part 4.3 assures that the conditions for adding the formulae can be derived.

Definition 12

- *A formula ϕ can be* derived *from a description S iff there is some π such that $\phi \in S^\omega_\pi$ (iff there is some π and $n \leq$* $\mathbf{card}(\mathcal{T}(S) \times \mathcal{T}(S))$ *such that $\phi \in S^n_\pi$).*

– *A* derivation *(in S) is an ordered subset of* $\{\neg t \lhd u, t \not\approx u \mid t, u \in \mathcal{T}(S)\}$ *meeting conditions 4.2 and 4.3.*

Then ϕ is derivable from S iff there is a derivation A such that $\phi \vee \bigvee A \in S^0_\pi$.

If $A = \langle \alpha_1, \ldots, \alpha_n \rangle$ is a derivation in S and α_i is either $\neg t_i \lhd u_i$ or $t_i \not\approx u_i$, let $S_A = S^n_\pi$, where $\pi = \langle \langle t_1, u_1 \rangle, \ldots, \langle t_n, u_n \rangle \rangle$.

We can now characterize the circumstances under which S^ω_π is unique in terms of the derivations in S.

Lemma 5 *For any finite set of formulae S, S^ω_π is unique (i.e., is independent of choice of π) iff there is no derivation $A = \langle \alpha_1, \ldots, \alpha_n \rangle$ such that, for some $\phi_1, \phi_2 \in \{t \lhd u, t \approx u \mid t, u \in \mathcal{T}(S)\}$*

$$A \cdot \neg\phi_1 \text{ and } A \cdot \neg\phi_2 \text{ are both derivations}$$

and

$$\bigvee A \vee \neg\phi_1 \vee \neg\phi_2 \in S^0_\pi.$$

This says that S^ω_π will be unique iff it is not possible to derive a set which the mechanism can extend either by ϕ_1 or ϕ_2 and for which $\neg\phi_2$ is a consequence of adding ϕ_1 and v.v.

The equivalence of uniqueness in the sequential mechanism and consistency in the simultaneous mechanism, then follows.

Proposition 2 *For S any satisfiable finite set of formulae, S^ω_π is unique if and only if* $\mathbf{Cn}(\bigcup_\pi S^\omega_\pi)$ *is consistent.*

With this, we can formally characterize when a description meets the conditions of the determinism hypothesis.

Proposition 3 *A finite set of literals S has a unique standard referent (relative to the mechanism of this section) iff S^ω_π is unique and is a tree model set.*

4. CONSEQUENCES FOR THE D-THEORY PARSERS

We now have a formal characterization of when descriptions meet the determinism hypothesis relative to a particular definition of the standard referent. This provides one route towards establishing conditions under which the hypothesis is guaranteed to be met. Given an account of the ambiguous descriptions that the parser must accommodate along with the defaults which should apply, one attempts to show for a class of descriptions including those which must be accommodated that there is a set of default rules which are consistent with the required defaults and which, when applied by the mechanism of Section 3.5, invariably result in a unique S^ω_π which is a tree model set. Conversely, if it can be shown that descriptions in that class can result in multiple S^ω_π, or S^ω_π that are not tree model sets, then the set of default rules is insufficient to disambiguate that class of descriptions. In such an event, either the class of descriptions must be further restricted or the default rules must be modified.

Given the kinds of ambiguity which occur in examples from the D-Theory literature, the rules we have assumed—$\triangleleft$-rule and $\approx$-rule —form an arguably minimally required set of default rules. In the next section we establish a number of properties of the descriptions which are consequences of the underlying parsing mechanism. These form a set of restrictions that are met implicitly by all descriptions built by deterministic parsers. In Section 4.2 we examine certain ambiguous descriptions which cannot meet the conditions of the determinism hypothesis regardless of the mechanism for extracting the standard referent. These lead to restrictions that must be met explicitly by the descriptions built by any deterministic parser. Thus we have lower bounds on both the defaults and the properties of the descriptions.

4.1. INHERENT PROPERTIES OF DESCRIPTIONS

We begin by exploring some of the properties common to all descriptions built by D-theory parsers. The most fundamental of these properties is that descriptions consist only of literals. In Section 2 we argued that this is a consequence of the requirement that the output of the parser make use of every part of the structure it builds in an essential way. Given the descriptions which occur in the literature (Marcus et al. 1983; Marcus 1987; Marcus and Hindle 1990) we might restrict which literals can occur as well. These descriptions explicitly use only proper domination, left-of and possibly equality. In addition, there is an implicit use of not-equal. While we will shortly argue that a $\neg\triangleleft$ formulae cannot occur in a description in an essential way, it does not appear that the use of any other formulae is incompatible with the determinism hypothesis. Thus we do not rule them out.

A second property follows from the fact that every individual in the description is known to dominate some terminal and that left-of totally orders those terminals. Thus there is a set L_S representing those terminals such that $L_S \subset \mathcal{T}(S)$ and[4]

$$(\forall t \in \mathcal{T}(S))(\exists l \in L_S)[t \triangleleft^* l \in \mathbf{Cn}(S)],$$
$$(\forall l \in L_S, t \in \mathcal{T}(S))[l = t \text{ or } \neg l \triangleleft^* t \in \mathbf{Cn}(S)],$$
$$(\forall l, k \in L_S)[l \prec k \in \mathbf{Cn}(S) \text{ or } k \prec l \in \mathbf{Cn}(S)].$$

[4]Such formulae are not generally explicitly included in the descriptions discussed in the literature. We assume that they are always added before the standard referent mechanism is applied.

Then for all $t, u \in \mathcal{T}(S)$ there exists some $l, k \in L_S$ such that $t \triangleleft^* l, u \triangleleft^* k \in \mathbf{Cn}(S)$ and either $l \prec k$ or $k \prec l$ is in $\mathbf{Cn}(S)$. It follows, by ***A16*** that for all t, u either

$$u \not\prec t \in \mathbf{Cn}(S) \text{ or } t \not\prec u \in \mathbf{Cn}(S).$$

A less obvious property is a consequence of the manner in which descriptions of fragments of the phrase-structure tree are combined. Every such fragment always names a minimal node with respect to domination. When two fragments are joined, it is always by asserting that some node in one of the fragments dominates the minimal node in the other (thus preserving the property of having a minimum node). (See Marcus (1987).) It follows that whenever it is known that a pair of terms both dominate a third, and thus must lie on the same branch, it is also known which dominates which. Thus we have

$$t \triangleleft^* v, u \triangleleft^* v \in \mathbf{Cn}(S) \Rightarrow t \triangleleft^* u \in \mathbf{Cn}(S) \text{ or } u \triangleleft^* t \in \mathbf{Cn}(S).$$

This latter characteristic is violated by the rootedness mechanism in Marcus (1987), and Marcus and Hindle (1990). It is clear, however, that this mechanism is intended to operate independently of the rest of the syntactic analysis. In fact, just the application of the $\triangleleft$-rule to descriptions which include rootedness nodes, before those nodes have been attached in their proper place by the rootedness mechanism, will often produce a tree which is not the intended reading of the input. Further, we show in the next section that every description that meets the conditions of the determinism hypothesis must include a root node. Thus we will assume that the rootedness mechanism has always been completed before any standard referent is extracted.

4.2. PROPERTIES REQUIRED OF ALL DESCRIPTIONS

We now turn to two classes of description which cannot meet the conditions of the determinism hypothesis regardless of the standard referent mechanism. These give us restrictions on the descriptions which must be met explicitly by every D-theory parser.

The first is

$$\neg t \triangleleft u \in \mathbf{Cn}(S) \Rightarrow \neg t \triangleleft^+ u \in \mathbf{Cn}(S) \text{ or } t \triangleleft^+ v, v \triangleleft^+ u \in \mathbf{Cn}(S) \text{ for some } v.$$

That is, whenever it is known that t cannot be the parent of u, it is also known either that t does not properly dominate u, or that there is an explicit witness to the fact that the length of the path between them is greater than one. To see this, suppose the contrary. Since $\neg t \triangleleft u \in \mathbf{Cn}(S)$, if S has a canonical model T then either $T \models \neg t \lhd^+ u$ or there is some v such that $T \models t \lhd^+ v \land v \lhd^+ u$. Since neither of these formulae are consequences of S, for each there is some tree in $\mathbf{Mod}(S)$ which fails to satisfy it. Thus one of these trees does not extend T and the description does not meet the determinism hypothesis.

Effectively, this rules out use of $\neg\lhd$ in descriptions, since formulae involving it can only be asserted under circumstances where they are implied by other formulae in the description. This also guarantees that, if S is restricted to literals, there are no unsaturated existentially quantified formulae in $\mathbf{Cn}(S)$. If such formulae were to occur, they would have to be a consequence of $\boldsymbol{A}_{11}$. But this would require that some $\neg\lhd$ occurs in $\mathbf{Cn}(S)$, a circumstance which can only occur if that existentially quantified formula is downward saturated.

A similar requirement is that the root be named in the description, although not necessarily as $\boldsymbol{r}$, i.e., there is some t such that $t \lhd^* u \in \mathbf{Cn}(S)$ for all u. Strictly speaking, if there is to be any tree for L_S then $\mathcal{T}(S)$ must include $\boldsymbol{r}$. We relax this, though, and count a tree to be a canonical model of S if it is a canonical tree for $L_{\mathcal{T}(S)\cup\{\boldsymbol{r}\}}$ in which $\boldsymbol{r} \approx t$ is true for some $t \in \mathcal{T}(S)$. That the requirement must be met by admissible descriptions follows from an argument similar to the argument proscribing $\neg\lhd$.

4.3. MEETING THE DETERMINISM HYPOTHESIS

These minimally required defaults do not suffice to disambiguate that class of all descriptions which can be built by D-theory parsers, i.e., which exhibit the properties discussed in the last two sections. The remaining gaps between the ambiguity that can occur in the descriptions and that which can be resolved by the minimally required defaults must be eliminated either by further restricting the class of descriptions or by modifying the default mechanism. In this section we look at how this can be done within the framework we have provided.

Formally, we have established that a given set of defaults fail to satisfy a given class of descriptions if there is some description S in that class for which the defaults either fail to construct a unique S_π^ω (independent of their order of application) or the S_π^ω they construct fails to be a tree model set. Recall, from the end of Section 3.4, that S_π^ω fails to be a tree model set iff it contains some disjunctive formula (i.e., either a disjunction or an existentially quantified formula) which is not downward saturated. Thus the mechanism for extracting standard referents can be seen as a process of saturating these formulae. In modifying the mechanism, one must, in essence, supply a rule which saturates the remaining formulae. Restricting the descriptions, on the other hand, resolves the ambiguity if such restriction implies that those formulae be downward saturated in the consequences of the description and in every S^i_π derivable from it.

The case in which S^ω_π is not unique is actually similar. In Section 3.5 we established that this is occurs only if an S^i_π can be obtained in which a disjunction $\neg\phi_1 \vee \neg\phi_2$ occurs where the default rules allow adding either ϕ_1 or ϕ_2. Again this is a process of downward saturating the disjunction, since adding ϕ_1 selects $\neg\phi_2$ and v.v. The failure then is that while the default rule saturates the disjunction it is insufficiently specific about *how* it should be saturated. Take, for example,

$$a \lhd^+ b, a \lhd^+ d, b \lhd^+ c \in \mathbf{Cn}(S).$$

The $\approx$-rule resolves the issues of whether $d \approx b$ or $d \not\approx b$ and whether $d \approx c$ or $d \not\approx c$. The problem is that the description implies $(d \not\approx b \vee d \not\approx c)$. Selecting $d \approx b$ implies $d \not\approx c$ and vice versa. The ambiguity can be resolved by modifying the default rules to give preference to one disjunct over the other. (One possibility is to restrict the $\approx$-rule to apply only to pairs which share a common immediate ancestor, which, in this case, ensures that d would be equated with the node higher in the tree.) Alternatively, it can be resolved by restricting the descriptions in such a way that no such unsaturated formulae can be derived (by requiring that in all descriptions built by the parser all pairs terms are related either by domination or left-of, for instance).

Modifications of the default rules which resolve ambiguity by giving preference to one opportunity to apply a rule over another essentially restrict the order of the pairs to which the rules are applied. While any reasonable restriction of this type can be incorporated into the conditions under which the rule applies, at least in the case where the order is a consequence of a general principle, the restriction can be expressed more naturally as a restriction on π. That is, rather than considering all π (in verifying the deterministic hypothesis) with a modified default rule, in this case it is more convenient to retain the original default rule but to get the equivalent effect by restricting consideration to some subset of the π.

In fact we conjecture that extending the minimal standard referent mechanism with such an ordering on π in which the pairs are considered "top-down" and either "left-to-right" or "right-to-left" will suffice to assure that our version of the determinism hypothesis is meet. Whether this has any linguistic justification is irrelevant to us here, we introduce it solely to suggest that, least for some classes of descriptions and definitions of standard referent, the machinery developed in Section 3 may be sufficient to prove that the determinism hypothesis is met.

5. CONCLUSION

We have examined the meaning of the determinism hypothesis in the context of D-theory parsers, and have proposed a definition which we believe preserves the intent of Marcus (1980). In light of this definition of determinism, D-theory parsers can be understood as a means of accommodating, through the use of descriptions, a degree of ambiguity which is strictly limited by the definition of the standard referent. Thus the definition of the standard referent determines the degree of ambiguity that can occur in the descriptions. Conversely the kinds of ambiguity required determines the kinds of defaults the standard referent must supply. The work reported here encompasses our first steps in a program to develop a formal understanding of these relationships.

Based on the ambiguity incorporated in the descriptions that occur in the literature on D-theory parsers, as well as the defaults assumed in extracting the standard referent, we have identified some minimal characteristics of its definition. We have introduced a formal framework within which particular notions of standard referent can be defined, and developed tools for reasoning about standard referents within that framework. This has led to a formal characterization of what it means for a description meet the conditions of the determinism hypothesis relative to a definition of standard referent.

With this formal foundation, we have identified a number of properties common to all descriptions built by D-theory parsers, as well as established certain requirements which must be met by every description which meets the determinism hypothesis. It is the gap between the ambiguity accommodated by the class of descriptions that meet these requirements and that which can be disambiguated by the minimal standard referent mechanism that must be addressed in the design of a D-theory parser. Finally, we have given a glimpse of how some of the issues involved in restricting the class of descriptions and extending the standard referent mechanism in order to close that gap can be approached within our formal framework.

Ultimately, we hope to develop methods sufficient to formally characterize the admissible descriptions given a particular definition of standard referent, and to characterize the ambiguities which must be resolved by the definition of the standard referent given a particular class of descriptions. For now, we are looking for a combination of default rules and restrictions on the descriptions under which the determinism hypothesis is guaranteed to be met. In particular, with a better understanding of the notion of standard referent assumed in current D-theory parsers and the kinds of ambiguity that can be present in the descriptions they build we hope to be able to identify such a combination as consistent with, or even implicitly assumed by, the D-theory parsers discussed in the literature.

We believe that this work delineates a number of issues in D-theory which have previously not been precisely formulated. We hope that it provides a foundation on which such issues can be explored.

References

Goodall, G. (1983) A three-dimensional analysis of coordination. In: A. Chuckerman, M. Marks, and J. Richardson, (eds.) *Papers from the 19th Regional Meeting of the Chicago Linguistic Society*, Chicago Linguistic Society, 146–154.

Lasnik, H. and Kupin, J. J. (1977) A restrictive theory of transformational grammar. *Theoretical Linguistics*, Vol. no. 4, 173–196.

Marcus, M. P. (1980) *A Theory of Syntactic Recognition for Natural Language*. MIT Press.

Marcus, M. P. (1987) Deterministic parsing and description theory. In: P. Whitelock, M. Wood, H. Somers, R. Johnson, and P. Bennett (eds.) *Linguistic Theory and Computer Applications*, Academic Press.

Marcus, M. P. and D. Hindle (1990) Description theory and intonation boundaries. In: G. Altmann (ed.) *Cognitive Models of Speech Processing: Psycholinguistic and Computational Perspectives*, MIT Press.

Marcus, Mitchell P., Donald Hindle, and Margaret M. Fleck (1983) D-theory: Talking about talking about trees. *Proceedings of the 21st Annual Meeting of the Association for Computational Linguistics*.

Rogers, J. and K. Vijay-Shanker (1993) *On the determinism hypothesis and D-theory parsers*. Technical report 94-01, University of Delaware, Newark DE, USA.

5. VARIETIES OF HEURISTICS IN SENTENCE PARSING

MAKOTO NAGAO
Department of Electronics and Communication
Kyoto University

Abstract.

In this chapter, a brief comparison is made among phrase structure grammar, dependency grammar, case grammar and some other kinds of grammar, and the reasons are considered why the sequential combination of dependency analysis and case frame analysis is the best for word-order-free languages such as Japanese. Methods of ambiguity resolution, anaphora and ellipsis estimation, and classification of referential property and number are also given.

1. KINDS OF GRAMMAR AND THEIR CHARACTERISTICS

There are lots of methods of sentence parsing, but parsing always presupposes a grammar, which is usually composed of a set of so-called grammatical rules or rewriting rules. Many different grammars have been proposed, and many parsing algorithms have been developed based on these grammars. Characteristically, these parsing algorithms are direct reflections of the features of the grammar formalisms, so that we have to clarify the basic characteristics of these grammars.

We can classify grammars so far proposed into the following few classes.

(i) Phrase Structure Grammar (PSG)
Context-free PSG, Context-sensitive PSG, Augmented Transition Network Grammar, Definite Clause Grammar, Categorial Grammar, Lexical Functional Grammar, Generalized PSG, Head Driven PSG, Tree Adjoining Grammar, ...

(ii) Dependency Grammar

(iii) Case Grammar

(iv) Systemic Grammar

H. Bunt and M. Tomita (eds.), Recent Advances in Parsing Technology, 79–90.

(v) Montague Grammar

In the following we will discuss the basic ideas behind these grammars, and compare them contrastively from the standpoint of parsing.

1.1. PHRASE STRUCTURE GRAMMAR

Phrase structure grammar was proposed by Chomsky from the standpoint of sentence generation. This means that this grammar formalism is not necessarily fitted to the analysis of sentences. This will become clear when we consider the meaning of a grammar rule such as $S \rightarrow NP \cdot VP$. This rule declares that a sentence *should* be composed of NP followed by VP, or that a sentence *presupposes* the existence of NP followed by the existence of VP. This means that a sentence which does not fit this definition is excluded from the scope of a language. In this way this grammar formalism gives the definition of a language.

There is always a gap between an existing language and a set of sentences which a grammar can produce. The gap is not small, but actually very big. Sentences which we speak or write are essentially free, and cannot be grasped by such an artificial framework. We encounter always sentences or expressions which cannot be explained by a grammar, and we are forced to improve or add rewriting rules constantly. When a grammar is proposed as a tool to give conceptual explanation of sentential structures of a language to a human being, a simple basic grammar will be sufficient. But when a grammar is to parse existing sentences by computer mechanically, there must be a very precise grammar, and its constant improvement will be required.

The Japanese language is quite different from English and many other European languages. Japanese is more free in word order change than these other languages, and there are varieties of omissions of essential components in a Japanese sentence. PSG has a difficulty in handling these phenomena because the grammar formalism presupposes the word (phrase) order as is specified in grammar rules. Basically this grammar formalism does not fit languages which are word order free, and where the notion of phrase structure does not hold.

Similar observations can be made concerning ellipsis. When PSG is used for the analysis of a language which has varieties of ellipsis, we have to try rule applications not only by the rules which have every component, but also by rules which do not have (or ignore) some of these components, because it is quite difficult to specify in what conditions a certain element can be omitted. This is almost impossible for practical parsing. And the concept of grammatical restriction will not hold in such a case, that is, the phrase structure grammar will have no meaning any more.

PSG thus has a serious problem in the analysis of sentences of at least a certain kind of languages such as Japanese. Nevertheless many people use PSG for parsing without such considerations. We must look for other grammar formalisms which may be better fitted for sentence parsing in Japanese.

1.2. DEPENDENCY GRAMMAR

Dependency grammar (DG) which was treated in detail first by Tesnière is a grammar which is called 'Kakariuke' grammar for Japanese, and which has been very popular in Japan for more than fifty years. This grammar is totally different from PSG in the sense that, while PSG is a kind of language definition tool, DG is a kind of interpretation tool of a given sentence. DG clarifies which word modifies or depends on which. It constructs the modifier-modifiee relations between the words in a sentence, and this is always possible because a word in a sentence always has a relation to another word in the same sentence. It does not presuppose anything, but just clarifies the word relations in a sentence. In this sense DG can be regarded as a grammar for interpretation.

The interpretation power of this grammar, however, is far weaker than that of PSG. DG does not say anything about subject, object, etc., but just says that this word modifies that, etc. This weak property however becomes profitable, for example, for word-order change in Japanese because the modifier-modifiee relation is not influenced by word-order change as shown in the following.

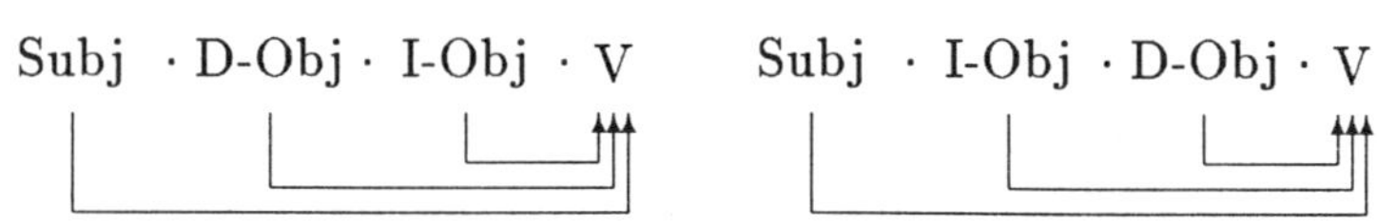

DG does not have any concern with omitted words, and the analysis process is always the same.

So far so good. But from the standpoint of machine translation or some other natural language processing, the role of each word or phrase in a sentence must be clarified more accurately. In Japanese this is known approximately by the information of verb conjugation, postpositions attached to nouns, and sometimes by the position of the word. So some additional analysis should follow DG analysis.

A serious problem in DG is an ambiguity problem, that a word can modify two or more words which follow the word in a sentence, and the decision is difficult. To solve this problem we have to prepare a good dictionary where the degree of affinity of two words is described. This is however not a particular problem for DG alone. It is a common problem for almost all grammars including PSG. This problem is relieved to a certain extent by the so-called non-crossing condition in the Japanese language, which can be illustrated as that

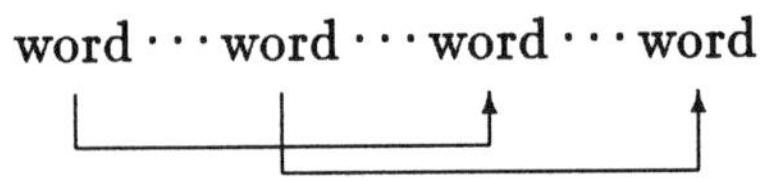

is impossible. This condition is useful for the elimination of redundant checks of modifier-modifiee relation in Japanese.

1.3. CASE GRAMMAR

Case grammar (CG), proposed by Fillmore, is quite different from the above two grammar formalisms in that CG aims to clarify the roles of words in a sentence from the standpoint of meaning or of conceptual function of a word in relation to a predicate. Therefore CG does not care about the word order in a sentence.

Case grammar interpretation of a sentence is represented by a case frame whose slots are filled in by words in a sentence. This case frame representation can be seen as a meaning representation of a sentence, so that it is comparatively language-neutral. That is, sentences in different languages which express the same contents may have the same case frame. This is the main reason that many machine translation systems have adopted the case frame representation as the goal of sentence analysis and the starting point of sentence generation.

One of the difficulties of CG is that we have to tackle a problem of formalizing the representation, because the grammar is based on meaning. Fillmore did not explicitly discuss this problem because he was not interested in machine processing but he relied on the human ability of interpretation. What he and his followers discussed seriously was what kind of cases (slot functions in case frame) must be set up, such as agent, object, instrument, etc. What we, natural language processing researchers, had to do was to establish a semantic marker system which is powerful enough to distinguish different usages of verbs and nouns. A case frame must specify what kind of nouns can be an agent, object, instrument, etc. of a particular verb in a particular usage or meaning. The verb *kakeru* in Japanese, for example, has more than thirty different usage patterns, and the semantic markers should be able to discriminate the meanings of nouns detailed enough to fit these usage patterns. It has been made clear by the effort of NTT researchers that two- to threethousand semantic markers are necessary for the satisfactory description of every different usage of verb patterns (Ikehara et al., 1991).

1.4. OTHER GRAMMAR FORMALISMS

There are many grammar formalisms which can be classified into PSG, and these have essentially the same problems, discussed in Section 1.1. Montague grammar is based on formal logic, and the meaning of a sentence is represented by a logical formula. Present-day formal logic has a limited power of representation and it is impossible to express the rich information of natural language in its limited formalism. There have been several trials of machine translation using Montague representation as a pivot, but all these attempts failed because of the poor expressive power of logic and also of the difficulty of transforming a sentential expression to a proper logical form.

Systemic grammar, proposed by Halliday, is unique in the sense that it distinguishes three components in a sentence, namely ideational function, textual function and interpersonal function. The Japanese language is rich in interpersonal functions. It has a sophisticated honorific expression system, for example, which uses specific words that affect sentential styles. Textual function corresponds roughly to discourse or contextual function. The problem will be whether we can write every detail of language expressions and word usages in this framework.

2. VARIETIES OF HEURISTIC COMPONENTS IN PARSING SENTENCES

2.1. AMBIGUITY RESOLUTION IN SENTENCE PARSING

In sentence parsing we are always confronted with a problem of ambiguity resolution of modifier-modifiee relations. To solve this problem we need such information as

(i) semantic consistency of modifier and modifiee.
(ii) word order and distance between modifier and modifiee. The kinds of words or symbols that we find in between the two words are important for the rejection of the modifier-modifiee relation.
(iii) consistency with contextual/situational information.

(i) is checked by the consistency of semantic markers. To realize this all the words in a dictionary must be given proper semantic markers for their distinctive meanings. We may be able to utilize inclusion relations of semantic markers for the consistency checking.

(ii) is not easy to handle. Basically, a modifier modifies the nearest possible modifiee, but this is not always true. We cannot specify a semantic relation so exactly as to accept just correct ones and reject the others. There always exist word pairs which cannot be accepted or rejected definitely. In these cases we have to look for other information. It is often very useful to look at words or symbols in between the two candidate words in a Japanese sentence. For example, the first word of a sentence which has - *wa* as a suffix usually modifies the last predicate of the sentence. But there are cases where this condition does not hold. The following is an example,

*Tokyo-*wa *bukka-ga takai-ga hito-ga atsumaru.*
(human being) (gather)
(Tokyo is high in consumer prices, but people come in.)
Tokyo-wa, *bukka-ga takai-ga hito-ga atsumaru.*
(Tokyo gathers people although consumer prices are high.)

In this sentence there is another *-wa* and the predicate *takai* in between *Tokyo-wa* and the final predicate *yasui*, and these prevent the relation of these two words. In the following sentences,

*Tokyo-*wa *bukka-ga takai-ga hito-ga atsumaru.*
Tokyo-wa, *bukka-ga takai-ga hito-ga atsumaru.*
(human being) (gather)

the first sentence permits two interpretations, that is, *Tokyo-wa* modifies either *takai* or *atsumaru* (gather). But the second usually has one interpretation, that is, *Tokyo-wa* modifies *atsumaru*. This is caused by the comma after *Tokyo-wa*. We have developed a sophisticated algorithm to solve these modifier-modifiee problems (Kurohashi and Nagao, 1994).

As for case (iii), a famous example is the following.

I saw a woman in the garden with a telescope.

Correct interpretation is possible only when we know the real situation of the utterance.

2.2. ANAPHORA AND ELLIPSIS

When we analyse a sentence morphologically, syntactically, and semantically, that is, we perform the transformation to case frame representation, anaphora and ellipsis are handled usually at the last stage of case frame construction. We can recognize that there is an ellipsis when we find out a vacant slot in a case frame representation of a sentence. We may be able to infer and recover this by utilizing contextual information (sometimes we have to see some more words or sentences after the ellipsis position). Inference and recovery of a proper word is not easy, but we can write varieties of inference rules which check grammatical and semantic information requested from the case slot default information and which utilize the contextual information so far obtained.

As for anaphora resolution, we can utilize grammatical information of pronominal words and write similar heuristic rules as above. We can of course also think of another analysis process, where anaphora determination is done just before the case frame transformation.

Looking for a proper word or concept for a pronominal reference or an ellipsis is a problem of language understanding. We have an example like the following.

Merikenko	*to*	*Satou-o*	*yoku*	*maze,*	*atatameru.*
(flour)	(and)	(sugar)	(well)	(mix)	(warm up)

where there is an omission of an object to the predicative verb, *atatameru.* When we trace back the sentence we encounter the nouns *Satou* and *Merikenko.* These are the candidates for the omitted object. However, the actual thing to warm up is neither of the two. It is the mixture of these materials, which does not appear explicitly in the sentence. We must introduce an inference mechanism that a mixture is created when two materials are 'mazeru-ed' (mixed). We have to have a mechanism to understand the meaning of a sentence and do the action which the sentence specifies, and get the result by applying an inference rule. In this way when there is a series of sentences which describe actions performed sequentially, each action is supposed to be applied to the object which is produced as the result of the previous actions. We have to write many heuristic rules to produce these objects.

We may be forced to infer more than this. For the above example we cannot warm up the mixture of flour and sugar directly. The mixture must be in a certain thing such as a bowl. The determination of pronominal reference and the recovery of omission are quite difficult. We have to clarify what the language understanding is and what the common sense reasoning is.

2.3. REFERENTIAL PROPERTY AND NUMBER

Besides the determination of pronominal reference and ellipsis we have to clarify the referential property (*definite, indefinite, generic*) and number (*singular, plural, uncountable*) of a noun in a sentence. In the Japanese language there is no such indications as articles and number suffixes as in English to show these properties of a noun. Therefore we must estimate the referential property and number of a noun in a Japanese sentence. This requires language understanding by contextual information. It is difficult to achieve this at the present level of research.

On the other hand we have to check how much information we can get to infer these properties of a noun from the sentence in which the noun appears. We have tried to construct a kind of expert system to solve this problem (Murata and Nagao, 1993). We formulated 84 heuristic rules to infer the referential property of a noun, and 48 heuristic rules to infer the number property.

Let us consider the following example.

Kinou *katta* piano-*no ichidai-wa choritsu-ga yokunai.*
(yesterday) (bought) (piano) (one unit) (tuning) (no good)
(One of the pianos which I bought yesterday is not tuned well.)

Piano in this sentence is modified by *kinou katta* (piano which I bought yesterday). So this piano is a concrete object which I have now, and the noun *piano* has the property *definite*. *Piano* is followed by *ichidai*, which means "one of ···", so that we can infer that *piano* is not singular. Many such heuristic rules are written in the form of expert system rules.

This system was tested for two different sample sentence sets. The first test was done for the nouns in a set of sentences which were referenced in the process of writing heuristic rules. The success rate were 85.5 % for the referential property and 89.0 % for the number property. The second test was done for the nouns in a set of newly given sentences. The success rates were 68.9 % and 85.6 % for the referential property and the number property, respectively. This kind of analysis of nouns in a sentence is important when we consider the design of better machine translation system.

2.4. TENSE, ASPECT, AND MODALITY

We have to write many heuristic rules to correctly interpret the tense, aspect and modality of a predicate. These are particularly important in the interpretation of tense, aspect and modality of two or more predicates in a sentence when one of these is in (i) embedded sentences, (ii) subordinate clauses, or (iii) coordinations. Many standard grammar books explain these relations in detail, but it is still very difficult to write expert system rules precisely for these relations.

Let us consider a pair of languages, for example English and Japanese. The categories and properties of tense, aspect and modality of Japanese are completely different from those of English. For example, the Japanese language has no present perfect tense. This tense is often expressed by adverbs in Japanese as follows.

Kare-wa ima *tuita.*
(he) (now) (arrived)
(He has just arrived.)

A more difficult situation exists where there is no such adverb and we have to infer the tense from the situation.

Kare-wa Kyoto-e kita. *Soshite ima kankou-o* shiteiru.
(he) (Kyoto) (came) (and) (now) (sight seeing) (do)
(He has come to Kyoto. And he is now doing sight seeing.)

Kare-wa Kyoto-e kita. *Soshite Kyoto daigaku-o* sotsugyo shita.
(he) (Kyoto) (came) (and) (Kyoto University) (graduate) (did)
(He came to Kyoto. And he graduated Kyoto University.)

Sometimes different tense expressions in Japanese correspond to the same tense in English. The following is an example.

Sore-wa	*10 nen*	*mae-no*	*koto-de*	aru.
(It)	(10 years)	(before)	(matter)	(is)
Sore-wa	*10 nen*	*mae-no*	*koto-de*	atta.
				(was)

(It was 10 years before.)

All these problems are related to the problem of discourse. We don't know how many problems of this kind there are and how many expert system rules we have to write. The first problem we have to tackle will be to clarify how many different categories of discourse problems there are.

3. STAGED DESIGN FOR PARSING SENTENCES

3.1. STEP-BY-STEP ANALYSIS

As mentioned in Section 1, each grammar formalism has its own characteristics, and so we have to choose carefully the best grammar formalism for a particular purpose. We consider that the following steps will be the best for the analysis of Japanese sentences for machine translation (Kurohashi and Nagao, 1996).

(i) morphological analysis
(ii) detection of parallel structures
(iii) dependency analysis
(iv) case frame analysis
(v) textual function analysis
(vi) interpersonal function analysis

We can design the analysis process in different ways, skipping the dependency analysis and obtaining the case frame from the result of morphological analysis, or merging the total process into one using the constraint programming methodology. However, we don't recommend such processes. We believe that the best way is to divide the entire process into many subprocesses, and to perform small transformations in each subprocesses . The reason is that the analysis is an *information loosing process*, which must be done very carefully in small steps, so that important information will not be lost. Another merit when the process is divided into many stages is that we can understand the details of each stage more easily and can improve each stage independently.

3.2. DETECTION OF PARALLEL STRUCTURES

Almost all current parsing systems fail in the analysis of long sentences, for example, of a sentence composed of more than thirty English words or more than seventy Japanese characters. Nobody has analyzed the reasons for this difficulty. Probably, very many factors are mixed up, all of which are equally possible causes of errors in the analysis. There is no single major reason for failure. We have to improve almost all the parts of the parsing process, particularly grammar rules.

On the other hand, the question may be raised why a sentence is so long. The main reason is that people write a long sentence by connecting phrases, clauses and sentences into one. Therefore an important point in the analysis of a long sentence is to find out such conjunctions. Serious efforts have been made to write grammar rules which check something like semantic similarities which may exist in the head nouns or main verbs of conjunctive structures. But there has been no significant improvement so far. This indicates that we have to think about an entirely new approach to find out parallel structures in a long sentence.

What we have recently developed (Kurohashi and Nagao 1992) is based on the assumption that parallel phrases/clauses /sentences will have a certain similarity in the sequence of words and their grammatical structures as a whole. We have to compare two word strings of arbitrary lengths in these aspects and get an overall similarity value. Because we had to compare word strings of arbitrary lengths in a sentence, we adopted the dynamic programming method to calculate overall similarity values for all the possible word-string pairs of arbitrary lengths to get the best one (for details see (Kurohashi and Nagao 1992)). The result was unexpectedly good. The algorithm has a success rate of more than 90% in finding parallel structures of different kinds, and many long Japanese sentences which were composed of more than 100 characters were successfully analyzed.

The idea behind this algorithm is just to find similar word strings in a sentence, which has nothing to do with the existing notion of grammatical rules. It is closer to human cognitive action which is vague, but which is very reliable in the global recognition process. The human brain may not work like the application of grammatical rules, but may work like the similarity detection mentioned here.

This algorithm was inserted in between the morphological analysis and the dependency analysis in our parsing system, and achieved a very good performance in sentence parsing.

3.3. DEPENDENCY ANALYSIS AND CONVERSION TO CASE FRAME REPRESENTATION

After the detection of conjunctive structures, the dependency analysis is first applied to these parts, and then to the whole sentential structure. By adding this parallel structure detection algorithm the accuracy of the dependency analysis has become very high.

The transformation of the dependency tree of a sentence to a case frame representation is not difficult because the noun-verb modifying relations have been obtained at the stage of the dependency analysis. The work to be done at this stage is to check in which case slots the nouns will come (Kurohashi and Nagao, 1996). If a vacant case slot remains after the assignment of words to suitable case slots, it is judged as an omission.

3.4. RECOGNITION OF A PHRASE UNIT

People utter a sentence not by word by word, but by phrase by phrase. This phrase unit is what Margaret Masterman called a 'breathgroup'. This phrase unit has a unique meaning, although each word in the phrase may have several meanings. This notion of phrase unit is different from that of PSG in the sense that a phrase in PSG is hierarchically recursive, but a phrase here is not.

Example-based machine translation, which has been recognized as giving better quality translation than other methods, memorizes lots of example phrases and their translations as pairs, and a target language sentence is composed of the phrasal translations. Example phrases in this case are just this phrase unit which corresponds to the breathgroup. There is a discussion in machine translation studies about the translation equivalence unit. Words are very ambiguous, and are therefore not a good choice of translation equivalence unit. Sentences have structural ambiguity and too big to be an equivalence unit. Therefore, phrases are good candidates.

Nowadays, there are many efforts to collect typical example phrases and to construct a phrasal dictionary, because such a dictionary could contribute very much to the improvement of machine translation quality. So to recognize phrases properly in a sentence has become an important task, particularly in example-based translation. When the phrases in a sentence are correctly recognized the analysis of a whole sentence becomes easy because the relations among these phrases are not so difficult to determine.

4. CONCLUSION

We have discussed the essential properties of various grammar formalisms, and suggested that an appropriate grammar must be chosen for a specific purpose. For example, generative grammar is not suitable for sentence analysis, so that the idea of bi-directional grammar, which aims at using the same grammar for analysis and synthesis of a sentence in machine translation, is not recommendable.

A sentence includes lots of information, such as syntactic information, semantic information, textual or rhetorical information, interpersonal information, and so on. We do not have any formal methods to detect this information. Even at the level of syntactic information PSG or any other grammar formalism is merely a framework for explaining the basic structures of a language. No one knows how human brain works to speak and recognize a language. We can only approximate various aspects of the human language mechanism to a certain extent. All these approximations are heuristic. Grammar formalisms, even PSG, are a kind of expert system. We have to write many expert systems to approximate a language at the levels of morphology, syntax, semantics, discourse, etc. Therefore, we have to consider a parallel or a pipeline execution structure of these expert systems, because the total system is too big and complex to be executed sequentially. This will be a very interesting software problem in the near future.

References

Ikehara, S. et al. (1991) Semantic Analysis Dictionaries for Machine Translation. *Information Processing Society of Japan SIG Notes*, NL–84–13 (in Japanese).

Kurohashi, S. and Nagao, M. (1992) Dynamic Programming Method for Analyzing Conjunctive Structures in Japanese, *Proc. 13th Int. Conference on Computational Linguistics*, Nantes.

Kurohashi, S. and Nagao, M. (1996) Structural Disambiguation in Japanese by Evaluating Case Structures based on Examples in Case Frame Dictionary. *This volume, 347–362.* An earlier version has appeared in *Proc. Third Int. Workshop on Parsing Technologies*, Tilburg/Durbuy, August 1993. ITK, Tilburg, 111–122.

Kurohashi, S. and Nagao, M. (1994) A Syntactic Analysis Method of Long Japanese Sentences based on the Detection of Conjunctive Structures. *Computational Linguistics* 20(4), 507–534.

Murata, M. and Nagao, M. (1993) Determination of referential property and number of nouns in Japanese sentences for machine translation into English, *Proc. Fifth Int. Conference on Theoretical and Methodological Issues in Machine Translation*, Kyoto.

6. PARSING AS DYNAMIC INTERPRETATION OF FEATURE STRUCTURES

HARRY BUNT AND KO VAN DER SLOOT
Institute for Language Technology and Artificial Intelligence
Tilburg University

Abstract.

In this chapter we develop a new approach to parsing through the recursive, model-theoretic interpretation of expressions representing linguistic knowledge. We argue that in particular the *dynamic* variant of model-theoretic semantics can be useful, which approaches interpretation in a constructive way.

On the theoretical side, we develop this approach by integrating feature structures in an existing formal language, defined and implemented for computational semantic purposes. The resulting language, called GEL, allows us to represent semantic as well as syntactic knowledge. In particular, we can represent grammatical rules as well as the phrase structures that they generate. Whereas a phrase-structure rule is traditionally viewed procedurally, as a recipe for phrase building, and a rule in the parsing-as-deduction approach is viewed declaratively, as a proposition which is true when the conditions for building the phrase are satisfied, a rule in GEL is viewed as a proposition in dynamic semantics: it can be evaluated recursively, not to true or false, but to the minimal changes in a model, needed to make the proposition true.

The viability of this idea has been demonstrated by an implementation of DPSG chart parsing and an emulation of HPSG parsing.

1. INTRODUCTION: THE STATUS OF FEATURE STRUCTURES

Feature structures are nowadays to many theoretical and computational linguists days what tree structures have been for decades: the natural form of

H. Bunt and M. Tomita (eds.), Recent Advances in Parsing Technology, 91–114.

describing linguistic structure. Feature matrices, in particular those called 'signs' in HPSG, indeed contain partly the same information as traditional syntactic trees; through the use of 'daughters' attributes, they describe the dominance aspect of constituent structure. They tend to contain *more* information then syntactic trees, as they contain besides syntactic features also a variety of features of semantic or pragmatic rather than syntactic significance. (In principle, a syntactic tree may also contain such information, however, if sufficiently rich information structures are used at the nodes). They contain *less* information then trees in that linear precedence information is not encoded in signs; they may, furthermore, be incomplete in that any feature attribute may have an unspecified value. Feature structures are thus inherently *partial* linguistic information structures; this partiality adds greatly to the flexibility they offer in their use. The absence of precedence information from signs is often advantageous, as it gives a natural possibility to describe order-independent regularities in constituent structure, thus allowing more easy expression of order-independent linguistic generalizations than frameworks without a dominance/precedence separation in their representations. It may be noted, though, that linear precedence relations could in principle be encoded in feature structures, just as dominance relations.

To many computational linguists, feature structures not only have a status comparable to that of traditional syntactic trees, but they also come as dignified descriptions of the kind of data structures that are familiar and useful in natural language processing. This is especially true for *typed* feature structures, where the type of a feature can be seen as corresponding to the notion of *data type* in traditional, typed programming languages or to the notion of *class* in object-oriented programming approaches. Two of the most salient features of feature structures, structure-sharing and the use of feature attributes that may have complex feature structures as values, are quite familiar as properties of data structures (and object classes); they correspond to the use of pointers to shared substructures and the use of nested or recursive data structures, respectively. The main operation on feature structures, finally, that of unification, has been inspired by the corresponding concept in Prolog.

To some computer scientists, AI people, and computational linguists, feature structures are a kind of *graphs*, that are particularly suitable as representation structures for partial knowledge. Graph unification, typing, and inheritance are considered essential properties. (In fact, the use of inheritance for dealing efficiently with a hierarchical system of typed features comes from the corresponding computational concept in AI.)

Closely related to this last view, finally, is that of some theoretically inclined formal linguists and logicians, who regard feature structures as a relatively new kind of language for representating linguistic knowledge. Studies concerned with feature structures from this perspective are, for example, Johnson (1988), Carpenter (1992), Dörre & Seiffert (1991), Kasper & Rounds (1986), Smolka (1989), Moss (1990). These studies are primarily concerned with formal definitions of languages of feature structures and their formal properties.

In the present chapter we consider feature structures also as formal-language objects, but our interest lies mainly in considering how such objects may be integrated in existing formal languages. In particular, we consider enriching a formal language, developed for the semantic representation of natural language, with feature structures. In this enriched language we can express both syntactic and semantic structures, and grammar rules. This opens the way to a new parsing paradigm if a *dynamic model-theoretic semantics* is defined for this language, which consists in computing the dynamic interpretations of grammar rules, their arguments instantiated by elements in an input string. Such an interpretation adds objects and structures to the pre-existing model in a minimal way, such that the grammar rules are satisfied; the syntactic side of this process corresponds to constructing a parse.

2. FEATURE STRUCTURES AS FORMAL-LANGUAGE EXPRESSIONS

Compared to expressions in the well-known languages of logic, feature structures[1] have three basic ingredients, not commonly found elsewhere:

1. the pairing of an attribute and a value to form a feature;[2]
2. the combination of features into 'bundles';
3. the use of markers to indicate re-entrancy, or 'structure sharing'.

These ingredients, plus the possibility to use features nested as attribute values, form the essence of feature structures. Additional constructions found in feature structures include lists, sets, negation, disjunction, and occasionally still others. Syntactically, a core language L_F of (untyped) feature structures can be defined as follows.

1. The vocabulary of L_F consists of:
   - a finite set of attribute symbols;
   - a finite set of atomic value symbols;

[1]Throughout most of this chapter we will focus on feature structures as they are used in HPSG, although most of what we have to say has a more general application.

[2]The term 'feature' is in the literature used sometimes for the combination of an attribute and a vale, like [CASE: `genitive`] and sometimes for an attribute alone, like CASE. In this chapter we will use the term in the former sense.

- a denumerable set of structure sharing markers;
- the auxiliary symbols $[\ ]\ (\ )\ <\ >\ :\ ,$

2. (a) If A is an attribute constant and v a value constant, then $[A : v]$ is a feature expression (*'atomic feature specification'*).

   (b) If A is an attribute constant and f a feature expression, then $[A : f]$ is a feature expression (*'complex feature specification'*).

   (c) If $f_1,.., f_k$ are feature expressions, then $< f_1, .., f_k >$ is a feature expression (*'feature bundle'*).

   (d) If e is a feature expression and i a structure sharing marker, then $(i : e)$ is a (*'marked'*) feature expression.

   (e) If A is an attribute constant and i a structure sharing marker, then $[A : i]$ is a feature expression (with structure sharing).

The familiar two-dimensional matrix notation for feature structures essentially differs from the linear notation introduced here in that the features in a feature bundel are ordered vertically and enclosed in large square brackets. Moreover, it is common to indicate structure sharing with small boxes, writing $\boxed{\mathrm{i}}\ e$ instead of $(i : e)$, and $[A\ \boxed{\mathrm{i}}]$ instead of $[A : i]$.

The heart of the semantic definition is that of the atomic feature specification. We view feature specifications as descriptions of predicates; regarding, for example, the feature specification [GENDER: neuter] as denoting the predicate of having neuter gender. The semantics of feature bundles can be regarded as the conjunction of the corresponding predicates. The semantics of feature nesting is more complex. To formulate it properly, a 3-way distinction must be made between:

- feature attributes that encode linguistic properties of words and phrases, such as GENDER, NUMBER, and CASE;
- those that serve to label parts of feature structures, such as LOC, SYNSEM, and HEAD, and in themselves do not encode linguistic properties;
- those that relate phrases to their constituents, such as SUBJ, HEAD-DTR and COMPLEMENT-DRS.

Attributes of the first kind typically correspond to traditional syntactic features, but sometimes they encode semantic or pragmatic properties; we will call them *base feature attributes.*

Attributes of the second kind allow one to refer to certain groups of features, like the head features, which is necessary to express grammatical principles like the Head Feature Principle. They may also help to make feature structures more readable. A feature structure like [SYNSEM: [SYN: [HEAD: [CAT: v]]]] is semantically equivalent to [CAT: v], which shows the semantic vacuity of these attributes.[3] Since these attributes label substructures in a feature structure, we will call them *label attributes*. (Notice, also, that these attributes do not allow atomic values.)

Attributes of the third kind describe relations of constituency between phrases and their components; hence we will call them *constituency attributes*. We will consider the semantics of the three kinds of features in section 3.3.

It is clearly possible to add syntactic rules like (2a-e) to the definition of a standard logical language, such as first-order predicate logic. To the rules defining the well-formed expressions of predicate logic we simply add the above rules, and we use feature specifications as predicates. The resulting language can be used to make statements about linguistic material. For instance, the following formula in 'extended predicate logic' would express that there is a singular noun with neuter gender in the sentence S:

$$(\exists x)\ (\ \mathrm{IN}(x, S) \wedge \mathrm{NOUN}(x) \wedge [\text{number: sing, gender: neuter}](x)\ )$$

In a similar way, we will add feature structures to a more complex language, designed specifically for representing natural language semantics, the EL language.

3. FEATURE STRUCTURES IN THE GEL LANGUAGE

3.1. ENSEMBLE LANGUAGE

The language EL ('Ensemble Language') combines typed lambda calculus with concepts from ensemble theory, an extension of set theory developed for dealing with mass terms (Bunt, 1985; see also Lewis, 1992), and having data structures and operations known to be useful from computational semantics, such as list, list projection, set, cartesian product, cardinality, etc. We will describe here a small part of the EL-language, sufficient to show the addition of feature structures to such a language.

Since EL has a great number of constructions, the usual kind of typography of formulas, with brackets and other delimiters to make the notation unambiguous, is not always convenient. Alternatively, we use explicit names for the constructions in the language, for example, instead of $P(a) \wedge \neg Q(a, b)$ we write, more explicitly:[4]

[3]When feature structures are typed, one may wish to assign different types to these structures. The 'labeling' feature attributes then have a type-changing effect. If type differences correspond to ontological differences at the level of denotations, this means that labeling attributes are not semantically vacuous. See also below on typing in GEL.

[4]Notice that in predicate logic, brackets are used as scope delimiters for connectives and quantifiers, for indicating the argument of a function or predicate, and for delimiting

conjunction (application(P, a), negation(application(Q,tuple(1:a, 2:b))))

We now give a somewhat simplified definition of the syntax of the relevant part of the EL language, and subsequently add the syntactic constructs for dealing with feature structures. The simplification is that we leave the typing of EL out of consideration. (EL is a heavily typed language, with complex types having a rather detailed syntactic structure; see Bunt, 1985).

Let us call the EL fragment considered here EL_0. Syntactic rules:

1. EL_0-constants and -variables are EL_0 expressions.
2. If $a_1, .., a_k$ are EL_0 expressions, then tuple(1:a_1,..k:a_k) is an EL_0 expression denoting a k-tuple of values.
3. If T is an EL_0 expression denoting an n-tuple, then projection(k, T) is an EL_0 expression, for $k \leq n$, denoting the kth object of that tuple.
4. If $a_1, .., a_k$ are EL_0 expressions, then set(1:a_1,..k:a_k) is an EL_0 expression denoting the set of objects denoted by $a_1, .., a_k$.
5. If S is a set-denoting EL_0 expression and ϕ an EL_0 expression denoting a proposition,[5] then selection(S, ϕ) is a set-denoting EL_0 expression.
6. If F^k is a k-ary function expression (function constant or complex EL_0 expression, denoting a function) and T^k an EL_0 expression denoting a k-tuple then application((F^k, T^k) is an EL_0 expression.
7. If ϕ, ψ and χ are proposition-denoting EL_0 expressions, then so are negation(ϕ); conjunction(ϕ, ψ); disjunction(ϕ, ψ), and conditional(ϕ, ψ).
8. If E is an EL_0 expression and x is a variable, then lambda(x, E) is a (function-) expression of EL_0.

Next we will consider the definition of GEL (Generalized EL), showing how the constructions for feature structures can be added to EL_0.

3.2. GEL EXPRESSIONS

To EL_0 we add attribute- and value constants, value variables, and structure sharing markers, and syntactic rules covering the core language L_F of feature structures defined above. We mentioned that, from a semantic point of view, a 3-way distinction must be made among features into *base-*, *label-*, and *constituency features*. This is made explicit in GEL by using the constructions bfeature, flabel, and fconstit, respectively.

n-tuples. In EL, brackets only serve to delimit the arguments of a construction.

[5]Conditions on the kind of entities denoted by an EL_0 expression correspond, in the formal definition of EL, with conditions on their types.

Some feature attributes take lists or sets of elements as values, which was not taken into account in L_F; since the EL_0 language already has list and set constructions, this is most easily taken into account now, when we consider the combination of EL_0 and features structures. For the sake of simplicity, we will leave set-valued attributes out of consideration here, and only consider *constituency* feature attributes taking list values.[6]

The relevant syntactic definitions are as follows.

1. If A is a base feature attribute constant and v a value constant or variable, then bfeature(A, v) is a feature-denoting GEL expression.[7]
2. (a) If A is a label attribute constant and e a feature-denoting GEL expression, then flabel(A, e) is a feature-denoting GEL expression.
   (b) If A is a constituency attribute constant and f a feature-denoting GEL expression, then fconstit(A, f) is a feature-denoting GEL expression.
   (c) If A is a list-valued constituency attribute constant and L a list of feature-denoting expressions, then fconstit(A, f) is a feature-denoting GEL expression.
3. If $f_1, ..., f_k$ are feature-denoting GEL expressions, then bundle$(f_1, .., f_k)$ is a feature-denoting GEL expression.
4. If e is a GEL expression and i a structure sharing marker, then fmark(i, e) is a GEL expression of the same type as e.
5. If A is an attribute constant and i a structure sharing marker, then bfeature(A, i), flabel(A, i), and fconstit(A, i), are feature-denoting GEL expressions.

[6]In HPSG the most important list-valued attributes are SUBCAT (or COMPS, as in Pollard & Sag 1994, chapter 9) and COMP-DTRS, of which the latter are constituency feature attributes. The SUBCAT attribute in Pollard & Sag 1987 also takes lists of signs as values; in Pollard & Sag 1994, on the other hand, SUBCAT takes lists of SYNSEM structures as values, which makes it conceptually slightly different; still, semantically it is a constituency attribute. See section 3.3 for the semantics of these attributes.

[7]As before, statements about the kind of entity denoted by an expression, are formally to be construed as statements about their types. In the case of feature-denoting expressions ('feature specifications'), we have to take into account the type system associated with the features we wish to include in EL, while on the other hand we want to regard features as predicates on words and phrases, which is the kind of thing that EL-types capture. Using the symbol ω for the type associated with words and phrases, features have the EL-type $(\omega \rightarrow tv)$, i.e. functions from words and phrases to **TRUE** and **FALSE**.

It may be noted here that the approach to typing in EL is strictly semantics-driven and inspired by the use of sparse ontologies. As such it differs from (Carpenter-) typing in feature structures, which is to some extent syntactically motivated and corresponds to more baroque ontologies. We bellieve that there is quite a lot of room for different approaches here. We have adopted the EL approach to typing in GEL. The combination of EL-typing and Carpenter-typing might be interesting to consider, but is outside the scope of the present chapter.

We will continue to use the notation $[A : f]$ for feature specifications involving any kind of attribute, in cases where the kind of attribute doesn't matter, or is obvious from the context.

3.3. GEL SEMANTICS

We define the semantics of GEL model-theoretically, as an extension of its EL base: for each construction of the language we define how its value can be computed from the values of its constituent expressions. The values of atomic constituents are looked up in the model, which is a structured specification of these values. In GEL one can talk about syntactic objects and their relations as well as about their semantics; therefore, GEL models contain linguistic entities besides the familiar kinds of semantic entities.

Concerning the semantics of feature structure expressions in GEL, the first point to consider is the semantics of a simple feature specification. We view a feature attribute as a mathematical function; this captures the idea that an attribute has a unique *value*.[8] These functions apply to words and phrases. A feature specification, pairing an attribute with a value, thus amounts to a predicate, which can be used to express a property of a word or phrase. The semantics of a predicate being (a characteristic function of) a set, a GEL expression like [GENDER: `fem`] receives as its interpretation the set of those words and phrases that have feminin gender. To formally interpret a feature specification, we apparently need a model which includes words and phrases as the objects to which features apply, and which also includes syntactic concepts like *feminin, interrogative, singular* and *mass* as individual objects that may occur as feature values.[9]

A model for the GEL sublanguage of feature structures is thus a 5-tuple:

$$M = < D, W, \Phi_W, \mathcal{A}, F >$$

where D is the domain of semantic individuals, W is a (finite) set of word tokens, Φ_W is a subset of the phrases that can be formed from W,[10] $\mathcal{A} = \{\mathcal{A}_1, .., \mathcal{A}_k\}$ is a finite collection of finite sets of objects called 'atomic feature values', and F is a function assigning interpretations to GEL constants as follows:

– to feature value constants, F assigns atomic feature values;

[8] Treating feature attributes as functions seems to us intuitively more satisfying than treating them as atomic entities, as Gazdar and Pullum (1987) have proposed.

[9] We will often use the same strings to denote GEL terms as well as their denotations in a model. Different type faces will be used to make the distinction where necessary; for instance, we will use *mass* for the denotation of `mass`.

[10] For simplicity, one may think of Φ_W as a set of finite sequences of elements from W. For DPSG the case is actually more complicated, as it allows phrases to be discontinuous.

- to a base feature attribute, F assigns a function from $W \cup \Phi_W$ to some value set $\mathcal{A}_i$;[11]
- to a constituent feature attribute A, F assigns a function from $W \cup \Phi_W$ to $W \cup \Phi_W$, or to lists of elements from $W \cup \Phi_W$, if A is list-valued;
- to label attributes, F assigns the identity function;

On the basis of the values assigned to attribute and value constants, the semantics of the different kinds of feature specifications is defined as follows by means of a recursive evaluation function $\mathcal{V}$, disregarding for a moment the complications related to structure sharing:

1. $\mathcal{V}(\mathsf{bfeature}(A, v)) = \lambda z : (\mathcal{V}(A))(z) = \mathcal{V}(v)$
2. $\mathcal{V}(\mathsf{flabel}(A, e)) = \mathcal{V}(e)$
3. $\mathcal{V}(\mathsf{fconstit}(A, f)) =$ if f is a feature specification then $(\lambda P : (\lambda z : P(\mathcal{V}(A)(z))))(\mathcal{V}(f))$ else (f is a list of feature specifications) $(\lambda P : (\lambda z : P_1(\mathcal{V}(A)(z)))(\mathcal{V}(f_1)) \wedge \ldots P_n(\mathcal{V}(A)(z)))(\mathcal{V}(f_n))$

Examples:

1. $\mathcal{V}(\mathsf{bfeature}(\text{GENDER}, \texttt{feminin})) =$
   $= \lambda z : gender'(z) = feminin$
   if $gender'$ is the function denoted by the attribute GENDER.
2. $\mathcal{V}(\mathsf{fconstit}(\text{HEAD-DTR}, \mathsf{bfeature}(\text{GENDER}, \texttt{feminin}))) =$
   $= (\lambda P : (\lambda z : P(head\text{-}dtr'(z))))(\lambda y : gender'(y) = feminin))$
   $= (\lambda z : gender'(head\text{-}dtr'(z)) = feminin)),$
   after lambda conversion.
   This expresses the property of having a head daughter with feminin gender.

The following example (strongly simplified compared to actual GEL models) illustrates the kind of models that goes with this semantics. In this model, we have a domain of discourse D consisting of four individuals (*jan*, *astrid*, *marie*, and *chris*), and eight word tokens $w_1, \ldots w_8$. The model says that *jan* is a boy, the other individuals are girls; except for *marie*, who's French, all are Dutch. This is formally accomplished by assigning to the

[11] To the special base attribute SEM, that relates a word or phrase to its semantic content, F assigns a function from $W \cup \Phi_W$ to the appropriate kind of entity (element of D, set of n-tuples from D, function from D to {TRUE, FALSE}, etc.).

word w_1, with phonological realization (PHON) 'Jan', the denotation (SEM) *jan*, to the word 'Dutch' (w_5) the denotation $\{jan, astrid, chris\}$, etc.

This model only exemplifies the model-theoretic treatment of base feature attributes and the SEM attribute, of which the functions they denote are represented by their extensions.[12] Label attributes are semantically trivial; constituency attributes are essential for representing phrase structure; we shall consider them in relation to parsing as GEL interpretation.

$$
\begin{array}{lcl}
M & = & < D, W, \Phi_W, \mathcal{A}, F > \\
D & = & \{jan, astrid, marie, chris\} \\
W & = & \{w_1, w_2, w_3, w_4, w_5, w_6, w_7, w_8\} > \\
\Phi_W & = & \emptyset \\
\mathcal{A} & = & \{\mathcal{A}_1, \mathcal{A}_2, \mathcal{A}_3\} \\
\mathcal{A}_1 & = & \{\text{`Jan', `Astrid', `Marie', `Chris', `Dutch', `French', `boys', `girls'}\} \\
\mathcal{A}_2 & = & \{ADJ, N, PN\} \\
\mathcal{A}_3 & = & \{sing, plur\} \\
F & = & <\text{PHON}, \{< w_1, \text{`Jan'}>, < w_2, \text{`Astrid'}>, < w_3, \text{`Marie'}>, \\
 & & \quad < w_4, \text{`Chris'}>, < w_5, \text{`Dutch'}>, < w_6, \text{`French'}>, \\
 & & \quad < w_7, \text{`boys'}>, < w_8, \text{`girls'}> \} \\
 & & <\text{CAT}, \{< w_1, PN >, < w_2, PN >, < w_3, PN >, < w_4, PN >, \\
 & & \quad < w_5, ADJ >, < w_6, ADJ >, < w_7, N >, < w_8, N > \} \\
 & & <\text{NUM}, \{< w_1, sing >, < w_2, sing >, < w_3, sing >, < w_4, sing >, \\
 & & \quad < w_7, plur >, < w_8, plur > \} \\
 & & <\text{SEM}, \{< w_1, jan >, < w_2, astrid >, < w_3, marie >, < w_4, chris >, \\
 & & \quad < w_5, \{jan, astrid, chris\} >, < w_6, \{marie\} >, \\
 & & \quad < w_7, \{jan\} >, < w_8, \{astrid, marie, chris\} >\}
\end{array}
$$

3.4. STRUCTURE SHARING SEMANTICS

Structure sharing markers serve to constrain the interpretation of feature structures. They may occur in two ways: as labels of substructures and as values of attributes. This means that three different situations may arise, corresponding to the possible combinations of kinds of occurrences:

1. a structure sharing marker i occurs twice or more as a label of a substructure, but does not occur as an attribute value;
2. a marker i occurs both as a label of a substructure and as an attribute value;

[12] Strictly speaking, for such models we should formulate the definition of $\mathcal{V}$ in terms of these extensions, e.g., we should say $\mathcal{V}(\mathsf{bfeature}(A,v)) = \lambda z :< z, \mathcal{V}(v) >\in (\mathcal{V}(A)$ instead of $\mathcal{V}(\mathsf{bfeature}(A,v)) = \lambda z : (\mathcal{V}(A))(z) = \mathcal{V}(v)$.

3. a marker i occurs twice or more as an attribute value, but does not occur as label of a substructure.

In the first case, the values of the substructures labeled with the same marker should be unified and the unification result used as the end result of evaluating each of the marked substructures. In the second case, the evaluation result of the labeled subexpression should be treated as the value of the markers occurring as attribute values. In the third case, the values of the attributes having the markers as 'values' are unspecified but required to be equal; this case is important in the formulation of ID-schemata and general principles. We will consider the first two cases here; the third case does not seem to arise in parsing in a significant way, since parsing is concerned with *instantiated* ID-schemata, as we will see below.

To deal with structure sharing in a formal way we introduce the concept of a *context-dependent* evaluation function, or *'covaluation'*. Such a function performs recursive evaluation, taking into account a certain set of expressions as 'context of evaluation'. The idea is that, when faced with the task of evaluating an expression labelled with a structure sharing marker, the specified context should be examined for possible other occurrences of the same marker. We therefore 'upgrade' the recursive evaluation function $\mathcal{V}$ to a covaluation function $\mathcal{V}^c$ which has two arguments: an expression ϕ to be evaluated, and a context C. We kick off the evaluation of a GEL expression ϕ by defining its interpretation in a model M to be:

$$\parallel \phi \parallel_M = \mathcal{V}^c(\phi, \sigma_\phi)$$

where σ_ϕ is the set of subexpressions of ϕ which are either *marked*, i.e. of the form $(i : e)$ (or '$\boxed{\text{i}}\ e$'), or just a structure sharing marker, occurring in the value of a feature attribute. The covaluation $\mathcal{V}^c$ now acts recursively just like the context-free evaluation $\mathcal{V}$ did before, except that it carries a context with it, which becomes relevant when it encounters a marked feature specification or a structure sharing marker used as a feature attribute value.

When $\mathcal{V}^c$ hits a marked subexpression $(i : \phi)$, it will look for other expressions $(i : \psi)$ in its context. If it finds such expressions, these ψ should be evaluated and unified with the evaluation result of ϕ. This is expressed in the first clause of the definition of the covaluation, given below. When $\mathcal{V}^c$ hits a structure sharing marker used in a feature attribute value, it will again look for expressions $(i : \psi)$ in its context. If it finds one, it evaluates it and takes the result to be the value of the structure sharing marker. If it finds more than one such expression, it takes the result of unifying their values. This is expressed in the second clause. The third clause says that covaluation with an empty context is the same as classical 'context-free' evaluation. The closing fourth clause says that for all GEL expressions that are not labelled by a structure sharing marker and that are not a structure sharing marker used as a value, the recursion in the covaluation is the same as that in the context-free evaluation, except that the context is carried along.[13]

1. $\mathcal{V}^c((\text{i: }\phi), C)) = \bigsqcup(\mathcal{V}^c(\phi, C - \{\phi\}), \bigsqcup_{(i:\psi)\in C} \mathcal{V}^c(\psi, C - \{\chi | (i:\chi) \in C\}))), \text{ if } C \neq \emptyset$

   $\mathcal{V}^c((\text{i: }\phi), \emptyset)) = \mathcal{V}^c(\phi, \emptyset))$
2. $\mathcal{V}^c(i, C)) = \bigsqcup_{(i:\psi)\in C} \mathcal{V}^c(\psi, C - \{\chi | (i:\chi) \in C\})) \text{ if } C \neq \emptyset$
3. $\mathcal{V}^c(\phi, \emptyset) = \mathcal{V}(\phi) \text{ if } \phi \neq (i:\psi) \text{ and } \phi \neq i$
4. **If ϕ is neither a structure sharing marker nor a marked expression, then $\mathcal{V}^c(\phi, C)$ is recursively defined in the same way as $\mathcal{V}$, keeping the context argument unchanged.**

4. PARSING AS MODEL-THEORETIC INTERPRETATION

In order to produce phrase-structure representations for input strings using GEL, we must first of all be able to formally interpret the corresponding parts of feature expressions.

Consider again the above toy model and suppose that we want to handle a token of the phrase *'Dutch girls'*. In terms of the model, this is a complex object formed by combining the objects w_5 and w_8; let p_1 denote the phrasal object having w_8 as its head daughter and w_5 as its adjunct daughter. This means that p_1 is an additional element in the model structure, and we have the following additional elements in Φ_W and F:

Φ_W : $\{p_1\}$
F: $< H-DTR, \{< p_1, w_8 >\} >$
$< ADJ-DTR, \{< p_1, w_5 >\} >$

From forming and interpreting GEL expressions describing phrase structure to the representation and interpretation of grammar rules is now a small step. Phrase-structure rules are traditionally viewed procedurally, as recipes for building phrases. In the parsing-as-deduction approach a rule is viewed declaratively, as a proposition which is true when the conditions for

[13]For instance, $\mathcal{V}^c(\text{tuple}(1{:}a_1,..,k{:}a_k), C) = < \mathcal{V}^c(a_1, C), .., \mathcal{V}^c(a_k, C) >$. Strictly speaking, instead of clause 4 in the definition we should define $\mathcal{V}^c$ for these cases by taking the definition of $\mathcal{V}$ and replacing $\mathcal{V}(..)$ everywhere by $\mathcal{V}^c(.., C)$. Notice, also, that $\mathcal{V}^c(i), \emptyset)$ is undefined; this situation may only occur in the covaluation of an ill-formed expression, with a 'free' structure-sharing marker.

building the phrase are satisfied. The constraint satisfaction approach of HPSG and related theories is also declarative; instead of PS-rules we have schemata and principles representing constraints on well-formedness, and parsing may be seen as proving that these constraints are satisfied.

GEL is also declarative in nature; when we use GEL to emulate a rule-based grammar formalism, like DPSG (see below), we get statements saying such things as: *'If we have a token of category DET and a token of category N, then (under certain further conditions) we also have a token of type NP'*. The model-theoretic semantics of GEL now leads to a 'parsing-as-evaluation' approach, where parsing amounts to evaluating the premises of such statements to TRUE. A *parsing-as-dynamic-interpretation* approach emerges when we treat such a statement in the fashion of dynamic semantics, as not denoting TRUE or FALSE, but as denoting the minimal changes to the model, needed to make the statement true.

When we apply GEL to the emulation of a constraint-based grammar, the situation is somewhat different. The constraint-based approach says that any string of words is well-formed if it satisfies all the constraints of the grammar. In HPSG, more specifically, any sequence of words that instantiates an ID-schema and satisfies the general principles as well as the language-particular LP-constraints, is a correct phrase in the language. Since an ID-schema is formally just a sign, it corresponds to a GEL feature expression denoting a complex predicate. To parse the phrase *Dutch girls* in HPSG comes down to showing first of all that it instantiates one of the ID-schemata; in this case a head-adjunct schema consisting of three objects, one for the phrase and two for its constituents, connected by HEAD-DTR and ADJ-DTR relations. The corresponding GEL task, in the traditional model-theoretic approach, is to recursively evaluate the GEL representation of this schema, the two daughter elements it contains instantiated by w_5 and w_8, and to show that the complex predicate denoted by this GEL expression delivers TRUE when applied to the phrasal object p_1. This is not very practical, as it presupposes the presence in the model of the phrasal object p_1 and, more generally, the presence of *all* word combinations that might be considered as candidate phrases. The dynamic approach is much more attractive, as it does not check the truth of the GEL predicate for an existing phrasal object in the model, but instead *constructs* a new object for which the predicate is true, if this can be done without violating any of the constraints of the grammar.

We will not spell out the dynamic form of the model-theoretic semantics for GEL here; it may suffice to note that every formal language which has a model-theoretic semantics defined in the classical sense, can be given a dynamic semantics; this has been demonstrated for predicate logic (Groenendijk & Stokhof, 1991), for modal logics (De Rijke, 1992), and as a matter of general principle (Van Benthem, 1991a; Van Benthem & Cepparello, 1994).

The viability of this approach to parsing has been demonstrated by a proof-of-concept implementation for DPSG chart parsing and an emulation of the STUF implementation of HPSG, which are described in the following sections.

4.1. DPSG PARSING USING GEL

4.1.1. *Discontinuous Phrase Structure Grammar*

DPSG, or 'Discontinuous Phrase Structure Grammar', has been developed over the years in the context of building natural-language understanding systems, such as the TENDUM dialogue system (Bunt et al., 1985), with the aim of handling discontinuous constituents in an elegant and effective manner. DPSG has been applied in experimental systems both for parsing and for generation (see Bunt, 1987; 1991). DPSG has grown out of the tradition of augmented context-free grammars, where the augmentations in this case are (1) the use of complex feature structures; (2) the formulation of semantic rules coupled to the syntactic rules in a rule-by-rule fashion.

The distinguishing property of DPSG is that its rules do not construct ordinary phrase-structure trees, but structures that allow crossing branches, called 'discontinuous trees'. Partly inspired by McCawley (1982), these constituent structures have been given a formal definition (see Bunt, 1991; 1996). The use of discontinuous trees provides an intuitively appealing and computationally simple treatment of bounded discontinuities. Figure 1 below gives an example.

To generate such a structure DPSG uses rules which, disregarding the augmentations with feature conditions and semantics, look as follows, where square brackets indicate 'internal context' elements of discontinuous constituents:

VP	→	VC	+	NP			DET	→	your
NP	→	DET	+	N			N	→	friend
VC	→	V	+	[NP]	+	PART	PART	→	up
							V	→	wake

See Bunt (1996) for more about the formalism, and Bunt (1991) for the description of a chart parser for DPSG.

The latest version of DPSG does not use the above rule format, but one where immediate dominance and linear precedence have been separated. A discontinuous rewrite rule like `VC --> V + [NP] + PART` is equivalent to the following combination of dominance- and precedence constraints, where

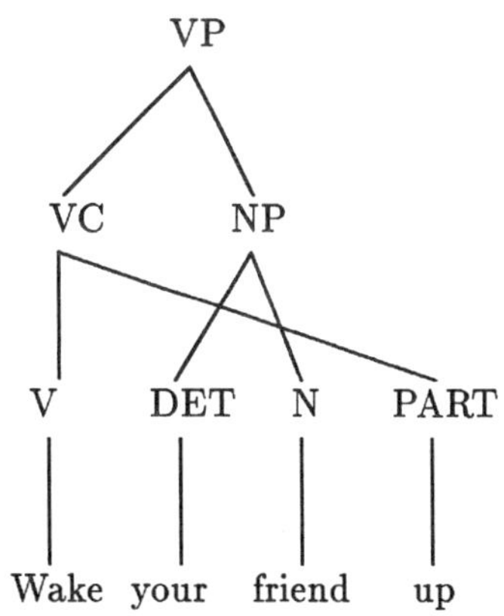

Figure 1. A discontinuous tree.

CD stands for context daughters:[14]

ID: VC $\rightarrow$ {V, PART}
CD: {NP}
LP: {VC $\prec$ NP, NP $\prec$ PART}

The dominance and precedence aspects of the rewrite rule have been separated here; the LP part can subsequently be factored out and made global for the entire grammar, as GPSG and HPSG do, or for a part of the grammar, as is done in the latest version of DPSG.

In this example, the ID/LP formulation has no advantages, since the original rule covered only one LP order; advantages can only be expected if the same dominance configuration allows various precedences. This is often the case with discontinuities; for example, in Dutch an intervening adverb can be placed on a great variety of positions in a clause.

In developing DPSG for implementing natural language fragments, we have chosen a rule format somewhat like that of Montague Grammar, where syntactic phrase-structure rules and feature conditions are coupled with semantic rules to build up semantic EL-representations in parallel with syntactic structures.

[14]The rules given here are strongly simplified compared to full-fledged DPSG-rules, which include local and global conditions on features, feature propagation constraints, and semantic composition rules. See below, section 4.1.2.

DPSG format:

NPCENTRE-2		
ID rule	:	r: NPCENTRE ⇒ a: CENTRALDET, b: NOM
CD rule	:	-
LP rule	:	<a,b>
Head	:	b
Local conds	:	a.form in {mass, ground, coll}
Global conds	:	a.form = b.form, a.gender = b.gender, a.defness = b.defness
SEM rule	:	r' = partselection(b', lambda(x, application(a', x)))

GEL format:

NPCENTRE-2
ID rule : r:NPCENTRE ⇒ a:CENTRALDET, b:NOM ;
CD rule : ;
LP rule : <a,b>;
GEL rule : conditional(

```
conjunction( eqel( Form-of( a ), Form-of( b ) ),
  eqel( Gender-of( a ), Gender-of( b ) ),
  eqel( Defness-of( a ), Defness-of( b ) ),
  in( Form-of(a), { Mass, Ground, Coll } ) ),
bundle(
  Head-Feature-Instantiation( b ),
  Form( Form-of( b ) ),
  Gender( Gender-of( b ) ),
  Person( Person-of( b ) ),
  Content( partselection(
    Content-of( b),
    lambda( -x, application( Content-of(a), -x ))) ) );
```

4.1.2. *DPSG rules in GEL*

To illustrate the use of GEL in the implementation of DPSG, we consider a (simplified) DPSG rule which combines a central determiner and a nominal into an 'npcentre'. We present the rule as formulated in DPSG and as expressed in GEL, respectively.

The GEL format has been chosen in such a way that the dominance and precedence conditions are kept separate from the other conditions, to facilitate the reuse of the parsing strategy developed for DPSG chart parsing (Bunt, 1991). Most of the work is done in the component called 'GEL rule', which combines the checking of local and global conditions on various features, the propagation of head features, and the semantic construction. In the conjunction describing the conditions for applying the rule, the equality relation of EL ('eqel') is used to test form and gender agreement of the constituents *a* and *b*. Similarly, the GEL predicate 'in' is used to test whether the form of constituent a belongs to an enumerated set of values.

When the parameters a and b in this rule are instantiated by feature structures representing constituents of category `CENTRALDET` and `NOM` (the ID-condition), where the central determiner immediately (CD-condition) precedes the nominal (LP-condition), then the GEL rule says that if the constraints on form and gender are satisfied, these constituents are the daughters of an NP centre whose head features, form feature, gender feature and person feature are inherited from the nominal constituent, and whose semantic content is constructed compositionally from the contents of the daughters.[15] Dynamic interpretation of the rule has the effect of creating an `NPCENTRE` node with these properties.

This approach has been implemented succesfully by extending the implemented machinery for EL evaluation with the GEL augmentations and merging this with the DPSG parser described in Bunt (1991).

4.2. HPSG PARSING USING GEL

4.2.1. *Grammatical information in HPSG*

In HPSG, grammatical rules come in three forms: as ID schemata, as LP restrictions, and as general principles, like the Subcategorization Principle and the Head Feature Principle.

ID schemata are constraints on the possible ways of using immediate dominance relations to build phrases. These constraints are expressed as signs, where some of the feature attributes have particular values such as an empty SUBCAT value, and where some attributes are required to have the same value, due to structure sharing. Being signs, ID schemata can be expressed in GEL.

LP restrictions are constraints on the order of the constituents of phrases, which are not treated in HPSG as feature attributes, as opposed to ID relations, and not part of a sign. LP restrictions are therefore not formalized within HPSG; they are formulated in the metalanguage. For dealing with LP restrictions in GEL we have three options:

1. we follow the HPSG strategy, leaving the linear precedence relation at the metalanguage and thus outside GEL:

2. we formalize what the theory says on linear precedence with the help of a GEL predicate constant denoting the LP relation;

3. we introduce a feature attribute ‘right neighbour’ and treat LP relations as parts of signs.

[15]The semantic part says, more specifically, that the NP centre denotes the union of those parts of the denotation of the (mass) nominal's denotation that satisfy the predicate denoted by the central determiner. For more explanation see Bunt, 1985.

To make our implementation close to other existing implementations (in particular to the STUF implementation of HPSG, discussed below), we take the first option, although theoretically the other options would perhaps be more interesting.

General principles, finally, describe how the values of certain feature attributes of phrases depend on those of their daughters. They can be seen as describing the propagation of feature values upon phrase building. These dependencies can be described in a first-order language and are thus easily expressed in GEL, as the above example of a DPSG rule in GEL illustrates.

4.2.2. *HPSG in STUF*

Our second implementation of parsing as dynamic interpretation is an emulation of the parser and grammar development environment called STUF (Stuttgart Type Unification Formalism), version of 1991, originally developed in the LILOG project (Herzog et al., 1986). In this section we outline the most relevant features of STUF and its use in implementing a fragment of English. In the next section we will describe the implementation of the same fragment using GEL.

STUF is a descendant of PATR-II, providing a formalism and a software environment for writing grammars of various kinds. STUF has a much richer language for specifying feature structures, based on Kasper and Rounds' feature logic (Kasper & Rounds, 1986). In STUF it is possible to directly specify complex embedded structures, including disjunctive and negative information. The core of the STUF language is formed by the following definition of the syntax of feature terms:[16]

```
atom              atomic value or template
_X                variable
attribute: S      feature selection
templ(S1,..,Sn)   parametrized template
[S1 S2 ..]        conjunction
{S1 S2 ..}        disjunction
not S             negation
```

Variables are used to describe structure sharing; they have the same interpretation as structure indices in the familiar matrix notation.

Templates are named complex feature terms, used to organize information more compactly. An example is the template for intransitive verbs, construed as objects that look for an NP to their left in order to form an S, and sharing its semantics with that S:

[16]We omit the use of semantic subsorts and paths here. For the full original definitions see Dörre & Seiffert, 1991 and Dörre & Raasch, 1991.

```
intransitive_verb :=
     [syntax [value: [ syntax: s
                       semantics: _X]
             direction: left
             argument:  syntax: np]
      semantics: _X]
```

Templates may be functional, having parameters which are substituted by actual values when applied. A simple example is the functional template `invert-boolean`, defined by:

```
invert_boolean(plus)  := minus.
invert_boolean(minus) := plus.
```

Lexical entries are simply feature term definitions where the name is interpreted as a word that may appear in an input sentence. Templates make these definitions very simple, as the following examples illustrate:

```
John := [ syntax: np ].
goes := intransitive_verb.
```

The STUF implementation of HPSG is not entirely faithful to the theory, in that (1) there is no ID/LP separation in STUF rules, which means that every ID schema has as many LP variants as the LP constraints allow; and (2) the general principles are instantiated for every ID schema.

The following elements, taken from an implementation of a fragment of English in the PLUS system (Black et al., 1991; Rentier, 1993) illustrate the actual use of STUF. In the next subsection we will illustrate the GEL emulation of STUF by describing the corresponding GEL structures.

1. Some functional templates:

```
head(X)    := synsem:local:head: X.
major(X)   := head(maj: X).
inv (X)    := head(maj: X).

comps(X)   := synsem:local:comps: X.
comps0     := comps(undef).

sat        := subj0, comps0.

ssat       := subj0, comps0, mod0.
unsat      := comps(def).

subj(X)    := synsem:local:subj: X.
subj0      := subj(undef).

mod(X)     := synsem:local:mod: X.
mod0       := mod(undef).
```

2. Some nonfunctional templates:

```
nominal    := major(n), mod0.

nphrase    := nominal, ssat.
```

3. Some general principles and auxiliary templates:

```
'HeadInherit'    := mother: head(X),
                    h_dtr: head(X).
'ContentInherit':= mother: content(X),
                    h_dtr: content(X).
'CompsInherit'   := mother: comps(X),
                    h_dtr: comps(X).
'GapInherit'     := mother: gap(X),
                    (( nonhead: gap0,
                       h_dtr: gap(X));
                     ( h_dtr: gap0,
                       nonhead: gap(X))).
'BindInherit'    := mother: bind(X),
                    (( nonhead: bind0,
                       h_dtr: bind(X));
                     ( h_dtr: bind0,
                       nonhead: bind(X))).

'NonLocalInherit':='GapInherit',
                   'BindInherit'.
'ModInherit'      := mother: mod( _X ),
                     h_dtr:  mod( _X ).
'ModCombine'      := mother:( mod0,
                              content(_X),
                              context(_Z)),
                     h_dtr:   _Y,
                     nonhead:(sat,
                              gap0,
                              mod(_Y),
                              content(_X),
                              context(_Z)).

'Complementation':= 'HeadInherit',
                    'ModInherit',
                    'ContentInherit',
                    'NonLocalInherit'.
'Adjunction'      := 'HeadInherit',
                     'CompsInherit',
                     'NonLocalInherit',
                     'ModCombine'.
```

4. Some ID/LP-rules (ID schemata with instantiated LP restrictions and general principles):

```
'RightComplementation' :=
    mother -> h_dtr, nonhead --
    'Complementation',
    nonhead: (major(not(d))).
'LeftComplementation'  :=
    mother -> nonhead, h_dtr --
    'Complementation',
    nonhead: (major(d)).
'LeftAdjunction'       :=
    mother -> nonhead, h_dtr --
    'Adjunction'.
```

5. Some lexical entries (slightly simplified):

```
car := nphrase,
       form(N),
       pers('3rd'),
       parm(P),
       restr1((rel:'CAR', arg0: P)).

who := nphrase,
       det(wh),
       pers('3rd'),
       gend(not(neut)),
       case(not(gen)),
       gap0,
       parm(P),
       restr1((rel:'WHO', arg0: P)).
```

4.2.3. *STUF emulated in GEL.*
To illustrate the emulation of STUF in GEL, we describe the GEL counterparts of the above STUF templates, ID rules instantiated for LP rules and general principles, and lexical entries.

1. Some functional templates

```
Head( _X )   := synsem:local:head: _X.
Major( _X )  := Head( maj: _X ).
Inv( _X )    := Head( inv: _X ).
Inv0         := Inv( undef ).

Comps( _X )  := synsem:local:comps: _X.
Comps0       := Comps( <> ).

Subj( _X )   := synsem:local:subj: _X.
```

```
Subj0        := Subj( undef ).

Sat          := bundle( Subj0,
                        Comps0 ).
Ssat         := bundle( Sat, Mod0 ).
Unsat        := Comps( Def ).

Mod( _X )    := synsem:local:mod: _X.
Mod0         := Mod( undef ).
```

2. Some nonfunctional templates:

```
Nominal := bundle( Major(N), Inv0,
                   Mod0, Subj0 ).
```

```
Nphrase := bundle( Nominal, Ssat ).
```

3. General principles:

```
HeadInherit( _HD ) :=
  if(testbundle(_HD, Head(_X)),
     Head(_X), undef ).

ContentInherit(_HD) :=
  if(testbundle(_HD, Content(_X)),
     Content(_X), undef).

CompsInherit(_HD) :=
  if(testbundle(_HD, Comps(_X)),
     Comps(_X), undef).

GapInherit(_HD, _N) :=
  if(testbundle(_N, Gap0),
     if(testbundle(_HD, Gap(_G1)),
        Gap(_G1), undef),
     if(testbundle(_HD, Gap0),
        if(testbundle(_N, Gap(_G2)),
           Gap(_G2), undef), undef)).

BindInherit(_HD, _N) :=
  if(testbundle(_N, Bind0),
     if(testbundle(_HD, Bind(_G1)),
        Bind(_G1), undef),
      if(testbundle(_HD, Bind0),
         if(testbundle(_N, Bind(_G2)),
            Bind(_G2), undef),
         undef)).

NonLocalInherit(_HD, _N) :=
  bundle(GapInherit(_HD, _N),
         BindInherit(_HD, _N)).
```

```
ModInherit(_HD) :=
  if(testbundle(_HD, Mod(_X)),
     Mod(_X),
     undef).

ModCombine(_HD, _N) :=
  if(testbundle(_N,
                Sat,
                Gap0,
                Mod(_HD),
                Content(_X),
                Context(_Z)),
     bundle(Mod0,
            Content(_X),
            Context(_Z)),
     undef).

Complementation(_HD, _N) :=
  bundle(HeadInherit(_HD),
         ModInherit(_HD),
         ContentInherit(_HD),
         NonLocalInherit(_HD, _N)).

Adjunction(_HD, _N) :=
  bundle(HeadInherit(_HD),
         SubjInherit(_HD),
         CompsInherit(_HD),
         ModCombine(_HD ,_N)).
```

4. Some ID/LP-rules (ID schemata with instantiated LP restrictions and general principles):

```
RightComplementation(_Head, _Comp) :=
  if(testbundle(_Comp, Major(notu(D))),
     Complementation(_Head, _Comp),
     undef).
```

```
LeftComplementation(_Comp, _Head) :=
  if(testbundle(_Comp, Major(D)),
     Complementation(_Head, _Comp),
     undef).
```

```
LeftAdjunction(_Adj, _Head) :=
    Adjunction(_Head, _Adj).
```

5. Some lexical entries:

```
car := bundle(Nphrase,
              Form(N),
              Pers(3rd),
              Parm(_1),
              Restr([rel:Car,
                     argzero:_1])).
```

```
who := bundle(Nphrase,
              Det(Wh),
              Pers(3rd),
              Gend(notu(Neut)),
              Case(notu(Gen)),
              Gap0,
              Parm(_1),
              Restr([rel:Who,
                     argzero:_1])).
```

Comparing the STUF and GEL descriptions, we see that, once the necessary functional templates and other auxiliary structures have been put in place, a relatively simple pattern of correspondences emerges. It my be noted that the GEL emulation has a clearer and more explicit representation of HPSG's general principles than the original STUF implementation, while the STUF representation is slightly more compact. A result of this explicitness is that the instantiation of the theory's general principles in every GEL rule (like in STUF) is hardly a drawback, although it is formally perhaps not in accordance with the theory. The principles are explicitly available in the implementation, ready for inspection and modification. Note also that the lexical representations in STUF and GEL are identical except for minor notational details; this is very important in practice, since most that an HPSG grammar writer is concerned with is the specification of lexical elements. In fact, the correspondence between lexical items in STUF and GEL is so straightforward that an automatic conversion from one format to the other would be possible.

Since the LP restrictions and general principles are instantiated in each ID-rule, application of STUF HPSG rules simply comes down to the application of these ID rules; there are no additional checks. Therefore, standard parsing procedures can be applied. We have implemented a simple chart parser for this purpose, using the matrix-driven parsing strategy described in Bunt (1991),[17] which applies the ID rules by invoking the implemented 'GEL machine' to evaluate the GEL rule.

5. CONCLUSIONS AND FUTURE WORK

Where STUF and similar formalisms and implementations developed in recent years, such as TFS, CUF and PLEUK, form an advance compared to PATR-II because of their more powerful languages for expressing linguistic information, GEL offers further extended possibilities to formalize grammatical information and represent it in a computationally attractive form. Not only ID-schemata and lexical entries can be given a formal representation, but LP-restrictions and general principles as well. At the same time, GEL retains the advantages of a fully declarative representation and of integrated representation of syntactic and semantic information.

Further work will have to make clear whether the approach described here offers, besides theoretical elegance, advantages for building efficient parsers and generators that work directly on the constraint-based representation of linguistic rules.

References

Van Benthem, J. (1991) General Dynamics. *Theoretical Linguistics 17: 159-201.*

Van Benthem, J. & Cepparello, G. (1994) Tarskian variations: dynamic parameters inclassical semantics. Technical Report CS-R9419, CWI, University of Amsterdam.

Black, W. et al. (1991) A Pragmatics-based Language Understanding System. In: *Information Processing Systems and Software, Selected Projects.* EC Brussels.

Bunt, H. (1985) *Mass terms and model-theoretic semantics.* Cambridge Univ. Press.

Bunt, H. (1987) Utterance generation from semantic representation augmented with pragmatic information. In G. Kempen (ed.) *Natural language generation.* Kluwer/Nijhoff, The Hague.

Bunt, H. (1991) Parsing with Discontinuous Phrase Structure Grammar. In M. Tomita (ed.) *Current Issues in Parsing Technology.* Kluwer, Dordrecht/Boston.

Bunt, H. (1995) Formal tools for modelling and processing discontinuous constituency. In H. Bunt & A. van Horck (eds.) *Discontinuous Constituency.* De Gruyter, Berlin.

Bunt, H., R.J. Beun, F. Dols, J. van der Linden & G. Schwartzenberg (1985) The TENDUM dialogue system and its theoretical basis. *IPO Annual Progress Report 19, 105–113.*

Carpenter, B. (1992) *The Logic of Typed Feature Structures.* Cambridge Univ. Press.

[17]The parser is simplified compared to the DPSG parser described in Bunt (1991) in that the particular provisions for dealing with discontinuous constituents have been left out. The implementation, carried out in C, is the work of Ko van der Sloot.

Dörre, J. & Raasch, I. (1991) *The Stuttgart Type Unification Formalism - User Manual.* IWBS Report 168, IBM Scientific Center, Stuttgart.

Dörre, J. & Seiffert, R. (1991) *Sorted Feature Terms and Relational Dependencies.* IWBS Report 153, IBM Scientific Center, Stuttgart.

Gazdar, G. & Pullum, G. (1987) *A Logic of Category Definition.* Cognitive Science Research Paper CSRP 072, University of Sussex.

Herzog, O. et al. (1986) *LILOG - Linguistic and logic methods for the computational understanding of German.* LILOG Report 1b, IBM Scientific Center, Stuttgart.

Johnson, M. (1988) *Attribute-Value Logic and the Theory of Grammar.* CSLI Lecture Notes 16.

Kasper, R. & Rounds, W. (1986) A logical semantics for feature structures. In: *Proc. ACL.* Columbia University, New York.

Lewis, D. (1992) *Parts of Classes.* Basil Blackwell, Oxford and Cambridge, MA.

McCawley, J. (1982) Parentheticals and Discontinuous Constituent Structure. *Linguistic Inquiry*, 13, 91–106

Moss, L.S. (1990) Completeness Theorems for Logics of Feature Structres. IBM Research Report RC 15737 (No. 69808), IBM Research, Yorktown Heights.

Pollard, C. & Sag, I. (1987) *Information-based Syntax and Semantics.* Vol I, Fundamentals. CSLI Lecture Notes 13, Stanford.

Pollard, C. & Sag, I. (1994) *Head-Driven Phrase Structure Grammar.* CSLI, Stanford, and University of Chicago Press

Rentier, G. (1993) The PLUS Grammar. *PLUS deliverable D3.2*, ITK, Tilburg.

De Rijke, M. (1992) A system of dynamic modal logic. Technical Report LP-92-08, ILLC, University of Amsterdam.

Sloot, K. van der (1990) The TENDUM 2.7 parsing algorithm for DPSG. *ITK Research Memo*, ITK, Tilburg.

Smolka, G. (1989) A feature logic with subsorts. LILOG Report 33, IWBS, IBM Germany, Heidelberg.

Tomita, M. (1986) *Efficient Parsing for Natural Language.* Kluwer Academic Publishers, Boston/Dordrecht.

7. PROOF THEORY FOR HPSG PARSING

STEPHAN RAAIJMAKERS
Institute for Language Technology and Artificial Intelligence
Tilburg University

Abstract.

A reinterpretation of Head-Driven Phrase Structure Grammar (HPSG) in a proof-theoretic context is presented. This approach yields a *decision procedure* which can be used to establish whether certain strings are generated by a given HPSG grammar. It is possible to view HPSG as a fragment of linear logic (Girard, 1987), subject to partiality and side conditions on inference rules. This relates HPSG to several categorial logics (Morrill, 1990). Specifically, HPSG signs are mapped onto quantified formulae, which can be interpreted as *second-order* types given the Curry-Howard isomorphism. The logic behind type inference will, aside from the usual quantifier introduction and elimination rules, consist of a partial logic for the undirected implication connective. It will be shown how this logical perspective can be turned into a parsing perspective. The enterprise takes the standard HPSG of Pollard & Sag (1987) as a starting point, since this version of HPSG is well-documented and has been around long enough to have displayed both merits and shortcomings; the approach is directly applicable to more recent versions of HPSG, however.

1. INTRODUCTION

The main concern of this chapter is building a parser for HPSG. The result of the enterprise should meet the following desiderata. First of all, the parser should interpret the original grammatical theory, or as close a dialect as possible. The parser should separate grammatical theory from parsing issues. Further, the parser should make an operationalisation of the grammatical theory explicit, as declaratively as possible. It should be easy to alter the grammatical theory, and, finally, the parser should have reasonable

H. Bunt and M. Tomita (eds.), Recent Advances in Parsing Technology, 115–144.

time/space complexity. Existing parsers for HPSG do not always conform to these requirements. For instance, the Popowich/Vogel parser (Popowich & Vogel, 1990) does not make a principled separation between the interpreted grammatical theory and the operation of the parser. This makes it relatively hard to adapt the grammar. Also, this parser is not impressingly efficient in terms of time and space. The LiLog STUF environment (Dörre & Raasch, 1991) does not interpret standard HPSG theory, and it is not entirely clear from the design of the parser how the grammatical theory is actually put to work.

In the *parsing-as-deduction* field, several parsing routines have arisen from proof-theoretic investigations (Moortgat, 1988; König, 1989). While these routines are not all among the most efficient, once a proof-theoretic formulation of HPSG has been made, one can benefit from these results. Some terminological remarks: we refer to HPSG as described by Pollard & Sag (1987) as '(classical, or standard) HPSG,' and to its type-theoretic (deductive) equivalent with '$\mathcal{D}$-HPSG'.

2. AN OVERVIEW OF HPSG

HPSG is a lexicalist, feature-based formalism for syntactic and semantic analysis of natural language. HPSG puts all relevant linguistic information in the lexicon, and has general rules, principles and constraints governing the construction of phrases from subphrases. As a syntactic formalism, HPSG divides the labour of tree construction into separate processes of *mobile construction* and *branch ordering.* A mobile is a tree-like structure with unordered trees; actually, a mobile can be interpreted as a description of a set of trees. So-called *immediate dominance* (ID) rules build these mobiles, which are then turned into trees by *linear precedence* (LP) constraints. HPSG is a feature-based formalism, employing various feature mechanisms transporting feature information through feature structures. In HPSG, lexemes are bundles of so-called attribute-value pairs

$$(1)\quad \begin{bmatrix} A_i & V_i \\ \vdots & \vdots \\ A_n & V_n \end{bmatrix}$$

where A_j is a certain linguistic (phonological/syntactic/semantic) property taking its specification from a set of values containing V_j. These bundles are called ***signs***. The reader is referred to Pollard & Sag (1987, 1994) for a full overview of the various attributes and their values. The generic structure of phrasal signs, describing phrases, in HPSG is shown in (2), where the *phon*, *syn*, *sem* and *dtrs* values describe respectively the phonological, syntactic, semantic and configurational properties of the sign. Attributes take either atomic or complex values; an attribute like *lex* (for lexicality) ranges over the set $\{+, -\}$, whereas an attribute like *dtrs*, describing daughters, which can be phrasal signs themselves, takes full signs as values.

$$(2)\quad \begin{bmatrix} phon & \ldots \\ syn & \begin{bmatrix} loc & \begin{bmatrix} head \ \ldots \\ subcat \ \ldots \\ lex \ \ldots \end{bmatrix} \\ bind \ \ldots & \end{bmatrix} \\ sem & \ldots \\ dtrs & \ldots \end{bmatrix}$$

The notion of *head* is a central concept in HPSG. Basically, a head of a phrase is a subphrase determining the relevant combinatorial properties of the sign. Heads can be phrasal or lexical; lexical heads are simply signs having no daughters. For instance, the head of a VP *sees Mary* is the verb *sees*. The grammatical properties of *sees* determine the properties (viz. agreement) of the VP as a whole, contrary to the properties of the direct object *Mary*. The head of the sentence *John sees Mary* is the VP *sees Mary*.

HPSG heavily leans on the notion of unification (Shieber, 1986). Simplifying matters somewhat, two signs S_1 and S_2 are unifiable with each other, written $S_1 \sqcup S_2$, if for any attribute they are both specified for, they bear non-conflicting values. Further, any fully disjunct parts of two signs (consisting of different attribute-value pairs) of the two signs can be combined directly. So,

$$(3)\quad \begin{bmatrix} A \begin{bmatrix} B & b \\ C & c \end{bmatrix} \end{bmatrix} \sqcup \begin{bmatrix} A \begin{bmatrix} B & b \\ D & d \end{bmatrix} \end{bmatrix} = \begin{bmatrix} A \begin{bmatrix} B & b \\ C & c \\ D & d \end{bmatrix} \end{bmatrix}$$

But the following fails if c_1 is not unifiable with c_2:

$$(4)\quad \begin{bmatrix} A \begin{bmatrix} B & b \\ C & c_1 \end{bmatrix} \end{bmatrix} \sqcup \begin{bmatrix} A \begin{bmatrix} B & b \\ C & c_2 \end{bmatrix} \end{bmatrix}$$

2.1. IMMEDIATE DOMINANCE RULES

Immediate dominance (ID) rules describe admissible dominance structures, which can be interpreted as mobiles: tree-like structures with unordered branches. The rules themselves take the form of partially specified HPSG signs, applying as felicity constraints to signs to be combined (see table 1).

Rule 1 licenses signs that have a non-lexical head daughter and are fully saturated, that is, signs having a *subcat*(egorisation) list of length zero,

TABLE 1. ID Rules as Signs

Rule Name	Sign Formulation
Rule 1 (**R1**)	$\begin{bmatrix} \mathit{syn} \mid \mathit{loc} \mid \mathit{subcat}\ \langle\rangle & \\ \mathit{dtrs} & \begin{bmatrix} \mathit{headdtr} \mid \mathit{syn} \mid \mathit{loc} \mid \mathit{lex}\ - \\ \mathit{compdtrs}\ \langle \_d \rangle \end{bmatrix} \end{bmatrix}$
Rule 2 (**R2**)	$\begin{bmatrix} \mathit{syn} \mid \mathit{loc} \mid \mathit{subcat}\ \langle \_s \rangle & \\ \mathit{dtrs} & \begin{bmatrix} \mathit{headdtr} \mid \mathit{syn} \mid \mathit{loc} \begin{bmatrix} \mathit{head} \mid \mathit{inv}\ - \\ \mathit{lex}\ + \end{bmatrix} \end{bmatrix} \end{bmatrix}$
Rule 3 (**R3**)	$\begin{bmatrix} \mathit{syn} \mid \mathit{loc} \mid \mathit{subcat}\ \langle\rangle & \\ \mathit{dtrs} & \begin{bmatrix} \mathit{headdtr} \mid \mathit{syn} \mid \mathit{loc} \begin{bmatrix} \mathit{head} \mid \mathit{inv}\ + \\ \mathit{lex}\ + \end{bmatrix} \end{bmatrix} \end{bmatrix}$

written as $\langle\rangle$. The configuration of this sign has one complement daughter, indicated with the variable '*_d*'; an example would be an S having a VP as head daughter and a subject as its single complement daughter. The *loc* attribute is used to describe "local" properties of a sign, such as lexicality and subcategorisation demands; this contrasts with the *bind* attribute, describing non-local coreference between signs, like anaphora binding. Rule 2 caters for instance for VP's, which have a lexical head daughter (the verb), and are one short of becoming saturated: they subcategorise for a subject. Rule 3 admits of saturated signs with a lexical, inverted head daughter, like in *Is John sleeping?*, the head daughter of which is the finite auxiliary *Is*, which subcategorises for both an infinitival VP and a nominative NP.

2.2. LINEAR PRECEDENCE CONSTRAINTS

Linear Precedence (or LP) constraints turn mobiles into genuine trees by imposing order on sister nodes (see table 2; the boxed integers used in this table denote variables ranging over attribute values, and $\prec$ denotes linear precedence between two nodes in an n-ary mobile configuration). The operation *order – constituents* produces the disjunction of all permutations of the phonology of the daughters. At least one of these permutations will have to be consistent with the constraints on order expressed by the LP constraints, which are specific for English and related languages.

LP1 says that lexical heads precede all their sisters (the empty sign [] acts like a "wildcard" symbol here, unifying with every sign). LP2 says that less *oblique* complements precede more oblique phrasal sisters; $\ll$ is

TABLE 2. LP Constraints

Name	Precedence Constraint
Constituent Order Principle	$\begin{bmatrix} \textit{phon order} - \textit{constituents}(\boxed{1}) \\ \textit{dtrs}\ \boxed{1} \end{bmatrix}$
LP Constraint 1 (**LP1**)	$\textit{head}[\textit{lex}\ +] \prec []$
LP Constraint 2 (**LP2**)	$\textit{complement} \ll \textit{complement}$

precedence between elements differing in obliqueness, where obliqueness corresponds inversely to degree of obligatoriness. Subjects, for instance, are in Germanic languages less oblique than direct objects, which means they are more obligatory: they cannot be omitted, in general (the asterisk indicating ungrammaticality):

(5) John eats.
⋆eats an apple.

The degree of obliqueness is mirrored (in reverse) by the order of complements on the *subcat* list of signs: the less oblique elements follow the more oblique elements.

2.3. FEATURE TRANSPORT PRINCIPLES

Various principles take care of the distribution of feature information in a feature structure, defining the paths along which information percolates upwards. Table 3 lists the most important of these principles, the Head Feature Principle (HFP), the Subcat Principle (SubcatP), and the Semantics Principle (SemP, simplified). Like the immediate dominance rules, these principles are formulated in sign format as well. The concept of *reentrancy*, expressing the sharing of information by several attributes across a sign, operates using boxed integers to identify attributes. The '+' operator is used as a string concatenation symbol. The HFP enforces identity between the head features of the head daughter and the mother sign. The Subcat Principle decomposes the *subcat* list of a head daughter in two parts of arbitrary (non-empty) length: the first part should correspond to the value of *compdtrs*, the second part becomes the value of the *subcat* attribute of the mother sign. The semantics principle states that the semantics of a mother sign must be composed of the combination of the semantics of the head daughter and the semantics of the complement daughters.

TABLE 3. Feature Transport

Name	Sign Formulation
HFP	$\begin{bmatrix} syn \mid loc \mid head\ \boxed{1} \\ dtrs \mid headdtr \mid syn \mid loc \mid head\ \boxed{1} \end{bmatrix}$
SubcatP	$\begin{bmatrix} sy \quad \square \quad n \mid loc \mid subcat\ 2 \\ dtrs \begin{bmatrix} headdtr \mid syn \mid loc \mid subcat\ \boxed{1} + \boxed{2} \\ compdtrs\ \boxed{1} \end{bmatrix} \end{bmatrix}$
SemP	$\begin{bmatrix} sem \begin{bmatrix} cont\ successively - combine - semantics(\boxed{1}, \boxed{2}) \end{bmatrix} \\ dtrs \begin{bmatrix} headdtr \mid sem \mid cont\ \boxed{1} \\ compdtrs \mid sem \mid cont\ \boxed{2} \end{bmatrix} \end{bmatrix}$

2.4. SAMPLE DERIVATION

The derivation in figure 1 shows the operation of the various principles, constraints and rules. Notice that HPSG as presented in Pollard & Sag (1987) assumes that nouns are heads selecting for determiners. Also, Pollard and Sag assume that heads themselves participate in the obliqueness hierarchy: they are more oblique than all their complements. Thus, LP2, once formulated as

(6) complement $\ll$ complement[lex -]

(Pollard & Sag, 1987:176) orders phrasal (non-lexical) heads after their complements (for instance VP's after subjects). In order to derive the order 'the cat' rather than 'cat the', Pollard and Sag assume that the head noun 'cat' becomes phrasal by the fact that Rule 2 is applicable to it as a lexical sign (cf. op. cit. p.153); so, rule application turns [*lex* +] into [*lex* -].

2.5. TREE ARITY

The HPSG theory as originally put forward by Pollard & Sag (1987) is not strictly binary-branching: the Subcat Principle allows for the combination of an *n*-ary functor with *n-1* arguments at once; e.g. the combination of a ditransitive verb taking three NP's (two complements and one subject) with two of its complements. This classical HPSG also is *non-monotonous*: as mentioned in the previous section, Rule 2 is able to change the lexicality of a sign by vacuously applying to that sign. This underdocumented fea-

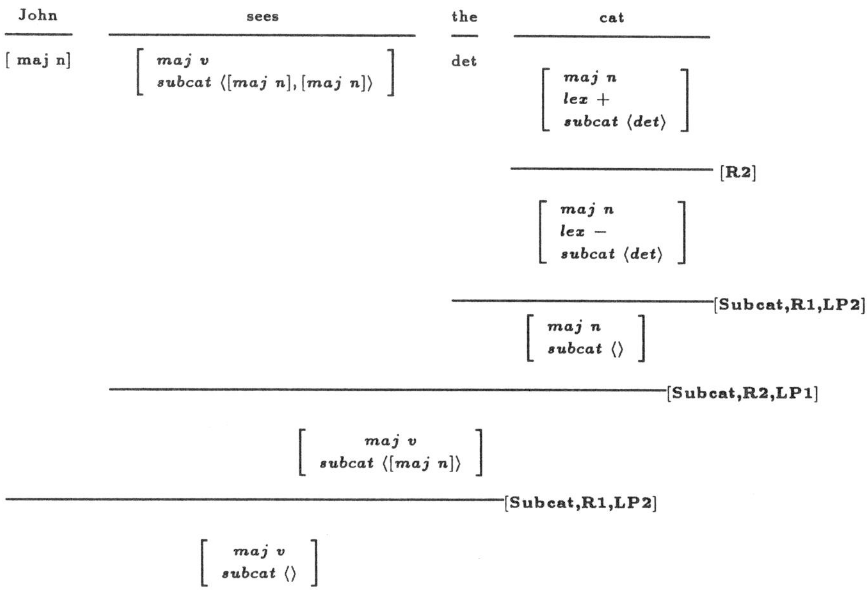

Figure 1. Sample derivation for 'John sees the cat'.

ture of HPSG has several drawbacks, most significantly, the fact that the operation is not structure preserving: usually, signs evolve from subsigns under unification; here, a + value becomes a − value, which unification cannot possibly account for. Conceptually, the lexicality feature seems to be *derivable*, since, only those signs are non-lexical which carry at least one daughter.

Classical HPSG does not lend itself directly to a proof-theoretic reconstruction. The theory, being declarative in a strong sense, has obscure operational aspects. Also, mainly for practical (but possibly also for theoretical) reasons, it appears to be desirable to have a version of HPSG building binary branching syntax trees. So, as a first step we present a binary version of HPSG.

3. BINARY-BRANCHING HPSG

The binary version of HPSG presented in this section removes some of the unattractive features of classical HPSG. Most significantly, this version makes no use of vacuous application of rules to signs, and thus allows for signs to monotonously evolve from lexical to non-lexical status. The theory remains very close to classical HPSG in all other aspects. The binarity is mainly motivated from practical reasons; it facilitates the linking of HPSG to a logical type calculus. Binarity is by no means a strong commitment, however. Focus is on the desire to analyse a fragment of Dutch declarative main clauses, although some examples illustrate the applicability of the binary apparatus on fragments of English as well.

First, we define lexicality in terms of daughters, using common predicate notation.

(7) *lexical*(Sign) if *dtrs*(Sign)= ⟨⟩,

parafrased as: Sign is lexical if Sign has zero daughters. We then define:

(8) $args_n$(Sign) if *length*(*subcat*(Sign))= $n, n \geq 1$,

parafrased as: Sign wants n arguments if the *subcat* list of Sign has length n (an empty list has length zero). We refer to a functor $\mathcal{F}$ with $args_n$ as $\mathcal{F}_n$.

The crucial observation for languages like Dutch and English is that the amount of saturation together with the lexicality of a functor (a sign with non-empty *subcat* list) determines the position of the functor with respect to its argument. A post-modifier like *with pictures*, modifying a noun like *book*, follows the noun: it is non-lexical, and has $args_1$. Similarly, intransitive verbs — assuming they are lexicalised as VP's, i.e. non-lexical, verbal $args_1$ functors — follow their subjects. Semi-saturated verbal functors like *gives John* precede their objects: they are $args_2$ functors. We can capture the order determiner-noun by assuming that determiners subcategorise for non-maximal noun projections (like *book*, *little book with black cover*), so they are $args_1$; they are lexical, and precede their argument. This contrasts with the view of Pollard & Sag (1987), which analyses nouns as subcategorising for determiners.[1] So, the generalisation seems to be that:

(9) (i) Ordering effects triggered by the lexicality of functors come into play only for $\mathcal{F}_1$ functors: a lexical $\mathcal{F}_1$ is ordered before its argument; a non-lexical $\mathcal{F}_1$ is ordered after its argument.
(ii) A functor $\mathcal{F}_n$ where $n > 1$ is ordered before its argument.

The LP constraints in table 3 make this precise[2]. The α is a variable ranging over a sister node in a binary mobile configuration. To see how these constraints work, consider the derivation in figure 2.

We also need the regular LP constraint for inverted phrases:

(10) (**BLP4**) $[\ inv + \ ] \prec \alpha$

This all works fine for concatenative phenomena, i.e. the combination of two phrases under adjacency. Certain adjuncts appear to be non-concatenative, however. In Dutch, one observes:

[1] We shall neglect the question on how to encode (non)-maximality of phrases here; a bar-level along the lines Cooper (1990) suggests may be necessary here.

[2] The signs in these constraints are only partly specified.

TABLE 4. LP Constraints

Name	Precedence Constraint
(BLP1)	$\begin{bmatrix} lex & + \\ args_1 & \end{bmatrix} \prec \alpha$
(BLP2)	$\alpha \prec \begin{bmatrix} lex & - \\ args_1 & \end{bmatrix}$
(BLP3)	$\begin{bmatrix} args_n \end{bmatrix} \prec \alpha$

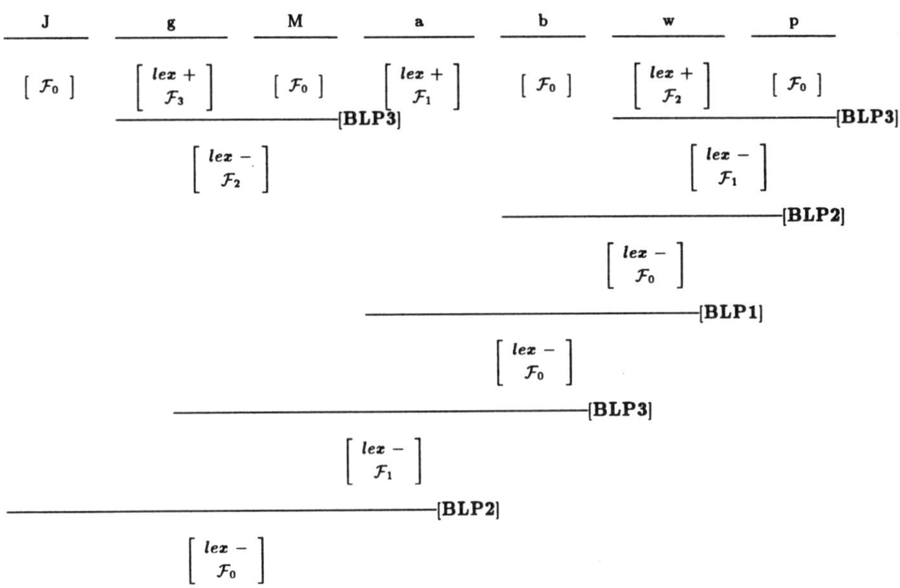

Figure 2. Sample derivation for 'John gives Mary a book with pictures'.

(11) Jan geeft met plezier Marie een boek.
'John gives with pleasure Mary a book'
John gives Mary a book with pleasure.
Jan geeft Marie met plezier een boek.
Jan geeft Marie een boek met plezier.

This suggests that the phonological operation associated with certain adverbial modifiers should not be concatenation but *infixation.* Reape (1990) has made similar remarks concerning semi-free word order phenomena. We then arrive at the following LP constraint

(12) (**BLP5**) $adv \Downarrow \alpha$

where $A \Downarrow B$ says that (the phonology of) A is infixed into (the phonology of) B. The non-concatenative connective $\downarrow$ was introduced in categorial grammar by Moortgat (Moortgat, 1988) for similar purposes; an expression of type $A \downarrow B$ infixes into expressions of type B to form an expression of type A (see section 4.4 below). The predicate *adv* flags the sign for a VP-level adverbial modifier, which is a sign subcategorising for a VP to yield a VP: it inherits the NP argument (the subject) its argument VP is still incomplete for. Complement order needs no longer be stipulated as a separate LP constraint: functors now combine with one argument at a time, and the order of arguments is expressed by the order on the *subcat* list. Further, the ID rules of original HPSG must be adapted: while Rules 1 and 3 can be kept, Rule 2 must now be altered to cater for generalised incompleteness: a sign with a lexical head daughter and more than one item on its *subcat* list should be a well-formed sign as well.

4. DEDUCTION FOR HPSG

With the binary version of HPSG we are set to give HPSG a deductive basis. First, we show that it is possible to reinterpret signs as types. Then we introduce a deductive apparatus performing type-deduction with these derived types. This calculus builds binary proof trees (*proof terms*), which are orthogonal to (binary-) HPSG derivation trees.

4.1. SIGNS AS FORMULAE

We propose to view signs as *types*, or, with the Curry-Howard isomorphism in mind, as *formulae* of a certain logic. Ideas in this spirit can already be found in work of Blackburn (interpreting signs as modal formulae), Morrill and others. The concept of types has many interpretations, but one particularly apt for linguistics is that a type is a set of expressions, or, in more traditional terms, a category. Together with a set of combinatorial principles, types form an algebra of expressions over a certain domain: a type system. Essentially, these combinatorial principles constitute a *derivability relation* between sequences of types '$\rightarrow$': $A \rightarrow B$ saying that from the type sequence A the type sequence B can be derived. An example of a type system would be any syntactic algebra consisting of a set of type formation rules (e.g. the production rules in a rewrite system) and a set of syntactic categories (types) containing expressions over some alphabet of strings. More fine-grained type systems make a distinction between atomic and complex types: atomic types being monadic objects and complex types being made up from (atomic or complex) subtypes with the use of so-called type-forming connectives which serve to express combinatorial properties. Type-forming connectives are relations over the set of type symbols; a familiar example are the slashes from categorial grammar $/, \backslash$: a *functor* type X/Y combines with a type Y to its *right* to form a type X; a functor type $Y\backslash X$ combines with a type Y to its *left* to form an X. There is a nice interpretation of linguistic types as propositional formulae in a logic: atomic types T correspond to formulae T; complex types like $A\backslash B$ correspond to $A \Rightarrow_l B$, with $\Rightarrow_l$ a left-oriented version of the implication arrow $\Rightarrow$ of propositional logic. The combination of a type A with a type $A \Rightarrow B$ to a type B then becomes an instance of Modus Ponens, of which we now have two versions: $A, A \Rightarrow_l B \rightarrow B$ and $A \Rightarrow_r B, A \rightarrow B$. This, in fact, is an operationalisation of the slogan *parsing as deduction*, which is basically the central theme of categorial deduction as in Lambek calculus (Moortgat, 1988).

The intuition that signs can be interpreted as types arises from the functionality expressed by the *subcat* feature: essentially, this feature expresses that a certain sign is *functionally (in-)complete* for one or more other signs. This immediately suggests a functional type equivalent (a functor) for these signs. Saturated signs then can be interpreted to correspond to saturated functors, or atomic types, i.e. types not being made up from a type-forming connective and one or more subtypes. HPSG's Subcat principle, which allows for the combination of a non-saturated sign with a subset of the signs it subcategorises for should then correspond to a combinatorial rule of type formation, i.c. an inference rule in a type calculus.

When we want to make a correspondence between the signs of HPSG and types of a certain kind, we immediately notice that HPSG signs encode much more information than the monadic categories of simple type systems like production grammars. A category like S, for instance, is represented in HPSG as a fine-grained specification of a verbal projection having various properties among which is an empty subcategorisation frame. Clearly, we need a more sophisticated type language than can be offered by monadic categories alone. Suppose, then, we switch from monadic types to types with internal structure: *predicational* types in stead of propositional types. The value of the category-determining $maj(or)$ attribute should become the top-level predicate constant. As in predicate logic, types (propositions) are made up from such a predicate constant and terms as arguments of the predicate. Signs having variable values, i.e. being *underspecified* for certain attributes, correspond to (universally) quantified formulae. E.g., a partial sign like

$$(13)\quad \begin{bmatrix} major & n \\ gender & neuter \\ person & \_x \end{bmatrix}$$

with $\_x$ a variable should correspond to the type

(14) $\forall(\_x).[n(gender(neuter), person(\_x))]$.

The choice between universal and existential quantification is mainly motivated from considerations regarding the proof terms for quantified formulae, which will be discussed in the next section. A related motivaton is the fact that universally quantified types have a straightforward connection with Prolog literals, facilitating implementation. It is important to notice that there is no deep, 'predicate-like' meaning behind such a formula: it is just a description of a certain kind of category, in the case above having a variable spot for the person value. Sign-valued attributes, i.e. attributes taking a full sign as value, or a list of signs, are treated the same: whenever such an attribute takes a variable sign as value, universal quantification over this variable occurs. This is responsible for the second-order nature of the type language we use.

Under the logical interpretation of types as formulae, types have *proof terms* associated with them; these proof terms are the *justification* for assuming the formula is true: they correspond to proofs for the propositions the types express. These proofs are constructed in a *calculus* of inference rules, the inference rules constituting a derivability relation over type sequences (like the combinatorial rules of production systems), where this derivability relation now gets a logical interpretation as well. An alternative, quite common point of view is that proof terms are a kind of procedures (or programs) and types are the specification of what these programs do. For instance, the formula

(15) $\forall(\_x).[n(gender(masc), number(\_x))]$

would be a specification of the program recognising singular and plural masculine noun phrases (this basically is what parsing is about).

A concept like *reentrancy* can easily be encoded by means of variable sharing, for example

(16) $\forall(\_x).[P_1(P_i(\_x), \ldots, P_n(\_x))]$

where each P_j is a predicate symbol.

We now turn to the translation from signs to types, where we let $\dagger(S)$ yield the formula (type) equivalent of the sign S. A few words on notation: $\mathcal{Q}^n$ denotes a sequence $\forall(\_v_i)\ldots\forall(\_v_n)$ of quantifiers. The empty quantifier sequence is written as $\mathcal{Q}^0$; $\mathcal{Q}^0.X = X$. Further, $\mathcal{Q}^n\mathcal{Q}^0 = \mathcal{Q}^0\mathcal{Q}^n = \mathcal{Q}^n$. We use the notation

$$\Sigma \begin{bmatrix} a_i & & b_i \\ & \vdots & \\ a_n & & b_n \end{bmatrix}$$

to refer to some sign Σ with all attribute–value pairs in the sign

$$\begin{bmatrix} a_i & & b_i \\ & \vdots & \\ a_n & & b_n \end{bmatrix}$$

present as subsigns. Likewise,

$$\Sigma - \begin{bmatrix} a_i & & b_i \\ & \vdots & \\ a_n & & b_n \end{bmatrix}$$

refers to some sign Σ complemented with respect to the subsign

$$\begin{bmatrix} a_i & & b_i \\ & \vdots & \\ a_n & & b_n \end{bmatrix}$$

Explicit feature paths are omitted in this notation where possible. Furthermore, $var(X)$, $atom(X)$, $number(X)$ express respectively that X is a variable, an atom or a number.

The crucial thing to note is that the *subcat* information of a sign is reformulated as the functional demands of a functor type: a *subcat* list of length n yields a functor with functional degree n, where n now indicates the number of arguments the functor is incomplete for.

The following example illustrates the mapping from signs to formulae. Variables are prefixed with an underscore; the positive value '+' is written as 1. The feature structure (17) then becomes the formula (18).

(17) $$\begin{bmatrix} syn & \begin{bmatrix} loc & \begin{bmatrix} head & \begin{bmatrix} maj\ n \\ case\ \_c \\ nform\ \_n \\ aux\ nil \\ inv\ nil \\ prd\ nil \end{bmatrix} \\ subcat\ [] & \\ lex\ 1 & \end{bmatrix} \\ bind\ \_b & \end{bmatrix} \end{bmatrix}$$

(18) $\forall(\_c)\forall(\_n)\forall(\_b).[n(syn(loc(head(case(\_c), nform(\_n), aux(nil), inv(nil), prd(nil)), lex(1)), bind(\_b)))]$

TABLE 5. From Signs to Types

$\dagger(Sign)$	Resultant Type	Condition
$\dagger(X)$	$\mathcal{Q}^0.X$	$var(X)$ **or** $atom(X)$ **or** $number(X)$ **or** $X = \langle\rangle$
$\dagger(\Sigma \begin{bmatrix} subcat\ \langle\rangle \\ maj\ M \end{bmatrix})$	$\mathcal{Q}^n.M(F)$	$\dagger(\Sigma - \begin{bmatrix} subcat\ \langle\rangle \\ maj\ M \end{bmatrix}) = \mathcal{Q}^n.F$
$\dagger(\Sigma \begin{bmatrix} subcat\ \langle X_1, .., X_n\rangle \\ maj\ M \end{bmatrix})$	$\mathcal{Q}^n\mathcal{Q}^m.A_1 \Rightarrow ..$ $..A_n \Rightarrow M(F)$	$\dagger(\Sigma - \begin{bmatrix} subcat\ \langle X_1, ..., X_n\rangle \\ maj\ M \end{bmatrix}) =$ $\mathcal{Q}^n_1.F$ **and** $\dagger(\langle X_1, .., X_n\rangle) :=$ $\mathcal{Q}^m.\langle A_1, .., A_n\rangle$
$\dagger([\ A\ V\ ])$	$\forall(V).A(V)$	$var(V)$
$\dagger([\ A\ V\ ])$	$\mathcal{Q}^n.A(X_1, .., X_n)$	$\dagger(V) := \mathcal{Q}^n.\langle X_1, .., X_n\rangle$
$\dagger(\langle X_1, .., X_n\rangle)$	$\mathcal{Q}^n\mathcal{Q}^m.$ $\langle F_1, F_2, .., F_n\rangle$	$\dagger(X_1) = \mathcal{Q}^n.F1$ **and** $\dagger(\langle X_2, .., X_n\rangle) =$ $\mathcal{Q}^m.\langle F_2, .., F_n\rangle$

4.2. TYPE DEDUCTION

In this section, we show how we can interpret the HPSG apparatus of ID rules, constraints and principles as an inference mechanism for type deduction, given the translation of signs into types. Before we do so, a few words on type deduction are necessary.

As mentioned in section 4.1, types have a truth-conditional interpretation: they correspond to *propositions* (formulae). This logical perspective makes it possible to identify type derivability relations with *logical* derivability relations from proof theory. A statement $A \rightarrow B$ expressing the derivability of type sequence B from type sequence A is then called a *sequent* (Gallier, 1986). A sequent $A_1, ..., A_n \rightarrow B$ can be interpreted as: the validity of the formulae $A_1, ..., A_n$ implies the validity of B; i.e., there is no model for the formulae $A_1, ..., A_n$ that is not also a model for B. The sequence $A_1, ..., A_n$ is called the *antecedent* of the sequent; the sequence B (in the present case of length 1) is called the *succedent* of the sequent.

The configuration $\dfrac{P_1 \quad \ldots \quad P_n}{C}$ is read as: the *conclusion sequent* C is valid iff the *premise sequents* $P_1, \ldots, P_n$ are valid. As an example, here is a fragment of so-called *linear non-commutative propositional logic*. 'Linear' (Girard, 1987) means here that this logic forces 'honest' bookkeeping: we are not allowed to duplicate nor delete types during derivation. From a linguistic perspective, linearity can be used to express the fact that the meaning of an utterance depends on the linear order of its words. Every Γ_i is a (possibly empty) type sequence; Λ is a non-empty type sequence, and X, Y, Δ are types. The comma denotes non-commutative concatenation: Γ_1, Γ_2 is the concatenation of the type sequences Γ_1 and Γ_2. This entails that antecedents are essentially lists of types.

$$\mathcal{I}\frac{}{X \rightarrow X}$$

$$\mathcal{R} \Rightarrow \frac{\Gamma, X \rightarrow Y}{\Gamma \rightarrow X \Rightarrow Y}$$

$$\mathcal{R} \Rightarrow \frac{X, \Gamma \rightarrow Y}{\Gamma \rightarrow X \Rightarrow Y}$$

$$\mathcal{L} \Rightarrow \frac{\Lambda \rightarrow X \qquad \Gamma_1, Y, \Gamma_2 \rightarrow \Delta}{\Gamma_1, X \Rightarrow Y, \Lambda, \Gamma_2 \rightarrow \Delta}$$

$$\mathcal{L} \Rightarrow \frac{\Lambda \rightarrow X \qquad \Gamma_1, Y, \Gamma_2 \rightarrow \Delta}{\Gamma_1, \Lambda, X \Rightarrow Y, \Gamma_2 \rightarrow \Delta}$$

The $\mathcal{L}$ rules are referred to as the *left rules* and the $\mathcal{R}$ rules as the *right* rules of the calculus. Here is a proof of the theorem $A \rightarrow (A \Rightarrow B) \Rightarrow B$.

$$\dfrac{\dfrac{\dfrac{}{A \rightarrow A}\mathcal{I} \quad \dfrac{}{B \rightarrow B}\mathcal{I}}{A, A \Rightarrow B \rightarrow B}\mathcal{L} \Rightarrow}{A \rightarrow (A \Rightarrow B) \Rightarrow B}\mathcal{R} \Rightarrow$$

As we alluded to in section 4.1, it is possible to associate with deductions *proof terms* encoding the proofs performed; these terms are λ-terms made up from the terms associated with the types in the sequents. The λ-terms come in various kinds; the ones we discuss are either *application terms* $t(t')$, saying that the functional term t is applied to the term t'; or *abstraction terms* $\lambda v.t$, a functional term taking a term v to a term t. Terms are in either *normal form* or *non-normal form*; in the latter case, terms contain subterms $(\lambda v.t)(t')$, so-called *redexes*. The relation called β-reduction allows the simplification of such a redex to $t[t'/v]$, which means that in term t, every occurrence of v is replaced by t'. The λ-terms for these deductions have the so-called *single-bind* property: every λ-bound variable v such that $\lambda v.t$ occurs exactly once in t; so we do not have terms $\lambda v.w$ where v does not occur in w, nor terms like $\lambda v.(t(v)(v))$. We then end up with the following rules:

$$\mathcal{I}\frac{}{t : X \to t : X}$$

$$\mathcal{R}\Rightarrow\frac{\Gamma, v : X \to t : Y}{\Gamma \to \lambda v.t : X \Rightarrow Y}$$

$$\mathcal{R}\Rightarrow\frac{v : X, \Gamma \to t : Y}{\Gamma \to \lambda v.t : X \Rightarrow Y}$$

$$\mathcal{L}\Rightarrow\frac{\Lambda \to t' : X \qquad \Gamma_1, t(t') : Y, \Gamma_2 \to \Delta}{\Gamma_1, t : X \Rightarrow Y, \Lambda, \Gamma_2 \to \Delta}$$

$$\mathcal{L}\Rightarrow\frac{\Lambda \to t' : X \qquad \Gamma_1, t(t') : Y, \Gamma_2 \to \Delta}{\Gamma_1, \Lambda, t : X \Rightarrow Y, \Gamma_2 \to \Delta}$$

The term for the proof above would be $\lambda P.P(t)$ giving the term t as a proof for A. Once one adds the so-called Cut rule to the calculus:

$$(19) \quad \text{Cut}\frac{\Gamma_2 \to \Lambda \quad \Gamma_1, \Lambda, \Gamma_3 \to \Delta}{\Gamma_1, \Gamma_2, \Gamma_3 \to \Delta}$$

λ-terms in non-normal form occur as proof terms. The Cut rule expresses the transitivity of the derivability relation $\to$.

Cut-free sequent calculus for the linear fragment of propositional logic has the so-called *subformula property*: premise sequents contain all and only subformulae of the conclusion sequent. Premise sequents have lower degree in terms of type-forming connectives: they contain one connective less than the conclusion sequents. From a top-down theorem proving regime, this means a steady reduction of complexity during deduction: one starts with a 'complex' sequent containing a multiplicity of connectives, breaking this sequent down into sequents of smaller degree, until one reaches the axiom sequents of type $A \to A$, thus settling the conjecture of the conclusion sequent. In calculi with Cut, the subformula property no longer holds, since Λ can be any type, possibly increasing the degree of the premise sequent $\Gamma_1, \Lambda, \Gamma_3 \to \Delta$. Fortunately, the Cut elimination theorem (Gentzen's *Hauptsatz* (Gentzen, 1934)) says that Cut is a derivable rule: every proof with Cut can be transformed into a Cut-free proof. Cut-elimination leads to normal-form proof terms.

Morrill (1990) has the following sequent rules for second-order quantifier types

$$\mathcal{L}\forall\frac{\Gamma_1, t(t') : \Lambda[t'/\_x], \Gamma_2 \rightarrow \alpha : X}{\Gamma_1, t : \forall(\_x).\Lambda, \Gamma_2 \rightarrow \alpha : X}$$

$$\mathcal{L}\exists\frac{\Gamma_1, \pi_2(t) : \Lambda[\pi_1(t)/\_x], \Gamma_2 \rightarrow \alpha : X}{\Gamma_1, t : \exists(\_x).\Lambda, \Gamma_2 \rightarrow \alpha : X}$$

$$\mathcal{R}\forall\frac{\Gamma \rightarrow t : \Lambda}{\Gamma \rightarrow \lambda\_x.t : \forall(\_x).\Lambda}$$

$$\mathcal{R}\exists\frac{\Gamma \rightarrow t_2 : \Lambda[t_1/\_x]}{\Gamma \rightarrow \langle t_1, t_2\rangle : \exists(\_x).\Lambda}$$

For $\{\mathcal{R}\forall, \mathcal{L}\exists\}$, the condition is that $\_x$ is not free in $\Gamma, \Gamma_1, \Gamma_2$; $t[\alpha/\beta]$ is the substitution of α for β in t and $\pi_i(t)$ is the i-th projection of the pair-term t: $\pi_1(\langle\alpha, \beta\rangle) = \alpha; \pi_2(\langle\alpha, \beta\rangle) = \beta$. The functional proof terms for $\forall$-types reflect the intuitionistic idea that a proof for a proposition $\forall(\_x).\Lambda$ consists of a method for proving the proposition expressed by Λ. This gives a more plausible interpretation of proofs for universal quantification once this quantification ranges over infinite domains: a mere truth-value then seems impossible to arrive at. The pair terms for $\exists$-types say that a proof for such a formula consists of an individual (a *witness*) and a term in which this individual is substituted for the bound variable. As noted earlier. the intuitionistic quantifier terms have a nice interpretation in our syntactic type calculus: a type $\forall(\_x).\Pi$ then becomes a specification of a method (proof) recognising all expressions of type Π on the basis of any (instantiation of) $\_x$. We shall be silent about proof terms from now on, as they do not play an evident role in parsing HPSG. They could be of use in proving meta-results about HPSG parsing, however.

It is a well-known fact from the proof-theory of predicate logic that once both kinds of quantification (universal and existential) are used, deductions are not invariant under permutation of rule application: the application of quantifier rules becomes order-sensitive (Wallen, 1990). This effect does not take place here, since we only have universal quantification. Given this complete and symmetric calculus, let us establish the fragment needed to perform deduction for HPSG.

4.3. ID RULES AS AXIOM SCHEMATA.

HPSG rules describe admissible, i.e. well-formed signs. In a type-theoretic setting, they can be interpreted as type checks, since here, signs become types. A simple way to implement these definitions, is to formulate them as *axiom schemata* in a type calculus. That is, every rule R defining the sign Σ becomes an axiom scheme:

(20) $(R)\ \dagger(\Sigma) \rightarrow \dagger(\Sigma)$.

So, every axiom sequent can be interpreted as an instance of an ID rule. This assures that, whenever an axiom schema is used during deduction, the type check is effective. For binary HPSG, this results in the axiom schemata of table 6, where X^n schematises over an argument sequence $X_j \ldots X_n$ of quantified (partially variable) types:

(21) $\forall(v_i)\ldots\forall(v_k)X_j \rhd \ldots \rhd \forall(v_l)\ldots\forall(v_m)X_n$ $(1 \leq i \leq k, 1 \leq j \leq n, 1 \leq l \leq m,\ \rhd \in \{\Rightarrow, \downarrow\})$

Irrelevant feature information is suppressed in table 6.

TABLE 6. Axiom Schemata

Name	Axiom Formulation
(I1)	$\forall(\_cat)\forall(\_phon)\forall(\_sem)\forall(\_d)$ $[\_cat(\_phon, syn(loc(subcat([\,]))), \_sem,$ $dtrs(headdtr(syn(loc(lex(0)))),$ $compdtrs(\_d)))] \rightarrow$ $\forall(\_cat)\forall(\_phon)\forall(\_sem)\forall(\_d)$ $[\_cat(\_phon, syn(loc(subcat([\,]))), \_sem,$ $dtrs(headdtr(syn(loc(lex(0)))),$ $compdtrs(\_d)))]$
(I2)	$\forall(\_cat)\forall(\_phon)\forall(\_syn)\forall(\_sem)X^n$ $[\_cat(\_phon, \_syn, \_sem,$ $dtrs(headdtr(syn(loc(head(inv(0)))))))] \rightarrow$ $\forall(\_cat)\forall(\_phon)\forall(\_syn)\forall(\_sem)X^n$ $[\_cat(\_phon, \_syn, \_sem,$ $dtrs(headdtr(syn(loc(head(inv(0)))))))]$
(I3)	$\forall(\_cat)\forall(\_phon)\forall(\_sem)\forall(\_d)$ $[\_cat(\_phon, syn(loc(subcat([\,]))), \_sem,$ $dtrs(headdtr(syn(loc(head(inv(1)),lex(1))))))] \rightarrow$ $\forall(\_cat)\forall(\_phon)\forall(\_sem)$ $[\_cat(\_phon, syn(loc(subcat([\,]))), \_sem,$ $dtrs(headdtr(syn(loc(head(inv(1)),lex(1))))))]$

It is not hard to recognise equivalents of the HPSG rules **R1, R2, R3** in the axiom schemata **I1, I2, I3**, once one remembers that functors now combine with their arguments one at a time: in classical HPSG, there were only two kinds of functional configurations: a functor having consumed all of its arguments (treated by **R1**) and a functor having consumed all of its arguments but one (**R2**). In $\mathcal{D}$-HPSG, many more configurations arise, generally speaking: $n - 1$ for any n-place functor. So, where the first axiom schema restores **R1**, the second can be seen to generalize **R2** to cover *any* kind of functional incompleteness. The lexicality demand on the head daughter **R2** vanishes here; functors consume one argument at a time, and once they have consumed one, they are no longer lexical. There is another option: the ID-rules could be compiled away by ensuring they are consequently applied to signs and their phrasal subsigns when the lexicon is created.

Although this idea hides the important concept of ID rules in the process of lexicon creation, it would allow for using the regular axiom scheme

$$\mathcal{I}\frac{}{t : X \rightarrow t : X} \; .$$

4.4. PRINCIPLES AND CONSTRAINTS AS INFERENCE RULES AND CONDITIONS

The various principles and constraints of HPSG appear to be easily reconciliable with the logical setting proposed. In HPSG, they do not form a homogenous class; some principles or constraints govern the flow of information in a feature structure, others create new information (like the LP constraints). This is reflected in their proof-theoretic reconstruction.

Head Feature Principle
The Head Feature Principle of HPSG instantiates the head features of a freshly projected 'mother sign' to the head features of the head daughter. The necessity for doing so vanishes in the type-theoretic HPSG equivalent. To see this, notice that in the latter, all necessary feature transport is encoded by means of variable sharing in the *type assignments* for the lexical entries. Where HPSG uses the Subcat Principle to create new sign projections, with new *compdtrs* and *subcat* values, $\mathcal{D}$-HPSG never creates new sign projections during analysis: types only become gradually more developed in the sense that more and more variable subtypes become instantiated. Therefore, the Head Feature Principle becomes totally redundant: the head features of a functor (a verb, or whatever) are preserved and developed all the way. This makes $\mathcal{D}$-HPSG in a way more lexical than original HPSG. The distinction among head daughters and their superordinating signs vanishes as well; one reasonable thing to say is that the Head Feature

Principle is 'compiled away' in the lexicon, making this distinction irrelevant. So, we can suppress the *headdtr* attribute in our signs.

Subcat Principle

The Subcat Principle is the motor behind syntactic combination in HPSG. Basically, what it does in original HPSG is to decompose the *subcat* list of a non-saturated sign, transferring a (non-fixed) number of entries on the list to the *compdtrs* attribute of a fresh mother sign, thus allowing the combination of the sign with suitable complements unifying with the *compdtrs* value.

In $\mathcal{D}$-HPSG, the Subcat Principle has a binary shape: it secures the combination of a functor $A \Rightarrow B$ and a (single) argument expression A to a result type B. As $A \Rightarrow B$ is an undirected functor, combining with an A either to its left or right to form a B, we will need two versions (left and right instances) of the Subcat Principle. These can be interpreted as *inference rules*, i.c. the *left rules* for the propositional connective $\Rightarrow$ for undirected implication we saw earlier. The (type) variable sharing in these rules must now be understood as demands for unification on type level:

$$(22) \quad \mathcal{L} \Rightarrow \frac{\Lambda \rightarrow X \qquad \Gamma_1, Y, \Gamma_2 \rightarrow \Delta}{\Gamma_1, X \Rightarrow Y, \Lambda, \Gamma_2 \rightarrow \Delta}$$

The Subcat Principle covers *concatenative* functors only, i.e. functors which either follow or precede their arguments. For non-concatenative functors, such as the adverbial modifiers of section 3, we cannot use the concatenative connective $\Rightarrow$.

Borrowing the connective $\downarrow$ from categorial grammar (Moortgat, 1988), then, $A \downarrow B$ is a expression wanting to penetrate in an expression of type B to form an A. The adverbial adjuncts are typed $vp \downarrow vp$, where vp is an abbreviation of a formula $n(\ldots) \Rightarrow v(\ldots)$. It turns out to be technically impossible to establish a full logic for this connective under the perspective of antecedents as lists; only the rule $\mathcal{L} \downarrow$ can be formulated.[3] See Moortgat (1988, 1990) for discussion resp. a solution. For our purposes, this is enough, however: HPSG displays partial logics (left rules only) for functional connectives. The rule becomes:

$$(23) \quad \mathcal{L} \downarrow \frac{\Gamma_2, \Gamma_3 \rightarrow t' : B \quad \Gamma_1, t(t') : A, \Gamma_4 \rightarrow \Lambda}{\Gamma_1, \Gamma_2, t : A \downarrow B, \Gamma_3, \Gamma_4 \rightarrow \Delta}$$

[3] A full logic for this connective would make the structural rule of Permutation a derivable theorem of the calculus: $\frac{\Gamma' \rightarrow \Delta}{\Gamma \rightarrow \Delta}$ where $Permutation(\Gamma) = \Gamma'$. This means that antecedents now become treated as multisets (sets with repetition) rather than lists, which is not desirable for linguistic purposes.

where Γ_i is a type sequence of length ≥ 0, with the exception that at least one of Γ_2, Γ_3 is non-empty. Notice that this rule generalizes over directed incompleteness (right incompleteness (/) and left incompleteness (\)) in the following way: if Γ_2 is empty, $\downarrow$ is an instance of /; if Γ_3 is empty, $\downarrow$ is an instance of \.

Semantics Principle

The Semantics Principle can be 'compiled away' as well, by putting in the lexicon the semantics of a sign as a product of the semantics of its daughter signs. This makes it possible to incorporate various kinds of semantics into lexical signs, for instance, a simple application semantics:

$$(24)\quad \begin{bmatrix} phon\ \ldots \\ syn \begin{bmatrix} \ldots \\ subcat\ [\ldots[sem\ X]] \end{bmatrix} \\ sem\ f(X) \\ dtrs\ \ldots \end{bmatrix}$$

LP Constraints

Once a functor combines with one of its arguments to form a mobile, the LP constraints apply to order the functor and argument branches by ordering the respective *phon* values to arrive at the *phon* value of the mother node. LP constraints can address both aspects of argument and functor, so they must be functions of a pair of types $\mathcal{T}$ to sets of types:

$$(25)\quad \mathcal{T} \times \mathcal{T} \longrightarrow POW(\mathcal{T}).$$

In case a concatenative functor combines with its arguments, the string ordering functions yield a singleton set of result types; for non-concatenative functors, this result set often has an arity greater than one, since there is generally more than one string position for a non-concatenative functor, and each separate string position determines a new sign.

The operationalisation of LP constraints in $\mathcal{D}$-HPSG is as follows. Once a functor has applied to its arguments, both functor and argument types are fed to the LP constraints, which figure out the *phon* value of the range subtype of the functor. This entails that LP constraints in $\mathcal{D}$-HPSG should operate as *side-conditions* on inference rules:[4]

$$(26)\quad \frac{P_1 \quad \ldots \quad P_n}{C}\ \textbf{if}\ \textbf{(B)LP}_i \vee \ldots \vee \textbf{(B)LP}_n$$

LP constraints operate on an argument type and a functor type. Table 7 presents the type-theoretic equivalents of the LP constraints of binary HPSG. We let $X^n \Rightarrow Y$ schematise over quantified types

[4]This relates the current enterprise to Gabbay's (Gabbay, 1991) *labelled deductive systems*, where side-conditions on inference rules occur as well.

(27) $\forall(v_i)\ldots\forall(v_k)X_j \Rightarrow \ldots\forall(v_l)\ldots\forall(v_m)X_n \Rightarrow Y \ (1 \leq i \leq k, 1 \leq j \leq n, 1 \leq l \leq m)$

where

(28) $X^1.Z = \forall(v_i)\ldots\forall(v_j)X \Rightarrow Z \ (1 \leq i \leq j).$

Further, $inv(X)$ says that X is inverted, and $adv(X)$ that X is an adverbial modifier. Irrelevant features are suppressed with '...', and quantifiers are omitted. The '+' operator denotes string concatenation, and the $\Downarrow$ operator infixation. The *phon* value of the functor is indicated with $\boxed{\mathrm{F}}$, and the *phon* value of the argument with $\boxed{\mathrm{A}}$. The notation $X \Rightarrow Y(lex(+))$ says that the functor $X \Rightarrow Y$ is lexical. Concluding, then, the set of axioms **I1, I2, I3**

TABLE 7. LP Constraints: functional notation

Constraint	Functor	Phonology after combination	Condition
(BLP1)	$X^1 \Rightarrow Y(lex(+))$	$\boxed{\mathrm{F}}+\boxed{\mathrm{A}}$	none
(BLP2)	$X^1 \Rightarrow Y(lex(-))$	$\boxed{\mathrm{A}}+\boxed{\mathrm{F}}$	none
(BLP3)	$X^n \Rightarrow Z$	$\boxed{\mathrm{F}}+\boxed{\mathrm{A}}$	$2 \leq n$
(BLP4)	$X^n \Rightarrow Z$	$\boxed{\mathrm{F}}+\boxed{\mathrm{A}}$	$1 \leq n$ **and** $inv(X^n \Rightarrow Z)$
(BLP5)	$X^n \Rightarrow Z$	$\boxed{\mathrm{F}}\Downarrow\boxed{\mathrm{A}}$	$1 \leq n$ **and** $adv(X^n \Rightarrow Z)$

(which can be interpreted as special instances of the general identity arrow $\mathcal{I}$) together with the rules $\mathcal{L} \Rightarrow, \mathcal{L} \downarrow, \mathcal{L}\forall, \mathcal{R}\forall$ constitute the minimal calculus necessary to "parse" HPSG. LP constraints apply as side-conditions to $\mathcal{L} \Rightarrow$. The lack of right rules for the functional connectives entails that this calculus does not enjoy Cut elimination, which can be performed only in symmetric calculi. Once one wants to introduce flexible constituency into the calculus, and leave the binary universe of $\mathcal{D}$-HPSG, these rules must be added. Adding $\mathcal{R} \Rightarrow$ would make the calculus structurally complete in generating all possible bracketings of the antecedent A for every provable sequent $A \rightarrow B$ (Moortgat, 1988).

5. IMPLEMENTATION

The ideas presented so far have been implemented in a prototypical system, allowing for parsing of a set of Dutch sentences. The system runs under X-windows on a Sun SPARCstation 1, and is programmed in Quintus Prolog and C.

5.1. DESIGN

The lexicon consists of lexeme-sign pairs. When a sentence $\_s$ is entered to be analysed, first the lexemes are looked up in the lexicon. The corresponding signs are compiled to a sequence Π of formulae according to the map † of section 4.1. Then, given the result category $\_c$, which the user is prompted to enter, the sequent $\Pi \rightarrow \_c(phon(\_s), \_syn, \_sem, \_dtrs)$ is formed, with $\_syn, \_sem, \_dtrs$ variables for syntactic, semantic and daughter information. The sequent is handed to the theorem prover, which is a meta-interpreter performing sequent deduction. Output is in both Prolog and graphical format: the derived type formula for an utterance is printed on screen as a Prolog term; in a separate window the sign equivalent of the formula is drawn in standard HPSG format.

5.2. TERM UNIFICATION AND UNIFORM SIGNS

Unification of feature structures is a computationally expensive tool, boiling down to extensive graph inspection and merging. This cost can be saved by adopting one uniform structure for the items to be unified, i.c. type-equivalents of signs: if we assume these types have a rigid term structure, we could directly make use of Prolog's built-in *term unification* mechanism for unifying them. This idea entails that every lexeme in the lexicon has a fixed sign type, with standard slots and values. The structure of this sign, following the standards of HPSG, is as shown in (29). Recall that the *subcat* feature is replaced by a functional specification by the map from signs to types. Lexemes can be unspecifiable for certain attributes; these attributes then carry the atomic value *nil*.

In Prolog, variables occurring in literals are implicitly universally quantified, which means that quantifiers are removed from them. This makes it possible to use Prolog's term unification mechanism directly to assign values to the variables; see Duffy (1991) for discussion. So, we can simply strip quantifiers from a formula, obtaining (30).

$$
(29)\quad \left[\begin{array}{ll}
phon & \ldots \\
syn & \left[\begin{array}{ll}
loc & \left[\begin{array}{ll}
head & \left[\begin{array}{ll}
maj & \ldots \\
case & \ldots \\
nform & \ldots \\
vform & \ldots \\
aux & \ldots \\
inv & \ldots \\
prd & \ldots
\end{array}\right] \\
subcat & \ldots \\
lex & \ldots
\end{array}\right] \\
bind & \ldots
\end{array}\right] \\
sem & \ldots \\
dtrs & \left[\begin{array}{ll}
headdtr & \ldots \\
compdtrs & \ldots
\end{array}\right]
\end{array}\right]
$$

(30) $\mathcal{Q}^n.X \mapsto X.$

Using this Prolog facility, it is not necessary to employ the $\forall$-rules in the implementation.

5.3. CALCULUS IN PROLOG FORMAT

In Prolog format, the axioms and rules of the calculus have the following shape:

(31)
```
axiom(Name,Antecedent--->Succedent
rule(Name,Antecedent--->Succedent (if C)
```

Given a functor type $A_1 \Rightarrow \ldots A_n \Rightarrow B$, which is right-associative, i.e. $A_1 \Rightarrow (\ldots(A_n \Rightarrow B)\ldots)$, it is necessary to inspect the properties of the ultimate range subtype B when applying the LP constraints. This would involve descending into the functor type, until one reaches the ultimate subtype B.

From a practical perspective, we would like to avoid such descent; we therefore notate such a functor as

(32) $[A_1, \ldots, A_n] \Rightarrow B$

where $[A_1, \ldots, A_n]$ is a list of types, and the range subtype B can be accessed directly. For the infix types $A \downarrow B$ we do likewise; they are usually of the form $([A_2, \ldots A_n] \Rightarrow B) \downarrow A_1$. In Prolog, we write `B@(_x,...,_y)` for B(_x, ..., _y). Sequents are written

(33) $(L_1, \ldots, L_n) \rightarrow X$ (if $P_1, \ldots, P_n$),

where each L_i is a subsequence (list) of types. The eventual premises of the inference are $P_1, \ldots, P_n$. Type sequences of length 1 are denoted as $[T]$, with T a type or type variable. Recall that, as every functor $X \Rightarrow Y$ is undirected, it can consume arguments either to its right, or to its left: the LP constraints serve to order the argument phonology with respect to the functor phonology. There will thus be two instances of the Subcat Principle, a `subcat_left` version, for argument cancellation to the left, and a `subcat_right` for argument cancellation to the right. Examples of the axiom and rule format are then (irrelevant feature information suppressed):

```
axiom(rule1,
 [Cat@(P1,
       syn(loc(H1,L),B1), S1,
       dtrs(headdtr(P2,syn(loc(H2,lex(0)),B2),S2,D1)),
            compdtrs([D2]))]
 --->
 [Cat@(P1
       syn(loc(H1,L),B1), S1,
       dtrs(headdtr(P2,syn(loc(H2,lex(0)),B2),S2,D1)),
            compdtrs([D2]))]).

rule(subcat_left,
(T1,T2,[[X|T]=>B@(S1,
                  syn(loc(W1,lex(L)),
                      W2),
                  S,D)],V) ---> Z
        if T2 ---> [X]
        and {lp(LP_Name, X,
                [X|T]=>B@(S1,syn(loc(W1,lex(L)),W2), S,D),
                [X|T]=>B@(S3,syn(loc(W1,lex(L)),W2), S,D))}
        and (T1,[T=>B@(S3,syn(loc(W1,lex(0)),W2), S,D)],V) ---> Z).
```

Notice how the lexicality value is changed to `0` in `subcat_left`, once the functor has combined with its argument. Above we argued that the lexicality feature is a derived feature, arising from the absence or presence of daughters in a tree. Since lexical signs already have (variable) daughters in $\mathcal{D}$-HPSG, checking for lexicality could (and should) be implemented here by inspection of the daughter specifications on the functor type: if the first daughter entry in the *compdtrs* attribute list has, say, a *variable phon* value, the sign as a whole can be concluded to be (still) lexical. For reasons of efficiency, we implement this view on lexicality by switching to non-lexicality the moment a functor combines with an argument. The variable `L` expresses the irrelevance of the (non-)lexicality of the functor symbol: no matter what value the functor has for the attribute *lex*, the range type will have the value `-` (`0`) for lexicality.

5.4. THEOREM PROVER

Various theorem proving techniques can be implemented quite easily in Prolog. As theorem prover, we use a simple sequent-proving device, implemented as follows: the prover is a set of clauses for a predicate `prove(+Goal, -Rules)`, where `Goal` is either a sequence of sequents of length minimally 1, or a structure $\{G_1, \ldots, G_n\}$ with each G_i $(1 \leq i \leq n)$ a non-sequent goal; `Rules` is a list encoding the inference rules and axioms used for proving `Goal`. Initially, `Goal` is the sequent to be proved. The predicate `prove/2` calls a routine matching the sequent against the database of inference rules, i.e. if `Goal` is of the form $(X_1, \ldots, X_n) \to Y$, it tries to match (resolve) the sequent against the rules and axioms of the calculus. Once a match has been made, the eventual premises of the inference are attempted to prove. Moortgat (1988) presents similar methods for categorial grammar.

```
prove({Goals},[]):- call(Goals).
prove(A--->B,[Rule|Rules]):-
        rule(Rule,(X ---> B if Y)),
        resolve(A,X),
        prove(Y,Rules).
prove(A and B,Rules):-
        prove(A,R1),
        prove(B,R2),
        conc(R1,R2,Rules).
prove(A--->B,[Ax]):-
        axiom(Ax,A1--->B),
        resolve(A,A1).
```

The linear precedence constraints are (as illustrated in section 5.3) encoded as goals $\{lp_i, \ldots, lp_n\}$, to be called before entering the eventual premise sequents.

5.5. CONSTRAINTS

Here are some linear precedence constraints. They are written as

(34) `lp(Name,Arg,Funct,NewFunct),`

with `Name` the name of the constraint, `Arg`, `Funct`, `NewFunct` types such that `NewFunct` has as its phonology value the ordered phonology values of `Arg` and `Funct`. Irrelevant variables are written as underscores. (Notice the use of *difference lists* for unit clause string concatenation (Pereira & Shieber (1987)).)

```
lp(lp1,
 X@(phon(S2-S3),_,_,_),
 [X@(_,_,_,_)]=>B@(phon(S1-S2), syn(loc(W1,lex(1)),W2), S,D),
 [X@(_,_,_,_)]=>B@(phon(S1-S3), syn(loc(W1,lex(1)),W2), S,D)).
```

```
lp(lp4,
  X@(phon(S2-S3),_,_,_),
  [X@(_,_,_,_)|T]=>B@(phon(S1-S2),P,Q,D),
  [X@(_,_,_,_)|T]=>B@(phon(S1-S3),P,Q,D))
        :-
  inv(B@(_,P,_,_)).
```

6. LEXICAL ENTRIES

Lexical entries are of the form

(35) `WORD := SIGN (← VAR_CONDITIONS)`

with `WORD,SIGN` resp. a lexeme and its sign representation, and the optional `<- VAR_CONDITIONS` encoding instantiations of variables mentioned in `SIGN` (this is just done to avoid having to type very complex signs when creating the lexicon). The sign structure of the lexical items is fully compliant with standard HPSG.

7. PERFORMANCE

The following overview lists real-time (not CPU-time) parsing results for a small set of Dutch sentences. The error rate for each of these sentences is zero. The results were generated by a compiled Prolog executable version of the program, running under X-windows on a Sun SPARCstation 1.

The sentences and their word-by-word translations are:

TABLE 8. Sample Input Sentences

Sentence	Translation
Jan loopt	*John walks*
De man loopt	*The man walks*
De man loopt graag	*The man walks gladly*
Jan heeft hard gelopen	*John has fast walked*
Jan slaat de man	*John hits the man*
John slaat graag de hond	*John hits gladly the dog*
De man koopt een boek met plaatjes	*The man buys a book with pictures*
Jan geeft Marie de hond	*John gives Mary the dog*
Jan geeft Marie een boek met plaatjes	*John gives Mary a book with pictures*
Jan geeft Marie graag een boek	*John gives Mary gladly a book*
dat Jan de hond slaat	*that John the dog hits*

TABLE 9. Parse Results (real time)

Sentence	Parse time
Jan loopt	0.000 sec.
de man loopt	0.000 sec.
de man loopt graag	0.050 sec.
Jan heeft hard gelopen	0.050 sec.
Jan slaat de man	0.067 sec.
Jan slaat graag de hond	0.450 sec.
de man koopt een boek met plaatjes	0.683 sec.
Jan geeft Marie de hond	0.117 sec.
Jan geeft Marie een boek met plaatjes	2.500 sec.
Jan geeft Marie graag een boek	1.316 sec.
dat Jan de hond slaat	0.017 sec.

As can be concluded from the output presented in the previous section, temporal performance is relatively good. Sentences taking a lot of time (say, over 1 second), invariably contain at least one adverbial modifier, or involve an NP closure problem. For instance, in

(36) John gives Mary a book with pictures

the phrase 'John gives Mary a book' can be erroneously analysed as a sentence before the PP 'with pictures' is attached to 'a book'. Once the parser detects the remaining phrase 'with pictures', it will have to backtrack and redo a lot of work. This performance is a consequence of the sequent formalism: for any configuration

(37) $X_1 \Rightarrow X_2, X_1, X_1 \Rightarrow X_1$

where each X_i is distinct, the analysis

(38) $((X_1 \Rightarrow X_2, X_1), X_1 \Rightarrow X_1)$

is tried. One idea would be to employ a wellformed substring table encoding intermediate parsing results, to avoid having to reparse too much once the parser starts backtracking.

Generally speaking, weak performance for long sentences is not surprising, since the various inference rules allow for blind alleys in the left premise deduction, by instantiating wrong subsequences of the antecedent to the factor reducing to an argument type. This effect arises from the non-deterministic nature of the procedure decomposing the antecedent into contexts around a functional type. The problem can be fixed by introducing so-called *proof invariants* (van Benthem, 1991) into the theorem prover.

Proof invariants are structural validities for antecedent-succedent pairs, which serve to prune blind alleys from the search space. The attractive feature of the current setting is that *any* optimalisation coming from proof theory can be used to optimise the parser.

8. CONCLUSIONS

We have shown that it is possible to give HPSG a deductive basis. The binary version of HPSG we have proposed, has been demonstrated to correspond to a fragment of second-order linear logic. The binarity of this HPSG dialect, which is faithful to classical HPSG in all other respects, is motivated from practical rather than theoretical reasons; in fact, the current approach is open to any version of HPSG. The parser we developed is, although relatively fast, in need of further optimalisation; the use of proof invariants may help to reduce the search space. Also, recently developed low-complexity theorem proving techniques such as *proof nets* (Roorda, 1991), may be of use here. Returning to the five desiderata of section 1, then, the last item, "The parser should have reasonable time/space complexity" has not fully been met yet, but its realisation should be feasible within the limits of current low–cost theorem proving techniques.

Acknowledgements

This research was carried out within the framework of the research programme 'Human-Computer Communication using natural language' (MMC). The MMC programme is sponsored by Senter, Digital Equipment, SUN Microsystems Nederland, and AND Software.

I thank my colleagues René Ahn, Miriam Mulders, Gerrit Rentier and Leon Verschuur for fruitful discussion and taking an active interest in the enterprise.

References

Benthem, J. van 1991 *Language in action*, Categories, Lambdas, and Dynamic Logic. Studies in logic and the foundations of mathematics, vol. 130. North-Holland, Amsterdam.

Cooper, R. 1990 Specifiers, Complements and Adjuncts in HPSG. Unpubl. ms., University of Edinburgh.

Dörre, J. & Raasch, I. 1991 *The Stuttgart Type Unification Formalism – User Manual.* IBM, Stuttgart.

Duffy, D.A. 1991 *Principles of automated theorem proving.* Wiley, Chichester.

Gabbay, D. 1991 *Labelled Deductive Systems.* Oxford University Press.

Gallier, J. 1986 *Logic for Computer Science*, Foundations of Automatic Theorem Proving. Harper and Row, New York.

Gentzen, G. 1934 Untersuchungen über das logische Schliessen. *Math. Zeitschrift* 39:176-210, 405-431.

Girard, J.-Y. 1987 Linear Logic. *Theoretical Computer Science*, 50: 1-102.

König, E. 1989 Parsing as natural deduction. In: *Proc. ACL'89*, Vancouver.

Moortgat, M. 1988 *Categorial Investigations*, logic and linguistic aspects of the Lambek calculus. Foris, Dordrecht.

Moortgat, M. 1990 Discontinuous Type Constructors. In: H.C. Bunt & A. van Horck (eds.) *Discontinuous Constituency*, Walter de Gruyter, Berlin.

Morrill, G. 1990 Grammar and logical types. Unpubl. ms., University of Edinburgh.

Pereira, F.C.N. & Shieber, S. 1987 *Prolog and Natural Language Analysis*. CSLI Lecture Notes, Stanford.

Pollard, C. & Sag, I. 1987 *Information-based syntax and semantics*, vol.1. CSLI Lecture Notes 13, Stanford.

Pollard, C. & Sag, I. 1994 *Head-Driven Phrase Structure Grammar*. CSLI, Stanford and University of Chicago Press, Chicago.

Popowich, F. & Vogel, C. 1990 A Logic-Based Implementation of Head-Driven Phrase Structure Grammar. In: *Proc. Third Intern. Workshop on Natural Language Understanding and Logic Programming*. Lidinogo, Stockholm.

Reape, M. 1990 Getting things in order. In: H.C. Bunt & A. van Horck (eds.) *Discontinuous Constituency*, Walter de Gruyter, Berlin.

Roorda, D. 1991 *Resource Logics*. Dissertation, University of Amsterdam.

Shieber, S. 1986 *An introduction to unification-based approaches to grammar*. CSLI Lecture Notes 4, Stanford.

Wallen, L.A. 1990 *Automated proof-search in non-classical logics*. MIT Press, Cambridge, Mass.

8. EFFICIENT PARSING OF COMPILED TYPED ATTRIBUTE VALUE LOGIC GRAMMARS

BOB CARPENTER AND GERALD PENN
Computational Linguistics Program
Philosophy Department, Carnegie Mellon University

Abstract.

The unification-based approach to processing attribute-value logic grammars, similar to Prolog *interpretation*, has become the standard. We propose an alternative, embodied in the Attribute-Logic Engine (ALE) [Carpenter and Penn 1994], based on the Warren Abstract Machine (WAM) approach to *compiling* Prolog [Aït-Kaci 1991]. Phrase structure grammars with procedural attachments, similar to Definite Clause Grammars (DCG) [Pereira and Warren 1980], are specified using a version of Rounds-Kasper logic extended with types, variables, and inequations [Carpenter 1992]. We argue for the benefits of a strong and total version of typing in terms of both clarity and efficiency. After discussing our term representations, we discuss the compilation of programs written in our logical language into a concise set of efficient, low-level instructions. We further discuss our implementation of inequations, which involves the delayed evaluation of underspecified inequations and the enforcement of extensional identity conditions for feature structures of certain user-specified types. We conclude our survey of ALE with a discussion of general type constraints, which allow arbitrary descriptions to be enforced on structures of user-specified types. Just as for Prolog programs themselves, the compilation of grammars leads to a boost in efficiency of at least an order of magnitude over interpreted code.

1. COMPILING TYPE DEFINITIONS

The first component of an ALE grammar is a type specification, which lays out the basic types of feature structures that will be employed in a grammar, along with the inheritance relations among these types and declarations of

H. Bunt and M. Tomita (eds.), Recent Advances in Parsing Technology, 145–168.

appropriate features and constraints on their values. Such a specification includes declarations such as the following for lists of atoms:

```
bot sub [atom,list].
  atom sub [a,b].
    a sub [].
    b sub [].
  list sub [ne_list,e_list].
    e_list sub [].
    ne_list sub []
            intro [hd:atom,tl:list].
```

This signifies that bot is the most general type, with two subtypes, atom and list. The type, atom, has two subtypes, a and b, which are maximally specific types. The list type also has two subtypes, ne_list and e_list, for non-empty and empty lists, respectively. Note that the ne_list type introduces two features, hd and tl, whose values are required to be atoms and lists. The only type which has any appropriate features is the ne_list type, and it is appropriate for exactly two features, hd and tl.

Inheritance of such appropriateness specifications is performed on the basis of the type hierarchy. Consider, for instance, the following declaration from HPSG:

```
sign sub [word,phrase]
     intro [phon:phon_list,
            synsem:synsem_obj,
            qstore:quant_list].
  word sub []
       intro [phon:singleton_phon_list].
  phrase sub []
         intro [dtrs:dtr_struct].
```

Here, the type sign introduces three features and provides value restrictions. The subtype for words inherits these features and the associated value restrictions, imposing the additional condition that the phonology value be a singleton list. The subtype for phrases introduces an additional feature for daughter signs. Thus, unlike the case for order-sorted terms (see, for instance, [Meseguer et al. 1987]), not every subtype of a type need have the same slots for values. This is significant for implementations, as memory cells are only allocated on a structure for appropriate features.

The initial stage of compilation in ALE involves just the type hierarchy. First, the transitive closure of subsumption is calculated using Warshall's algorithm (see [O'Keefe 1990]). Second, least upper bounds are computed for each pair of consistent types. One condition we impose on type hierarchies is that they form a bounded-complete partial order (BCPO), or in other words, that every pair of bounded (consistent) types, i.e. every pair of types with a common subtype, has a least upper bound. This ensures that the unification of two types produces a unique value. This reduces non-determinism at run time, but might require additional types to be declared by the user (see [Carpenter 1992]). Such hierarchies can be compiled automatically from either systemic networks or ISA/ISNOTA hierarchies, as shown in [Carpenter and Pollard 1991]. The final stage involves calculating, for each type, which features are appropriate and what their appropriate values. This is done by collecting all of the declared features on subtypes and unifying their value restrictions. In addition to requiring a type hierarchy to form a BCPO, we also require that they introduce each feature at a unique most general type. This, along with the BCPO condition, ensures a unique solution to the type inference problem. If the only information we had about an object was that it was defined for the feature, `f`, we would infer that it was of the type that introduced the feature, `f`. If, however, there were two maximally general types for which `f` was appropriate, a decision could not be made as to which type it was and non-determinism would be introduced. As with the BCPO condition, this condition can be accommodated automatically by introducing a new type appropriate for the feature, which is more general than the two existing ones (see [Carpenter 1992]). We also forbid appropriateness cycles such as:

```
person sub [male,female]
      intro [father:male,
             mother:female].
   male sub [].
   female sub [].
```

We rule out this situation because type inference, as we define it below, cannot find most general well-typings in such cases. To be a well-formed object of type `male`, the `father` feature must be defined and filled by an object of type `male`; such a procedure clearly does not halt. But if we wish to represent people with parents, the problem can be solved by adding types which are not required to have parents, as we have done for lists. In the list domain, a non-empty list structure can have a non-empty list as a substructure, but it is not required to have one; in general a non-empty list's tail is only required to be a list.

During the compilation of the type system, many different kinds of errors are detected, such as: two types which mutually subsume one another, violations of the BCPO condition where two types have multiple unifiers, cases where inconsistent constraints are inherited by a feature, where there are appropriateness cycles, where there is no most general type appropriate for a feature, and so on. Other errors, such as undeclared types and multiple declarations, are also recognized. In addition, a number of warnings are raised for potentially undesirable cases, such as a type with only one subtype or where dynamic type-inference during unification will be necessary.

This latter condition arises when types `s` and `t` are both appropriate for `f`, with value restrictions `s'` and `t'`, but the unification of `s` and `t`, `s+t`, has a more specific restriction than `s'+t'`. In this case, when an `s` and `t` object are unified, the additional constraints on their value for `f` must be checked.

2. COMPILING BASIC OPERATIONS

As with other grammar formalisms based on attribute-value logics, the primary data structure used in ALE is the feature structure. The structures used in ALE are similar to those in other systems, with the primary difference being that they are required to be totally well-typed (see [Carpenter 1992]). In other words, every feature structure must be assigned a type and every feature appropriate for that type must appear with an appropriate value. This can be contrasted with sorted, but untyped systems, that allow sorts to label feature structures and participate in unification, but don't enforce any typing conditions. It can also be contrasted with systems that only perform type inference on values, but do not require every appropriate feature to be present.

Typing a programming language can be motivated from many perspectives. For development and debugging, the ability to detect errors at compile time is crucial. In ALE, rules that cannot be satisfied and lexical entries that are not well-typed are flagged as such. Fine-grained error reports, furthermore, can isolate the exact structures in which a type error occurred. Practice has shown that this reduces grammar development time significantly, because one of the most prevalent grammar-writing errors is being inconsistent about which features appear at which level in a structure and how they are bundled together, especially when grammar formalisms approach the 200 node range for lexical entries, as found in significant fragments of HPSG (see [Penn 1993]).

Typing can also be motivated from the standpoint of efficiency. With typing, the features appropriate for a feature structure can be determined at compile time. This has three advantages. First, arrays can be used to represent structures very compactly. Second, memory allocation and deallocation can be handled efficiently, as the type and, hence, size of each structure are known. Third, unification can be performed much more quickly, as there is no need to merge list representations of feature-value pairs — the positions of relevant features are known at compile time. We consider these two benefits in turn.

ALE is currently implemented in Prolog.[1] The WAM implementation of

[1]Plans are underway to implement ALE in C, using WAM-like byte coding and evaluation of instructions. The basic feature-description commands of a true abstract machine have been implemented by [Qu 1994] and [Wintner 1994].

Prolog is exploited heavily to develop a WAM-like behavior for ALE. Using Prolog for feature structure unification systems has its advantages and drawbacks. The drawback is that there are no pointers in Prolog, and thus path compression during dereferencing cannot be carried out efficiently (though it is carried out on inactive edges during parsing). The advantage is that Prolog is very good at structure copying, last call optimization, incremental clause evaluation and search. We will consider all these topics. First, we note that the data structure used for feature structures in ALE is:

```
Tag-foo(V1,...,Vn)
```

`Tag` is a reference pointer, signaling the token identity of the structure, much as a position in memory in an imperative language would do. `foo` is the name of the type of the structure, which must be a Prolog atom, of course. The terms `V1` through `Vn` are the values for the features `F1` through `Fn` that are appropriate for type `foo`. Given Prolog's WAM-compilation, this amounts to having the following kind of record structure for feature structures:

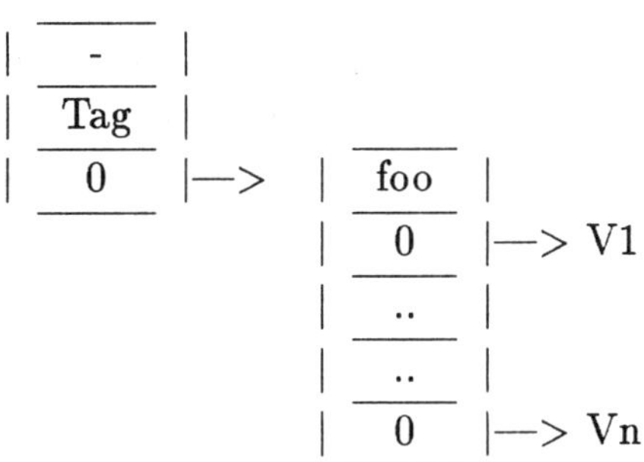

Contrast this with a representation such as:

```
Tag-foo([F1:V1,...,Fn:Vn])
```

where the features are encoded explicitly in a list. Here the structure required is as pictured below (ignoring the tag).

In general, our representation requires $4+n$ cells for a structure with n features, while the latter one requires $4+6n$ cells for the same structure. This constitutes a huge discrepancy when we consider the increase in overhead this induces, throughout the grammar, in areas such as lexical retrieval and copying edges into the chart. Note that this difference between using record-like structures and lists of feature-value pairs is Prolog-independent.

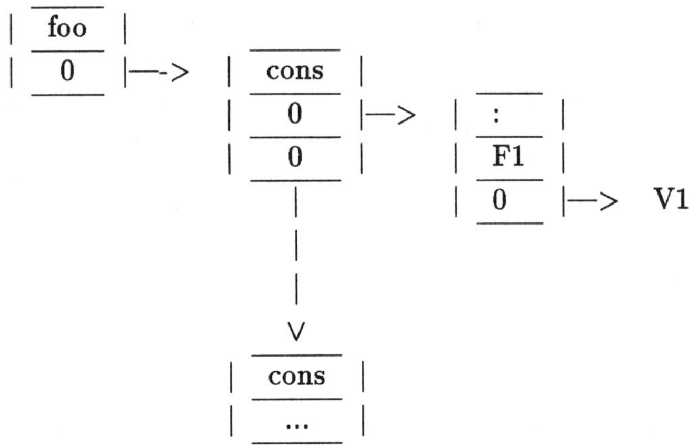

We have not said much about the tag. It is based on the same principle as O'Keefe's method of encoding arrays in Prolog using variables, which provides constant time access and update (see the Quintus library). Each slot in an array is associated with a value and a pointer, which is either a variable or a structure consisting, in turn, of another value and a pointer. Updates are performed by instantiating the variable to a new pair consisting of a variable and a value. Values are, thus, found by following the pointer until it is a variable. To maintain constant time, the entire array must regularly be updated by path compression. In our case, the tag plays the role of the pointer, and dereferencing is performed by following the tag value until it is a variable. The predicate `deref/3` performs dereferencing and deconstructs the resulting structure.

```
deref(Tag-FS,Tag,FS):-
  var(Tag), !.
deref(FSIn-_,Tag,FS):-
  deref(FSIn,Tag,FS).
```

Note that the number of dereferencing steps needed at any stage is bounded by the depth of the inheritance hierarchy (of course, Prolog does its own internal dereferencing, so we cannot statically bound the total number of dereferencing steps needed during unification). Path compression is then the equivalent of O'Keefe's array updating, and is performed when a completed edge is found during parsing. We will see examples of the use of tags shortly.

The second benefit we mentioned for typing structures is that we can carry out unification without merging feature-value lists. The standard method in unifying feature structures is to take two lists of features, find the common elements, unify them, take both symmetric differences, and copy the results of this into the final result. Such tasks are, comparatively, quite costly, especially as the number of features grows. Instead, our compiler will produce the following kind of code to perform unification (which has been simplified here, but will be expanded upon later):

```
unify(T-ne_list(H,R),T-ne_list(H2,R2)):-
  unify(H,H2),  unify(R,R2).
```

The positional encoding of feature values means that, at compile time, we know which features any two types have. Also note that the tags are identified to make sure any update of one structure is reflected in the other. Compare the number of operations required in the above procedure to one that must look through two lists of feature-value pairs, act conditionally depending on the results of comparisons, and detect termination conditions. While our unification, in the above case, requires only two logical operations in Prolog, the list merging method would require at least two comparisons, a termination test and the same two logical operations as our method, more than doubling the cost in the best possible instance. Of course, matters are much worse if the features are out of order or do not match up exactly in the two structures.

Having motivated our approach, we now consider two operations on feature structures which are calculated at compile time. The first of these involves adding type information to a feature structure. For instance, we might have a feature structure of type `list`, and want to add the information that it is non-empty. In this case, the system produces the following code:

```
add_to(ne_list,Tag-FVs):-
  add_to_ne_list(FVs,Tag).

add_to_ne_list(list,
               _-ne_list(T1-bot,
                         T2-bot)):-
  add_to_atom(bot,T1),
  add_to_list(bot,T2).
```

Note that to add the information that a structure is an `ne_list` at the top level, we incorporate the first argument into the name of the predicate and move the type-value term into first-argument position. This enhances the first-argument indexing that the WAM already performs. This means that, given the current structure of type `list`, hashing is done to find the code to add the fact that it is a non-empty list to it. In fact, the clauses for `add_to/2` are never called by the system, as can be seen from the second of the above clauses, which calls `add_to_atom(TVs,Tag1)` rather than `add_to(atom,Tag1-TVs)`.

For completely fresh features, such as the head (`T1`) and tail (`T2`) above, there is really no reason to create a structure `Tag-bot` and then immediately add a type to it. A more efficient version of `add_to_list/2` is:

```
add_to_ne_list(list,
               _-ne_list(_-atom,_-list)).
```

Such an optimization is straightforward and statically computable.

Consider the more complicated case of adding the type word to a feature structure of type sign given above:

```
add_to_word(sign(T-Phon,SynSem,QSt),
            _-word(T-Phon,SynSem,QSt)):-
  add_to_singleton_phon_list(Phon,T).
```

Here, we see that (pointers to) the feature values for sign are copied over into the new word structure, and the additional constraint that the Phon value be a singleton list must also be resolved. Note that this extra bit of (pointer) copying is something that is also done in encodings using lists of feature-value pairs.

The basic unification procedure simply checks if two structures are equal, and if so, succeeds, and if not, decomposes the structures into a tag and type-value structure, sending it to unify/4.

```
unify_deref(FS1,FS2):-
  deref(FS1,Tag1,TVs1),
  deref(FS2,Tag2,TVs2),
  ( Tag1 == Tag2, !
  ; unify(TVs1,TVs2,Tag1,Tag2)
  ).
```

The clauses of unify/4 responsible for unifying two ne_lists produced by the compiler are:

```
unify(ne_list(H1,T1),TVs2,Tag1,Tag2):-
  unify_ne_list(TVs2,H1,T1,Tag1,Tag2).

unify_ne_list(ne_list(H2,T2),H1,T1,T,T):-
  unify_deref(H1,H2),
  unify_deref(T1,T2).
```

The argument order and extra level of indirection exploit the first-argument indexing of the WAM. In effect, when two structures are unified, they are first dereferenced, then two hashings are performed, one on each one's type; and, finally, their shared feature values are unified. This illustrates one of the simplest cases of unification. Note that absolutely no type inference is required at run time because the compiler knows that, when two structures of the same type are unified, their feature values already meet the type's constraints, and hence, the result of unifying them will. Other cases might involve add_to_*type*/2 goals being called and tags being instantiated, when unifying two structures leads to a new structure with a type higher than either of the inputs. For instance, suppose we have:

```
b sub [c] intro [f:x,h:u].
d sub [c] intro [g:y,h:v].
  c sub [] intro [f:x2,h:u+v,j:z].
```

where u+v is the type unification of u and v. Then we would have:

```
unify(b(V1,V2),TVs2,Tag1,Tag2):-
  unify_b(TVs2,V1,V2,Tag1,Tag2).

unify_b(d(V3,V4),V1,V2,
        Tag-c(V1,V3,V2,T-z),
        Tag-c(V1,V3,V2,T-z)):-
  unify_deref(V2,V4),
  deref(V1,Tag1,TVs1),
  add_to_x2(TVs1,Tag1).
```

When unifying structures of type b and d, we must instantiate both of their reference pointers to a new structure of type c, with a new feature j, and in addition, perform the extra type inference on the value of f. It is worth noting that all and only the necessary type inference is determined at compile-time. For instance, the fact that the h value for c is required to satisfy the unification of the constraints on h in b and d is enough to let the compiler determine that no additional type inference will be required.

3. COMPILING DESCRIPTIONS

In this section, we consider compiling descriptions taken from ALE's attribute-value logic (we postpone the discussion of inequations for now):

```
<desc> ::= <type>
         | <var>
         | <feat>:<desc>
         | <desc> and <desc>
         | <desc> or <desc>
```

As shown in [Smolka 1988], a lack of variables can lead to a quadratic increase in the size of descriptions that use only path equations; with variables, path equations are no longer necessary. A complete proof theory for entailment between descriptions with respect to a set of type declarations can be found in [Carpenter 1992].

Descriptions are compiled into the operations, `add_to_`*type*, `unify`, `deref`, conjunction and disjunction in Prolog. In addition, to handle constraints of the form `<feat>:<desc>`, which tell us to add a description to the value of a feature, we need a procedure for extracting a feature's value from a structure. This is done with clauses such as:

```
featval(hd,FS,Val):-
  deref(FS,Tag,TVs),
  featval_hd(TVs,Tag,Val).
```

```
featval_hd(ne_list(Tag-H,_),Tag,H).
```

Again, we present the first clause for convenience; only the second is used at run-time, combined with the necessary dereferencing. Note that if we look for the hd value of a structure of type, list, we must coerce the type, list, to ne_list:

```
featval_hd(list,_-ne_list(T-atom,_-list),
                T-atom).
```

Here, we create a new structure of type ne_list, with a fresh head and tail, and return the fresh head as the result. In general, this might require additional type inference, as can be seen by considering what would happen if we extracted the value of the feature, j, from an object of type, d, in the type system introduced above. In this case, the type d object would be coerced to one of type, c, which, in turn, requires boosting the type of its h value, and adding new f and j values:

```
featval_j(d(V1,T2-TVs2),
          _-c(T3-x2,V1,T2-TVs2,T-z),
          T-z):-
  add_to_u(TVs2,T2).
```

The compiler has enough information to determine exactly which type inferences to perform as part of finding a feature's value. As with add_to_*type* itself, no calls to add_to_*type* are necessary for f or j and their arguments simply instantiated appropriately at compile time.

We are now in a position to see how descriptions get compiled into Prolog clauses. To add a description of the kind found on the left to a dereferenced structure, Tag-TVs, the Prolog code on the right is generated:

```
type         add_to_type(TVs,Tag)

V            deref(V,Tag2,TVs2),
             unify(TVs,TVs2,Tag,Tag2)

f:D          featval_f(TVs,Tag,Val),
             deref(Val,Tag2,TVs2),
             [ add D to Tag2-TVs2 ]

D1 and D2    [ add D1 to Tag-TVs ],
             deref(Tag-TVs,Tag2,TVs2),
             [ add D2 to Tag2-TVs2 ]

D1 or D2     ( [ add D1 to Tag-TVs]
             ; [ add D2 to Tag-TVs]
             )
```

Types are straightforward, and simply invoke the appropriate `add_to` goal. Variables are instantiated to the feature structures which they describe. Adding a variable to a structure, thus, involves dereferencing the variable, which is instantiated to its current value, and unifying it with the structure to which it is being added. All variables are initialized to `Tag-bot` at compile-time for compatibility with the basic operations over feature structures. The last three cases are recursive. Adding a description to a feature's value requires finding the feature's value, dereferencing it, and adding the embedded description. Conjunction and disjunction in descriptions are translated into the corresponding Prolog control structures. In particular, this means that we treat disjunction in descriptions non-deterministically. In this way, Prolog backtracking, and its attendant efficient implementation of search and variables, will take care of the disjunction without any need for explicit copying in the program. Of course, the non-determinism is still there — but Prolog is handling it. Conjunction, on the other hand, is treated as goal sequencing in Prolog. Again, backtrack points and their attendant instantiations of variables are reduced directly to Prolog's implementation. In a non-Prolog implementation of conjunction and disjunction, presumably the design of the WAM itself would be followed (see [Aït-Kaci 1991]).

4. COMPILING GRAMMARS AND PROGRAMS

This compilation of descriptions into Prolog code rather than into feature structures is where ALE departs most radically from other attribute-value-based parsers with which we are familiar. The traditional method, for chart parsing, for example, involves taking an inactive edge which has just been created and trying to unify it with the feature structures corresponding to the heads of rules in the grammar. Instead, our system will execute the Prolog code compiled from the description of the head of a grammar rule. There are two principal benefits to our approach. These stem from the fact that we reduce the copying and search methods to those of the WAM itself by compiling the Prolog clauses generated. The first benefit is that early failures in matching a description to a goal do not result in any excess copying — in fact there is really no copying done at all — it is all handled in the heap mechanism of the WAM. The second benefit of our approach to search is that, if we have deeply embedded disjunctions in our descriptions, we do not need to expand to a disjunctive normal form or invoke one of the many approaches to disjunctive unification. In particular, if we have a description with an embedded disjunction and the first disjunct fails, then we only backtrack to the second disjunct, not all the way back to the beginning of the structure. The quest for efficiency of just this kind of backtracking is at the heart of the design of the WAM. It should be noted that nothing here depends on using a chart parser as the control strategy — similar benefits would accrue for any other parsing strategy. In fact, the same benefits could also be gained by using this kind of strategy in generation, e.g. along the lines of [van Noord et al. 1992].

The chart parsing strategy used in ALE is not particularly significant qua parser, as it was primarily motivated by Prolog considerations. What is significant is the way in which descriptions are compiled and made available to the parser, a strategy which can be maintained using many different parsers. For instance, a left-corner or shift-reduce parser would not require any copying or manipulation of the database. The most significant property to note about ALE's parser is that it employs a dynamic chart, where inactive edges are asserted into the database,[2] and it parses according to a bottom-up strategy, from right to left in the chart, and from left to right through individual rules. Active edges are truly active, being represented only by the current position in a Prolog clause compiled from a rule description. Rules are of the form:

```
D0 ===> D1, ..., DN.
```

where D0 is the description of the mother category and the other Di are descriptions of the daughter categories. The grammar rules are then compiled into the rule/3 predicate. The goal, rule(C,L,R), is called whenever an inactive edge, C, is added from position L to R in the chart, either by the lexicon or by rule/3 itself. The code produced for the above rule is:

```
rule(C1,Left,Mid1):-
  [ add D1 to C1 ],
  edge(Mid1,Mid2,C2),
  [ add D2 to C2 ],
  ...
  edge(MidN-1,Right,CN),
  [ add DN to CN ],
  [ add D0 to Tag-bot ],
  path-compress(Tag-bot,C0),
  assert(edge(Left,Right,C0)),
  rule(C0,Left,Right).
```

When rule(C1,Left,Mid1) is called, the first thing that happens is that the description D1 is added to the feature structure, C1. Assuming this fails, no other work is done, and no copying is performed. Instead, the code generated by the description D1 is simply executed, and failure

[2]Current versions of the WAM in SICStus and Quintus index asserted clauses on their first arguments. This allows the edges beginning at a particular position to be retrieved easily by hashing. Using the copying predicate and hashing predicates directly in a system like SICStus should, in fact, be faster than assert.

causes Prolog backtracking either to earlier disjunctions in the description D1, or to other clauses for rule/3 generated by other rules. Assuming D1 is successfully added to C1, rule/3 looks for an inactive edge, C2, directly to the right of C1 in the chart. The fact that parsing is done right to left ensures that the chart has been completed to the right of any inactive edge which is being considered. If an inactive edge of category C2 is found on the right, rule/3 attempts to add the description, D2, to a copy of C2. The current bottleneck in this process is the inordinate amount of copying required, especially when many empty categories are present. Every inactive edge that is considered as an extension of an active edge is eagerly copied in full. A better solution would be to add the descriptions to the edges, keeping some kind of trail, but Prolog does not provide such fine control of its database. The process of extending the rule with inactive edges continues until the sequence of category descriptions on the right-hand side of the rule is completely exhausted. At this point, the mother category is constructed by adding the compiled description, D0, to a fresh category, path compressing the reference chains, asserting it into the database of inactive edges, and recursively calling rule/3. There are no base cases to rule/3; it will eventually fail and backtrack through all of the disjunctive choice points and alternative rules.

The input string is consumed from right to left, with inactive edges being added at each step until no more edges can be added. This gives the parser as a whole a mix of breadth-first and depth-first search, to best exploit the inherent behavior of the WAM. The top level control strategy is quite straightforward. The words are reversed and counted; and the chart is built from the right to left, using all lexical entries for each word to fire rule/3. Before considering lexical entries, empty categories are asserted into the chart and processed using rule/3. All lexical and empty category alternatives will be considered during backtracking before proceeding leftward to the previous word. We should also mention that lexical entries and empty categories are fully expanded as path-compressed feature structures at compile time.

```
parse(Words,C):-
  reverse(Words,WordsRev),
  length(Words,N),
  build_chart(Words,N),
  edge(0,N,C).

build_chart(_,N):-
  empty(C),
  assert(edge(N,N,C)),
  rule(C,N,N).
build_chart([],_).
build_chart([W|Ws],N):-
```

```
M is N-1,
( lex(W,C),
  assert(edge(M,N,C)),
  rule(C,M,N)
; build_chart(Ws,M)
).
```

In addition to allowing categories in a rule, ALE also allows definite clause goals to be invoked, as in a DCG rule such as:

```
f(Z) ---> h(Y), g(X), {foo(X,Y,Z)}, j(Z).
```

In this rule, as soon as the `h(Y)` and `g(X)` categories are found, the goal, `foo(X,Y,Z)`, is invoked and solved before going on to consider `j(Z)`. The change to `rule/3` is minimal; the code for solving `foo(X,Y,Z)` is simply inserted in between the code generated by the categories `g(X)` and `j(Z)`.

Definite clause programs can be defined in ALE, where instead of Prolog terms, feature structure descriptions are used. For instance, we can define standard predicates such as:

```
append(e_list,X,X) if true.
append(hd:X and tl:Xs,
       Ys,
       hd:X and tl:Zs) if
  append(Xs,Ys,Zs).
```

The logical variables are used as in Prolog, with the result being an instance of constraint logic programming over the typed feature structure logic. This bears a close similarity to the LOGIN language of [Aït-Kaci and Nasr 1986], who point out a number of benefits of using an order-sorted notion of feature structures, rather than first-order terms, for logic programming. A general CLP scheme suiting this application was defined by [Höhfeld and Smolka 1988] and this particular application is detailed in [Carpenter 1992]. The previous two clauses will translate into the following pieces of code, following [O'Keefe's 1990] meta-interpreters (and omitting all of the dereferencing):

```
solve([]).
solve([G|Gs]):-
  solve(G,Gs).

solve(append(Tag1-TVs1,FS2,FS3),Goals):-
  add_to_e_list(TVs1,Tag1),
  unify(FS2,FS3),
  solve(Goals).
solve(append(Tag1-TVs1,FS2,Tag3-TVs3),Goals):-
  featval_hd(TVs1,Tag1,FS1H),
  featval_hd(TVs3,Tag3,FS3H),
  unify(FS1H,FS3H),
```

```
featval_tl(TVs1,Tag1,FS1T),
featval_tl(TVs3,Tag3,FS3T),
solve(append(FS1T,FS2,FS3T),Goals).
```

The encoding used, with `Goals` threaded, is to ensure that last call optimization takes place. While ALE does not perform its own first-argument indexing, it does fully support cut, disjunction, negation by failure, and last call optimization.

Definite clause procedural attachments can be interspersed into rules just as in DCGs. This mechanism has been used in ALE grammars for purposes such as quantifier scoping using Cooper Storage, for treating the maximal onset principal in syllabification in attribute-value phonology [Mastroianni 1993], and for implementing principles such as the non-local feature principle (for slashes) of HPSG [Penn 1993]. Procedures can even be used to postpone some of the unifications in a rule until after all of the categories have been found, thus encoding a form of restriction similar to that used by [Shieber 1985]. The definite clause component can also be used for interleaving on-line semantic processing with syntactic processing as suggested by [Pereira and Pollack 1990].

ALE has a number of other useful features. One of the most interesting of these is its use of lexical rules, which are loosely based on those of PATR-II, in that they map one lexical entry to another at compile-time. In ALE, such rules may also involve procedural attachments, or contain a rudimentary morphological component based on string unification. ALE also fully supports parametric macros which are statically compiled out into the descriptions they abbreviate. Finally, ALE admits general hooks to Prolog, to allow the developer a larger degree of flexibility.

5. EXTENSIONAL TYPES

ALE observes the distinction between *intensional* and *extensional* types [Carpenter 1992:Chapter 8]. Extensional typing for feature structures is related both to extensionality for (possibly non-well-founded sets), and to equality over first-order terms. In the latter case, two terms, $s(x_1, \ldots, x_n)$ and $t(y_1, \ldots, y_n)$, are equal if and only if $s = t$ and $x_i = y_i$ for all $1 \leq i \leq n$ (the conditions are more subtle for cyclic terms in some Prologs). This kind of extensional identity condition is not normally assumed for feature structures (though it is often assumed for atomic values). It is, for example, possible to have two feature structures of type `list` with the same `hd` and `tl` values, without necessarily requiring them to be one and the same object. In ALE, by declaring `list` to be an extensional type, the identity conditions between structures of this type will be as for Prolog terms.

In standard treatments of feature structures (though not in ALE), there can only be one copy of any *atom* (a feature structure with no appropriate features) in a feature structure. Thus, if path π_1 leads to atom a, and path π_2 leads to atom a, then the values for those two paths are *token-identical*. Token-identity refers to an identity between two feature structures with respect to the objects themselves, as opposed to *structure-identity*, which refers to an identity between two feature structures with respect to the information they contain, i.e. whether their combined information could be construed as information about the same object. Another motivation for adding extensional types to ALE is found in their interaction with inequations (discussed below).

[Smolka 1988a] partitioned his atoms according to whether more than one copy could exist or not. In ALE, following [Carpenter 1992], this notion of copyability has been extended to arbitrary types – loosely speaking, those types which are copyable we call *intensional*, and those which are not, we call *extensional*. Thus, it is possible to have two feature structures of the same intensional type which, although they may be structurally isomorphic, are not token-identical.

Given the set of types, **Type**, defined by an ALE signature, we designate a subset, $\mathbf{ExtType} \subseteq \mathbf{Type}$, as the set of extensional types. This set consists only of *maximally specific types*, i.e. for each $\sigma \in \mathbf{ExtType}$, there is no type τ such that σ subsumes τ. The restriction of **ExtType** to maximally specific types is peculiar to ALE, and is levied in order to reduce the computational complexity of enforcing extensionality. In principle, we could require that this set must only be *upward closed*, which means that if $\sigma \in \mathbf{ExtType}$, and σ subsumes τ, then $\tau \in \mathbf{ExtType}$ [Carpenter 1992].

We need one more definition to formally state the effect which an extensional type has on feature structures in ALE. Given a set of extensional types, **ExtType**, an equivalence relation, $\asymp$, is said to be a *collapsing relation* on well-typed feature structures such that $F_1 \asymp F_2$ for $F_1 \neq F_2$ only if:

- F_1 has the same type, σ, as F_2, and $\sigma \in \mathbf{ExtType}$, and
- for every feature f appropriate to σ, F_1^f, the value of f in F_1, and F_2^f, the value of f in F_2, are defined, and $F_1^f \asymp F_2^f$.

In ALE, all feature structures are *collapsed*, which is to say that the only collapsing relation which exists over feature structures is the trivial collapsing relation, i.e. $F_1 \asymp F_2$ if and only if F_1 is token-identical to F_2.

In the case of acyclic feature structures, this definition is equivalent to saying that two intensional descriptions of feature structures refer to the same extensionally typed feature structure if and only if, for every feature appropriate to that type, their respective values on that feature are token-identical. So, for example, suppose we have:

```
bot sub [a,b,c,g].
  a sub [] intro [f:b,g:c].
  g sub [] intro [h:a,j:a].
```

If a, b, and c are extensional, any feature structure of type g must have token-identical h and j values. But if only a, and b are extensional, and c is intensional, then only the f values of the h and j values are necessarily token-identical.

Our formulation of extensionality above is stronger than the simple acyclic definition, though it reduces to the acyclic definition if there are no cycles in a structure. Furthermore, this definition amounts to the same as [Colmerauer's 1987] infinite tree unfolding for Prolog, if all types are extensional.

To the user, it appears that ALE works in a domain of feature structures where only the trivial collapsing relation exists. Internally, ALE works in the broader domain of all totally well-typed feature structures, and only periodically enforces the restriction on collapsings. The first stage of enforcement is to collect all possibly non-trivially collapsible pairs of feature structures. This stage is potentially expensive for large feature structures, since ALE must collect all pairs of feature values with the same extensional type. As a result, the enforcement is only performed just before ALE displays an answer to a top-level query and just before it adds an edge to its parsing chart.

To determine whether a pair of structures is extensionally identical or not, ALE builds a stack of pairs of feature values, initially with only this pair itself. For each pair of feature values on this stack, ALE must verify that if the feature values are collapsible, then they are trivially collapsible, i.e. the pair consists of the same feature structure twice. In doing so, ALE ensures that the only collapsing relation that exists is the trivial one. This verification is conducted by the predicate, iso_seq, on an argument consisting of a list of structures to test for extensional equality.

```
iso_seq([]).
iso_seq([iso(Tag1,TVs1,Tag2,TVs2)|Isos]):-
  ( Tag1 == Tag2,
    !, iso_seq(Isos)
  ; Tag1 = Tag2,
    iso_sub_seq(TVs1,TVs2,Isos)
  ).
```

The first disjunct corresponds to the case where the same feature structure occurs twice (token-identity in ALE is given by identical tags). The second corresponds to the case where the two are distinct, but since the only collapsing relation after enforcement should be the trivial one, their tags are unified. By specifying these two separate cases and by unifying these pointers before recursively checking feature values, this method will enforce our strong version of extensionality on cyclic feature structures.

The predicate, iso_sub_seq, takes two feature structures of the same extensional type, and for every feature appropriate to that type, adds the pair of their respective values for that feature to the stack, and recursively calls iso_seq. Thus, according to the definition of extensionality above, if the initial pair on the stack was not collapsible, then iso_seq will fail, unwinding any tag unifications that it made, since no token-identity assertions are needed for extensionality to be observed. If iso_seq succeeds, then the initial pair was collapsible, but since all of the respective tags in the two feature structures have been unified, it is now trivially collapsible.

The type information available to ALE at compile-time can be used to create one simple iso_sub_seq clause for every extensional type. If, for example, we have declared e to be extensional and appropriate for two features, then, the corresponding clause would be:

```
iso_sub_seq(e(V1,V2),e(V3,V4),V0) :-
    iso_seq(iso(V1,V3,iso(V2,V4,V0))).
```

Testing for extensional identity is, thus, no more expensive computationally than performing unification, and usually much more efficient, because substructures of intensional types need not be explored, in general.

6. INEQUATIONS

ALE provides one additional description in its attribute-value logic for inequality:

```
<desc> ::=  (=\= <desc>)
```

An inequation is satisfied by any feature structure which is not token-identical with the feature structure picked out by its argument. Inequations are only useful if the argument is a multiply-occurring variable or a description satisfied by an extensionally typed feature structure, since otherwise, the feature structure constructed for the argument description can never be encountered again, and the inequation never violated.

Inequation is an instance of general negation which requires the feature structures given by two paths *never* to be unified. [Penn and Carpenter 1993] argue that inequations plus finite disjunctions of types and appropriateness conditions are not only sufficient for encoding negation within linguistic contexts (as well as many other constraint puzzles), but are often also more precise formulations of what is intended than unrestricted negation. More general forms of negation have simply not been well motivated within a linguistic setting.

It is also worth mentioning that an inequation between two feature structures is a requirement for them not to be ***token-identical***. It is, thus, possible for two feature structures of the same intensional type to be structurally isomorphic, and still satisfy an inequation between them. In the case of an extensional type, an inequation between two feature structures of that same type is equivalent to a disjunction of inequations on their feature's values. For example, in the above signature, if only the type, a, is extensional, then the inequational description:

```
(h:H,
 j:=\= H)
```

would be satisfied by the same feature structures as the disjunctive description:

```
(h:(f:F,
    g:G),
 j:(f:=\=F
   ;g:=\=G)).
```

On the other hand, an inequation of the form `=\= t` for an extensional atomic type, `t`, amounts to the requirement that the value take some type other than `t`. Because there are no appropriate features, `=\= t` reduces to a trivially satisifed disjunction. Operationally, however, the two descriptions above are not equivalent. In fact, extensional types combined with inequations can be used to eliminate certain disjunctions, which is desirable since the use of explicitly disjunctive descriptions drastically increases the search space traversed by many of ALE's operations. Instead of requiring a particular verbal form to be `pers:(first;second)`, for example, we can simply make `third` extensional, and then require `pers:(=\= third)`.

Inequations in ALE are *persistent*: they require that two feature structures *never* be unified. Consider, for example, the following signature:

```
bot sub [a,b].
  a sub [] intro [f:b].
  b sub [c,d].
```

Because ALE evalutes conjuncts and disjuncts from left to right, if inequations were not persistent, then the description `(a,f:=\=c,f:c)` would be satisfiable. At the time the second conjunct is evaluated, the value of `f` has not yet been promoted to `c`, because `a` only restricts the value of `f` to `b`. Then, if inequations were not persistent, the next conjunct would be evaluated with no regard to the previously encountered inequation, and `f`'s value would be promoted. If we were to use the description, `(a,f:c,f:=\=c)`, instead, no feature structure would satisfy it. Because ALE uses persistent inequations, this description is not satisfied by any feature structure, regardless of which ordering of conjuncts is used. The persistence of inequations preserves the monotonicity of ALE's attribute-value logic.

The maintenance of persistent inequations requires the following operations to be performed upon evaluating an inequation:

- **deletion**: performed when the two feature structures involved are of two non-unifiable types, and hence, can never be unified;
- **addition**: when a new inequation is encountered in any description, e.g. a type constraint, a lexical item, the category of a rule;
- **failure**: when two inequated feature structures are unified;
- **splitting**: which is used when the two feature structures are of the same extensional type.

In the last, if two inequated feature structures are of the same extensional type, then the inequation is satisifed if and only if their respective values for at least one feature are not unified. As a result, we can "split" such an inequation into a disjunction of inequations, with each disjunct corresponding to one feature.

It is tempting to try to maintain information about inequations directly on the feature structures they inequate. This way, when the feature structure is modified, the inequation can be tested immediately. But this fails to take into account the fact that a feature structure can become extensionally identical to another one after having a deeply embedded substructure further instantiated. A second problem in locally representing inequations is that inequations often split into a disjunctive array of inequations between substructures. It would be prohibitively expensive to induce choice points from inequations in this way.

By far, the easiest way to maintain inequations is to use Prolog freezing. By freezing the tags of the inequated feature structures, they can be checked whenever they are instantiated to be sure that the new tags are not identical (i.e. the two structures have been unified), and to perform deletion or splitting when appropriate. Unfortunately, ALE does not always instantiate a new tag for a feature structure in a unification. For instance, to minimize reference chains, if an input is of the same type as the result, its tag is not instantiated to a new structure. Similarly, embedded substructures can be further instantiated without modifying the tag of the embedding structure.

The strategy employed by ALE is to keep a single representation of the relevant inequations for each top-level query or edge. When a rule is applied to a set of edges, the inequations on the result can be gathered from those on the daughters and those introduced by the rule scheme used. ALE's representation is not just a simple list, but rather a logical encoding of constraints in a conjunctive normal form. The concrete representation is a list of conjuncts, each of whose members is a list of disjuncts. Because the inequation representations can grow rapidly with this strategy, it is important to prune the list such that only those inequations which are pertinent remain. An inequation is *pertinent* to an edge if both of its feature structures occur as substructures of the feature structure for that edge, or if only one occurs as a substructure, and the other is of an extensional type. The latter case is necessary, since the feature structure which occurs as a substructure may eventually acquire the same extensional type as the one which is not, and they may be unified by the extensionality property above. This pertinency check is made just after ALE destructively dereferences an edge's entire feature structure by copying it (to path-compress the reference chains) and just before it asserts that edge. At this time, the substructure check is essentially free, since the old tags of all of the substructures can be marked specially to preserve re-entrancy.

Of course, these representations are checked for the consistency of their inequations at this time, and also before the answer to any top-level query is given. Each individual inequation is checked before it is added to the representation, regardless of whether it is added as the result of an addition or a split. The representation is also checked after each daughter in a rule is recognized, and once per resolution step when solving procedural attachments (to simulate Prolog's treatment of its own inequations).

The conjunctive normal form set of inequations is processed pointwise over its conjuncts, evaluating each one. Each conjunct, being a list of disjuncts, is also processed pointwise. The code to thread the logical operations is straightforward. The evaluation of each inequation leads to either failure, success, splitting, or postponement:

```
check_ineq(Tag1,_,Tag2,_,fail):-
  Tag1 == Tag2.
check_ineq(_,TVs1,_,TVs2,succeed):-
   functor(TVs1,Type1,_),
   functor(TVs2,Type2,_),
   \+unify_type(Type1,Type2,_), !.
check_ineq(_,TVs1,_,TVs2,Ineqs):-
  ( functor(TVs1,Type1,_),
    extensional(Type1),
  ; functor(TVs2,Type2,_),
    extensional(Type2)
  ),
  !, residuate(TVs1,TVs2,Ineqs).
check_ineq(Tag1,TVs1,Tag2,TVs2,postpone).
```

The first clause states that an inequation between extensionally identical structures fails. The second clause states that an inequation succeeds between two structures of inconsistent type. The third clause applies to pairs of structures of identical extensional type, and returns a list of inequations between their substructures (i.e. splitting). A recursive call on the new inequations in this case. The last clause applies to postpone the inequation if none of the other clauses have applied. An example of `residuate/3` would be:

```
residuate(index(P,N,G), index(P2,N2,G2),
          [ineq(P,P2), ineq(N,N2), ineq(G,G2)]).
```

We need one such clause for each extensional type. The actual code used by ALE for evaluating an inequation is significantly more complicated than this; like all ALE predicates, it is both highly threaded and highly unfolded to exploit indexing and last call optimization.

7. TYPE CONSTRAINTS

ALE allows arbitrary attribute-value logic formulae to be attached as constraints on types. Such constraints are indicated in the signature using the cons operator, e.g.:

```
bot sub [a,b].
  a sub [c,d] intro [f:bot].
  b sub [d] intro [g:bot].
d cons (f:X,g:X).
```

The constraint on the type d requires all feature structures of type d to have token-identical values for features f and g. The type a has no constraints expressed, which produces the same behavior as the trivial constraint bot. A type constraint may use any of the operators in the description language, including type descriptions. The type descriptions may not be used in a cyclic manner, however. For example, the following constraints could not be added to this signature:

```
a cons f:b.
b cons g:c.
```

because a subsumes c. Notice, however, that type constraints can be used to provide additional information regarding value restrictions on appropriate features. In general, type constraints can encode a greater variety of restrictions.

Type constraints are simply compiled into extra goals for the compiled add_to_*type* and unify_*type* predicates. So, in the above example, the clause for unifying a feature structure of type a with a feature structure of type b is:

```
unify_a(b(GV),FV,Tag-d(FV,GV),
                 Tag-d(FV,GV)) :-
  unify_deref(FV,GV).
```

where the `unify_deref` goal comes from the general type constraint on d. This is an eager evaluation strategy for constraints.

8. CONCLUSION

We have shown how grammars based on attribute-value logic descriptions can be compiled efficiently into low-level Prolog instructions which exploit the inherent efficiency of the WAM. Unfortunately, there are a few inefficiencies stemming from this encoding, due to Prolog's logical variables and its lack of control over copying structures from the database. The ideal solution is to build a WAM-like abstract machine language directly for typed feature structures and their associated descriptions ([Qu 1994], [Wintner 1994]). The WAM has proven to be the most efficient architecture yet developed for implementing parsers for "unification-based" grammars.

With the current implementation, ALE performs at about one percent of the speed of the SICStus compiler itself on the naive reverse benchmark. In [Penn's 1993] HPSG grammar for English, with lexical entries ranging between 100 and 200 node feature structures, and with all of the local and nonlocal principles implemented, is able to process 15 word sentences, creating approximately 40-50 inactive edges, in seconds, at about 3,000 feature structure unifications per second, on a DEC 5100, running SICStus 2.1#8.

ALE Version 2.0, as described in this paper, is available from the authors without charge for research purposes. It runs under SICStus and Quintus Prologs. It is distributed with roughly 100 pages of documentation and sample grammars, including a preliminary version of Penn's HPSG grammar for English.

Acknowledgement

This chapter is based upon work supported under a National Science Foundation Graduate Research Fellowship. Any opinions, findings, conclusions or recommendations expressed in this publication are those of the authors and do not necessarily reflect the views of the National Science Foundation.

References

Aït-Kaci, H. (1986a). An algebraic semantics approach to the effective resolution of type equations. *Theoretical Computer Science*, 45.

Aït-Kaci, H. and R. Nasr (1986) LOGIN: A logic programming language with built-in inheritance. *Journal of Logic Programming* 3.

Aït-Kaci, H. (1991) *Warren's Abstract Machine: A Tutorial Reconstruction.* MIT Press, Cambridge, Mass.

Carpenter, B. (1992) *The Logic of Typed Feature Structures.* Cambridge University Press.

Carpenter, B. and G. Penn (1994) ALE User's Guide Version 2.0. Laboratory for Computational Linguistics Technical Report, Carnegie Mellon University, Pittsburgh.

Carpenter, B. and C. Pollard (1991) Inclusion, disjointness and choice: the logic of linguistic classification. *Proceedings of the ACL.*

Colmerauer, A. (1987) Theoretical Models of Prolog II. In van Canegham, M. and D. Warren, eds., *Logic Programming and its Applications*, 1–31, Ablex, Norwood.

Höhfeld, M. and G. Smolka (1988) Definite relations over constraint languages. LILOG Report 53, IBM Scientific Centre, Stuttgart.

Kasper, B. and B. Rounds (1990) The logic of unification in grammar. *Linguistics and Philosophy* 13.

Mastroianni, M. (1993) Attribute-logic Phonology. MS Thesis, Computational Linguistics Program, Carnegie Mellon University, Pittsburgh.

Meseguer, J., J. Goguen and G. Smolka (1987) Order-sorted unification. CSLI Report 87-86, Stanford.

O'Keefe, R. (1990) *The Craft of Prolog.* MIT Press, Cambridge, Mass.

Penn, G. (1993) A utility for typed feature structure-based grammatical theories. MS Thesis. Computational Linguistics Program, Carnegie Mellon University, Pittsburgh. Available as Laboratory for Computational Linguistics Technical Report.

Penn, G. and B. Carpenter (1993). Three sources of disjunction in a typed feature structure-based resolution system. In *Feature Formalisms and Linguistic Ambiguity.* Ellis Horwood.

Pereira, F. and D.H.D. Warren (1980) Definite clause grammars for language analysis. *Artificial Intelligence* 13.

Pereira, F. and M. Pollock (1991) Incremental interpretation. *Artificial Intelligence* 50.

Pollard, C. and I. Sag (1994) *Head-Driven Phrase Structure Grammar.* CSLI/University of Chicago Press.

Qu, Y. (1994) An abstract machine for typed attribute-value logic. MS Thesis, Computational Linguistics Program, Carnegie Mellon University. Available as Laboratory for Computational Linguistics Technical Report.

Shieber, S. (1985) Using restriction to extend parsing algorithms for complex-feature-based formalisms. Proceedings of the ACL.

Smolka, G. (1988) A feature logic with subsorts. LILOG Report 55. IBM Scientific Centre, Stuttgart.

Wintner, S. (1994) An abstract machine for HPSG. PhD Thesis Proposal. Computer Science Department, Technion University, Haifa.

9. PREDICTIVE HEAD-CORNER CHART PARSING

KLAAS SIKKEL
GMD – Forschungszentrum Informationstechnik
Schloß Birlinghoven, Sankt Augustin, Germany

AND

RIEKS OP DEN AKKER
Department of Computer Science, University of Twente

Abstract.
Head-Corner (HC) parsing has come up in computational linguistics a few years ago, motivated by linguistic arguments. This idea is a heuristic, rather than a fail-safe principle, hence it is relevant indeed to consider the worst-case behaviour of the HC parser. We define a novel predictive head-corner chart parser of cubic time complexity.

We start with a left-corner (LC) chart parser, which is easier to understand. Subsequently, the LC chart parser is generalized to an HC chart parser. It is briefly sketched how the parser can be enhanced with feature structures.

1. INTRODUCTION

"Our Latin teachers were apparently right", Martin Kay (1989) remarks. "You should start [parsing] with the main verb. This will tell you what kinds of subjects and objects to look for and what cases they will be in. When you come to look for these, you should also start by trying to find the main word, because this will tell you most about what else to look for".

Head-driven or *head-corner* parsing has been addressed in several publications (Proudian and Pollard, 1985; Kay 1989; Satta and Stock 1989; van Noord 1991; Bouma and van Noord 1993). As the head-driven approach is a heuristic, rather than a fail-safe principle, it is important to pay attention to the worst-case behaviour. This is best taken care of in a tabular approach

H. Bunt and M. Tomita (eds.), Recent Advances in Parsing Technology, 169–182.

like the bottom-up head-driven parser by Satta and Stock. We enhance the tabular head-driven parser with top-down prediction.

The algorithmic details of the head-corner parser are not easy. Therefore we will make some effort to convey the intuition behind the parser. To that end, we first define a *left-corner* chart parser in Section 3 and afterwards generalize this to a head-corner parser in 4. A complexity analysis is given in 5. We sketch extension with feature structures in 6 and briefly discuss related approaches in 7.

2. CHART PARSING

Chart parsing, first introduced by Kay (1980), is a well-known parsing technique in computational linguistics. We will present a conventional Earley chart parser in a slightly unconventional way. Thus the reader who is familiar with the Earley parser will get a feeling for the notation used in this chapter.

We use the following notational conventions. Nonterminals are denoted by $A, B, \ldots \in N$; terminals by $a, b, \ldots \in \Sigma$. We write V for $N \cup \Sigma$ with $X, Y, \ldots$ as typical elements. Strings in V^* are denoted by $\alpha, \beta, \ldots$. A context-free grammar G is a 4-tuple (N, Σ, P, S), with P a set of productions and S the start symbol. The sentence to be parsed is denoted $a_1 \ldots a_n$. We make extensive use of *place markers* $i, j, k \ldots$, indicating positions in the sentence. The symbol a_i is located between positions $i-1$ and i.

A chart parser is characterized by the following entities: a *domain of items*, that can be added to the chart by the parser using an agenda; some *operators* that specify how combinations of items on the chart can lead to recognition of other items; an *initial chart* and an *initial agenda*. Items represent (the existence of) partial parse trees for the given sentence. At each step some current item is selected from the agenda, and moved to the chart. If the chart contains items that, in combination with the current item, allow recognition of other items not yet present on the chart or on the agenda, these are added to the agenda. This continues until the agenda is empty.

A context-free chart parser does not really construct parse trees. But a representation of all parse trees can easily be obtained when items in the chart are annotated with pointers to the items that caused their recognition. Various forms of sophistication can be added by structuring the chart or by providing a strategy to select the next item from the agenda.

The Earley chart parser uses two types of items:

$[A \to \alpha \bullet \beta, i, j]$: *Earley items* (for $A \to \alpha\beta \in P$ and $0 \le i \le j \le n$),

$[a, j-1, j]$: *terminal items*, representing a_j $(1 \leq j \leq n)$.

An Earley item $[A \rightarrow \alpha{\bullet}\beta, i, j]$ is to be recognized by the chart parser iff

$\alpha \Rightarrow^* a_{i+1} \dots a_j$, and
$S \Rightarrow^* a_1 \dots a_i A\gamma$ for some $\gamma \in V^*$.

The initial chart contains the terminal items representing the string.[1]

When the j-th word belongs to different categories, say a and b, then both items $[a, j-1, j]$ and $[b, j-1, j]$ are present in the initial chart. The initial agenda contains items $[S \rightarrow {\bullet}\gamma, 0, 0]$ for all productions $S \rightarrow \gamma \in P$. The following operators are defined for the Earley chart parser:

predict: for $B \rightarrow \gamma \in P$:

$$[A \rightarrow \alpha{\bullet}B\beta, i, j] \vdash [B \rightarrow {\bullet}\gamma, j, j];$$

scan:

$$[A \rightarrow \alpha{\bullet}b\beta, i, j], [b, j, j+1] \vdash [A \rightarrow \alpha b{\bullet}\beta, i, j+1];$$

complete:

$$[A \rightarrow \alpha{\bullet}B\beta, i, j], [B \rightarrow \gamma{\bullet}, j, k] \vdash [A \rightarrow \alpha B{\bullet}\beta, i, k].$$

The turnstyle ($\vdash$) notation is a convenient shorthand, meaning that the left-hand side items licence the recognition of the right-hand side item. As a running example we will use the sentence `the cat caught a mouse`, represented by the lexical categories

$$*det \ *n \ *v \ *det \ *n.$$

The example grammar is

$$S \rightarrow NP \ VP,$$
$$NP \rightarrow *det \ *n,$$
$$VP \rightarrow *v \ NP.$$

Due to lack of ambiguity, the example will nicely illustrate the difference between the chart parsers that are presented in this chapter. Initially, the chart contains $\{[0, *det, 1], [1, *n, 2], [2, *v, 3], [3, *det, 4], [4, *n, 5]\}$ and the agenda is $\{[S \rightarrow {\bullet}NP \ VP, 0, 0]\}$. In Table 1 the completed chart is shown (excluding terminal items), annotated with how the items were recognized.

The items on the chart can be seen as *the trace of a left-to-right walk through the parse tree*. This walk is shown in Figure 1, annotated with the item numbers. (In the general case things are rather more complicated. There could be different parse trees and also partial left-to-right walks

TABLE 1. The final Earley chart

#	item	recognized by
0	$[S \to \bullet NP\ VP, 0, 0]$	initial
1	$[NP \to \bullet {*det}\ {*n}, 0, 0]$	*predict*(0)
2	$[NP \to {*det}\bullet {*n}, 0, 1]$	*scan*(1)
3	$[NP \to {*det}\ {*n}\bullet, 0, 2]$	*scan*(2)
4	$[S \to NP\bullet VP, 0, 2]$	*compl*(0,3)
5	$[VP \to \bullet {*v}\ NP, 2, 2]$	*predict*(4)
6	$[VP \to {*v}\bullet NP, 2, 3]$	*scan*(5)
7	$[NP \to \bullet {*det}\ {*n}, 3, 3]$	*predict*(6)
8	$[NP \to {*det}\bullet {*n}, 3, 4]$	*scan*(7)
9	$[NP \to {*det}\ {*n}\bullet, 3, 5]$	*scan*(8)
10	$[VP \to {*v}\ NP\bullet, 2, 5]$	*complete*(6,9)
11	$[S \to NP\ VP\bullet, 0, 5]$	*complete*(4,10)

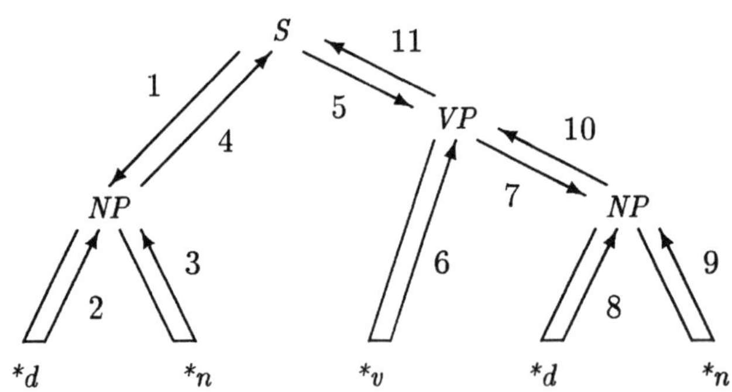

Figure 1. The Earley tree walk

of valid prefixes that can't be extended to a parse. All trese traces are interlaced and may partly coincide.)

3. LEFT-CORNER CHART PARSING

We will now specify a Left-Corner (LC) parser as a chart parser; it is to be generalized to a head-corner parser in the next section. The deterministic LC algorithm originally stems from Rosenkrantz and Lewis (1970).

[1]In general we could allow that items $[X, j, k]$, with $k > j$ and X either a terminal or a nonterminal, are initially on the chart. These 'initial' items could be constructed then by preprocessing the input sentence by a lexical analyser, or some other substring parser.

We describe a generalized LC parser[2] for context-free grammars that is similar to, but subtly different from the Earley parser. *Scan* and *complete* operations remain unchanged, predicting is handled differently. We start with a *predict item* $[0, S]$ meaning that we are to look for a constituent S starting at position 0. We proceed bottom-up, starting from $[*det, 0, 1]$. We can 'climb up' from **det* to an *NP* because this moves us nearer to the goal S. Or, to put it more formally, because a leftmost derivation

$$S \Rightarrow^* NP\gamma \Rightarrow *det\,*n\gamma$$

exists, we may extend $[*det, 0, 1]$ to $[NP \rightarrow *det \bullet *n, 0, 1]$.

A few steps later we have recognized $[S \rightarrow NP \bullet VP, 0, 2]$. Here we set a *sub-goal*, represented by the predict item [2, *VP*]. In Figure 2 it is shown how the LC chart parser steps through a parse tree:

- Steps up correspond to a *scan* or *complete* as in the Earley case.
- Steps down to the leftmost child are skipped because these are implicitly encoded in the *transitive left-corner relation* that is encorporated in the parser.
- Steps down to *non-leftmost nonterminal* children correspond to setting a new sub-goal.

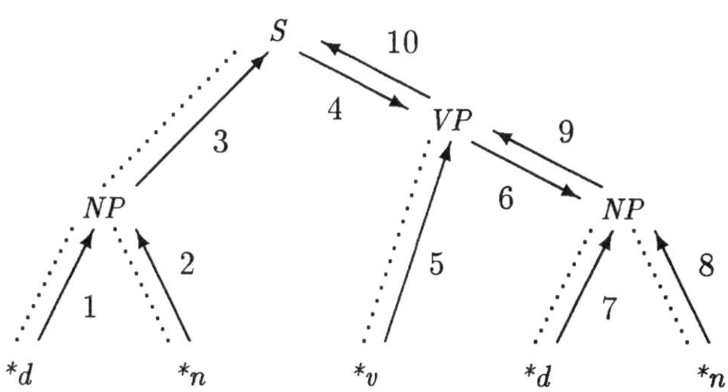

Figure 2. The left-corner tree walk

[2]The term 'Generalized LC' has been introduced by Demers (1977) for a rather different concept. He generalized the notion of Left Corner, deriving a framework that describes a class of parsers and associated grammars ranging from LL(k) via LC(k) to LR(k). We generalize the LC(0) parser by dropping the restriction that the grammar be LC(0). The nondeterminism is handled by a dynamic programming technique, as in Generalized LR parsing (Tomita, 1985). Note that the semantic ambiguity of the noun phrase "Generalized LC parsing" duly reflects the syntactic ambiguity: we are concerned with [Generalized [Left-Corner Parsing]], whereas Demers discussed [[Generalized Left-Corner] parsing].

In Table 2 the final chart is shown of the LC chart parser that will be formally defined next. Each item on the final chart corresponds to an arrow in the tree walk.

TABLE 2. The final LC chart

#	item	recognized by
0	$[0, S]$	initial
1	$[NP \rightarrow *det{\bullet} *n, 0, 1]$	$lc(i)$ (0)
2	$[NP \rightarrow *det *n{\bullet}, 0, 2]$	*scan* (1)
3	$[S \rightarrow NP{\bullet} VP, 0, 2]$	$lc(ii)$ (0,2)
4	$[2, VP]$	*predict* (3)
5	$[VP \rightarrow *v{\bullet} NP, 2, 3]$	$lc(i)$ (4)
6	$[3, NP]$	*predict* (5)
7	$[NP \rightarrow *det{\bullet} *n, 3, 4]$	$lc(i)$ (6)
8	$[NP \rightarrow *det *n{\bullet}, 3, 5]$	*scan* (7)
9	$[VP \rightarrow *v\ NP{\bullet}, 2, 5]$	*complete* (5,8)
10	$[S \rightarrow NP\ VP{\bullet}, 0, 5]$	*complete* (3,9)

The intuition behind the LC parser should be clear now, and we present the formal definition rather terse. The *left corner* of a production is the leftmost symbol in the right-hand side of that production (and ε for an empty production). We write $A >_\ell U$ if A has left corner $U \in (V \cup \{\varepsilon\})$ We write $>_\ell^*$ for the transitive closure of $>_\ell$. Hence we have, for example, $S >_\ell^* *det$.
The LC chart parser uses the following kinds of items:

$$
\begin{array}{ll}
[i, A] & : \text{ predict items,} \\
[B \rightarrow \alpha{\bullet}\beta, i, j]: & \text{Earley items -- only those with } \alpha \neq \varepsilon \text{ or } \alpha = \beta = \varepsilon, \\
[a, j-1, j] & : \text{ terminal items as usual.}
\end{array}
$$

The initial chart contains the terminal items representing the sentence, the agenda is initialized to $\{[0, S]\}$. The operators of the LC chart parser are defined as follows. We distinguish separate left-corner (lc) operators for left corners a, C, and ε.

$lc(i)$: for $A >_\ell^* B$, $B \rightarrow a\beta \in P$:

$$[i, A],\ [a, i, i{+}1] \ \vdash\ [B \rightarrow a{\bullet}\beta, i, i{+}1],$$

$lc(ii)$: for $A >_\ell^* B$, $B \rightarrow C\beta \in P$:

$$[i, A], [C \rightarrow \gamma{\bullet}, i, j] \ \vdash\ [B \rightarrow C{\bullet}\beta, i, j],$$

$lc(iii)$: for $A >_\ell^* B$, $B \rightarrow \varepsilon \in P$:

$[i, A] \vdash [B \to \bullet, i, i]$;

predict:

$[B \to \alpha{\bullet}C\beta, i, j] \vdash [j, C]$;

scan:

$[B \to \alpha{\bullet}a\beta, i, j], [a, j, j{+}1] \vdash [B \to \alpha a{\bullet}\beta, i, j{+}1]$;

complete:

$[B \to \alpha{\bullet}C\beta, i, j], [C \to \gamma\bullet, j, k] \vdash [B \to \alpha C{\bullet}\beta, i, k]$.

Thus we have characterized the LC chart parser by defining the initial chart and agenda and the operators. The reader may verify that these operators produce the chart shown in Table 2 for our example sentence. For a proof of the correctness of the algorithm we refer to Sikkel and op den Akker (1992) or Sikkel (1993).

4. HEAD-CORNER CHART PARSING

We introduce the head-corner chart parser by analogy to the left-corner parser. While the LC parser makes a left-to-right walk through a parse tree, the HC parser makes a *head-first* walk through a parse tree[3], as shown in Figure 3. With this very simple idea in mind we can fix the formal details.

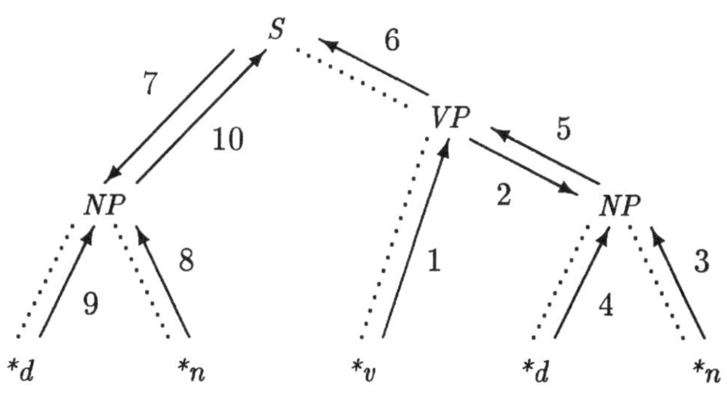

Figure 3. The head-corner tree walk

A *context-free head grammar* is a 5-tuple (N, Σ, P, S, r), with r a function that assigns a natural number to each production in P. Let $|p|$ denote the length of the right-hand side of p. Then r is constrained to $r(p) = 0$ for

[3]In the general case, to be precise, the HC parser makes interlacing and partially coinciding walks through all full parse trees, as well as 'valid infixes' starting from a feasible lexical head of the sentence.

$|p| = 0$ and $1 \leq r(p) \leq |p|$ for $|p| > 0$. The *head* of a production p is the $r(p)$-th symbol of the right-hand side; an ε-production has head ε. It is up to the grammar writer to choose heads for the productions.

In a practical notation, we give a head grammar as a set of productions with the heads underlined. We have extended the example grammar to a head grammar with the following head assignments:

$$S \to NP\ \underline{VP},$$
$$VP \to \underline{{}^*v}\ NP,$$
$$NP \to {}^*det\ \underline{{}^*n}.$$

The relation $>_h$ is defined by $A >_h U$ if there is a production $p = A \to \alpha \in P$ with U the head of p; the transitive and reflexive closure of $>_h$ is denoted $>_h^*$. Hence we have, for example, $S >_h^* {}^*v$. For the head-corner parser we distinguish the following kinds of items:

$[l, r, A]$: *predict items*
$[B \to \alpha{\bullet}\beta{\bullet}\gamma, i, j]$: *double dotted* (DD) *items,*
$[a, j-1, j]$: terminal items.

A predict item $[l, r, A]$ will be recognized if a constituent A is being looked for that must be located somewhere between l and r. Such a constituent should either stretch from l to some j (if we are working to the right from the head of some production) or from r downto some j (if we are working to the left from the head of some production), with $l \leq j \leq r$. A double dotted item $[B \to \alpha{\bullet}\beta{\bullet}\gamma, i, j]$ is recognized if there is a goal $[l, r, A]$ such that $A >_h^* B$, $l \leq i$, $j \leq r$ and $\beta \Rightarrow^* a_{i+1} \ldots a_j$ has been established.

The initial chart contains the terminal items that represent the string as usual; the agenda is initialized with a single predict item $[0, n, S]$. If the string is correct, we will be able to derive an item $[S \to {\bullet}\gamma{\bullet}, 0, n]$. The operators, are defined as follows. We distinguish three different head-corner (hc) operators for terminal heads b, for nonterminal heads C and for heads being ε.

$hc(i)$: for $A >_h^* B,\ B \to \alpha\underline{b}\gamma \in P,\ l < j \leq r$:
$$[l, r, A],\ [b, j-1, j]\ \vdash\ [B \to \alpha{\bullet}b{\bullet}\gamma, j-1, j],$$

$hc(ii)$: for $A >_h^* B,\ B \to \alpha\underline{C}\gamma \in P, l \leq i \leq j \leq r$:
$$[l, r, A],\ [C \to {\bullet}\delta{\bullet}, i, j]\ \vdash\ [B \to \alpha{\bullet}C{\bullet}\gamma, i, j],$$

$hc(iii)$: for $A >_h^* B,\ B \to \varepsilon \in P,\ l \leq j \leq r$:
$$[l, r, A]\ \vdash\ [B \to {\bullet}{\bullet}, j, j];$$

predict: for $A >_h^* B,\ l \leq i \leq j \leq r$:

$[l,r,A],\ [B \to \alpha C{\bullet}\beta{\bullet}\gamma, i, j] \ \vdash\ [l,i,C],$
$[l,r,A],\ [B \to \alpha{\bullet}\beta{\bullet}C\gamma, i, j] \ \vdash\ [j,r,C];$

scan: for $A{>}_h^*B$, $l < j \leq k \leq r$:

$[l,r,A],\ [a,j-1,j],\ [B \to \alpha a{\bullet}\beta{\bullet}\gamma, j, k] \ \vdash\ [B \to \alpha{\bullet}a\beta{\bullet}\gamma, j-1, k],$
$[l,r,A],\ [B \to \alpha{\bullet}\beta{\bullet}a\gamma, i, j-1],\ [a,j-1,j] \ \vdash\ [B \to \alpha{\bullet}\beta a{\bullet}\gamma, i, j];$

complete: for $A{>}_h^*B$, $l \leq i \leq j \leq k \leq r$:

$[l,r,A],\ [C \to {\bullet}\delta{\bullet}, i, j],\ [B \to \alpha C{\bullet}\beta{\bullet}\gamma, j, k] \ \vdash\ [B \to \alpha{\bullet}C\beta{\bullet}\gamma, i, k],$
$[l,r,A],\ [B \to \alpha{\bullet}\beta{\bullet}C\gamma, i, j],\ [C \to {\bullet}\delta{\bullet}, j, k] \ \vdash\ [B \to \alpha{\bullet}\beta C{\bullet}\gamma, i, k].$

Head-corner analysis of the example sentence illustrates how the chart parser may jump up and down the sentence. The completed HC chart is shown in Table 3. Each item corresponds to a step in the head-corner tree walk for the parse of our example sentence, cf. Figure 3.

TABLE 3. The final HC chart

#	item	recognized by
0	$[0,5,S]$	*initial*
1	$[VP \to {\bullet}{*}v{\bullet}NP, 2, 3]$	*hc*(*i*) (0)
2	$[3,5,NP]$	*predict*(0,1)
3	$[NP \to {*}det{\bullet}{*}n{\bullet}, 4, 5]$	*hc*(*i*) (2)
4	$[NP \to {\bullet}{*}det\ {*}n{\bullet}, 3, 5]$	*scan* (2,3)
5	$[VP \to {\bullet}{*}v\ NP{\bullet}, 2, 5]$	*complete* (0,1,4)
6	$[S \to NP{\bullet}VP{\bullet}, 2, 5]$	*hc*(*ii*) (0,5)
7	$[0,2,NP]$	*predict*(0,6)
8	$[NP \to {*}det{\bullet}{*}n{\bullet}, 1, 2]$	*hc*(*i*) (7)
9	$[NP \to {\bullet}{*}det\ {*}n{\bullet}, 0, 2]$	*scan* (7,8)
10	$[S \to {\bullet}NP\ VP{\bullet}, 0, 5]$	*complete* (0,6,9)

5. COMPLEXITY ANALYSIS AND FURTHER OPTIMIZATIONS

The number of items that can be recognized is $O(n^2)$, but the work involved for an arbitrary current item is more than linear. The most problematic operation is *complete* (with *scan* as a special sub-case) with 5 place markers involved. *Complete* can be reduced to 3 place markers with some special extra bookkeeping. As a consequence, the number of place markers involved in *scan* and *predict* will drop from 4 to 3. We keep a *goal table*, in the form of a CYK table, for storage of the predicted goals. Whenever an item $[l,r,C]$ is predicted, we write a C in goal table entry (l,r). Furthermore, we write a C in every entry (i,j) with $l \leq i \leq j \leq r$ in which no C is present. A typical case is presented in Figures 4 and 5. A goal $[1,7,C]$ is to be added, the entry (1,7) is marked + in Figure 4. One adds C symbols column by column, stopping each time when an C is found. In Figure 5 "+" indicates the entries where a C is written and "−" indicates the entries that were inspected but already contained an C. During the course of the algorithm only $O(n^2)$ C symbols are written, per symbol only $O(n)$ entries are inspected that already did contain C. Using the goal table, the place markers l, r in the *complete* can be replaced by i, k.

	0	1	2	3	4	5	6	7	8 (right)
0	C	C	C						
1		C	C					+	
2			C	C	C				
3				C	C				
4					C				
5						C	C	C	C
6							C	C	C
7								C	C
8 (left)									C

Figure 4. Adding $[1,7,C]$ to the goal table...

	0	1	2	3	4	5	6	7	8 (right)
0	C	C	C						
1		C	−	+	+	+	+	+	
2			C	−	−	+	+	+	
3				C	C	+	+	+	
4					C	+	+	+	
5						−	−	−	C
6							C	C	C
7								C	C
8 (left)									C

Figure 5. ... successful (+) and unsuccessful (−) accesses

Using the goal table as explained above, one can straightforwardly verify that the overall complexity in the length of the sentence is $O(n^2)$ space and $O(n^3)$ time as usual, assuming that the chart is structured likewise as a triangular matrix. When the size of the grammar is taken into account the analysis gets somewhat more complicated. For the sake of brevity we only state the results. A detailed analysis is given by Sikkel (1993). For an optimal worst-case complexity we have to make a small change to the implementation and represent fully completed DD items $[A \rightarrow \bullet\beta\bullet, i, j]$ by CYK items $[A, i, j]$. An Earley chart parser — using the same optimization — has a time complexity $O(|G|n^3)$, with $|G|$ the number of productions multiplied by the average length of a production. *Without prediction* the HC parser has a time complexity of $O(|G|rn^3)$, with r the size of the longest production. This extra factor r is because we use double dotted, rather than single dotted items. Prediction usually speeds up a parser but may slow it down in pathological cases. In the worst case it adds a factor $|N|$, the number of nonterminal symbols, yielding a time complexity of $O(|N||G|rn^3)$. The space complexity is $O(|G|rn^2)$ for the chart and agenda, and $O(|N|^2 \times |N||\Sigma|)$ for storage of the $>_h^*$ relation in tabular form.

The obtained worst-case complexity is optimal, in the sense that all complexity factors are properly accounted for. The factor $|N|$ in addition to an optimal Earley parser is a necessary consequence of (the worst-case behaviour of) prediction. The factor r for right-hand side length can be eliminated by a simple optimization:

- When an item $[A \rightarrow \alpha\bullet B\bullet\gamma, i, j]$ has been recognized by the head-corner rule, with $\alpha \neq \varepsilon \neq \gamma$, it should be expanded *either* to $[A \rightarrow \bullet\alpha B\bullet\gamma, h, j]$ *or* to $[A \rightarrow \alpha\bullet B\gamma\bullet, i, k]$ but not both; from either one a completed item $[A \rightarrow \bullet\alpha B\gamma\bullet, h, k]$ can be obtained. This idea is taken from Satta and Stock (1989).

By imposing the restriction that right expansion is to be allowed only for items that cannot further expand to the left, the time complexity is reduced by a factor r to $O(|N||G|n^3)$.

A large percentage of computing time can be saved by adding some more sophistication to the algorithm. Another optimization that can be added straightforwardly is the following:

- A predicted item should fit to the left, fit to the right, or both. This can be expressed by using predict items of the form $[= l, = r, A]$, $[\geq l, = r, A]$ and $[= l, \leq r, A]$ with the obvious interpretation. For example, if $A >_h^* X$ and X occurs only at the left (i.e., if $A \Rightarrow^* X\beta$) then $[X, i, j]$ fits to $[= l, \leq r, A]$ only if $i = l$. The head-corner operator can be adapted accordingly.

If the grammar is limited to Chomsky Normal Form, the first saving doesn't apply but the second is more effective. Further optimizations are possible, but beyond the scope of this chapter.

6. EXTENSION WITH FEATURE STRUCTURES

Feature information according to any unification based grammar can be added to recognized items. For bottom-up composition of constituents this is straightforward. Using feature information for top-down prediction is more subtle, as we can only use so-called ***transitive features***. A feature is transitive if every constituent shares the feature with its head. Hence, a constituent transitively shares such a feature with its lexical head. This is important, because sub-goals are parsed from the lexical head upwards. If, for example, a *VP* has been found with *agreement* 3sg (third person singular), then the *NP* that is set as a goal must also have *agreement* 3sg. Because *agreement* is a transitive feature, only a noun with *agreement* 3sg can be the lexical head.

Practically this works as follows. Double dotted items $[B \rightarrow \alpha \bullet \beta \bullet \gamma, i, j]$ are replaced by items $[l, r, A; B \rightarrow \alpha \bullet \beta \bullet \gamma, i, j]$, with A the predicted goal symbol. The transitive features of A are shared with B. If we have an item $[l, r, A; A \rightarrow \bullet \alpha \bullet, l, j]$ we can unify the predicted and parsed A if the nontransitive features match as well.

7. RELATED APPROACHES

The left-corner chart parser of Section 3, although rather different in style of presentation, is closely related to the predictive chart parsing framework introduced by Kay (1980). First ideas of generalized LC parsing, although not under that name, can be traced back to Pratt (1975). A left-corner style parser in Prolog was presented by Matsumoto *et al.* (1983). This BUP parser is limited to acyclic, ε-free grammars. Nederhof (1992) defines a generalized LC parser by analogy to the generalized LR parser of Tomita (1985). Nederhof's parser is more efficient than our LC chart parser, but it doesn't generalize to HC.

The head-driven parser of Satta and Stock (1989) is similar to ours, but does not make use of prediction. The use of a head-driven approach to enhance the efficiency of prediction was first suggested by Kay (1989).

The context-free head grammars in Section 4 should not be confused with Head Grammars as introduced by Pollard (1984), that handle discontinuous constituents by means of 'head wrapping'. (Van Noord, 1991) describes a Prolog implementation of a head-corner parser for languages with discontinuous constituents.

Bouma and van Noord (1983) have experimented with various parsing strategies for unification grammars and conclude that for important classes of grammars it is fruitful to apply parsing strategies that are sensitive to the linguistic notion of a head.

A Head-Corner parser for typed feature structures has been implemented by Moll (1995). It is used as a parser in an experimental natural language dialogue System. See op den akker *et al.* (1995) for more details.

8. CONCLUSIONS

We have given a formal treatment of a predictive head-corner parser. The item-based description of (predictive) chart parsers is a useful formalism for such a formal treatment. This is exemplified by the fact that we cover grammars with ε-productions with hardly any additional effort, while these are usually left out for the sake of simplicity. Enhancing a head-corner chart parser with prediction is new.

The head-corner approach cannot be claimed to be more efficient in general than the (generalized) left-corner approach or other parsers. It is indeed a heuristic, that can be expected to be effective when most of the feature information of a constituent is located in the head. Hence, *because* it is a method based on a heuristic, rather than a fail-safe principle, it is important to consider what happens if the heuristic doesn't pay off. Therefore we have made some effort to make sure that the worst-case behaviour conforms to the usual complexity bounds for context-free parsing algorithms: $O(n^3)$ time and $O(n^2)$ space.

Acknowledgements

We are grateful to Anton Nijholt, Mark-Jan Nederhof, Gertjan van Noord and Giorgio Satta for constructive comments on earlier drafts of this chapter. We thank Margriet Verlinden, Gert Veldhuijzen van Zanten, and Marc Moll for their work on the implementation of the Head-Corner Parser.

References

op den Akker R., ter Doest H., Moll M. and Nijholt A. (1995) Parsing in dialogue systems using typed feature structures. Memoranda Informatica 95-25, Department of Computer Science, University of Twente, Enschede, the Netherlands.

Bouma, G. and van Noord, G. (1993) Head-driven Parsing for Lexicalist Grammars: Experimental Results. *Proc. 6th European Chapter of the ACL*, 71–80.

Demers, A.J. (1977) Generalized Left Corner Parsing. *4th ACM Symp. on Principles of Prog. Lang.*, 170–182.

Kay, M. (1980) Algorithm Schemata and Data Structures in Syntactic Processing. Report CSL-80-12, Xerox PARC, Palo Alto, Ca.
Reprinted in: Grosz, B.J. et al. (Eds.), *Readings in Natural Language Processing*, Morgan Kaufmann, Los Altos, Ca. (1982).

Kay, M. (1989) Head Driven Parsing. *Int. Workshop on Parsing Technologies (IWPT'89)*, 52–62.

Matsumoto, Y., Tanaka, H., Hirakawa, H., Miyoshi, H. and Yasukawa, H. (1983) BUP: a bottom-up parser embedded in Prolog. *New Generation Computing* **1**, 145–158.

Moll M. (1995) Head-Corner Parsing using Typed Feature Structures. M.Sc. Thesis, University of Twente, Dept. of Computer Science, Enschede, the Netherlands.

Nederhof, M.-J. (1993) Generalized Left-Corner Parsing. *Proc. 6th European Chapter of the ACL*, 305–314.

Noord, G. van (1991) Head Corner Parsing for Discontinuous Constituency. *Proc. 29th Ann. Meeting of the ACL*, 114–121.

Pollard, C. (1984) Generalized Context-Free Grammars, Head Grammars and Natural Languages. Ph.D. Thesis, Dept. of Linguistics, Stanford University.

Pratt, V.R. (1975) LINGOL — A Progress Report. *Proc. 4th Int. Joint Conf. on Artificial Intelligence (IJCAI'75)*, 422–428.

Proudian, D. and Pollard, C. (1985) Parsing head-driven phrase structure grammar. *Proc. 23th Ann. Meeting of the ACL*, 167–171.

Rosenkrantz, D.J. and Lewis, P.M. (1970) Deterministic Left Corner Parsing. *Proc. 11th Ann. Symp. on Switching and Automata Theory*, 139–152.

Satta, G. and Stock, O. (1989) Head-Driven Bidirectional Parsing: A Tabular Method. *Proc. Int. Workshop on Parsing Technologies (IWPT'89)*, 43–51.

Sikkel, K. (1993) Parsing Schemata. Ph.D. Thesis, Dept. of Computer Science, University of Twente, Enschede, the Netherlands.

Sikkel, K. and op den Akker, R. (1992) Left-Corner and Head-Corner Chart Parsing. Memoranda Informatica 92-55, University of Twente, Enschede, the Netherlands.

Tomita, M. (1985) *Efficient Parsing for Natural Language.* Kluwer, Boston, Mass.

10. GLR* – AN EFFICIENT NOISE-SKIPPING PARSING ALGORITHM FOR CONTEXT-FREE GRAMMARS

ALON LAVIE AND MASARU TOMITA
School of Computer Science
Carnegie Mellon University

Abstract.

This chapter describes GLR*, a parser that can parse *any* input sentence by ignoring unrecognizable parts of the sentence. Using an efficient algorithm, the parser is capable of finding and parsing a maximal subset of the original input that is parsable, and therefore return the parse with fewest skipped words. The parser returns some parse(s) for any input sentence, unless no part of the sentence can be recognized at all.

Formally, the problem can be defined in the following way: Given a context-free grammar G and a sentence S, find and parse S' - the largest subset of words of S, such that $S' \in L(G)$.

The algorithm described in this chapter is a modification of the Generalized LR (Tomita) parsing algorithm (Tomita, 1986). The parser accommodates the skipping of words by allowing shift operations to be performed from inactive state nodes of the Graph Structured Stack. A heuristic similar to beam search makes the algorithm computationally tractable.

The modified parser, GLR*, has been implemented and integrated with the latest version of the Generalized LR Parser/Compiler (Tomita et al., 1988; Tomita, 1990).

We discuss an application of the GLR* parser to spontaneous speech understanding and present some preliminary tests on the utility of the GLR* parser in such settings.

1. INTRODUCTION

In this chapter, we introduce a technique for substantially increasing the robustness of parsers to two particular types of extra-grammaticality: noise in

H. Bunt and M. Tomita (eds.), Recent Advances in Parsing Technology, 183–200.

the input, and limited grammar coverage. Both phenomena cause a common situation, where the input contains words or fragments that are unparsable. The distinction between these two types of extra-grammaticality is based to a large extent upon whether or not the unparsable fragment, in its context, can be considered grammatical by a linguistic judgment. This distinction may indeed be vague at times, and of limited practical importance.

Our approach to the problem is to enable the parser to overcome these forms of extra-grammaticality by ignoring the unparsable words and fragments and focusing on the maximal subset of the input that is covered by the grammar. Although presented and implemented as an enhancement to the Generalized LR parsing (GLR) paradigm, our technique should be applicable to most phrase-structured based parsing formalisms. However, the efficiency of our parser is due in part to several particular properties of GLR parsing, to which there may not be direct equivalents in other parsing formalisms.

The problem can be formalized in the following way: Given a context-free grammar G and a sentence S, find and parse S' - the largest subset of words of S, such that $S' \in L(G)$.

A naive approach to this problem is to exhaustively list and attempt to parse all possible subsets of the input string. The largest subset can then be selected from among the subsets that are found to be parsable. Such an algorithm is clearly computationally infeasible, since the number of subsets is exponential in the length of the input string. We thus devise an efficient method for accomplishing the same task, and pair it with an efficient search approximation heuristic that maintains runtime feasibility.

The algorithm described in this chapter, which we have named GLR*, is a modification of the Generalized LR (Tomita) parsing algorithm. It has been implemented in Lucid Common Lisp as an updated version of the GLR Parser/Compiler (Tomita, 1986; Tomita, 1990).

There have been several other approaches to robust parsing, most of which have been special purpose algorithms. Some of these approaches have abandoned syntax as a major tool in handling extra-grammaticalities and have focused on domain dependent semantic methods (Carbonell and Hayes, 1984; Ward, 1991.) Other systems have constructed grammar and domain dependent fall-back components to handle extra-grammatical input that causes the main parser to fail (Stallard and Bobrow, 1992; Seneff, 1992).

Our approach can be viewed as an attempt to extract from the input the maximal grammatical structure that is possible, within a domain independent setting. Because the GLR* parsing algorithm is an enhancement to the standard GLR context-free parsing algorithm, all of the techniques and grammars developed for the standard parser can be applied as they are. In particular, the standard LR parsing tables are compiled in advance from the grammar and used "as is" by the parser in runtime. The GLR* parser inherits the benefits of the original parser in terms of ease of grammar development, and, to a large extent, efficiency properties of the parser itself. In the case that the input sentence is by itself grammatical, GLR* returns the exact same parse as the standard GLR parser.

The remaining sections of the chapter are organized in the following way: Section 2 presents an outline of the basic GLR* algorithm itself, followed by a detailed example of the operation of the parser on a simple input string. In section 3 we discuss the search heuristic that is added to the basic GLR* algorithm, in order to ensure its runtime feasibility. We discuss an application of the GLR* algorithm to spontaneous speech understanding, and present some preliminary test results in section 4. Finally, our conclusions and further research directions are presented in section 5.

2. THE GLR* PARSING ALGORITHM

In this section, we provide an informal outline of the basic GLR* parsing algorithm. This algorithm is designed to find and parse all possible grammatical substrings of a given input. As an extension of the GLR parsing algorithm, GLR* uses the same data structures. Particularly, GLR* uses the same parsing tables that are pre-compiled from the grammar. It is only the run-time parsing part of the algorithm that is different.

The key difference between GLR and GLR* is in their use of the Graph Structured Stack (GSS). GLR uses the GSS as an extended version of a stack, where only the active nodes at the top of the stacks are accessible. GLR*, on the other hand, views the GSS as a chart that records partial parses and the state of the parser when they were created. GLR* thus maintains a structure representing the complete GSS throughout the parsing process, and allows access to all nodes in this structure, not merely the active ones.

GLR* pursues the parses of all possible subsets of the input by allowing the parser to skip over words of the input in a controlled way. With an LR style parser that uses lookaheads into the input, allowing the parser to skip over words has implications on the lookaheads used by the parser, which complicates the algorithm considerably. However, a number of studies have demonstrated that with practical natural language grammars, using a GLR parser with extended lookaheads can in fact damage the parser's efficiency (Billot and Lang, 1989). For these reasons, GLR* was designed to work with no lookaheads. It therefore uses LR(0) parsing tables.

GLR* accommodates skipping words of the input string by allowing shift operations to be performed from inactive state nodes in the GSS.

Shifting an input symbol from an inactive state is equivalent to skipping the words of the input that were encountered after the parser reached the inactive state and prior to the current word being shifted. Since the parser is LR(0), reduce operations need not be repeated for skipped words (the reductions do not depend on any lookahead). Information about skipped words is maintained in the symbol nodes that represent parse sub-trees.

2.1. INFORMAL OUTLINE OF THE BASIC GLR* ALGORITHM

We now present an informal high-level outline of the basic GLR* parsing algorithm. Similar to the GLR algorithm, GLR* parses the input on a single left-to-right scan of the input, processing one word at a time. The processing of each input word is called *a stage*. Each stage consists of two main *phases*, a *reduce phase* and a *shift phase*. The reduce phase always precedes the shift phase. The outline of each stage of the algorithm is shown in Figure 1. `RACT(st)` denotes the set of reduce actions defined in the parsing table for state *st*. Similarly, `SACT(st,x)` denotes the shift actions defined for state *st* and symbol x, and `AACT(st,x)` denotes the accept action.

The last stage of the algorithm, in which the end-of-input symbol "$" is processed, is somewhat different. The `READ`, `DISTRIBUTE-REDUCE` and `REDUCE` steps are identical to those of previous stages; a `DISTRIBUTE-ACCEPT` replaces the `DISTRIBUTE-SHIFT` step, however. In the `DISTRIBUTE-ACCEPT` step, accept actions are distributed to all state nodes *st* in the GSS (active and inactive), for which `AACT(st,$)` is true. Pointers to these state nodes are then collected into a list of final state nodes. If this list is not empty, GLR* accepts the input, otherwise, the input is rejected. Finally, a `GET-PARSES` step creates and returns a list of all symbol nodes that are direct descendents of the final state nodes. These symbol nodes are the roots of the parse forest.

2.2. AN EXAMPLE

To clarify how the GLR* algorithm actually works, we present a step by step runtime example. Figure 2 contains a simple natural language grammar that we use for this example. The terminal symbols of the grammar are depicted in lower-case, while the non-terminals are in upper-case. The grammar is compiled into an SLR(0) parsing table, which is displayed in Table 1. Note that since the table is SLR(0), the reduce actions are independent of any lookahead. The actions on states 10 and 11 include both a shift and a reduce.

To understand the operation of the parser, we now follow some steps of the GLR* parsing algorithm on the input `x = det n v n det p n`. This input is ungrammatical due to the second "`det`" token. The maximal par-

```
(1) READ:
    Read the next input token x.

(2) DISTRIBUTE-REDUCE:
    For each active state node st, get the set of reduce
    actions RACT(st) in the parsing table, and attach it
    to the active state node.

(3) REDUCE:
    Perform all reduce actions attached to active state
    nodes. Recursively perform reductions after distributing
    reduce actions to new active state nodes that result
    from previous reductions.

(4) DISTRIBUTE-SHIFT:
    For each state node st in the GSS (active and inactive),
    get SACT(st,x) from the parsing table. If the action is
    defined attach it to the state node.

(5) SHIFT:
    Perform all shift actions attached to state nodes of
    the GSS.

(6) MERGE:
    Merge active state nodes of identical states into a
    single active state node.
```

Figure 1. Outline of a Stage of the Basic GLR* Parsing Algorithm

(1) S → NP VP
(2) NP → det n
(3) NP → n
(4) NP → NP PP
(5) VP → v NP
(6) PP → p NP

Figure 2. A Simple Natural Language Grammar

sable subset of the input in this case is the string that includes all words

	Reduce	Shift					Goto			
State		det	n	v	p	$	NP	VP	PP	S
0		sh3	sh4				2			1
1						acc				
2				sh7	sh8			5	6	
3			sh9							
4	r3									
5	r1									
6	r4									
7		sh3	sh4				10			
8		sh3	sh4				11			
9	r2									
10	r5				sh8				6	
11	r6				sh8				6	

TABLE 1. SLR(0) Parsing Table for Grammar in Figure 1

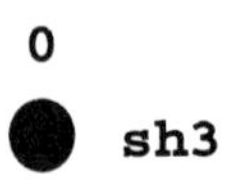

Figure 3. GSS Prior to SHIFT Step of Stage 1

other than this second "det".

In the figures ahead, we graphically display the GSS constructed by the parser in various stages of the parsing process. The following notation is used in these figures:

- An *active* state node is represented by a black circle with the state number indicated above it. Actions attached to the node are marked on the right.
- An *inactive* state node is represented by a clear circle. The state number is indicated above the node and attached actions are indicated above the state number.
- Symbol nodes are represented as squares. The symbol label is marked above the node.
- *Reduce* actions are denoted by **r**n, where n is the index number of the grammar rule.
- *Shift* actions are denoted by **sh**n, where n is the new state into which the parser moves after the shift action.

We follow the GSS of the parser prior to the reduce and shift phases of each stage of the algorithm, while processing the input string. The

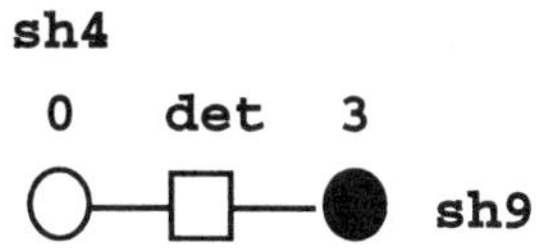

Figure 4. GSS Prior to SHIFT Step of Stage 2

initial GSS contains the single active state node of state 0. Since there are no reduce actions from state 0, the first reduce phase is empty. With the first input token being "det", the DISTRIBUTE-SHIFT step attaches the action "sh3" to state node 0. Figure 3 shows the GSS following this DISTRIBUTE-SHIFT step and just prior to the SHIFT step of stage 1.

In the following SHIFT step, the "det" is shifted, a symbol node is created and the parser moves into a new active state node of state 3. The algorithm then proceeds to the next stage to process the next input token "n". Since there are no reduce actions from state 3, the reduce phase of this stage is empty. In the following DISTRIBUTE-SHIFT step, shift actions are distributed by the algorithm to both the active node of state 3 and the inactive node of state 0. Figure 4 shows the GSS after this step, just prior to the SHIFT step of stage 2.

In the following SHIFT step, the input token "n" is shifted from both state nodes, creating new active state nodes of states 9 and 4. The shifting of the input token "n" from state 0 corresponds to a parse in which the first input token "det" is skipped. Stage 3 begins to process the next input token "v". First, in the DISTRIBUTE-REDUCE step, reduce actions are distributed to the existing active nodes. Figure 5 shows the GSS at this point in time, just prior to the REDUCE step of stage 3.

The following REDUCE step reduces both branches into noun phrases. The two "NP"s are packed together by a local ambiguity packing procedure. In the following DISTRIBUTE-SHIFT step, shift actions for the input token "v" are distributed to all the state nodes. However, in this case, only state 2 allows a shift of "v" (into state 7). The resulting GSS, prior to the SHIFT step of stage 3, is displayed in Figure 6.

The following SHIFT step creates an active state node of state 7. The next stage begins by reading the next input token "n". The state 7 node is the only active node at this point. Since no reduce actions are specified for this state, the following reduce phase is empty. Shift actions are then distributed in the DISTRIBUTE-SHIFT step. The resulting GSS is shown in Figure 7.

The subsequent SHIFT step then shifts the input token "n" from the three nodes that were marked with shift actions. The next input token is "det". Figure 8 shows the GSS just prior to the next REDUCE step and

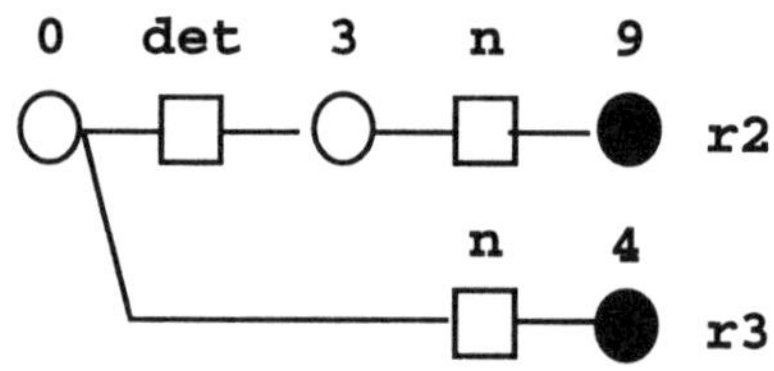

Figure 5. GSS Prior to REDUCE Step of Stage 3

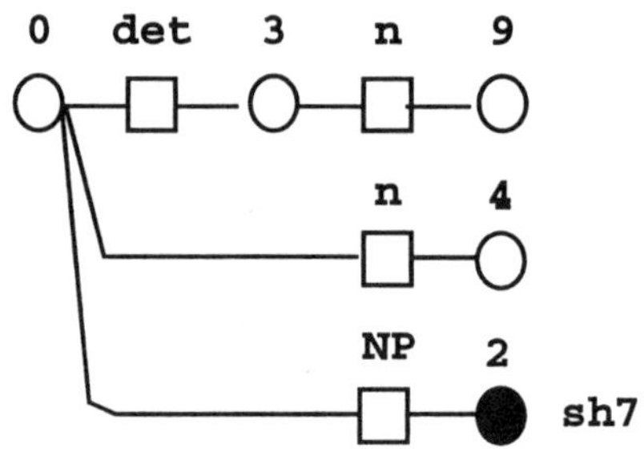

Figure 6. GSS Prior to SHIFT Step of Stage 3

Figure 9 after the `REDUCE` and `DISTRIBUTE-SHIFT` steps, just before the `SHIFT` step. Note that the current input token "`det`" cannot be shifted from either of the two active state nodes at this point. A GLR parser would have thus failed at this point. However, the GLR* algorithm succeeds in distributing the shift actions to two inactive state nodes in this case. The token "`det`" is then shifted from these two nodes.

The next stage then begins, and the input token "p" is read. Since no reduce actions can be distributed to the active state node 3, the reduce phase is empty. `DISTRIBUTE-SHIFT` then distributes shift actions to all state nodes. The GSS at this point is shown in Figure 10. Note that once again, shift actions could not be distributed to the active state node, since the grammar does not allow "p" to follow "`det`". However, a shift action was distributed to the node of state 10. This branch skips over the previous "`det`", and eventually leads to the desired maximal parse.

For the sake of brevity we do not continue to further follow the parsing step by step. The final GSS, following the `DISTRIBUTE-ACCEPT` step, is displayed in Figure 11. Several different parses, corresponding to different subsets of skipped words are actually packed into the "`S`" symbol node seen at the bottom of the figure. The parse that corresponds to the maximal subset of the input is one in which the second "`det`" is the only word that was skipped.

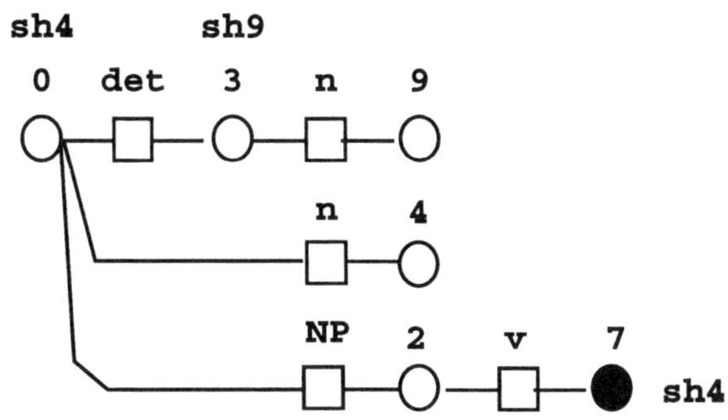

Figure 7. GSS Prior to SHIFT Step of Stage 4

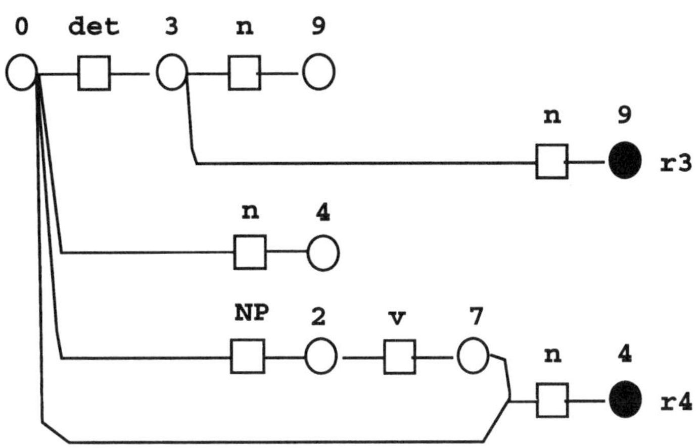

Figure 8. GSS Prior to REDUCE Step of Stage 5

2.3. EFFICIENCY OF THE PARSER

Efficiency of the parser is achieved by a number of different techniques. The most important of these is a sophisticated process of local ambiguity packing and pruning. A local ambiguity is a part of the input sentence that corresponds to a phrase (thus, reducible to some non-terminal symbol of the grammar), and is parsable in more than one way. The process of skipping words creates a large number of local ambiguities. For example, the grammar in Figure 2 allows both determined and undetermined noun phrases (rules 2 and 3). As seen in the example presented earlier, this results in the creation of two different noun phrase symbol nodes for the initial fragment "`det` n". The first node is created for the full phrase after a reduction according to the first rule. A second symbol node is created when the determiner is skipped and a reduction by the second rule takes

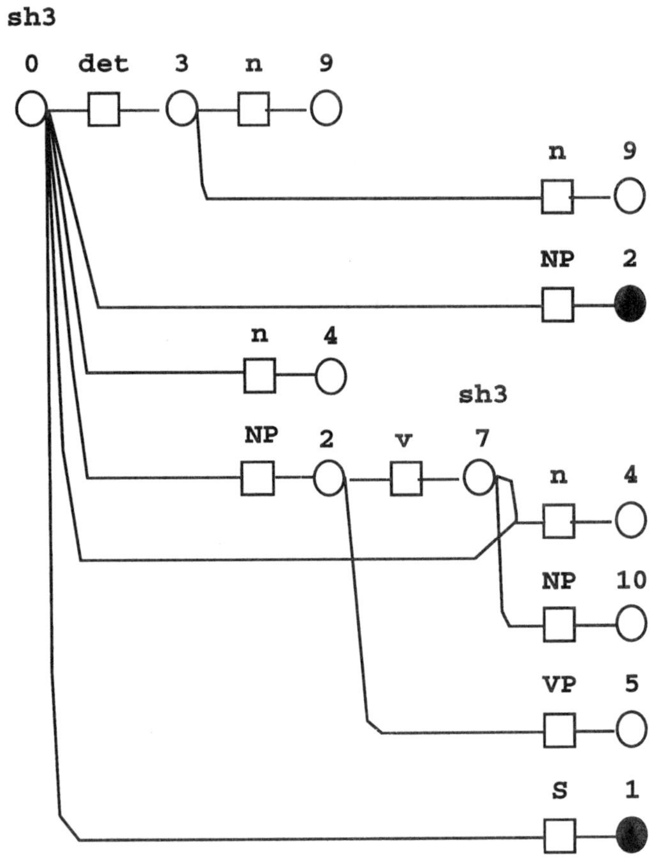

Figure 9. GSS Prior to SHIFT Step of Stage 5

place.

Locally ambiguous symbol nodes are detected as nodes that are surrounded by common state nodes in the GSS. The original GLR parser detects such local ambiguities and packs them into a single symbol node. This procedure was extended in the GLR* parser. Locally ambiguous symbol nodes are compared in terms of the words skipped within them. In cases such as the example described above, where one phrase has more skipped words than the other, the phrase with more skipped words is discarded in favor of the more complete parsed phrase. This operation drastically reduces the number of parses being pursued by the parser.

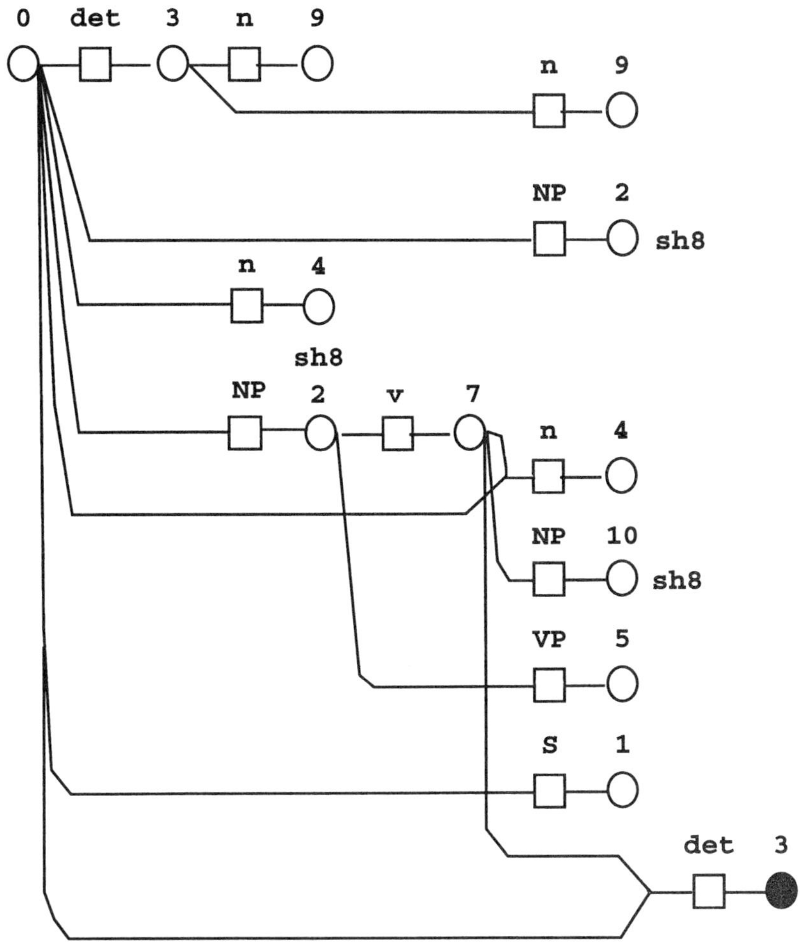

Figure 10. GSS Prior to SHIFT Step of Stage 6

2.4. SELECTING THE BEST MAXIMAL PARSE

The basic GLR* parsing algorithm constructs parses for all parsable subsets of a given input sentence. In principle, we are only interested in finding the maximal parsable subset of the input string (and its parse). However, in many cases there are several distinct maximal parses, each consisting of a different subset of words of the original sentence. Additionally, there are cases where a parse that is not maximal in terms of the number of words skipped may be deemed preferable.

To select the "best" parse from the set of parses returned by the parser, we use a scoring procedure that ranks each of the parses found. We then

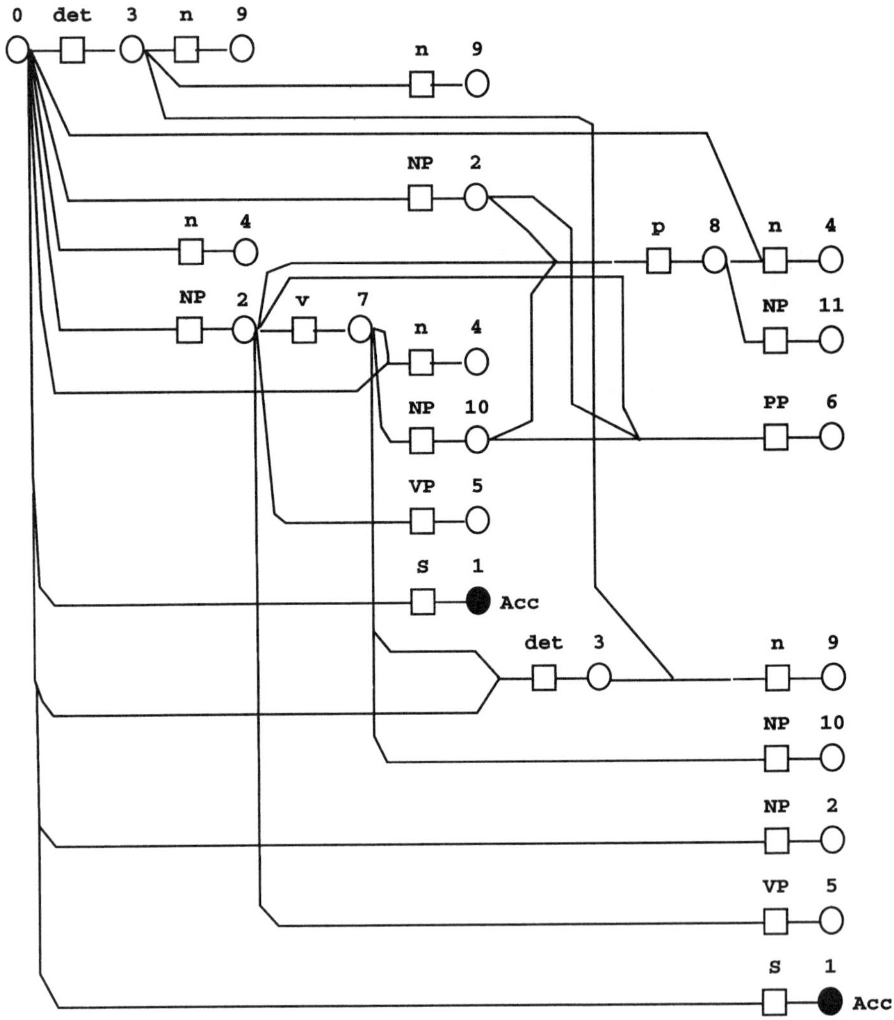

Figure 11. Final GSS after DISTRIBUTE-ACCEPT Step

select the parse that was ranked best [1]. Presently, our scoring procedure is rather simple. It takes into account the number of words skipped and the fragmentation of the parse. Both measures are weighed equally. Thus a parse that skipped one word but parsed the remaining input as a single sentence is preferred over a parse that fragments the input into three sentences, without skipping any input word.

[1]The system will display the n best parses found, where the parameter n is controlled by the user at runtime. By default, we set n to one, and the highest ranking parse is displayed.

We are in the process of enhancing this simple scoring mechanism. We plan on adding to our scoring function several additional heuristic measures that will reflect various syntactic and semantic properties of the parse tree. We will measure the effectiveness of our enhanced scoring function in ranking the parse results by their desirability.

3. THE BEAM SEARCH HEURISTIC

Although implemented efficiently, the basic GLR* parser is still not guaranteed to have a feasible running time. The basic GLR* algorithm described earlier computes parses of all parsable subsets of the original input string, the number of which is potentially exponential in the length of the input string. We are interested in finding parses of maximal subsets of the input string (or almost maximal subsets). We have therefore developed and added to the parser a heuristic that prunes parsing options that are not likely to produce a maximal parse. This process has been traditionally called "beam search".

A direct way of adding a beam search to the parser would be to limit the number of active state nodes pursued by the parser at each stage, and continue processing only active nodes that are most promising in terms of the number of skipped words associated with them. However, the structure of the GSS makes it difficult to associate information on skipped words directly with the state nodes [2]. We have therefore opted to implement a somewhat different heuristic that has a similar effect.

Since the skipping of words is the result of performing shift operations from inactive state nodes of the GSS, our heuristic limits the number of inactive state nodes from which a input symbol is shifted. At each shift stage, shift actions are first distributed to the active state nodes of the GSS. This corresponds to not skipping any words at this stage. If the number of state nodes that allow a shift operation at this point is less than a predetermined constant threshold (the "beam-limit"), then shift operations from inactive state nodes are also considered. Inactive states are processed in an ordered fashion, so that shifting from a more recent state node that will result in fewer skipped words is considered first. Shift operations are distributed to inactive state nodes in this way until the number of shifts distributed reaches the threshold.

Using the beam search heuristic reduces the runtime of the GLR* parser to within a constant factor of the original GLR parser. Although it is not

[2]This is due to the fact that state nodes are merged. Therefore, a state node may be common to several different sub-parses, with different skipped words associated with each sub-parse.

guaranteed to find the desired maximal parsable subset of the input string, our preliminary tests have shown that it works well in practice.

The threshold (beam-limit) itself is a parameter that can be dynamically set to any constant value at runtime. Setting the beam-limit to a value of 0 disallows shifting from inactive states all together, which is equivalent to the original GLR parser. In preliminary experiments that we have conducted (see next section) we have achieved good results with a setting of the beam-limit to values in the range of 5 to 10. There exists a direct tradeoff between the value of the beam-limit and the runtime of the GLR* parser. With a set value of 5, our tests have indicated a runtime that is within a factor of 2-3 times that of the original GLR parser, which amounts to a parse time of only several seconds on sentences that are up to 30 words long.

4. PARSING OF SPONTANEOUS SPEECH USING GLR*

4.1. THE PROBLEM OF PARSING SPONTANEOUS SPEECH

As a form of input, spontaneous speech is full of noise and irrelevances that surround the meaningful words of the utterance. Some types of noise can be detected and filtered out by speech recognizers that process the speech signal. A parser that is designed to successfully process speech recognized input must however be robust to various forms of noise, and be able to weed out the meaningful words from the rest of the utterance.

When parsing spontaneous spoken input that was recognized by a speech recognition system, the parser must deal with three major types of extra-grammaticality:

- Noise due to the spontaneity of the speaker, such as repeated words, false beginnings, stuttering, and filled pauses (i.e. "ah", "um", etc.).
- Ungrammaticality that is due to the language of the speaker, or to the coverage of the grammar.
- Errors of the speech recognizer.

We have conducted two preliminary experiments to evaluate the GLR* parser's ability to overcome the first two types of extra-grammaticality. We are in the process of experimenting with the GLR* parser on actual speech recognized output, in order to test its capabilities in handling errors produced by the speech recognizer.

4.2. PARSING OF NOISY SPONTANEOUS SPEECH

The first test we conducted was intended to evaluate the performance of the GLR* parser on noisy sentences typical of spontaneous speech. The parser was tested on a set of 100 sentences of transcribed spontaneous speech dialogues in a conference registration domain. The input is hand-coded tran-

	Robust Parser
Parsable	99
Unparsable	1
Good/Close Parses	77
Bad Parses	22

TABLE 2. Performance of the GLR* Parser on Spontaneous Speech

scribed text, not processed through any speech recognizer. The grammar used was an upgraded version of a grammar for the conference registration task, developed and used by the JANUS speech-to-speech translation project at CMU [Waibel et al. 1991]. Since the test sentences were drawn from actual speech transcriptions, they were not guaranteed to be covered by the grammar. However, since the test was meant to focus on spontaneous noise, sentences that included verbs and nouns that were beyond the vocabulary of the system were avoided. Also pruned out of the test set were short opening and closing sentences (such as "hello" and "goodbye"). The transcriptions include a multitude of noise in the input. The following example is one of the sentences from this test set:

```
"fckn2_10 /ls/ /h#/ um okay {comma}
then yeah I am disappointed {comma}
*pause* but uh that is okay {period}"
```

The performance results are presented in Table 2. Note that due to the noise contaminating the input, the original parser is unable to parse a single one of the sentences in this test set. The GLR* parser succeeded to return some parse result in all but one of the test sentences. However, since returning a parse result does not by itself guarantee an analysis that adequately reflects the meaning of the original utterance, we reviewed the parse results by hand, and classified them into the categories of "good/close" and "bad" parses. The results of this classification are included in the table.

4.3. GRAMMAR COVERAGE

We conducted a second experiment aimed exclusively on evaluating the ability of the GLR* parser to overcome limited grammar coverage. In this experiment, we compared the results of the GLR* parser with those of the original GLR parser on a common set of sentences using the same grammar. We used the grammar from the spontaneous speech experiment for this test as well. The common test set was a set of 117 sentences from

	Original Parser		Robust Parser	
	number	percent	number	percent
Parsable	71	61%	114	97%
Unparsable	46	39%	3	3%
Good/Close Parses	61	52%	82	70%
Bad Parses	10	9%	32	27%

TABLE 3. Performance of the GLR* Parser vs. the Original Parser

the conference registration task of the JANUS project. These sentences are simple synthesized text sentences. They contain no spontaneous speech noise, and are not the result of any speech recognition processing. Once again, to evaluate the quality of the parse results returned by the parser, we classified the parse results of both parsers by hand into two categories: "good/close parses" and "bad parses". The results of the experiment are presented in Table 3.

The results indicate that using the GLR* parser results in a significant improvement in performance. The percentage of sentences, for which the parser returned good or close parses increased from 52% to 70%, an increase of 18%. Fully 97% of the test sentences (all but 3) are parsable by the GLR* parser, an increase of 36% over the original parser. However, this includes a significant increase (from 9% to 27%) in the number of bad parses found. Thus, fully half of the additional parsable sentences of the set return with parses that may be deemed bad.

The results of the two experiments clearly point to the following problem: Compared with the GLR* parser, the original GLR parser, although fragile, returned results of relatively good quality, when it succeeded in parsing the input. The GLR* parser, on the other hand, will succeed in parsing almost any input, but this parse result may be of little or no value in a significant portion of cases. This indicates a strong need for the development of methods for discriminating between good and bad parse results. We intend to try and develop some effective heuristics to deal with this problem. The problem is also due in part to the ineffectiveness of the simple heuristics currently employed for selecting the best parse result from among the large set of parses returned by the parser. As mentioned earlier, we are currently working on developing more sophisticated and effective heuristics for selecting the best parse.

5. CONCLUSIONS AND FUTURE RESEARCH DIRECTIONS

Motivated by the difficulties that standard syntactic parses have in dealing with extra-grammaticalities, we have developed GLR*, an enhanced version of the standard Generalized LR parser, that can effectively handle two particular problems that are typical of parsing spontaneous speech: noise contamination and limited grammar coverage.

Given a grammar G and and input string S, GLR* finds and parses S', the maximal subset of words of S, such that S' is in the language $L(G)$. The parsing algorithm accommodates the skipping of words and fragments of the input string by allowing shift operations to be performed from inactive states of the GSS (as well as from the active states, as is done by the standard parser). The algorithm is coupled with a beam-search-like heuristic, that controls the process of shifting from inactive states to a limited beam, and maintains computational tractability.

Most other approaches to robust parsing have suffered to some extent from a lack of generality and from being domain dependent. Our approach, although limited to handling only certain types of extra-grammaticality, is general and domain independent. It attempts to maximize the robustness of the parser within a purely grammatical setting. Because the GLR* parsing algorithm is a modification of the standard GLR context-free parsing algorithm, all of the techniques and grammars developed for the standard parser can be applied as they are. In the case that the input sentence is by itself grammatical, GLR* returns the same parse as the standard GLR parser. The techniques used in the enhancement of the standard GLR parser into the robust GLR* parser are in principle applicable to other phrase-structure based parsers.

Our preliminary experiments on the effectiveness of the GLR* parser in handling noise contamination and limited grammar coverage have produced encouraging results. However, they have also pointed out a need for developing effective heuristics that can select the best parse result from a potentially large set of possibilities produced by the parser. Since the GLR* parser is likely to succeed in producing some parse in practically all cases, successful parsing by itself can no longer be an indicator to the value and quality of the parse result. We are therefore developing additional heuristics for evaluating the quality of the selected best parse.

We are in the process of conducting extensive experiments with speech recognized input to evaluate our system and guide its further development. We are also investigating the potential of the GLR* parser in several other application areas and domains.

References

Billot, S. and Lang, B., The Structure of Shared Forests in Ambiguous Parsing. In *Proceedings of the 27th Annual Meeting of the Association for Computational Linguistics (ACL-89)*, Vancouver, BC, Canada, June 1989.

Carbonell, J. G. and Hayes, P. J., Recovery Strategies for Parsing Extragrammatical Language. *Technical Report CMU-CS-84-107*, 1984.

Seneff, S., A relaxation method for understanding spontaneous speech utterances. In *Proceedings of DARPA Speech and Natural Language Workshop*, pages 299–304, February 1992.

Stallard, D. and Bobrow, R., Fragment processing in the DELPHI system. In *Proceedings of DARPA Speech and Natural Language Workshop*, pages 305–310, February 1992.

Tomita, M., Mitamura, T., Musha, H., and Kee, M., The Generalized LR Parser/Compiler - Version 8.1: User's Guide. *Technical Report CMU-CMT-88-MEMO*, 1988.

Tomita, M., *Efficient Parsing for Natural Language.* Kluwer Academic Publishers, Hingham, Ma., 1986.

Tomita, M., The Generalized LR Parser/Compiler - Version 8.4. In *Proceedings of International Conference on Computational Linguistics (COLING-90)*, pages 59–63, Helsinki, Finland, 1990.

Ward, W., Understanding spontaneous speech: The Phoenix system. In *Proceedings of IEEE International Conference on Acoustics, Speech and Signal Processing (ICASSP)*, pages 365–367, April 1991.

11. EVALUATION OF THE TAGGED TEXT PARSER

A PRELIMINARY REPORT

TOMEK STRZALKOWSKI
GE Corporate Research & Development
Schenectady, NY

AND

PETER G. N. SCHEYEN
Department of Computer Science
The University of Western Ontario

Abstract.
TTP, the Tagged Text Parser, is a fast and robust natural language parser specifically designed to process vast quantities of unrestricted text. TTP can analyze written text at the speed below 0.2 sec/sentence, or more than 80 words per second. An important novel feature of TTP is that it is equipped with a skip-and-fit recovery mechanism that allows for fast closing of more difficult sub-constituents after a preset amount of time has elapsed without producing a parse. Although a complete analysis is attempted for each sentence, the parser may occasionally ignore fragments of input to resume 'normal' processing after skipping a few words. These fragments are later analyzed separately and attached as incomplete constituents to the main parse tree. TTP has recently been evaluated against several leading parsers. While no formal numbers were released (a formal evaluation is planned later this year), TTP has performed surprisingly well. The main argument of this chapter is that TTP can provide a substantial gain in parsing speed giving up relatively little in terms of the quality of output it produces. This property allows TTP to be used effectively in parsing large volumes of text.

1. OVERVIEW

Recently, there has been a growing demand for fast and reliable natural language processing tools, capable of performing reasonably accurate syn-

H. Bunt and M. Tomita (eds.), Recent Advances in Parsing Technology, 201–220.

tactic analysis of large volumes of text within an acceptable time. A full sentential parser that produces complete analysis of input, may be considered reasonably fast if the average parsing time per sentence falls anywhere between 2 and 10 seconds. A large volume of text, perhaps a gigabyte or more, would contain as many as 7 million sentences. At the speed of say, 6 sec/sentence, this much text would require well over a year to parse. While 7 million sentences is a lot of text, this much may easily be contained in a fair-sized text database. Therefore, the parsing speed would have to be increased by at least a factor of 10 to make such a task manageable.

In this chapter we describe TTP, a fast and robust natural language parser that can analyze written text and generate regularized parse structures at a speed of below 1 second per sentence. In the experiments conducted on variety of natural language texts, including technical prose, news messages, and newspaper articles, the average parsing time varied between 0.3 sec/sentence and 0.5 sec/sentence, or between 2500 and 4300 words per minute, as we tried to find an acceptable compromise between parser's speed and precision.[1] Original experiments were performed within an information retrieval system with the recall/precision statistics used to measure effectiveness of the parser.

In the second part of this chapter, the linguistic accuracy of TTP is discussed based on the partial results of a quantitative evaluation of its output using the Parseval method (Harrison *et al.*, 1991). This method calculates three scores of 'closeness' as it compares the bracketed parse structures returned by the parser against a pre-selected standard. These scores are: the crossings rate which indicates how many constituents in the candidate parse are incompatible with those in the standard; recall which is the percentage of candidate constituents found in the standard; and precision which specifies the percentage of standard constituents in the candidate parse. Parseval may also be used to compare the performance of different parsers. In comparison with NYU's Proteus parser, for example, which is on average two levels of magnitude slower than TTP, the crossing score was only 6 to 27% higher for TTP, with recall 13% lower, and approximately the same precision for both parsers.

In addition we discuss the relationships between allotted parse time per sentence, the average parsing time, crossings rate, and recall and precision scores.

[1]These results were obtained in early 1993 on a Sun's SparcStation 2; more recent results of less than 0.2 sec/sentence or more than 80 words per second were obtained when parsing 3.3 GBytes of Tipster collection on a Sun's SparcStation 10.

2. INTRODUCTION TO TAGGED TEXT PARSER

It has long been assumed that in order to gain speed, one may have to trade in some of the parser's accuracy. For example, we may have to settle for partial parsing that would recognize only selected grammatical structures (e.g. noun phrases; Ruge *et al.*, 1991), or would avoid making difficult decisions (e.g. pp-attachment; Hindle, 1983). Much of the overhead and inefficiency comes from the fact that the lexical and structural ambiguity of natural language input can only be dealt with using limited context information available to the parser. Partial parsing techniques have been used with a considerable success in processing large volumes of text, for example AT&T's Fidditch (Hindle *et al.*, 1991) parsed 13 million words of Associated Press news messages, while MIT's parser (De Marcken, 1990) was used to process the 1 million word Lancaster/Oslo/Bergen (LOB) corpus. In both cases, the parsers were designed to do partial processing only, that is, they would never attempt a complete analysis of certain constructions, such as the attachment of pp-adjuncts, subordinate clauses, or coordinations. This kind of partial analysis may be sufficient in some applications because of a relatively high precision of identifying correct syntactic dependencies, for example Church *et al.* (1990) used partial parses generated by Fidditch to study word co-occurrence patterns in syntactic contexts. On the other hand, applications involving information extraction or retrieval from text will usually require more accurate parsers.

An alternative is to create a parser that would attempt to produce a complete parse, and would resort to partial or approximate analysis only under exceptional conditions such as an extra-grammatical input or a severe time pressure. Encountering a construction that it couldn't handle, the parser would first try to produce an approximate analysis of the difficult fragment, and then resume normal processing for the rest of the input. The outcome is a kind of 'fitted' parse, reflecting a compromise between the actual input and grammar-encoded preferences. One way to accomplish this is to adopt the following procedure: (1) close (reduce) the obstructing constituent (one which is being currently parsed), then possibly reduce a few of its parent constituents, removing corresponding productions from further consideration, until a production is reactivated for which a continuation is possible; (2) jump over the intervening material so as to restart processing of the remainder of the sentence using the newly reactivated production.

As an example, consider the following sentence where the highlighted fragment is likely to cause problems, and may be better off ignored in the first pass:

"The method is illustrated by the automatic construction of both re-

> *cursive and iterative programs operating on natural numbers, lists, and trees, in order to construct a program satisfying certain specifications* a theorem induced by those specifications is proved, *and the desired program is extracted from the proof.*"

Assuming that the parser now reads the article 'a' following the string 'certain specifications', it may proceed to reduce the current NP, then SI → 'to'+V+NP, SI → SA, SA → NP+V+NP+SA, until finally S → S+'and'+S is reached on the stack. Subsequently, the parser skips input to find 'and', then resumes normal processing. The key point here is that TTP decides (or is forced) to reduce incomplete constituents rather than to backtrack or otherwise select an alternative analysis. However, this is done only after the parser is thrown into the panic mode, which in case of TTP is induced by the time-out signal. In other words, while there is still time TTP will proceed in regular top-down fashion until the time-out signal is received. Afterwards, for some productions early reduction will be forced and fragments of input will be skipped if necessary. If this action does not produce a parse within a preset time (which is usually much longer than the original 'regular' parsing time), the second time-out signal is generated which forces the parser to finish even at the cost of introducing dummy constituents into the parse tree. The skipped-over fragments of input are quickly processed by a simple phrasal analyzer, and then attached to the main parse tree at the points where they were deleted.

Figure 1 illustrates an example parse structure returned by TTP (note that "(vrbtm X)" surround all un-parsed tokens in the input).

As may be expected, this kind of action involves a great deal of indeterminacy which, in case of natural language strings, is compounded by the high degree of lexical ambiguity. If the purpose of this skip-and-fit technique is to get the parser smoothly through even the most complex strings, the amount of additional backtracking caused by the lexical level ambiguity is certain to defeat it. Without lexical disambiguation of input, the parser's performance will deteriorate, even if the skipping is limited only to certain types of adverbial adjuncts. The most common cases of lexical ambiguity are those of a plural noun (nns) vs. a singular verb (vbz), a singular noun (nn) vs. a plural or infinitive verb (vbp,vb), and a past tense verb (vbd) vs. a past participle (vbn), as illustrated in the following example.

> "*The notation used* (vbn or vbd?) *explicitly associates* (nns or vbz?) *a data structure* (vb or nn?) *shared* (vbn or vbd?) *by concurrent processes* (nns or vbz?) *with operations defined* (vbn or vbd?) *on it.*

We use a stochastic tagger to process the input text prior to parsing. The tagger, developed at BBN (Meteer *et al.*, 1991) is based upon a bi-gram model and it selects most likely tag for a word given co-occurrence

Sentence:

Mrs. Hills said that the U.S. is still concerned about "disturbing developments in Turkey and continuing slow progress in Malaysia."

TTP Approximate Parse:

```
(sent
   (np
      (name mrs . hills))
   (vp
      (verb said)
      (thats
         (compl that)
         (sent
            (np
               (t_pos the)
               (name u.s.))
            (vp
               (verb
                  is
                  (adv still))
               (venpass
                  (verb concerned)))))
      ((vrbtm about)
         (vrbtm ")
         (((np
            (adj disturbing)
            (n developments)))
            (pp
            (prep in)
            (np
               (np
                  (name turkey))
               and
               (np
                  (a_pos_v continuing)
                  (adj slow)
                  (n progress))))
            (pp
            (prep in)
            (np
               (name malaysia .))))
         (vrbtm "))))
```

Figure 1. An example TTP parse

probabilities computed from a relatively small training set. The input to TTP looks more like the following:

> "The/dt notation/nn used/vbn explicitly/rb associates/vbz a/dt data/nns structure/nn shared/vbn by/in concurrent/jj processes/nns with/in operations/nns defined/vbn on/in it/pp ./."

In a 'normal' operation, TTP produces a regularized representation of each parsed sentence that reflects the sentence's logical structure. This representation may differ considerably from a standard parse tree, in that the constituents get moved around (e.g., de-passivization), and the phrases are organized recursively around their head elements. However, for the purpose of the evaluation with Parseval an 'input-bracketing' version has been created. In this version the skipped-over material is simply left unbracketed.

As the parsing proceeds, each sentence receives a new slot of time during which its parse is to be returned. The amount of time allotted to any particular sentence can be regulated to obtain an acceptable compromise between parser's speed and accuracy. In our experiments we found that 0.5 sec/sentence time slot was appropriate for the Wall Street Journal articles (the average length of the sentence in our WSJ collection is 17 words).[2] We must note here that giving the parser more time per sentence doesn't always mean that a better (more accurate) parse will be obtained. For complex or extra-grammatical structures we are likely to be better off if we do not allow the parser wander around for too long: the most likely interpretation of an unexpected input is probably the one generated early (the grammar rule ordering enforces some preferences). In fact, our experiments indicate that as the 'normal' parsing time is extended, the accuracy of the produced parse increases at an ever slowering pace, peaking for a certain value, then declining slightly to eventually stabilize at a constant level. This final level-off indicates, we believe, an inherent limit in the coverage of the underlying grammar.

3. THE TTP TIME-OUT MECHANISM

The time-out mechanism is implemented using a straightforward parameter passing and is limited to only a subset of nonterminals used by the grammar. Suppose that X is such a nonterminal, and that it appears on the right-hand side of a production $S \rightarrow X\ Y\ Z$. The set of "starters" is computed for Y, which consists of the word tags that can occur as the left-most constituent of Y. This set is passed as a parameter while the parser attempts to recognize

[2] For parsing the Tipster collection we used 0.3 sec timeout. Except for the Wall Street Journal, this collection also contains material from Associated Press newswire, Federal Register, Ziff Communications periodicals, Department of Energy abstracts, San Jose Mercury News daily, and U.S. Patents.

X in the input. If X is recognized successfully within a preset time, then the parser proceeds to parse a Y, and nothing else happens. On the other hand, if the parser cannot determine whether there is an X in the input or not, that is, it neither succeeds nor fails in parsing X before being timed out, the unfinished X constituent is closed (reduced) with a partial parse, and the parser is restarted at the closest element from the starters set for Y that can be found in the remainder of the input. If Y rewrites to an empty string, the starters for Z to the right of Y are added to the starters for Y and both sets are passed as a parameter to X. As an example consider the following clauses in TTP:

```
sentence(P) :-
    assertion([],P).
assertion(SR,P) :-
    clause(SR,P1),
    s_coord(SR,P1,P).
clause(SR,P) :-
    sa([pdt,dt,cd,pp,ppS,jj,jjr,jjs,nn,nns,np,nps],P2),
    subject([vbd,vbz,vbp],P1),
    verbphrase(SR,P1,P2,P).
thats(SR,P) :-
    that,
    assertion(SR,P).
```

In the above code, P, P1, and P2 represent partial parse structures, while SR is a set of starter word tags where the parsing will resume should the present nonterminal be timed-out. First arguments to 'assertion', 'sa', and 'subject' are also sets of starter tags. In the 'clause' production above, a (finite) clause rewrites into a left sentence adjunct ('sa'), a 'subject', and a 'verbphrase'. If 'sa' is aborted before its evaluation is complete, the parser will jump over some elements of the unparsed portion of the input looking for a word that could begin a subject phrase: a pre-determiner (pdt), a determiner (dt), a count word (cd), a pronoun (pp,ppS), an adjective (jj, jjr, jjs), a noun (nn, nns), or a proper name (np, nps). Likewise, when 'subject' is timed out, the parser will restart with 'verbphrase' at either vbz, vbd or vbp (finite forms of a verb). Note that if 'verbphrase' is timed out both 'verbphrase' and 'clause' will be closed, and the parser will restart at an element of set SR passed down to 'clause' from assertion. Note also that in the top-level production for a sentence the starter set for 'assertion' is initialized to be empty: if the failure occurs at this level, no continuation is possible.

The forced reduction and skip-over are carried out through special productions that are activated only after a preset amount of time has elapsed since the start of parsing. For example, 'subject' is defined as follows:

```
subject(SR,PG) :-
    timed_out,!,
    skip(SR),
    store(PG).
subject(SR,P) :-
    noun_phrase(SR,P).
```

When a non-terminal is timed out and the parser jumps over a non-zero length fragment of input, it is assumed that the skipped part was some sub-constituent of the reduced non-terminal (e.g., subject). Accordingly, a place holder (PG) is left in the parse structure under the node dominated by this non-terminal. This placeholder will be later filled by some material recovered from the skipped-over fragment which is put aside by store(PG). In the bracketing-only version of TTP unparsed fragments are placed verbatim within the outmost bracket of the timed-out constituent, e.g.,

```
(S
    (NP we)
    (VP
        (V receive)
        (NP more pro letters
            (VRBTM than) (VRBTM con))
    ...
    ))
```

Note that (VRBTM *) brackets are invisible to the evaluation program, as will be explained in the next section.

There are a few caveats in the skip-and-fit parsing strategy just outlined which warrant further explanation. In particular, the following problems must be resolved to assure parser's effectiveness:

1. how to select starter tags for non-terminals, and
2. how to select non-terminals at which input skipping can occur.

Obviously some tags are more likely to occur at the left-most position of a constituent than others. Theoretically, a subject phrase can start with a word tagged with any element from the following list (still not a complete list): pdt (pre-determiner), dt (determiner), cd (numerical), jj, jjr, jjs (adjective), pp, ppS (pronoun), nn, nns (noun), np, nps (name), vbg, vbn (participle), rb (adverb), in (preposition). In practice, however, we may select only a subset of these, as shown in the 'clause' production above. Although we now risk missing the left boundary of the subject phrase in some sentences, while skipping an adjunct to their left, most cases are still covered and the chances of making a serious misinterpretation of input are significantly lower.

On the other hand certain adjunct phrases may be of little interest, possibly because of their typically low information content, and we may choose to ignore them altogether. Thus in the 'ntovo' object string production below (where 'to' is the tag of word 'to'):

```
ntovo(SR,[P—PSA]) :-
    subject([to],P1),
    sa([to],PSA),
    tovo(SR,P1,P).
```

'sa' (sentential adjunct) material is skipped entirely if 'subject' is timed out. We must note here that this scheme will behave as expected only if there is no other 'to' tag between the skip point and the beginning of 'tovo' phrase, e.g.,

"Financial planners often urge
investors to diversify ... "

└── NTOVO ──┘

N(P) + TO + V(P)

When this is not the case, skipping may have to be redone. As an example, consider the following fragment:

"... *urge*
those flying to New York to take ... "

└─── NTOVO ──────────┘

└─── NP ─────────┘ to └ VP ┘

If 'subject' of 'ntovo' is timed-out, the parser will first jump to "to (New York)", and only after failing to find a verb ("New") will redo skip in order to take a longer leap to the next 'to'. This example shows that a great deal of indeterminacy still remains even in the tagged text, and that the final selection of skip points and starter tags may require some training.

A related problem is the selection of non-terminals that can be allowed to time out. This is normally restricted to various less-than-essential adjunct-type constituents, including adverbials, some prepositional phrases, relative clauses, etc. Major sentential constituents such as subject or verb phrase should not be timed (though their sub-constituents can), or we risk to generate very uninteresting parses. Note that a timed-out phrase is not lost, but its links with the main parse structure (e.g., traces in relative clauses) may be severed, though not necessarily beyond repair. Another important restriction is to avoid introduction of spurious dummy phrases, for example, in order to force an object on a transitive verb. The time-out points must be placed in such a way that while the above principles are observed, the parser is guaranteed a swift exit when in the skip-and-fit mode. In other words, we do not want the parser to get trapped in inadvertently created dead ends, hopelessly trying to fit the parse.

As an additional safety valve, a second time-out signal can be issued to catch any processes still operating beyond a reasonable time after the first time-out. In this case, a relaxed skipping protocol is adopted with skips to only major constituents, or outright to the end of the input. Dummy constituents may be introduced if necessary to close a parse fast. This, however, happens rarely if the parser is designed carefully. While parsing 4 million sentences (85 million words) of Wall Street Journal articles, the second time-out was invoked less than 10 times.

4. PARSER EVALUATION WITH PARSEVAL

Parseval is a quantitative method of parser evaluation which compares constituent bracketings in the parse's output with a set of 'standard' bracketings. A parse is understood as a system of labeled brackets imposed upon the input sentence, with no changes in either word order or form permitted. Using three separate scores of 'crossings', recall and precision assigned to each parse (and explained in more detail below) the measure determines parser's accuracy indicating how close it is to the standard. For the purpose of this evaluation Penn Treebank bracketings have been adopted as standard.

In the rest of this section we demonstrate how Parseval typically processes a sentence. The example used here is sentence 337 from Brown Corpus, one of the set of 50 sentences used in initial evaluation. In this example, the sentence has been processed with TTP time-out set at 700 msecs. Figure 2 shows the parse as output by TTP.

The first two steps that the evaluator takes is to delete certain kinds of lesser constituents. This is done because of a great variety of treatment of these items across different parsers, and their relatively minor role in deciding correctness of a parse. The first phase deletes the following types of token strings from the parse:

1. Auxiliaries – "might have been understood" → "understood"
2. "Not" – "should not have come" → "come"
3. Pre-infinitival "to" – "not to answer" → "answer"
4. Null categories – (NP ()) → (NP)
5. Possessive endings – "Lori's mother" → "Lori mother"
6. Word-external punctuation (quotes, commas, periods, dashes, etc.)

Sentence 337

"Mr. Nixon, for his part, would oppose intervention in Cuba without specific provocation."

TTP PARSE (lispified)

```
(S
  (NP (NAME mr. nixon))
  (VP
     ,
     (PP
        (PREP for)
        (NP (T_POS (POSS his)) (N part)))
     ,
     (VERB would)
     (VO
        (VERB oppose)
        (NP (N intervention)))
     (PP
        (PREP in)
        (NP (N cuba)))
     (PP
        (PREP without)
        (NP (ADJ specific) (N provocation))))
  .)
```

Figure 2. TTP parse with a time-out of 700 msecs

The revised parse of sentence 337 is shown in figure 3.

Subsequently, certain pairs of brackets are recursively deleted, namely those that enclose either a single constituent or word, or an empty string. Figure 4 illustrates sentence 337 after this phase.

Now the parse can be compared against the standard, which is shown in figure 5.

We may note that there are several differences between the two structures: the most apparent is that various PP phrases are made part of VP in one of them while not in the other. In addition, TTP's VO constituent creates a "crossing" fault with respect to the standard, as it encompasses neither a subset nor a superset of any standard bracketing.

...(VO oppose intervention) ...

...(VP oppose (NP intervention ...

```
(S
   (NP (NAME mr nixon))
   (VP
      (PP
         (PREP for)
         (NP (T_POS (POSS his)) (N part)))
      (VERB )
      (VO
         (VERB oppose)
         (NP (N intervention)))
      (PP
         (PREP in)
         (NP (N cuba)))
      (PP
         (PREP without)
         (NP (ADJ specific) (N provocation))))
   )
```

Figure 3. TTP parse after first phase in Parseval evaluation

```
(S
   (NP mr nixon)
   (VP
      (PP for
         (NP his part))
      (VO oppose intervention)
      (PP in cuba)
      (PP without
         (NP specific provocation))))
```

Figure 4. TTP parse after second phase in Parseval evaluation

```
(S
   (NP mr nixon)
   (PP for
      (NP his part))
   (VP oppose
      (NP intervention
         (PP in cuba)
         (PP without
            (NP specific provocation)))))
```

Figure 5. Standard parse of sentence 337

Other measures of closeness between these two structures are recall and precision, defined as follows:

$$recall = \frac{\#\ standard\ constituents\ in\ candidate}{\#\ constituents\ in\ standard}$$

$$prec = \frac{\#\ candidate\ constituents\ in\ standard}{\#\ constituents\ in\ candidate}$$

In the current example, both the candidate and the standard parses have 9 constituents. Seven of these constituents are common to one another, and there is one crossing fault. Therefore this TTP parse is evaluated as follows:

crossings	=	1
recall	=	77.78%
precision	=	77.78%

5. EVALUATION OF TTP

Two sets of evaluations were performed with TTP. In the first set, 50 sentences from Brown Corpus were used. In the series of runs with time-out value ranging from 100 to 2500 msecs, TTP scores varied from average crossing rate of 1.38 (for 100 msec time-out) to 0.82 (at 1700 msec); recall from the low of 59.37 (at 1800 msec!) to 62.02 (at 500 msec); and precision from 70.52 (at 100 msec) to 77.06 (at 1400 msec). The mean scores were: crossing rate 0.92, recall 60.57% and precision 75.69%. These scores reflect both the quality of the parser as well as the differences between grammar systems used in TTP and in preparing the standard parses. For example, average recall scores for hand parsed Brown sentences varied from 79% (for LSP grammar on which TTP is based; Sager, 1981) to 97%, with the average of 94%. We also plotted average parsing time per sentence for various time-out values. This is summarized in table 1 (timing values are in milliseconds). These results were obtained on Sun SparcStationELC.

The second set of tests involved 100 sentences from Wall Street Journal. Since WSJ sentences were usually longer and more complex than the 50 Brown sentences, we used time-outs of 250 msecs and more. Table 2 summarizes average crossings, recall and precision scores for TTP. Note that the performance peaks at time-out 500 and 750 msecs. These results are for a Sun SparcStation2.

T/O	C	R	P	TIME
100	1.38	61.54	70.52	160
200	1.24	60.10	72.05	200
500	1.00	62.02	75.22	300
600	0.88	62.02	76.33	316
1000	0.90	61.78	76.49	380
1500	0.86	59.86	75.91	420
2000	0.86	59.37	76.00	460
2500	0.82	60.34	76.76	490
Mean	0.92	60.57	75.69	

TABLE 1. Summary of Parseval results on the Brown Corpus

T/O	C		R	P	TIME
	TOT	PER			
250	71	2.91	55.08	61.50	305
500	70	2.60	55.22	63.16	438
600	72	2.68	54.20	62.51	477
750	69	2.57	55.22	63.85	540
1500	68	2.60	54.57	64.01	797
30000	59	2.17	51.79	66.26	2930

TABLE 2. Summary of Parseval results on 100 sentences from the WSJ

The above statistics can be compared with those obtained parsing the same set of 100 sentences with a 'regular' parser: NYU's Proteus Parser (Grishman, 1990). Both parsers are based on the same grammar system (although Proteus grammar provides a much better coverage of English). Table 3 summarizes these results.

One should note that the per-sentence crossing ratio and recall score indicate how good the parser is at discovering the correct bracketings (precision is less useful as it already includes crossing errors). Clearly, both the crossing ratio and precision improves as we let the parser take more time to complete its job. On the other hand, the recall, after an initial increase, declines somewhat for larger values of time-out. This, we believe, points to the limitations of the underlying grammar used in these tests: initial correct hypotheses (enforced by preferences within the parser) are replaced

Proteus Statistics

C TOT	C PER	R	P	TIME
56	2.34	63.74	62.87	24000

TTP Best Statistics

T/O	C TOT	C PER	R	P	T
500	70	2.60	55.22	63.16	438
% change					
	+25%	+11	-13	+0.4	
750	69	2.57	55.22	63.85	540
% change					
	+23%	+9.8	-13	+1.5	
30000	59	2.17	51.79	66.26	2930
% change					
	+5%	-7	-19	+5	

TABLE 3. Comparison between TTP and Proteus, a 'traditional' parser.

by less likely ones when the parser is forced to backtrack.

6. CONCLUSIONS

At present, TTP is a part of a natural language information retrieval system. Along with a stochastic part-of-speech tagger, morpho-lexical stemmer and phrase extractor, it constitutes the linguistic pre-processor built on top of the statistical information retrieval system PRISE, developed at NIST. During the database creation process, TTP is used to parse documents so that appropriate indexing phrases can be identified with a high degree of accuracy. Both phrases and single-word terms are selected, along with their immediate syntactic context which is used to generate semantic word associations and create a domain-specific level-1 thesaurus.

For the TREC-1 conference, concluded in November 1992, a total of 500 MBytes of Wall Street Journal articles have been parsed, which is approximately 4 million sentences. It took about 2 workstation-weeks to process this material. While the quality of parsing was less than perfect, it was nonetheless quite good. In various experiments with the final database we noted an increase of retrieval precision over the purely statistical base system that ranged from 6% (notable) to more than 13% (significant).

For the recent TREC-3 conference of November 1994, we processed 3.3 GBytes of Tipster collection material, extracting both single-word indexing terms as well as phrases and names.

Further experiments have shown that phrasal terms, when properly weighted relative to other terms, can improve the retrieval precision in excess of 20% when compared with the performance of statistical indexing schemes. Therefore, at least in applications such as document retrieval or information extraction, TTP-level parsing appears quite sufficient, while its high speed and robustness makes an otherwise impractical task of linguistic text processing quite manageable and, moreover, at par with other statistical parts of the system.

Further development of TTP will continue, especially expanding its base grammar to bring the coverage closer to Sager's LSP or Grishman's Proteus. We are also investigating ways of automated generation of skipping parsers like TTP out of any full grammar parser, a process we call 'ttpization'.

TTP is available for research purposes; it has been used in a variety of applications ranging from information retrieval to optical readers to speech recognition support.

Acknowledgements

This article is based upon work supported by the Advanced Research Projects Agency under Contract N00014-90-J-1851 from the Office of Naval Research, under Contract N00600-88-D-3717 from PRC Inc., under ARPA's Tipster Phase-2 Contract 94-FI57900-000, and the National Science Foundation under Grant IRI-93-02615. We also acknowledge a support from the Canadian Institute for Robotics and Intelligent Systems (IRIS). The PRISE information retrieval system used in this project has been developed at NIST. We would like to thank Donna Harman and Will Rogers for valuable assistance. We would also like to thank Ralph Weischedel, Heidi Fox and Constantine Papageorgiou of BBN for providing and assisting in the use of the part of speech tagger.

References

Church, K.W. and Hanks, P. (1990) Word association norms, mutual information, and lexicography. *Computational Linguistics*, Vol. 16 No. 1, MIT Press, 22–29.

De Marcken, C.G. (1990) Parsing the LOB corpus. *Proceedings of the 28th Meeting of the ACL*, Pittsburgh, PA. , 243–251.

Grishman, R. (1990) *Proteus Parser Reference Manual.* Proteus Project Memorandum 4-C, Courant Institute of Mathematical Sciences, Courant Institute of Mathematical Sciences, New York University.

Harrison, P., Abney, S., Black, E., Flickinger, D., Gdaniec, C., Grishman, R., Hindle, D., Ingria, R., Marcus, M., Santorini, B. and Strzalkowski, T. (1991) Evaluating Syntax Performance of Parser/Grammars of English. *Natural Language Processing Systems Evaluation Workshop*, Berkeley, CA., 71–78.

Hindle, D. (1983) *User manual of Fidditch, a deterministic parser.* Naval Research Laboratory Technical Memorandum 7590-142.

Hindle, D. and Rooth M. (1991) Structural Ambiguity and Lexical Relations. *Proceedings of the 29th Meeting of the ACL*, Berkeley, CA., 229–236.

Meteer, M., Schwartz R., and Weischedel, R. (1991) Studies in Part of Speech Labeling. *Proceedings of the 4th DARPA Speech and Natural Language Workshop*, Morgan-Kaufman, San Mateo, CA., 331–336.

Ruge, G., Schwarz, C., Warner, A.J. (1991) Effectiveness and Efficiency in Natural Language Processing for Large Amounts of Text. *Journal of the ASIS*, Vol. 42 No. 6, 450–456.

Sager, N. (1981) *Natural Language Information Processing.* Addison-Wesley.

Strzalkowski, T. and Vauthey, B. (1992) Information Retrieval Using Robust Natural Language Processing. *Proceedings of the 30th ACL Meeting*, Newark, DE, June–July, 104–111.

Strzalkowski, T. (1992) TTP: A Fast and Robust Parser for Natural Language. *Proceedings of COLING-92*, Nantes, France, July 23–28.

Strzalkowski, T. (1993) Natural Language Processing in Large-Scale Text Retrieval Tasks. *First Text Retrieval Conference (TREC-1)*, NIST Special Publication 500-207, 173–188

Strzalkowski, T. and Perez-Carballo, J. (1994) Recent Developments in Natural Language Text Retrieval. *Second Text Retrieval Conference (TREC-2)*, NIST Special Publication 500-217, 123–136.

Strzalkowski, T. (1995) Natural Language Information Retrieval. *Information Processing and Management*, Vol. 31 No. 3, 397–417.

A. APPENDIX: Example Parses Produced by TTP

All sentences in the examples below are from Wall Street Journal sample. Parses obtained at 750 msecs time-out on Sun SparcStation2.

Sentence:

Mr. McGovern, 63, had been under intense pressure from the board to boost Campbell's mediocre performance to the level of other food companies.

TTP PARSE:

```
((sent
  (np
    (name mr . mcgovern)
    (rn
      (((punct ,))
        (appos
          (np
            (count 63)))
        ,)))
  (vp
    (verb had)
    (veno
      (verb been)
      ((pp
        (prep under)
        (np
          (adj intense)
          (n pressure))))
      ((pp
        (prep from)
        (np
          (t_pos the)
          (n board))))
      (tovo
        (prep to)
        (tvp
          (verb boost)
          (np
            (t_pos
              (poss
                ((name campbell))
                's))
            (adj mediocre)
            (n performance))
          ((pp
            (prep to)
            (np
              (t_pos the)
              (n level)
              (rn
                (pp
                  (prep of)
                  (np
                    (adj other)
                    (n_pos
                      (np
                        (n food)))
                    (n companies))))))))))))
  .)
```

CROSSINGS: 1
RECALL : 86.67%
PRECISION: 81.25%

Sentence:

Any money in excess of $40 million collected from the fees in fiscal 1990 would go to the Treasury at large.

TTP PARSE:

```
((sent
  (np
    (t_pos any)
    (n money))
  (vp
    ((pp
      (prep in)
      (np
        (n excess)
        (rn
          (pp
            (prep of)
            (np
              (n $ 40 million)
              (rn
                (rn_wh
                  (venpass
                    (verb collected)
                    ((pp
                      (prep from)
                      (np
                        (t_pos the)
                        (n fees))))
                    ((pp
                      (prep in)
                      (np
                        (count
                          fiscal 1990))))))))))))
    (verb would)
    (vo
      (verb go)
      (pp
        (prep to)
        (np
          (t_pos the)
          (n treasury))))
    ((pp
      (prep at)
      (np
        (n large))))))
  .)
```

CROSSINGS: 7
RECALL : 50.00%
PRECISION: 47.06%

Sentence:

RJR Nabisco Inc. and American Brands Inc. say they have no plans to follow Philip Morris's lead.

TTP PARSE:

```
((sent
  (np
    (np
      (name rjr nabisco inc .))
      and
      (np
        (name american brands inc .)))
  (vp
    (verb say)
    (thats
      (compl ())
      (sent
        (np
          (n they))
        (vp
          (verb have)
          (np
            (t_pos no)
            (n plans)
            (rn
              (rn_wh
                (tovo
                  (prep to)
                  (tvp
                    (verb follow)
                    (np
                      (t_pos
                        (poss
                          ((name
                              philip
                              morris))
                          's))
                      (n lead))))))))))))
 .)
```

CROSSINGS: 0
RECALL : 100%
PRECISION: 100%

Sentence:

All three major creditors – the IRS, Minpeco and Manufacturers Hanover – voted against and effectively doomed a reorganization plan proposed by Mr. Hunt.

TTP PARSE:

```
(((np
    (t_pos all)
    (count three)
    (adj major)
    (n creditors)))
  (vrbtm -)
  ((np
      (t_pos the)
      (name irs)))
  (vrbtm ,)
  ((np
      (name minpeco)))
  (vrbtm and)
  ((np
      (name manufacturers hanover)))
  (vrbtm -)
  (vrbtm voted)
  (vrbtm against)
  (vrbtm and)
  (vrbtm effectively)
  (wh_rel
      (venpass
        (verb doomed)))
  ((np
      (t_pos a)
      (n_pos
        (np
          (n reorganization)))
      (n plan)
      (rn
        (rn_wh
          (venpass
            (verb proposed)
            (pp
              (prep by)
              (np
                (name mr . hunt))))))))
 .)
```

CROSSINGS: 0
RECALL : 57.14%
PRECISION: 100.00%

Sentence:

The Health Insurance Association of America, an insurers' trade group, acknowledges that stiff competition among its members to insure businesses likely to be good risks during the first year of coverage has aggravated the problem in the small-business market.

TTP PARSE:

```
((sent
 (np
  (t_pos the)
  (n_pos
   (np
    (n health))
   (n_pos
    (np
     (n insurance))))
  (n association)
  (rn
   (pp
    (prep of)
    (np
     (name america)))
   (rn
    (((punct ,))
     (appos
      (np
       (t_pos an)
       (n_pos
        (poss
         (n insurers)
         ')
        (n_pos
         (np
          (n trade))))
       (n group)))
     ,))))
 (vp
  (verb acknowledges)
  (np
   (t_pos that)
   (adj stiff)
   (n competition))
  ((pp
   (prep among)
   (np
    (t_pos
     (poss its))
    (n members)
    (rn
     (rn_wh
      (tovo
       (prep to)
       (tvp
        (verb insure)
        (np
         (n businesses)
         (rn
          (rn_wh
           ((verb likely)))
          (rn
           (rn_wh
            (tovo
             (prep to)
             (tvp
                (verb be)
                (objbe
                  ((np
                     (adj good)
                     (n risks)))))))))))))))))
((pp
 (prep during)
 (np
  (t_pos the)
  (adj first)
  (n year)
  (rn
   (pp
    (prep of)
    (np
     (n coverage)
     (((vrbtm has))
      ((wh_rel
       (venpass
        (verb aggravated))))
      (((np
        (t_pos the)
        (n problem)))
       ((pp
        (prep in)
        (np
         (t_pos the)
         (n_pos
          (np
           (n small-business)))
         (n market))))))))))))))
.)
```

CROSSINGS: 13

RECALL : 38.46%

PRECISION: 37.04%

12. LEARNING TO PARSE WITH TRANSFORMATIONS

ERIC BRILL
Department of Computer Science
Johns Hopkins University

Abstract.

In this chapter we describe a new technique for parsing free text: a transformational grammar[1] is automatically learned that is capable of accurately parsing text into binary-branching syntactic trees. The algorithm works by beginning in a very naive state of knowledge about phrase structure. By repeatedly comparing the results of bracketing in the current state to proper bracketing provided in the training corpus, the system learns a set of simple structural transformations that can be applied to reduce the number of errors. After describing the algorithm, we present results and compare these results to other recent results in automatic grammar induction.

1. INTRODUCTION

There has been a great deal of interest of late in the automatic induction of natural language grammar. Given the difficulty inherent in manually building a robust parser, along with the availability of large amounts of training material, automatic grammar induction seems like a path worth pursuing. A number of systems have been built that can be trained automatically to bracket text into syntactic constituents. In Magerman and Marcus (1990) mutual information statistics are extracted from a corpus of text and this information is then used to parse new text. Sampson (1986) defines a function to score the quality of parse trees, and then uses simulated annealing to heuristically explore the entire space of possible parses for a given sentence. In Brill (1992), distributional analysis techniques are applied to a large corpus to learn a context-free grammar.

[1]Not in the traditional sense of the term.

H. Bunt and M. Tomita (eds.), Recent Advances in Parsing Technology, 221–240.

The most promising results to date have been based on the inside-outside algorithm, which can be used to train stochastic context-free grammars. The inside-outside algorithm is an extension of the finite-state based Hidden Markov Model (by Baker, 1979), which has been applied successfully in many areas, including speech recognition and part of speech tagging. A number of recent papers have explored the potential of using the inside-outside algorithm to automatically learn a grammar (Lari and Young, 1990; Sharman et al., 1990; Pereira and Schabes, 1992; Briscoe and Waegner, 1992; Carroll and Charniak, 1992; Schabes et al., 1993).

Below, we describe a new technique for grammar induction. The algorithm works by beginning in a very naive state of knowledge about phrase structure. By repeatedly comparing the results of parsing in the current state to the proper phrase structure for each sentence in the training corpus, the system learns a set of ordered transformations which can be applied to reduce parsing error. The trained transformational parser is completely symbolic and can bracket text in linear time with respect to sentence length. In addition, since some tokens in a sentence are not even considered in parsing, the method could prove to be considerably more robust than a CFG-based approach when faced with noise or unfamiliar input. After describing the algorithm, we present results and compare these results to other recent results in automatic phrase structure induction.

2. TRANSFORMATION-BASED, ERROR-DRIVEN LEARNING

The phrase structure learning algorithm is an application of a general learning technique called transformation-based error-driven learning. This learning paradigm, illustrated in figure 1, has been applied to a number of different natural language applications, including part of speech tagging and prepositional phrase attachment disambiguation (Brill, 1994; Brill and Resnik, 1994). First, unannotated text is passed through the initial-state annotator. The initial-state annotator can range in complexity from assigning random structure to assigning the output of a sophisticated manually created annotator. Once text has been passed through the initial-state annotator, it is then compared to the *truth*,[2] and transformations are learned that can be applied to the output of the initial state annotator to make it better resemble the *truth*.

A greedy search strategy is used to learn transformations: at each stage of learning, the *best scoring* transformation is learned. Three components must be defined to completely specify a transformation-based learner:

1. The initial-state annotator.

[2] As specified in a manually annotated corpus.

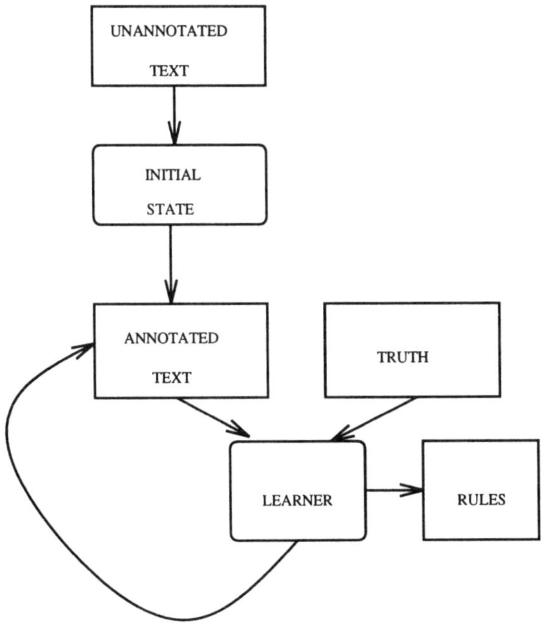

Figure 1. Transformation-Based Error-Driven Learning.

2. The list of allowable transformations.
3. The scoring function.

3. LEARNING PHRASE STRUCTURE

The phrase structure learning algorithm is trained on a small corpus of partially bracketed text which is also annotated with part of speech information. All of the experiments presented below were done using the Penn Treebank annotated corpus (Marcus et al., 1993). The learner begins in a naive initial state, knowing very little about the phrase structure of the target corpus. In particular, all that is initially known is that English tends to be right branching and that final punctuation is final punctuation. Transformations are then learned automatically which transform the output of the naive parser into output which better resembles the phrase structure found in the training corpus. Once a set of transformations has been learned, the system is capable of taking sentences tagged with parts of speech (either manually tagged text, or the output of an automatic part of speech tagger) and returning a binary-branching structure with nonterminals unlabelled.[3]

[3]This is the same output given by systems described in Magerman and Marcus, 1990; Brill, 1992; Pereira and Schabes, 1992; Schabes, 1993.

3.1. THE INITIAL STATE OF THE PARSER

Initially, the parser operates by assigning a right-linear structure to all sentences. The only exception is that final punctuation is attached high. So, the sentence "*The dog and old cat ate .*" would be incorrectly bracketed as:

((The (dog (and (old (cat ate))))) .)

The parser in its initial state will obviously not bracket sentences with great accuracy. In some experiments below, we begin with an even more naive initial state of knowledge: sentences are parsed by assigning them a random binary-branching structure with final punctuation always attached high.

3.2. STRUCTURAL TRANSFORMATIONS

The next stage involves learning a set of transformations that can be applied to the output of the naive parser to make these sentences better conform to the proper structure specified in the training corpus. The list of possible transformation types is prespecified. Transformations involve making a simple change triggered by a simple environment. In the current implementation, there are twelve allowable transformation types:

– (1-8) (*Add*|*delete*) a (*left*|*right*) parenthesis to the (*left*|*right*) of part of speech tag X.
– (9-12) (*Add*|*delete*) a (*left*|*right*) parenthesis between tags X and Y.

To carry out a transformation by adding or deleting a parenthesis, a number of additional simple changes must take place to preserve balanced parentheses and binary branching. To give an example, to delete a left paren in a particular environment, the following operations take place (assuming, of course, that there is a left paren to delete):

1. Delete the left paren.
2. Delete the right paren that matches the just deleted paren.
3. Add a left paren to the left of the constituent immediately to the left of the deleted left paren.
4. Add a right paren to the right of the constituent immediately to the right of the deleted left paren.
5. If there is no constituent immediately to the right, or none immediately to the left, then the transformation fails to apply.

Structurally, the transformation can be seen as follows. If we wish to delete a left paren to the right of constituent X,[4] where X appears in a subtree of the form:

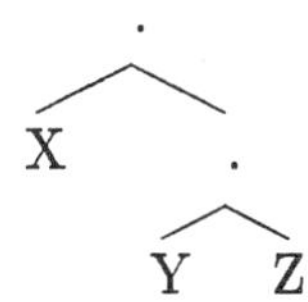

carrying out these operations will transform this subtree into:

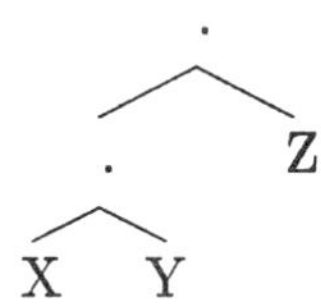

Given the sentence:[5]

The dog barked .

this would initially be bracketed by the naive parser as:

((The (dog barked)) .)

If the transformation *delete a left paren to the right of a determiner* is applied, the structure would be transformed to the correct bracketing:

(((The dog) barked) .)

To add a right parenthesis to the right of Y, Y must once again be in a subtree of the form:

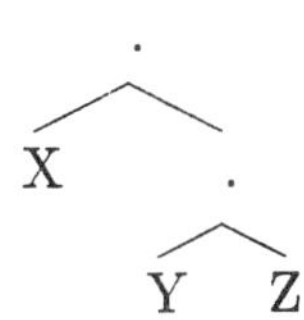

If it is, the following steps are carried out to add the right paren:

1. Add the right paren.
2. Delete the left paren that now matches the newly added paren.

[4] To the right of the rightmost terminal dominated by X if X is a nonterminal.
[5] Input sentences are also labelled with parts of speech.

3. Find the right paren that used to match the just deleted paren and delete it.
4. Add a left paren to match the added right paren.

This results in the same structural change as deleting a left paren to the right of X in this particular structure.

Applying the transformation *add a right paren to the right of a noun* to the bracketing:

((The (dog barked)) .)

will once again result in the correct bracketing:

(((The dog) barked) .)

The transformation list specifies two possible structural transformations: subtree

(X (Y Z))

is transformed to

((X Y) Z)

or

((X Y) Z)

is transformed to

(X (Y Z))

These transformations can be triggered by preterminals dominated by the root of this subtree, as well as preterminals immediately preceding and following the frontier of the subtree.

3.3. LEARNING TRANSFORMATIONS

Learning proceeds as follows. Sentences in the training set are first parsed using the naive parser which assigns right linear structure to all sentences, attaching final punctuation high. Next, for each possible instantiation of the twelve transformation templates, that particular transformation is applied to the naively parsed sentences. The resulting structures are then scored using some measure of success that compares these parses to the correct structural descriptions for the sentences provided in the training corpus. The transformation resulting in the overall best scoring structures then becomes the first transformation of the ordered set of transformations that are to be learned. That transformation is applied to the right-linear structures, and then learning proceeds on the corpus of improved sentence bracketings. The following procedure is carried out repeatedly on the training corpus until no more transformations can be found whose application reduces the error in parsing the training corpus:

1. The best transformation is found for the structures output by the parser in its current state.[6]
2. The transformation is applied to the output resulting from bracketing the corpus using the parser in its current state.
3. This transformation is added to the end of the ordered list of transformations.
4. Go to 1.

After a set of transformations has been learned, it can be used to effectively parse fresh text. To parse fresh text, the text is first naively parsed and then every transformation is applied, in order, to the naively parsed text.

One nice feature of this method is that different measures of bracketing success can be used: learning can proceed in such a way as to try to optimize any specified measure of success. The measure we have chosen for our experiments is the same measure described in Pereira and Schabes (1992), which is one of the measures that arose out of a parser evaluation workshop (Black et al., 1991). The measure is the percentage of constituents (strings of words between matching parentheses) from sentences output by our system which do not cross any constituents in the Penn Treebank structural description of the sentence. For example, if our system outputs:

(((The big) (dog ate)) .)

and the Penn Treebank bracketing for this sentence was:

(((The big dog) ate) .)

then the constituent *the big* would be judged correct whereas the constituent *dog ate* would not.

Figure 2 shows the first ten transformations found from one run of training on the Wall Street Journal corpus, which was initially bracketed using the right-linear initial-state parser.

The first two transformations, as well as transformation number 4, 5, 7, 8 and 9 all extract noun phrases from the right linear initial structure. After bracketing in the initial state, every word will be the leftmost terminal of a phrase containing the entire remainder of the sentence to its right. The first two transformations effectively remove singular and plural common nouns

[6]The *state* of the parser is defined as naive initial-state knowledge plus all transformations that currently have been learned.

#	Add/ Delete	Left/ Right Paren	Environment
1	D	L	Left of NN
2	D	L	Left of NNS
3	A	R	Left of ,
4	D	L	Btwn NNP and NNP
5	D	L	Right of DT
6	A	R	Left of ,
7	D	R	Left of NNS
8	D	R	Btwn NN and NN
9	D	L	Btwn JJ and JJ
10	D	L	Right of $

Figure 2. The first 10 learned transformations.

from such a structure and bracket them with the preceding constituent instead. The sentence "The cat meowed ." would initially be bracketed as:

((The/DT (cat/NN meowed/VBD)) ./.)

Applying the first transformation to this bracketing (or the second transformation to the same bracketing with *cats* replacing *cat*) would result in:

(((The cat) meowed) .)

If there is a left parenthesis between two proper nouns, then the second proper noun is initially bracketed with constituents that follow it rather than with the preceding proper noun. The fourth transformation fixes this. The sentence *General Motors is very profitable* . would initially be bracketed as:

((General/NNP (Motors/NNP (is (very profitable)))) .)

Applying the fourth transformation would convert this structure to:

(((General Motors) (is (very profitable))) .)

The following example demonstrates the interaction between transformations. The sentence *The fastest cars won .* would initially be bracketed as:

((The/DT (fastest/JJ (cars/NNS won/VBD))) .)

The first transformation to apply to this sentence would be number 2, resulting in:

((The ((fastest cars) won)) .)

The next applicable transformation is number 5, whose application results in:

(((The (fastest cars)) won) .)

After this transformation is applied, no other transformations can be applied to the sentence, and the correct structure is produced.

Transformation number 10 results from the fact that a number usually follows a dollar sign, and these two lexical items should be bracketed together. Transformations 3 and 6 result from the fact that a comma is a good indicator of the preceding phrase being terminated. Since each transformation is carried out only once per environment, multiple listings of a transformation are required if the transformation is to be applied multiple times to a single environment. The sentence *We called them , but they left .* would initially be bracketed as:

((We/PP (called/VBD (them/PP (,/, (but (they left)))))) .)

The first applicable transformation is number 3, whose application results in:

((We ((called them) (, (but (they left))))) .)

The next applicable transformation is number 6, whose application results in the correct structure:

(((We (called them)) (, (but (they left)))) .)

4. RESULTS

In the first experiment we ran, training and testing were done on the Texas Instruments Air Travel Information System (ATIS) corpus (Hemphill et al., 1990).[7] In table 1, we compare results we obtained to results cited in Pereira and Schabes (1992) using the inside-outside algorithm on the same

[7]In all experiments described in this chapter, results are calculated on a test corpus which was not used in any way in either training the learning algorithm or in developing the system.

corpus. Accuracy is measured in terms of the percentage of noncrossing constituents in the test corpus, as described above. Our system was tested by using the training set to learn a set of transformations, and then applying these transformations to the test set and scoring the resulting output. In this experiment, 64 transformations were learned (compared with 4095 context-free rules and probabilities used in the inside-outside algorithm experiment). We obtain comparable performance using a training corpus only 20% as large as that used to train the inside-outside algorithm.

Method	# Training Corpus Sentences	Accuracy
Inside-Outside	700	90.4%
Transformation Learner	150	91.1%

TABLE 1. Comparing two learning methods on the ATIS corpus.

After applying all learned transformations to the test corpus, 60% of the sentences had no crossing constituents, 74% had fewer than two crossing constituents, and 85% had fewer than three. The mean sentence length of the test corpus was 11.3. Figure 3 shows accuracy as a function of the number of transformations that have been applied to the test corpus. As the transformation number increases, overtraining sometimes occurs. In the current implementation of the learner, a transformation is added to the list if it results in *any* positive net change in the training set. Toward the end of the learning procedure, transformations are found that only affect a very small percentage of training sentences. Since small counts are less reliable than large counts, we cannot reliably assume that these transformations will also improve performance in the test corpus. One way around this overtraining would be to set a threshold: specify a minimum level of improvement that must result for a transformation to be learned. Another possibility is to use additional training material to prune the set of learned transformations.

We next ran an experiment to determine what performance could be achieved if we dropped the initial right-linear assumption. Using the same training and test sets as above, sentences were initially assigned a random binary-branching structure, with final punctuation always attached high. Since there was less regular structure in this case than in the right-linear case, many more transformations were found, 147 transformations in to-

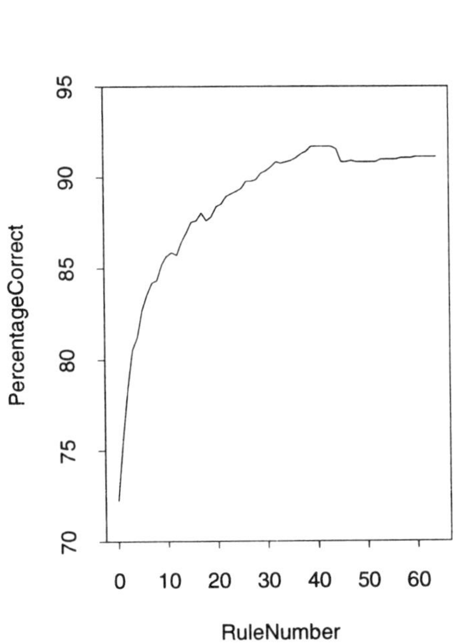

Figure 3. Accuracy as a function of transformation number for the ATIS Corpus.

tal. When these transformations were applied to the test set, a bracketing accuracy of 87.1% resulted.

The ATIS corpus is structurally fairly regular. To determine how well our algorithm performs on a more complex corpus, we ran experiments on the Wall Street Journal. Results from this experiment can be found in table 2.[8] Accuracy is again measured as the percentage of constituents in the test set which do not cross any Penn Treebank constituents.[9]

In the corpus we used for the experiments of sentence length 2-15, the mean sentence length was 10.80. In the corpus used for the experiment of sentence length 2-25, the mean length was 16.82. As would be expected, performance degrades somewhat as sentence length increases. In table 3, we show the percentage of sentences in the test corpus that have no crossing constituents, and the percentage that have only a very small number of crossing constituents.[10]

In table 4, we show the standard deviation measured from three different

[8]For sentences of length 2-15, the initial right-linear parser achieves 69% accuracy. For sentences of length 2-20, 63% accuracy is achieved and for sentences of length 2-25, accuracy is 59%.

[9]In all of our experiments carried out on the Wall Street Journal, the test set was a

Sent. Length	# Training Corpus Sentences	# of Trans- formations	% Accuracy
2-15	250	83	88.1
2-15	500	163	89.3
2-15	1000	221	91.6
2-20	250	145	86.2
2-25	250	160	83.8

TABLE 2. WSJ Sentences

Sent. Length	# Training Corpus Sentences	% of 0-error Sents.	% of ≤2-error Sents.
2-15	500	53.7	84.6
2-15	1000	62.4	87.8
2-25	250	29.2	59.9

TABLE 3. WSJ Sentences.

randomly chosen training sets of each sample size and randomly chosen test sets of 500 sentences each, as well as the accuracy as a functionof 500 sentences each, as well as the accuracy as a function of training corpus size for sentences of length 2 to 20.

In Schabes et al. (1993), an experiment was run using the inside-outside algorithm to train a grammar from the partially bracketed Wall Street Journal corpus. As in the experiment with the ATIS corpus, all possible binary context-free rules were initially allowed, and random probabilities were assigned to each rule. A comparison of this approach to the transformation-based approach is shown in tables 5 and 6. The inside-outside experiment was carried out on sentences of length 1-15, and the transformation-based experiment was carried out on sentences of length 2-15. The inside-outside experiment had a grammar of 4095 probabilistic context free rules, which could be trimmed down to 450 rules without changing performance. 221

randomly selected set of 500 sentences.

[10]For sentences of length 2-15, the initial right linear parser parses 17% of sentences with no crossing errors, 35% with one or fewer errors and 50% with two or fewer. For sentences of length 2-25, 7% of sentences are parsed with no crossing errors, 16% with one or fewer, and 24% with two or fewer.

# Training Corpus Sents	% Correct	Std. Dev.
0	63.0	0.69
10	75.8	2.95
50	82.1	1.94
100	84.7	0.56
250	86.2	0.46
750	87.3	0.61

TABLE 4. WSJ Sentences of length 2 to 20.

symbolic transformations were learned in the transformation-based experiment. In table 5, a comparison is shown between the transformation-based learner and the inside-outside algorithm when parsing accuracy is measured in terms of crossing brackets. In table 6, accuracy is measured as the percentage of sentences with no crossing bracket violations.

Method	# Training Corpus Sents	% Accuracy
Inside-Outside	1095	90.2
Transformation Learner	1000	91.6

TABLE 5. Comparison of Two Learning Algorithms on the Wall Street Journal: Crossing Bracket Accuracy

Method	# Training Corpus Sents	Sentence Accuracy
Inside-Outside	1095	57.1
Transformation Learner	1000	62.4

TABLE 6. Comparison of Two Learning Algorithms on the Wall Street Journal: Sentence Accuracy

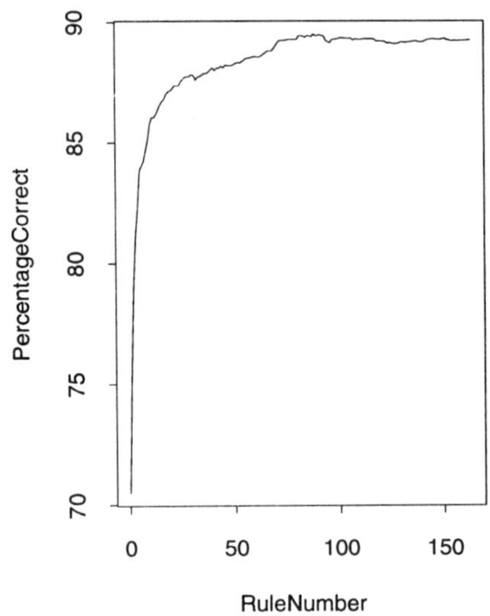

Figure 4. Accuracy as a function of transformation number for the WSJ Corpus.

A graph showing parsing performance for a WSJ run trained on a 500-sentence training corpus (training and testing on sentences of length 2-15) is shown in figure 4. We also ran an experiment on WSJ sentences of length 2-15 starting with random binary-branching structures with final punctuation attached high. In this experiment, 325 transformations were found using a 250-sentence training corpus, and the accuracy resulting from applying these transformations to a test set was 84.7%.

Finally, in figure 5 we show the sentence length distribution in the Wall Street Journal corpus.

While the numbers presented above allow us to compare the transformation learner with systems trained and tested on comparable corpora, these results are all based upon the assumption that the test data is tagged fairly reliably (manually tagged text was used in all of these experiments, as well in the experiments of Pereira and Schabes, 1992, and Schabes et al., 1993.) When parsing free text, we cannot assume that the text will be tagged with the accuracy of a human annotator. Instead, an automatic tagger would have to be used to first tag the text before parsing. To address this issue, we ran one experiment where we randomly induced a 5% tagging error rate beyond the error rate of the human annotator. Errors were induced in such a way as to preserve the unigram part of speech tag probability

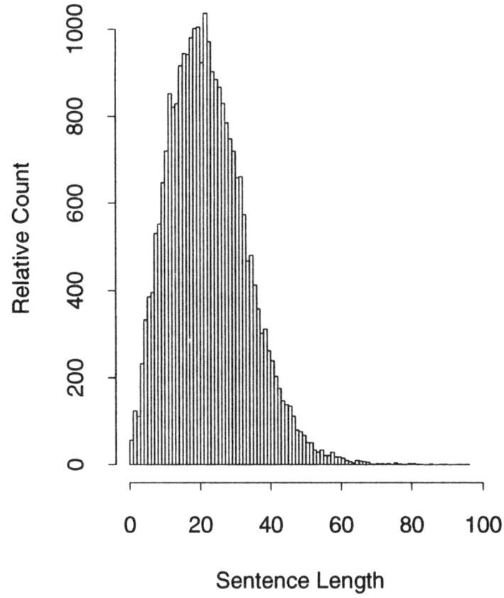

Figure 5. The Distribution of Sentence Lengths in the WSJ Corpus.

distribution in the corpus. The experiment was run for sentences of length 2-15, with a training set of 1000 sentences and a test set of 500 sentences. The resulting bracketing accuracy was 90.1%, compared to 91.6% accuracy when using an unadulterated training corpus. Accuracy only degraded by a small amount when training on the corpus with adulterated part of speech tags.

5. SAMPLE OUTPUT

Below are ten randomly chosen parses from the Wall Street Journal. In each case, the output of the bracketing program is listed first, and the Penn Treebank bracketing is listed second. Crossing brackets are marked with a star.

((But (if *((a raider) *(takes *((over (when ((the stock) (is weak))))) (, ((the shareholder) (never (gets (his recovery))))))*)*)*)) .)
((But (if ((a raider) (takes over (when ((the stock) (is weak)))))) , ((the shareholder) (never gets (his recovery)))) .)

(((The company) (expects (to (resume *((full operations) (by today))*)))) .)
(((The company) (expects (to (resume (full operations)) (by today)))) .)

(((" It) *(('s *((very likely) *((((the next) (five years)) (will (be (strong (for funds))))) (, "))*)*) (he says))*) .)
(((" It ('s (very likely ((the next five years) will (be strong (for funds))))) , ") (he says)) .)

(((The (latest report)) (compares (with (((a modest) (9.9 (% increase))) (in *((July (machine orders)) (from ((a year) earlier)))*))))) .)
(((The latest report) (compares (with (a modest 9.9 % increase (in (July machine orders)) (from ((a year) earlier)))))) .)

(((The goal) (was (to (boost ((the circulation) (above ((the (500,000 level)) ((considered significant) (by advertisers))))))))) .)
(((The goal) (was (to (boost (the circulation) (above ((the 500,000 level) (considered significant (by advertisers)))))))) .)

(((Mr. Jones) (ran *((((for (the Senate)) (as (a Democrat))) (in 1986)) (, (but (lost (to ((incumbent Sen.) (Don Nickles)))))))*)) .)
(((Mr. Jones) ((ran (for (the Senate)) (as (a Democrat)) (in 1986)) , but (lost (to (incumbent Sen. Don Nickles))))) .)

((Then (((the ((auto paint) shop)) fire) (sent ((an (evil-looking cloud)) *(of *((black smoke) (into (the air)))*)*))))) .)
((Then ((the auto paint shop fire) (sent (an evil-looking cloud (of (black smoke))) (into (the air))))) .)

((He (*(used *(to (be ((a boiler-room) salesman)))*)* (, (peddling (investments (*(in oil)* *(*((and (gas wells)) and)* (rare coins))*))))))) .)
((He (used (to (be (a boiler-room salesman) , (peddling (investments (in ((oil and gas wells) and (rare coins)))))))))) .)

(((The board) (is (scheduled (to (meet Tuesday))))) .)
(((The board) is (scheduled (to (meet Tuesday)))) .)

((Ignore (the (present condition))) .)
((Ignore (the present condition)) .)

In the first example, there are three bracketing errors, all arising from the failure to end the clause following *if* at the comma. The second sentence has one error, which is a prepositional phrase attachment error. The third sentence has three bracketing errors, arising from crossing matching quotes. Perhaps a number of meta-rules, either learned or manually coded, such as information about matching parentheses and quotes, would significantly improve performance. The fourth sentence has one error, which is again a prepositional phrase attachment error. The sixth sentence has one error, from attaching the clause following (and including) the comma to the preposition *for* instead of the verb *ran*. The seventh sentence has two errors, both due to prepositional phrase attachment. The eighth sentence has five errors, one of which is due to prepositional phrase attachment and two arising from a difficult coordinate structure. In addition to meta-rules, postprocessors addressing particular parsing problems such as prepositional phrase attachment and coordination could lead to significant system performance improvements. Progress has already been made on a transformation-based prepositional phrase attachment program (see Brill and Resnik, 1994).

6. ASSIGNING NONTERMINAL LABELS

Once a tree is bracketed, the next step is to label the nonterminal nodes. Transformation-based error-driven learning is once again used for learning how to label nonterminals. Currently, a node is labelled based solely on the labels of its children. Therefore, an unlabelled tree can be labelled in a bottom-up fashion. Instead of addressing the problem of labelling the unlabelled tree output of the previous section, we have addressed a slightly different problem. The problem is to assign a tag to a node of a properly bracketed tree given the proper labels for the child nodes. This problem can be more easily evaluated and solving it is a significant step toward solving the problem of labelling the output of the transformation-based bracketer.

The Penn Treebank bracketed Wall Street Journal corpus was used for this experiment.[11] Two training sets were used (training set A had 1878 sentences and training set B had 1998), as well as a test set of 1971 sentences. In the first experiment, the initial state annotator assigned the label *noun phrase* to all nodes. Then, transformations were learned to improve accuracy. The transformation templates are:

1. Change the node label to X if Y is a child.[12]
2. Change the node label to X if Y and Z are adjacent children.

[11]Thanks to Rich Pito for providing corpus processing tools for running this experiment.

[12]Y can be a nonterminal or preterminal (and need not be the only child).

Transformation Number	Tag As	If Children Include
1	PP	IN
2	S	VP
3	VP	VBD
4	VP	VB
5	VP	VBN
6	VP	VBG
7	VP	VBZ
8	S	, S
9	S	VP
10	SBar	-NONE- S
11	PP	TO NP
12	SBar	IN S
13	VP	VBP
14	S	VP
15	S	CC S
16	WHNP	WDT
17	SBar	WHNP
18	VP	CC VP
19	WHNP	WP
20	ADJP	JJR

TABLE 7. Transformations For Labelling Nonterminals.

Transformations were learned using training set A. A total of 115 transformations were learned. Initially assigning the label *noun phrase* to all nonterminal nodes in the test set resulted in an accuracy of 44.9%. Applying all learned transformations to the test set resulted in an accuracy of 94.3%. Table 7 shows the first twenty learned transformations. Transformations 15 and 18, as well as a number of similar transformations in the entire list capture the general rule:

$$X \rightarrow \text{X and X}$$

for coordination. It appears that the transformation *Change a label to S if VP is a child* is particularly effective, appearing as transformation 2, 9 and 14. After the second transformation is applied, the transformations that follow could undo the second transformation as a side-effect. So, this transformation applies a number of times to remedy this.

Next, a less naive start state was used. A nonterminal node is assigned the most likely tag for its children, as indicated in a second training set (training set B). Unseen child sequences are tagged with a default tag (noun phrase). Transformations were learned after applying the start state annotator to training set A. On the test set, initial state accuracy was 92.6%. Applying the transformations resulted in an accuracy of 95.9%. A total of 107 transformations were learned.

We are very encouraged by the accuracy obtained using such a simple learning algorithm that only makes use of very local environments without recourse to any lexical information. Hopefully, adding richer environments such as *the word X is a child*, or *the nonterminal to the left is Y* will lead to an even more accurate nonterminal labeller. By first bracketing text and then labelling nonterminals, we can produce labelled parse trees in linear time with respect to sentence length. The bracketer runs in $O(|n| * |T|)$, where $|n|$ is the length of the sentence and $|T|$ is the number of bracketing transformations. The nonterminal labeller also runs in $O(|n| * |T|)$, as all transformations are tried at every nonterminal node. Therefore, parsing run time is: $O(|n| * |T|) + O(|n| * |T|) = O(|n| * |T|)$.

7. CONCLUSIONS

In this chapter, we have described a new approach for learning a grammar to automatically parse text. The method can be used to obtain high parsing accuracy with a very small training set. Instead of learning a traditional grammar, an ordered set of structural transformations is learned that can be applied to the output of a very naive parser to obtain binary-branching trees with unlabelled nonterminals. Experiments have shown that these parses conform with high accuracy to the structural descriptions specified in a manually annotated corpus. Unlike learners based on the inside-outside algorithm which attempt to find a grammar to maximize the probability of the training corpus in hope that this grammar will match the grammar that provides the most accurate structural descriptions, the transformation-based learner can readily use any desired success measure in learning.

The transformation-based learner can easily be extended simply by adding transformation templates. In the future, we plan to experiment with other types of transformations. Currently, each transformation in the learned list is only applied once in each appropriate environment. For a transformation to be applied more than once in one environment, it must appear in the transformation list more than once. One possible extension to the set of transformation types would be to allow for transformations of the form: add/delete a paren as many times as is possible in a particular environment. We also plan to experiment with other scoring functions and control strategies for finding transformations and to use this system as a postprocessor to other grammar induction systems, learning transformations to improve their performance. We hope these future paths will lead to a trainable and very accurate parser for free text.

References

Black, E., Abney, S., Flickinger, D., Gdaniec, C., Grishman, R., Harrison, P., Hindle, D., Ingria, R., Jelinek, F., Klavans, J., Liberman, M., Marcus, M., Roukos, S., Santorini, B., and Strzalkowski, T. (1991) A procedure for quantitatively comparing the syntactic coverage of English grammars. In *Proc. Fourth DARPA Speech and Natural Language Workshop*, 306–311.

Baker, J. (1979) Trainable grammars for speech recognition. In *Speech communication papers presented at the 97th Meeting of the Acoustical Society of America.*

Brill, E., and Marcus, M. (1992) Automatically acquiring phrase structure using distributional analysis. In *Darpa Workshop on Speech and Natural Language*, Harriman, N.Y.

Brill, E., and Resnik, P. (1994) A transformation-based approach to prepositional phrase attachment disambiguation. In *Proc. Fifteenth International Conference on Computational Linguistics (COLING-1994)*, Kyoto.

Brill, E. (1992) A simple rule-based part of speech tagger. In *Proceedings of the Third Conference on Applied Natural Language Processing, ACL*, Trento.

Brill, E.. (1994) Some advances in rule-based part of speech tagging. In *Proc. Twelfth National Conference on Artificial Intelligence (AAAI-94)*, Seattle.

Briscoe, T. and Waegner, N. (1992) Robust stochastic parsing using the inside-outside algorithm. In *Workshop notes from the AAAI Statistically-Based NLP Techniques Workshop.*

Carroll, G. and Charniak, E. (1992) Learning probabilistic dependency grammars from labelled text. In *Proc. of Fall Symposium on Probabilistic Approaches to Natural Language.* American Association for Artificial Intelligence (AAAI), 1992.

Hemphill, C., Godfrey, J. and Doddington, G. (1992) The ATIS spoken language systems pilot corpus. In *Proc. of DARPA Speech and Natural Language Workshop*, 1990.

Lari, K. and Young, S. (1990) The estimation of stochastic context-free grammars using the inside-outside algorithm. *Computer Speech and Language*, 4.

Magerman, D. and Marcus, M. (1990) Parsing a natural language using mutual information statistics. In *Proc. 8th National Conference on Artificial Intelligence.*

Marcus, M., Santorini, B., and Marcinkiewicz, M. (1993) Building a large annotated corpus of English: the Penn Treebank. *Computational Linguistics*, 19(2).

Pereira, F. and Schabes, Y. (1992) Inside-outside reestimation from partially bracketed corpora. In *Proceedings of the 30th Annual Meeting of the Association for Computational Linguistics*, Newark, De.

Sampson, G. (1986) A stochastic approach to parsing. In *Proc. COLING'86*, Bonn.

Sharman, R., Jelinek, F., and Mercer, R. (1990) Generating a grammar for statistical training. In *Proc. of the 1990 Darpa Speech and Natural Language Workshop.*

Schabes, Y., Roth, M., and Osborne, R. (1993) Parsing the Wall Street Journal with the inside-outside algorithm. In *Proc. of the 1993 European ACL*, Utrecht.

13. ESTIMATION OF VERB SUBCATEGORIZATION FRAME FREQUENCIES BASED ON SYNTACTIC AND MULTIDIMENSIONAL STATISTICAL ANALYSIS

AKIRA USHIODA, DAVID A. EVANS, TED GIBSON
AND ALEX WAIBEL

Computational Linguistics Program
Carnegie Mellon University

Abstract.
We describe a mechanism for automatically estimating frequencies of verb subcategorization frames in a large corpus. A tagged corpus is first partially parsed to identify noun phrases and then a regular grammar is used to estimate the appropriate subcategorization frame for each verb token in the corpus. In an experiment involving the identification of six fixed subcategorization frames, our current system showed more than 80% accuracy. In addition, a new statistical method enables the system to learn patterns of errors based on a set of training samples and substantially improves the accuracy of the frequency estimation.

1. INTRODUCTION

When we construct a grammar, there is always a trade-off between the coverage of the grammar and the ambiguity of the grammar. If we hope to develop an efficient high-coverage parser for unrestricted texts, we must have some means of dealing with the combinatorial explosion of syntactic ambiguities. While a general probabilistic optimization technique such as the Inside-Outside algorithm (Baker 1979, Lauri and Young 1990, Jelinek *et al.* 1990, Carroll and Charniak 1992) can be used to reduce ambiguity by providing estimates on the applicability of the context-free rules in a

H. Bunt and M. Tomita (eds.), Recent Advances in Parsing Technology, 241–253.

grammar (for example), the algorithm does not take advantage of lexical information, including such information as verb subcategorization frame preferences. Discovering or acquiring lexically-sensitive linguistic structures from large corpora may offer an essential complementary approach.

Verb subcategorization (verb-subcat) frames represent one of the most important elements of grammatical/lexical knowledge for efficient and reliable parsing. At this stage in the computational-linguistic exploration of corpora, dictionaries are still probably more reliable than automatic acquisition systems as a source of subcategorization (subcat) frames for verbs. The Oxford Advanced Learners Dictionary (OALD) (Hornby 1989), for example, uses 32 verb patterns to describe a usage of each verb for each meaning of the verb. However, dictionaries do not provide quantitative information such as how often each verb is used with each of the possible subcat frames. Since dictionaries are repositories, primarily, of what is possible, not what is most likely, they tend to contain information about rare usage (de Marken 1992). But without information about the frequencies of the subcat frames we find in dictionaries, we face the prospect of having to treat each frame as equiprobable in parsing. This can lead to serious inefficiency. We also know that the frequency of subcat frames can vary by domain; frames that are very rare in one domain can be quite common in another. If we could automatically determine the frequencies of subcat frames for domains, we would be able to tailor parsing with domain-specific heuristics. Indeed, it would be desirable to have a subcat dictionary for each possible domain.

This chapter describes a mechanism for automatically acquiring subcat frames and their frequencies based on a tagged corpus. The method utilizes a tagged corpus because (i) we don't have to deal with a lexical ambiguity (ii) tagged corpora in various domains are becoming readily available and (iii) simple and robust tagging techniques using such corpora recently have been developed (Church 1988, Brill 1992).

Brent reports a method for automatically acquiring subcat frames but without frequency measurements (Brent and Berwick 1991, Brent 1991). His approach is to count occurrences of those unambiguous verb phrases that contain no noun phrases other than pronouns or proper nouns. By thus restricting the 'features' that trigger identification of a verb phrase, he avoids possible errors due to syntactic ambiguity. Although the rate of false positives is very low in his system, his syntactic features are so selective that most verb tokens fail to satisfy them. (For example, verbs that occurred fewer than 20 times in the corpus tend to have no co-occurrences with the features.) Therefore his approach is not useful in determining verb-subcat frame frequencies.

To measure frequencies, we need, ideally, to identify a subcat frame for each verb token in the corpus. This, in turn, requires a full parse of the corpus. Since manually parsed corpora are rare and typically small, and since automatically parsed corpora contain many errors (given current parsing technologies), an alternative source of useful syntactic structure is needed. We have elected to use partially parsed sentences automatically derived from a lexically-tagged corpus. The partial parse contains information about minimal noun phrases (without PP attachment or clausal complements). While such derived information about syntactic structure is less accurate and complete than that available in certified, hand-parsed corpora, the approach promises to generalize and to yield large sample sizes. In particular, we can use partially parsed corpora to measure verb-subcat frame frequencies.

2. METHOD

The procedure to find verb-subcat frequencies, automatically, is as follows.

1) Make a list of verbs out of the tagged corpus.
2) For each verb on the list (the 'target verb'),
   (2.1) Tokenize each sentence containing the target verb in the following way:
   All the noun phrases except pronouns are tokenized as "n" by a noun phrase parser and all the rest of the words are also tokenized following the schema in Table 1 (see below). For example, the sentence *The corresponding mental-state verbs do not* follow [target verb] *these rules in a straightforward way* is transformed to a sequence of tokens "bnvaknpne".
   (2.2) Apply a set of subcat extraction rules to the tokenized sentences. These rules are written as regular expressions and they are obtained through the examination of occurrences of a small sample of verbs in a training text.

Note that in the actual implementation of the procedure, all of the redundant operations are eliminated. Our NP parser also uses a finite-state grammar. It is designed especially to support identification of verb-subcat frames. One of its special features is that it detects time-adjuncts such as *yesterday, two months ago*, or *the following day*, and eliminates them in the tokenization process. For example, the sentence *He told the reporters the following day that...* is tokenized to "bivnc..." instead of "bivnnc...".

3. EXPERIMENT ON WALL STREET JOURNAL

We used the above method in experiments involving a tagged corpus of Wall Street Journal (WSJ) articles, provided by the Penn Treebank project. Our

b:	sentence initial maker	e:	sentence final maker
k:	target verb	t:	*to*
i:	pronoun	m:	modal
n:	noun phrase	w:	relative pronoun
v:	finite verb	a:	adverb
u:	participial verb	x:	punctuation
d:	base form verb	c:	complementizer *that*
p:	preposition	s:	the rest

TABLE 1. List of Symbols/Categories

experiment was limited in two senses. First, we treated all prepositional phrases as adjuncts. (It is generally difficult to distinguish complement and adjunct PPs.) Second, we measured the frequencies of only six fixed subcat frames for verbs in non-participle form. (This does not represent an essential shortcoming in the method; we only need to have additional subcat frame extraction rules to accommodate participles.)

We extracted two sets of tagged sentences from the WSJ corpus, each representing 3-MBytes and approximately 300,000 words of text. One set was used as a training corpus, the other as a test corpus. Table 2 gives the list of verb-subcat frame extraction rules obtained (via examination) for four verbs *expect, reflect, tell*, and *give*, as they occurred in the training corpus. Sample sentences that can be captured by each set of rules are attached to the list. Table 3 shows the result of the hand comparison of the automatically identified verb-subcat frames for *give* and *expect* in the test corpus. The tabular columns give actual frequencies for each verb-subcat frame based on manual review and the tabular rows give the frequencies as determined automatically by the system. The count of each cell ($[i, j]$) gives the number of occurrences of the verb that are assigned the i-th subcat frame by the system and assigned the j-th frame by manual review. The frame/column labeled 'REST' represents all other subcat frames, encompassing such subcat frames as those involving wh-clauses, verb-particle combinations (such as *give up*), and no complements.

Despite the simplicity of the rules, the frequencies for subcat frames determined under automatic processing are very close to the real distributions. Most of the errors are attributable to errors in the noun phrase parser. For example, 10 out of the 13 errors in the [NP,NP+NP] cell under *give* are due to noun phrase parsing errors such as the misidentification of a N–N sequence (e.g., **give* [$_{\mathrm{NP}}$ *government officials rights*] *against the press*

	Frame	Rule
1.	NP+NP	`k(i|n)n`
2.	NP+CL	`k(i|n(pn)*)c`
		`k(i|n)(i|n)a*(m|v)`
3.	NP+INF	`k(i|n(pn)*)ta*d`
4.	CL	`kc`
		`k(i|n)a*(m|v)`
5.	NP	`k(i|n)/[^mvd]`
		`#pw(i|n(pn)*)a*m?a*k/[^t]`
6.	INF	`kta*d`

Notes:

NP: noun phrase
CL: that-clause with and without the complementizer *that*
INF: *to* + infinitive

`x*` matches a sequence of any number of x's including zero
`x?` is either x or empty
`(x|y)` matches either x or y
`[^xyz]` matches any token except x, y, and z
`#x`(sequence) matches (sequence) that is not directly preceded by x
`x/y` matches x if x is immediately followed by y

Sample Sentences:

Frame 1. "...gives *current management enough time to work on...*"

Frame 2. "...tell *the people in the hall that...*"; "...told *him the man would...*"

Frame 3. "...expected *the impact from the restructuring to make...*"

Frame 4. "...think *that...*"; "...thought *the company eventually responded...*"

Frame 5. "...saw *the man...*"; "*...which the president of the company* wanted*...*" *but not*
"...saw *him swim...*"; "*...(hotel) in which he* stayed*...*"; "*...(gift) which he* expected *to get...*"

Frame 6. "...expects *to gain...*"

Table 2: Set of Subcategorization Frame Extraction Rules

Outpput of System
Give

Real Occurrences

	NP+NP	NP+CL	NP+INF	NP	CL	INF	REST	Total
NP+NP	52	0	0	0	0	0	0	52
NP+CL	1	0	0	0	0	0	0	1
NP+INF	2	0	0	0	0	0	0	2
NP	13	0	0	27	0	0	0	40
CL	0	0	0	0	0	0	0	0
INF	0	0	0	0	0	0	0	0
REST	1	0	0	4	0	0	9	14
Total	69	0	0	31	0	0	9	109

Output of System
Expect

Real Occurrences

	NP+NP	NP+CL	NP+INF	NP	CL	INF	REST	Total
NP+NP	0	0	0	0	0	0	0	0
NP+CL	0	0	0	0	0	0	0	0
NP+INF	0	0	55	1	0	0	0	56
NP	0	0	4	28	0	0	0	32
CL	0	0	0	0	8	0	0	8
INF	0	0	0	0	0	40	0	40
REST	0	0	1	6	0	0	7	14
Total	0	0	60	35	8	40	7	150

TABLE 3. Subcategorization Frame Frequencies

acquire	end	like	spend
build	expand	need	total
close	fail	produce	try
comment	file	prove	use
consider	follow	reach	want
continue	get	receive	work
design	help	reduce	
develop	hold	see	
elect	let	sign	

TABLE 4. Verbs Tested

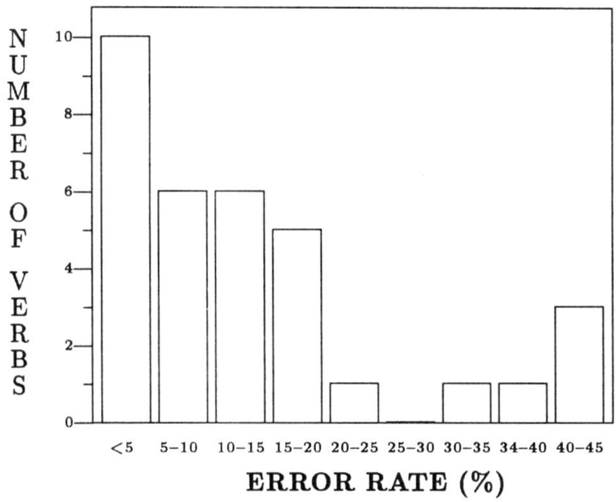

Figure 1. Distribution of Errors

vs. *give* [$_{\text{NP}}$ *government officials*] [$_{\text{NP}}$ *rights*] *against the press*).

To measure the total accuracy of the system, we randomly chose 33 verbs from the 300 most frequent verbs in the test corpus (given in Table 4), automatically estimated the subcat frames for each occurrence of these verbs in the test corpus, and compared the results to manually determined subcat frames.

The overall results are quite promising. The total number of occurrences of the 33 verbs in the test corpus (excluding participle forms) is 2,242. Of these, 1,933 were assigned correct subcat frames by the system. (The 'correct'-assignment counts always appear in the diagonal cells in a comparison table such as in Table 3.) This indicates an overall accuracy for the method of 86%.

If we exclude the subcat frame 'REST' from our statistics, the total number of occurrences of the 33 verbs in one of the six subcat frames is 1,565. Of these, 1,311 were assigned correct subcat frames by the system. This represents 83% accuracy.

For 30 of the 33 verbs, both the first and the second (if any) most frequent subcat frames as determined by the system were correct. For all of the verbs except one (*need*), the most frequent frame was correct.

Figure 1 is a histogram showing the number of verbs within each error-rate zone. In computing the error rate, we divide the total 'off-diagonal'-cell counts, excluding the counts in the 'REST' column, by the total cell counts, again excluding the 'REST' column margin. Thus, the off-diagonal cell counts in the 'REST' row, representing instances where one of the six actual subcat frames was misidentified as 'REST', are counted as errors. This formula, in general, gives higher error rates than would result from simply dividing the off-diagonal cell counts by the total cell counts.

Overall, the most frequent source of errors, again, was errors in noun phrase boundary detection. The second most frequent source was misidentification of infinitival 'purpose' clauses, as in *he used a crowbar to open the door.* The phrase *to open the door* is a 'purpose' adjunct modifying either the verb phrase *used a crowbar* or the main clause *he used a crowbar.* But such adjuncts are incorrectly judged to be complements of their main verbs by the subcat frame extraction rules in Table 2. In formulating the rules, we assumed that a 'purpose' adjunct appears effectively randomly and much less frequently than infinitival complements. This is true for our corpus in general; but some verbs, such as *use* and *need*, appear relatively frequently with 'purpose' infinitivals. In addition to errors from parsing and 'purpose' infinitives, we observed several other, less frequent types of errors. These, too, pattern with specific verbs and do not occur randomly across verbs.

4. STATISTICAL ANALYSIS

For most of the verbs in the experiment, our method provides a good measure of subcat frame frequencies. However, some of the verbs seem to appear in syntactic structures that cannot be captured by our inventory of subcat frames. For example, *need* is frequently used in relative clauses without relative pronouns, as in *the last thing they need.* Since this kind of relative clauses cannot be captured by the rules in Table 2, each occurrence of these relative clause causes an error in measurement. It is likely that there are many other classes of verbs with distinctive syntactic preferences. If we try to add rules for each such class, it will become increasingly difficult to write rules that affect only the target class and to eliminate undesirable rule interactions.

In the following sections, we describe a statistical method which, based on a set of training samples, enables the system to learn patterns of errors and substantially increase the accuracy of estimated verb-subcat frequencies.

4.1. GENERAL SCHEME

The method described in Section 2 is wholly deterministic; it depends only on one set of subcat extraction rules which serve as filters. Instead of treating the system output for each verb token as an estimated subcat frame, we can think of the output as one feature associated with the occurrence of the verb. This single feature can be combined, statistically, with other features in the corpus to yield more accurate characterizations of verb contexts and more accurate subcat-frame frequency estimates. If the other features are capturable via regular-expression rules, they can also be automatically detected in the manner described in the Section 2. For example, main verbs in relative clauses without relative pronouns may have a higher probability of having the feature "nnk", i.e., "(NP)(NP)(VERB)".

More formally, let Y be a response variable taking as its value a subcat frame. Let $X_1, X_2, \ldots, X_N$ be explanatory variables. Each X_i is associated with a feature expressed by one or a set of regular expressions. If a feature is expressed by one regular expression (R), the value of the feature is 1 if the occurrence of the verb matches R and 0 otherwise. If the feature is expressed by a set of regular expressions, its value is the label of the regular expression that the occurrence of the verb matches. The set of regular expressions in Table 2 can therefore be considered to characterize one explanatory variable whose value ranges from (NP+NP) to (REST).

Now, we assume that a training corpus is available in which all verb tokens are given along with their subcat frames. By running our system on the training corpus, we can automatically generate a $(N + 1)$-dimensional contingency table. Table 3 is an example of a 2-dimensional contingency table with $X =$ <OUTPUT OF SYSTEM> and $Y =$ <REAL OCCURRENCES>. Using loglinear models (Agresti 1990), we can derive fitted values of each cell in the $(N+1)$-dimensional contingency table. In the case of a saturated model, in which all kinds of interaction of variables up to $(N + 1)$-way interactions are included, the raw cell counts are the Maximum Likelihood solution. The fitted values are then used to estimate the subcat frame frequencies of a new corpus as follows.

First, the system is run on the new corpus to obtain an N-dimensional contingency table. This table is considered to be an $X_1 - X_2 - \cdots - X_N$ marginal table. What we are aiming at is the Y margins that represent the real subcat frame frequencies of the new corpus. Assuming that the training corpus and the new corpus are homogeneous (e.g., reflecting similar subdomains or samples of a common domain), we estimate the Y margins using Bayes theorem on the fitted values of the training corpus by the formula given in Table 5.

4.2. LEXICAL HEURISTICS

The simplest application of the above method is to use a 2-way contingency table, as in Table 3. There are two possibilities to explore in constructing a 2-way contingency table. One is to sum up the cell counts of all the verbs in the training corpus and produce a single (large) general table. The other

$$E(Y = k \mid X_1 - X_2 - \cdots - X_N \textit{ marginal table of the new corpus})$$

$$= \sum_{i_1} \sum_{i_2} \cdots \sum_{i_N} \mathcal{N}_{i_1 i_2 \cdots i_N +} P(Y = k \mid X_1 = i_1, X_2 = i_2, \cdots, X_N = i_N)$$

$$= \sum_{i_1} \sum_{i_2} \cdots \sum_{i_N} \mathcal{N}_{i_1 i_2 \cdots i_N +} \frac{P(X_1=i_1, X_2=i_2, \cdots, X_N=i_N \mid Y=k)\, P(Y=k)}{\sum_{k'} [P(X_1=i_1, X_2=i_2, \cdots, X_N=i_N \mid Y=k')\, P(Y=k')]}$$

$$= \sum_{i_1} \sum_{i_2} \cdots \sum_{i_N} \mathcal{N}_{i_1 i_2 \cdots i_N +} \frac{\mathcal{M}_{i_1 i_2 \cdots i_N k}}{\sum_{k'} \mathcal{M}_{i_1 i_2 \cdots i_N k'}}$$

where $\mathcal{N}_{i_1 i_2 \cdots i_n +}$ is the cell count of the $X_1 - X_2 - \cdots - X_N$ marginal table of the new corpus obtained as the system output, and $\mathcal{M}_{i_1 i_2 \cdots i_N k}$ is the fitted value of the $(N+1)$-dimensional contingency table of the training corpus based on a particular log-linear model.

TABLE 5. Multidimensional Statistical Estimation of Subcat Frame Frequencies.

is to construct a table for each verb. Obviously the former approach is preferable if it works. Unfortunately, such a table is typically too general to be useful; the estimated frequencies based on it are less accurate than raw system output. This is because the sources of errors, viz., the distribution of off-diagonal cell counts of 2-way contingency tables, differ considerably from verb to verb. The latter approach is problematic if we have to make such a table for each domain. However, if we have a training corpus in one domain, and if the heuristics for each verb extracted from the training corpus are also applicable to other domains, the approach may work.

To test the latter possibility, we constructed a contingency table for the verb from the test corpus described in the Section 3 that was most problematic (least accurately estimated) among the 33 verbs—*need.* Note that we are using the test corpus described in the Section 3 as a training corpus here, because we already know both the measured frequency and the hand-judged frequency of *need* which are necessary to construct a contingency table. The total occurrence of this verb was 75. To smooth the table, 0.1 is added to all the cell counts. As new test corpora, we extracted another 300,000 words of tagged text from the WSJ corpus (labeled "W3") and also three sets of 300,000 words of tagged text from the Brown corpus (labeled "B1", "B2", and "B3"), as retagged under the Penn Treebank tagset. All the training and test corpora were reviewed — and judged — by hand.

Table 6 gives the frequency distributions based on the system output, hand judgement, and statistical analysis. (As before, we take the hand judgement to be the gold standard, the actual frequency of a particular frame.) After the Y margins are statistically estimated, the least estimated Y values less than 1.0 are truncated to 0. (These are considered to have appeared due to the smoothing.)

W3	NP+NP	NP+CL	NP+INF	NP	CL	INF	REST
Measured	2.4	0.0	10.6	44.7	1.2	31.8	9.4
By Hand	0.0	0.0	0.0	69.4	0.0	30.6	0.0
Estimated	0.0	0.0	0.0	66.3	0.0	30.1	3.6
Total Occurrences: 85							

B1	NP+NP	NP+CL	NP+INF	NP	CL	INF	REST
Measured	1.8	0.9	7.9	38.6	1.8	14.9	34.2
By Hand	0.0	0.0	0.0	72.8	0.0	15.8	11.4
Estimated	0.0	0.0	0.0	76.6	0.0	14.4	9.1
Total Occurrences: 114							

B2	NP+NP	NP+CL	NP+INF	NP	CL	INF	REST
Measured	0.0	1.4	8.7	40.6	1.4	17.4	30.4
By Hand	0.0	0.0	0.0	73.9	0.0	18.8	7.2
Estimated	0.0	0.0	0.0	76.1	0.0	16.4	7.5
Total Occurrences: 69							

B3	NP+NP	NP+CL	NP+INF	NP	CL	INF	REST
Measured	3.3	0.0	1.7	30.0	3.3	31.7	30.0
By Hand	0.0	0.0	0.0	60.0	0.0	28.3	11.7
Estimated	0.0	0.0	0.0	61.4	0.0	29.8	8.8
Total Occurrences: 60							

TABLE 6. Statistical Estimation (Unit = %) for the Verb *Need*

In all of the test corpora, the method gives very accurate frequency distribution estimates. Big gaps between the automatically-measured and manually-determined frequencies of “NP” and ‘REST’ are shown to be substantially reduced through the use of statistical estimation. This result is especially encouraging because the heuristics obtained in one domain are shown to be applicable to a considerably different domain. Furthermore, by combining more feature sets and making use of multi-dimensional analysis, we can expect to obtain more accurate estimations.

5. CONCLUSION AND FUTURE DIRECTION

We have demonstrated that by combining syntactic and multidimensional statistical analysis, the frequencies of verb-subcat frames can be estimated with high accuracy. Although the present system measures the frequencies of only six subcat frames, the method is general enough to be extended to many more frames. Since our current focus is more on the estimation of the frequencies of subcat frames than on the acquisition of frames themselves, using information on subcat frames in machine-readable dictionaries to guide the frequency measurement can be an interesting direction to explore.

The traditional application of regular expressions as rules for deterministic processing has self-evident limitations since a regular grammar is not powerful enough to capture general linguistic phenomena. The statistical method we propose uses regular expressions as filters for detecting specific features of the occurrences of verbs and employs multi-dimensional analysis of the features based on loglinear models and Bayes Theorem.

We expect that by identifying other useful syntactic features we can further improve the accuracy of the frequency estimation. Such features can be regarded as characterizing the syntactic context of the verbs, quite broadly. The features need not be linked to a local verb context. For example, a regular expression such as "`w[^vex]*k`" can be used to find cases where the target verb is preceded by a relative pronoun such that there is no other finite verb or punctuation or sentence final period between the relative pronoun and the target verb.

If the syntactic structure of a sentence can be predicted using only syntactic and lexical knowledge, we can hope to estimate the subcat frame of each occurrence of a verb using the context expressed by a set of features. We thus can aim to extend and refine this method for use with general probabilistic parsing of unrestricted text.

Acknowledgements

We thank Teddy Seidenfeld, Jeremy York, and Alex Franz for their comments and discussions with us.

References

Agresti, A. (1990) *Categorical Data Analysis*. John Wiley and Sons, New York, NY.

Baker, J. (1979) Trainable grammars for speech recognition. In D.H. Klatt and J.J. Wolf (eds.), *Speech Communication Papers for the 97th Meeting of the Acoustic Society of America*, 547–550.

Brent, M.R. (1991) Automatic acquisition of subcategorization frames from untagged text. *Proceedings of the 29th Annual Meeting of the ACL.*

Brent, M.R. and Berwick, R.C. (1991) Automatic acquisition of subcategorization frames from tagged text. *Proceedings of the DARPA Speech and Natural Language Workshop*, Morgan Kaufmann.

Brill, E. (1992) A simple rule-based part of speech tagger. *Proceedings of the DARPA Speech and Natural Language Workshop*, Morgan Kaufmann.

Carroll, G. and Charniak, E. (1992) Learning probabilistic dependency grammars from labelled text. *Working Notes of the Symposium on Probabilistic Approaches to Natural Language*, AAAI Fall Symposium Series.

Church, K.W. (1988) A stochastic parts program and noun phrase parser for unrestricted text. *Proceeding of the Second Conference on Applied Natural Language Processing.*

deMarcken, C.G. (1990) Parsing the LOB corpus. *Proceedings of the 28th Annual Meeting of the ACL*, 243–251.

Hornby, A.S. (ed.). (1989) *Oxford Advanced Learner's Dictionary of Current English.* Oxford University Press, Oxford, UK.

Jelinek, F., Lafferty, J.D., and Mercer, R.L. (1990) *Basic Method of Probabilistic Context Free Grammars*. Technical Report RC 16374 (72684), IBM, Yorktown Heights, NY 10598.

Lari, K. and Young, S.J. (1990) The estimation of stochastic context-free grammars using the Inside-Outside algorithm. *Computer Speech and Language*, Vol. 4, 35–56.

14. MONTE CARLO PARSING

RENS BOD
Department of Computational Linguistics
University of Amsterdam

Abstract.
In stochastic language processing, we are often interested in the most probable parse tree of an input sentence. Since there can be exponentially many parses, comparing all of them is not efficient. The Viterbi algorithm (Viterbi, 1967; Jelinek et al., 1990) provides a tool to calculate in cubic time the most probable derivation of a sentence. However, in stochastic language models that allow a tree to be generated by different derivations - like Data-Oriented Parsing (DOP) or Stochastic Lexicalized Tree-Adjoining Grammar (SLTAG) - the most probable derivation does not necessarily produce the most probable tree. In such cases, a Viterbi-style optimization is not applicable to finding the most probable parse tree. In this chapter, we show that by employing Monte Carlo techniques, the most probable parse tree can be estimated as accurately as desired in polynomial time. Monte Carlo parsing is not only relevant to DOP or SLTAG, but also provides for other stochastic language models an interesting alternative to Viterbi. Experiments on a set of manually corrected trees from the Penn Treebank yield 96% parse accuracy.

1. INTRODUCTION

As soon as a formal grammar characterizes a non-trivial part of a natural language, almost every input sentence of reasonable length gets an unmanageably large number of different analyses. Since most of these analyses are not perceived by a human language user, there is a need for distinguishing the appropriate parse(s) of a sentence from the inappropriate ones. In stochastic language processing, it is assumed that the appropriate parse of an input string can be estimated by the most probable parse.

H. Bunt and M. Tomita (eds.), Recent Advances in Parsing Technology, 255–280.

Many instantiations of this idea estimate the probability of a parse by assigning application probabilities to the rewrite rules of a context-free grammar (Suppes, 1970; Fujisaki et al., 1989; Jelinek et al., 1990; Pereira and Schabes, 1992; Schabes et al., 1993). By definition of a context-free derivation, each rewriting is independent of the context within which the nonterminal appears; therefore the probability of a context-free derivation (and its corresponding parse tree) is the product of the probabilities of its context-free rewritings.

It has been widely recognized that unconditional application probabilities of context-free rewrite rules are not adequate for estimating the probability of a parse, since they do not describe how the probability of syntactic structures or lexical items depends on their context. In order to overcome this lack of context-sensitivity, several alternative approaches have been proposed. In (Magerman & Marcus, 1991) and (Magerman & Weir, 1992), a stochastic CFG is combined with part-of-speech trigram statistics. Another approach applies probabilities to elementary trees (Resnik, 1992; Schabes, 1992; Schabes and Waters, 1993), while in (Black et al., 1993), the probability of a rewrite rule is taken to be stochastically dependent on the rules that generated its lefthand side.

The Data-Oriented Parsing (DOP) approach, suggested in (Scha, 1990) and developed in (Bod, 1992, 1993), distinguishes itself from the other statistical approaches in that it omits the step of articulating a formal grammar. Instead, it uses a manually analyzed corpus directly as a stochastic tree grammar. An input string is parsed by combining subtrees from the corpus in the most probable way. In this view, every corpus-subtree can be considered as an elementary tree. As a consequence, one parse tree can usually be generated by several derivations that involve different subtrees. This leads to a statistics where the probability of a parse is equal to the sum of the probabilities of all its derivations. It is hoped that such an approach can accommodate all statistical properties of a language corpus.

We will show that conventional parsing techniques can be applied to DOP. However, in order to calculate the most probable parse, a Viterbi-style optimization is not applicable, since the most probable derivation does not necessarily produce the most probable parse. We will show that by using Monte Carlo techniques, the most probable parse can be estimated in polynomial time. In the following, we first outline the DOP framework in a more general fashion, after which we deal with the parsing and disambiguation problem. Finally, we report on experiments with the Air Travel Information System (ATIS) corpus.

2. THE DATA-ORIENTED PARSING FRAMEWORK

Following (Bod, 1995), the Data-Oriented Parsing (DOP) framework is characterized by the following parameters:

1. definition of the corpus analyses
2. definition of the sub-analyses
3. definition of the combination operations between sub-analyses
4. definition of the combination probabilities between sub-analyses

By means of these parameters a wide range of DOP models can be instantiated. In this article, we will instantiate above parameters only in as far as the resulting model can be implemented and tested with actually available corpora. As these corpora consist of syntactically labeled phrase structure trees, we make the following choices among the parameters:

1. *corpus analyses:* syntactically labeled phrase structure trees
2. *sub-analyses:* subtrees
3. *combination operations:* composition: the identification of the root-node of one subtree with the leftmost nonterminal leaf node of another subtree (in other words: the "substitution" of one subtree on the leftmost nonterminal leaf node of another subtree)
4. *combination probabilities:* the probability of substituting a subtree on a leftmost nonterminal leaf node of another subtree; this is defined as the probability of selecting a subtree among all corpus-subtrees that could be substituted on a certain nonterminal leaf node.

Ad (2): A *subtree* of a tree T is a connected subgraph U of T such that, (1) for every node in U holds that it has either zero daughter nodes or all daughter nodes of the corresponding node in T, and, (2) U consists of more than one node. The example in figure 1 clarifies this definition. This definition of subtree defines exactly all partial analyses that could be generated by the 'underlying' phrase structure grammar.

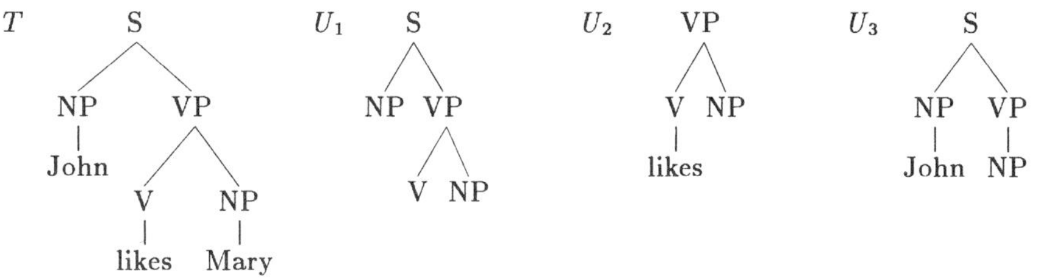

Figure 1. U_1 and U_2 are *subtrees* of T, but U_3 is not.

Ad (3): The *composition* operation (also called *leftmost substitution* operation) is defined as follows.

The composition of subtrees t and u, $t \circ u$, yields a copy of t in which its leftmost nonterminal leaf node has been identified with the root node of u (i.e., u is *substituted* on the leftmost nonterminal leaf node of t). We may define several other combination operations between subtrees, but as a first realization of DOP we will only use this one. Notice the analogy of the substitution operation with rule-application in context-free grammars. The addition of *leftmost* serves to make the composition for two subtrees unique, such that we can speak of a (partial) function.

The composition operation is illustrated by figure 2.

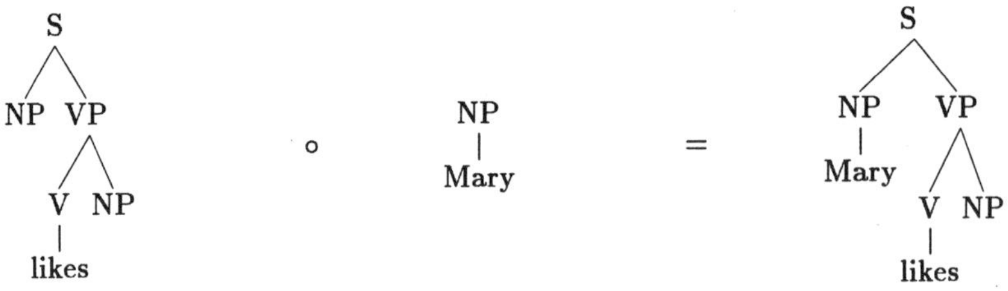

Figure 2. Illustration of the *composition* or *substitution* operation.

We will write in the following $(t \circ u) \circ v$ as: $t \circ u \circ v$. Note, however, that composition is not associative.

Ad (4): The substitution of a subtree on a leftmost nonterminal node is independent of the subtree in which this leftmost nonterminal node appears. This means that we can simply talk about the substitution probability of a certain subtree t given a node of a category C; that is, we can write this substitution probability as $P(X = t|root(X) = C)$. If we consider only the cases where the substitution operation is defined, i.e. where C is equal to the root of t, we can write the substitution probability of a subtree t as $P(X = t|root(X) = root(t))$. By applying Bayes' rule, we obtain $P(X = t)P(root(X) = root(t)|X = t)/P(root(X) = root(t))$. Since $P(root(X) = root(t)|X = t)$ is equal to 1 for all t, we get $P(X = t|root(X) = root(t)) = P(X = t)/P(root(X) = root(t))$. If we directly use our corpus for the probability estimations, we can evaluate the above formula as follows: $P(X = t)/P(root(X) = root(t)) = (N_{X:X=t}/N_X)/(N_{X:root(X)=root(t)}/N_X) = N_{X:X=t}/N_{X:root(X)=root(t)}$. Thus, the substitution probability of a subtree t is computed as the ratio between the number of occurrences of t and the total number of occurrences of subtrees that have the same root as t. Note that this implies that the substitution probabilities of subtrees with the same root-node sum up to one.

Now that we have instantiated the parameters of our DOP model (which for reasons of conciseness we will often call "DOP"), we want to know how we can compute the probability of an analysis of an input sentence from the substitution probabilities of the subtrees that make up the analysis. In order to deal with this, it is convenient to illustrate DOP with an example. Suppose that a corpus of sentence analyses consists of only two trees given in figure 3.

Figure 3. A corpus of two trees.

This means that we have the following space of subtrees (figure 4):

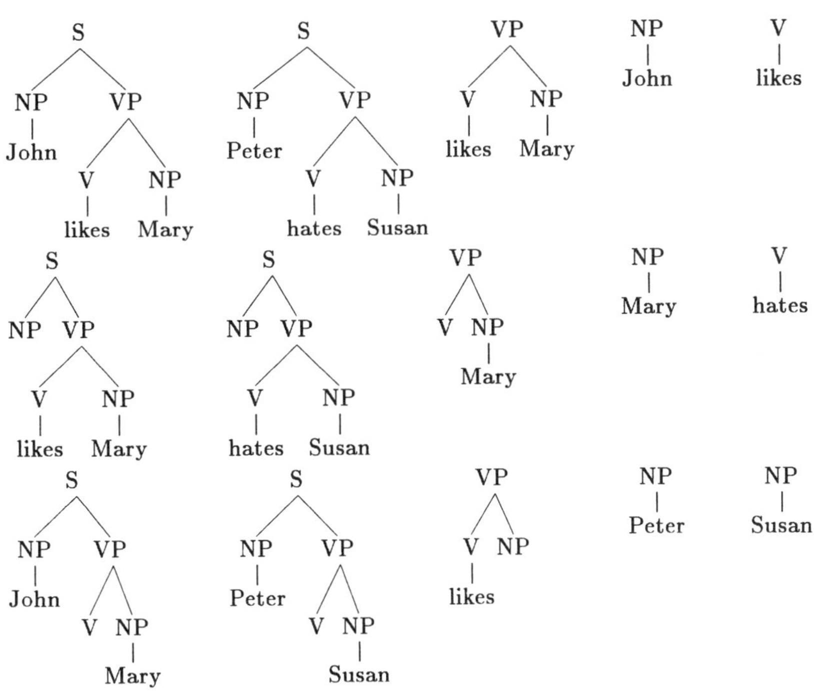

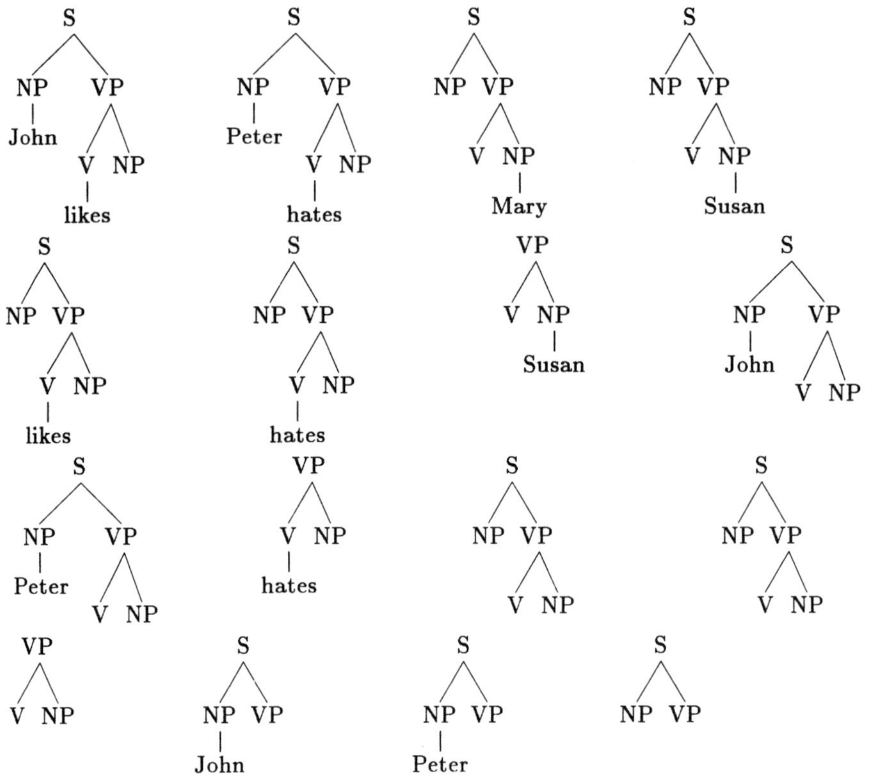

Figure 4. The space of subtrees corresponding to the corpus in Figure 3.

By means of the substitution operation, a new input sentence *"Mary likes Susan"* can be analyzed by combining subtrees as in figure 5, for instance.

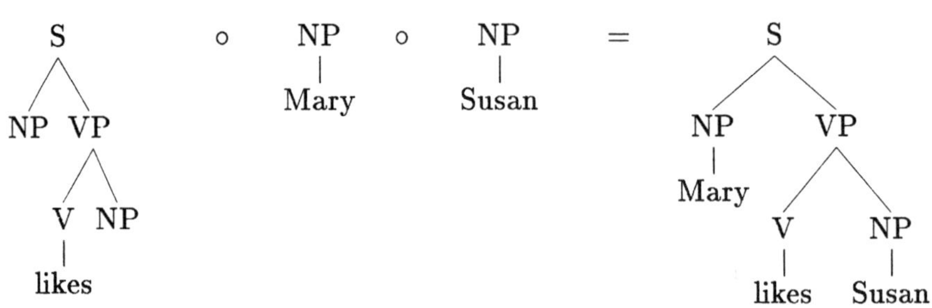

Figure 5. Analyzing *"Mary likes Susan"* by combining corpus-subtrees.

Such a combination of subtrees will be called a *derivation*. We notice that other derivations may yield the same parse tree; for instance, the one in figure 6 or that in figure 7 below.

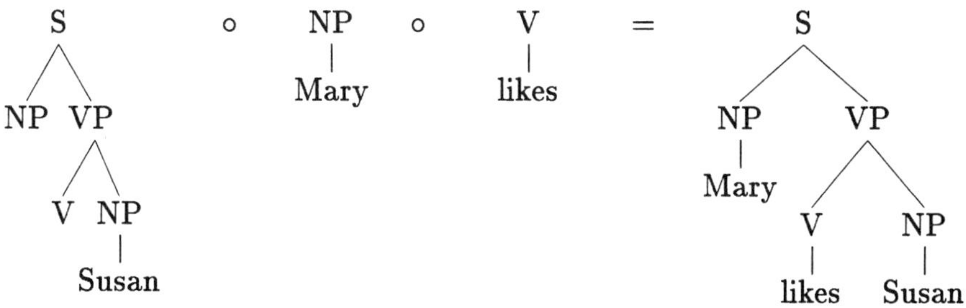

Figure 6. Different derivation yielding the same parse tree.

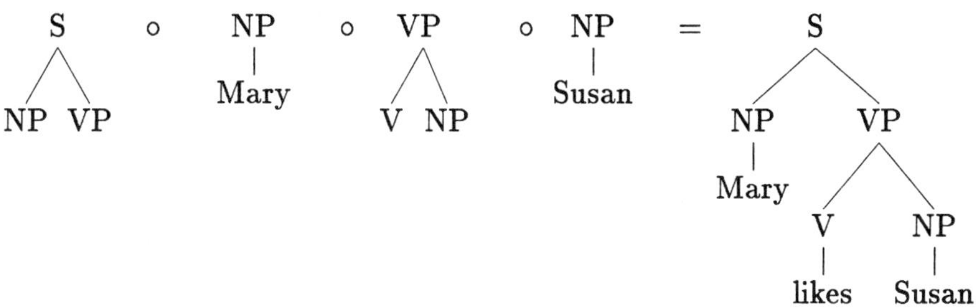

Figure 7. Another derivation yielding the same parse tree.

Thus, a parse tree can be generated by several derivations involving different subtrees.[1] How can we compute the probability of a derivation and that of a parse tree from the substitution probabilities of the subtrees? Let us start with the probability of a derivation, which is the joint probability of the subtrees that make up the derivation. Since the substitution of each subtree on a nonterminal is independent of the subtree in which this nonterminal appears, the probability of a derivation is equal to the product of the substitution probabilities of its subtrees.

As an example, we calculate the substitution probabilities of the subtrees in figure 7 together with the probability of their resulting derivation. The subtree $S(NP, VP)$ occurs twice among a total of 20 subtrees rooted with an S (see figure 4). Thus, its substitution probability is $2/20$.[2] The

[1] We might call this 'spurious ambiguity'. Note that in this imaginary example, the sentence "Mary likes Susan" is not structurally ambiguous.

[2] The term 'substitution probability' may seem inappropriate for subtrees rooted with an S, since they are not substituted on any other subtree. One should therefore assume a

subtree $NP(Mary)$ occurs once among a total of 4 subtrees that can be substituted on the category NP, hence, its substitution probability is 1/4. The probability of selecting the subtree *VP(V(likes),NP)* is 1/8, since there are 8 subtrees rooted with a VP, among which this subtree occurs once. Finally, the probability of selecting *NP(Susan)* is equal to 1/4. The probability of the resulting derivation is then equal to $2/20 \cdot 1/4 \cdot 1/8 \cdot 1/4 = 1/1280$. Table 1 shows the probabilities of all three derivations given above.

P(figure 5)	=	1/20	1/4	1/4		=	1/320
P(figure 6)	=	1/20	1/4	1/2		=	1/160
P(figure 7)	=	2/20	1/4	1/8	1/4	=	1/1280

TABLE 1. The probabilities of the derivations in figures 5, 6 and 7.

This table shows that a model which defines probabilities over parse trees by taking into account only one derivation, does not accommodate the frequencies of all subtrees that may contribute to the generation of a parse tree. We should take into account the probabilities of all derivations of a parse tree, such that no subtree that might possibly be of statistical interest is ignored. How can we compute the probability of a parse tree? The probability that a parse occurs is equal to the probability that any of its derivations occurs. Therefore, the probability of a parse is the sum of the probabilities of all its derivations. (This marks the difference with 'normal' stochastic grammars, where usually no distinction is made between the probability of a parse tree and the probability of a derivation which generates that tree). The calculation of the probability of the above parse tree for *Mary likes Susan* is left to the reader. Note that the probability of a sentence or string is the sum of the probabilities of all its parses.

We conclude this section with an emerging property of DOP, which will turn out to be of interest. In DOP, the probability of a parse depends on all derivations that generate that parse; therefore, other things being equal, the more different ways in which a parse can be generated, the higher its probability tends to be; this implies that a parse which can (also) be generated by relatively large corpus-subtrees tends to be favored over a parse which can only be generated by relatively small corpus-subtrees. Thus, given a sentence, there is a preference for the parse which can be generated by the largest possible subtrees.

start-symbol S on which the first subtree of a derivation is substituted. This will be made rigorous in the following section, where we describe DOP as a 'stochastic tree-substitution grammar'.

3. DOP AS A STOCHASTIC TREE-SUBSTITUTION GRAMMAR

For dealing with the problem of computing the most probable parse of a sentence, it is convenient to define our DOP model within the context of Formal Stochastic Language Theory as a stochastic tree-substitution grammar (STSG). Formally, a *Stochastic Tree-Substitution Grammar* G is a five-tuple $< V_N, V_T, S, R, P >$ where

- V_N is a finite set of nonterminal symbols;
- V_T is a finite set of terminal symbols;
- $S \in V_N$ is the distinguished symbol;
- R is a finite set of elementary trees whose top nodes and interior nodes are labeled by nonterminal symbols, and whose yield nodes are labeled by terminal or nonterminal symbols;
- P is a function which assigns to every elementary tree $t \in R$ a probability $p(t)$. For a tree t with a root α, $p(t)$ is interpreted as the probability of substituting t on α. We require, therefore, that $0 < p(t) \leq 1$ and $\Sigma_{t:root(t)=\alpha} p(t) = 1$.

If t_1 and t_2 are trees such that the *leftmost nonterminal yield node* of t_1 is equal to the root of t_2, then $t_1 \circ t_2$ is the tree that results from substituting t_2 for this leftmost nonterminal yield node in t_1. The partial function $\circ$ is called *leftmost substitution.* We will write $(t_1 \circ t_2) \circ t_3$ as $t_1 \circ t_2 \circ t_3$, and in general $(..((t_1 \circ t_2) \circ t_3) \circ ..) \circ t_n$ as $t_1 \circ t_2 \circ t_3 \circ ... \circ t_n$. For reasons of conciseness we will use the term *substitution* for leftmost substitution. Notice that the value $p(t)$ for an elementary tree with root α is the probability of substituting t for any nonterminal leaf node α in any elementary tree in R.

A *leftmost derivation* generated by an STSG G is a tuple of trees $< t_1, ..., t_n >$ such that $t_1, ..., t_n$ are elements of R, the root of t_1 is labeled by S, and the yield of $t_1 \circ ... \circ t_n$ is labeled by terminal symbols. The set of leftmost derivations generated by G is thus given by $\mathsf{Derivations}(G) = \{< t_1, ..., t_n > | t_1, ..., t_n \in R \wedge root(t_1) = S \wedge yield(t_1 \circ ... \circ t_n) \in V_T^+\}$. For convenience we will use the term *derivation* for leftmost derivation. A derivation $< t_1, ..., t_n >$ is called a derivation of tree T, iff $t_1 \circ ... \circ t_n = T$. A derivation $< t_1, ..., t_n >$ is called a derivation of string s, iff $yield(t_1 \circ ... \circ t_n) = s$. The probability of a derivation $< t_1, ..., t_n >$ is defined as $p(t_1) \cdot ... \cdot p(t_n)$.

A parse tree generated by an STSG G is a tree T such that there is a derivation $< t_1, ..., t_n > \in \mathsf{Derivations}(G)$ for which $t_1 \circ ... \circ t_n = T$. The set of parse trees, or tree language, generated by G is given by $\mathsf{Parses}(G) = \{T | < t_1, ..., t_n > \in \mathsf{Derivations}(G) : t_1 \circ ... \circ t_n = T\}$. For reasons of conciseness we will often use the terms *parse* or *tree* for a parse tree. A parse whose yield is equal to string s, is called a parse of s. The probability of a parse is defined as the sum of the probabilities of all its derivations.

A *string* generated by an STSG G is an element of V_T^+ such that there is a parse generated by G whose yield is equal to the string. The set of strings, or *string language*, generated by G is given by $\mathsf{Strings}(G) = \{s | \exists T : T \in \mathsf{Parses}(G) \wedge s = yield(T)\}$. The probability of a string is defined as the sum of the probabilities of all its parses. This means that the probability of a string is also equal to the sum of the probabilities of all its derivations.

It may be evident that STSG is a generalization over our DOP model: DOP projects a corpus of tree structures into an STSG, where the subtrees of DOP are the elementary trees of the STSG, and the substitution probabilities are the probabilities of the corresponding elementary trees in STSG. In (Bod, 1995), it is shown that STSG is stochastically stronger than stochastic context-free grammar (Fujisaki et al., 1989; Jelinek et al., 1990), stochastic history-based grammar (Black et al., 1993) and (current instantiations of) stochastic tree-adjoining grammar (Schabes, 1992; Resnik, 1992).

4. PARSING AND DISAMBIGUATION IN DOP

In order to deal with the problem of computing the most probable parse tree of a sentence in DOP or STSG, we distinguish between parsing and disambiguation. By parsing we mean the creation of a parse forest for an input sentence. By disambiguation we mean the selection of the most probable parse[3] from the forest. The creation of a parse forest is seen as an intermediate step for computing the most probable parse.

4.1. PARSING

From the way STSG combines elementary trees by means of substitution, it follows that an input sentence can be parsed by the same algorithms as (stochastic) context-free grammar ((S)CFG). Every elementary tree t is used as a context-free rewrite rule: $root(t) \rightarrow yield(t)$. Given a cubic time context-free parsing algorithm, an input sentence of n words can be parsed in n^3 time. Most cubic time parsers make use of a chart or well-formed substring table. A chart parser takes as input a set of context-free rewrite rules and a sentence and produces as output a chart of labeled phrases. A labeled phrase is a sequence of words labeled with a category symbol which denotes the syntactic category of that phrase. A chart-like parse forest can

[3]Note that there can be more than one most probable parse for an input sentence; however, for non-trivial corpora, an input sentence tends to get exactly one most probable parse. In the following, we will assume that the most probable parse is unique.

be obtained by including pointers from a category to the other categories which caused it to be placed in the chart. Algorithms that accomplish this can be found in (Kay, 1980; Winograd, 1983; Jelinek et al., 1990).

In order to obtain a chart-like forest for a sentence parsed by STSG, we need to label the phrases not only with the syntactic categories of that phrase but with the full elementary trees t that correspond to the use of their derived rules $root(t) \rightarrow yield(t)$. Note that in a chart-like forest generated by an STSG, different derivations that generate a same tree do not collapse. We will therefore talk about a derivation forest generated by an STSG (cf. Sima'an et al., 1994).

The following formal example illustrates what a derivation forest of a sentence may look like for STSG. In the example, we leave out the probabilities of the elementary trees, that are needed only in the disambiguation process. The visual representation comes from (Kay, 1980): every entry (i, j) in the chart is indicated by an edge and spans the words between the ith and the jth position of a sentence. Every edge is labeled with the elementary trees that denote the underlying phrase. The example STSG consists of the elementary trees of figure 8. For the input string *abcd*, the derivation forest obtained is shown in figure 9.

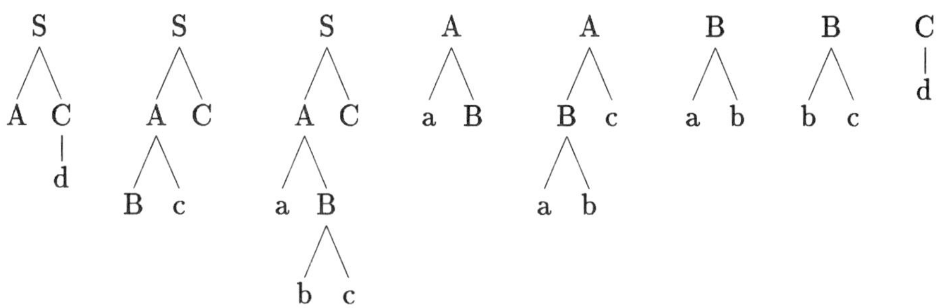

Figure 8. Elementary trees of an example STSG.

Note that different derivations in the forest produce the same tree. By exhaustively unpacking the forest, four different derivations generating two different trees are obtained. Thus, every tree is represented twice in the forest by different derivations (with possibly different probabilities). We may ask whether we can pack the forest by collapsing spurious derivations, summing up their probabilities. Unfortunately, no efficient procedure is known that accomplishes this (remember that there can be exponentially many derivations for one tree).

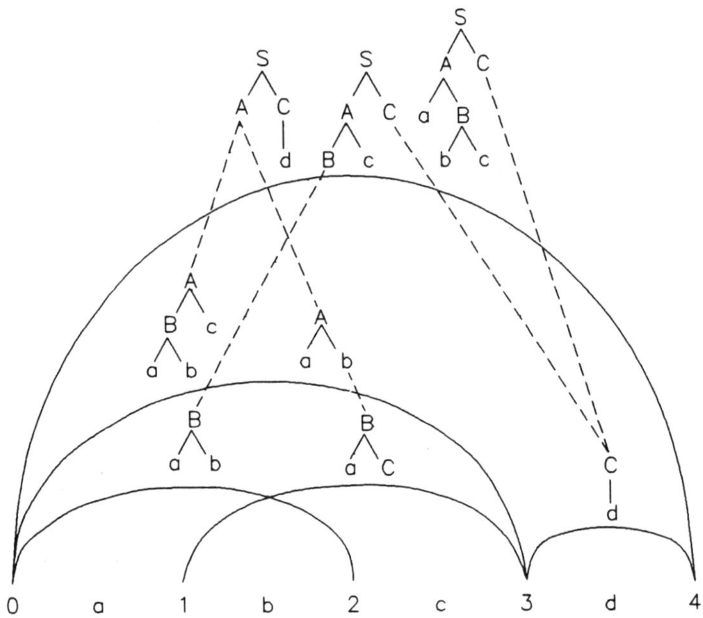

Figure 9. Derivation forest for the string abcd.

4.2. DISAMBIGUATION

Cubic time parsing does not guarantee cubic time disambiguation, as a sentence may have exponentially many parses and any such parse may have exponentially many derivations. Therefore, in order to find the most probable parse of a sentence, it is not efficient to compare the probabilities of the parses by exhaustively unpacking the chart. Even for determining the probability of one parse, it is not efficient to add the probabilities of all derivations of that parse.

Viterbi optimization and finding the most probable parse

There exists a heuristic optimization algorithm, known as Viterbi optimization, which selects on the basis of an SCFG the most probable derivation of a sentence in cubic time (Viterbi, 1967; Fujisaki et al., 1989; Jelinek et al., 1990). In STSG, however, the most probable derivation does not necessarily generate the most probable parse, as the probability of a parse is defined as the sum of the probabilities of all its derivations. Thus, there is an important question as to whether we can adapt the Viterbi algorithm for finding the most probable parse.

To understand the difficulty of the problem, we look in more detail at the Viterbi algorithm. The basic idea of the Viterbi algorithm is the pruning of low probability subderivations in a bottom-up fashion. Two

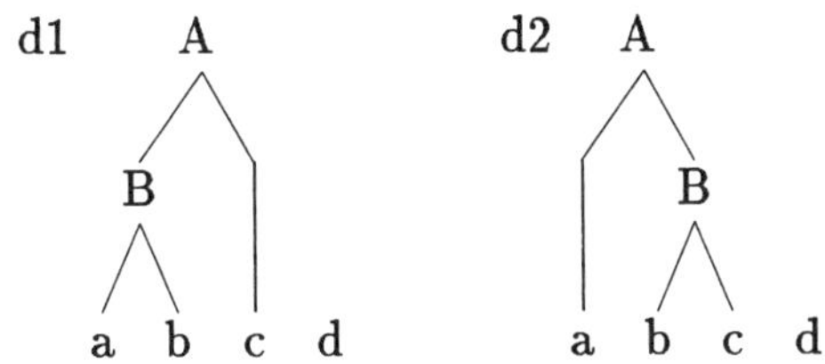

Figure 10. Two subderivations for the substring *abc*.

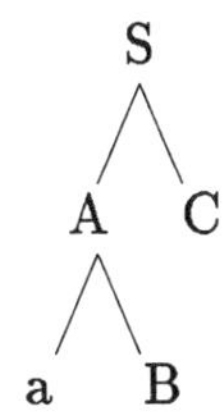

Figure 11. Elementary tree

different subderivations of the same part of the sentence and whose resulting subparses have the same root can both be developed (if at all) to derivations of the whole sentence in the same ways. Therefore, if one of these two subderivations has a lower probability, then it can be eliminated. This is illustrated by a formal example in figure 10. Suppose that during bottom-up parsing of the string abcd the following two subderivations *d1* and *d2* have been generated for the substring *abc*. (Actually represented are their resulting subparses.)

If the probability of *d1* is higher than the probability of *d2*, we can eliminate *d2* if we are only interested in finding the most probable *derivation* of *abcd*. But if we are interested in finding the most probable *parse* of *abcd* (generated by STSG), we are not allowed to eliminate *d2*. This can be seen by the following. Suppose that we have the additional elementary tree given in figure 11.

This elementary tree may be developed to the same tree that can be developed by *d2*, but not to the tree that can be developed by *d1*. And since the probability of a parse tree is equal to the sum of the probabilities of all its derivations, it is still possible that *d2* contributes to the generation of the most probable parse. Therefore we are not allowed to eliminate *d2*.

This counter-example does not prove that there is no heuristic optimization that allows for a polynomial time selection of the most probable parse. But it makes clear that a *'select-best'* search, as accomplished by Viterbi, is not adequate for finding the most probable parse in STSG. In (Sima'an et al., 1994), it is shown that there exists an optimization technique for finding the most probable parse in STSG, but that this technique still takes exponential time. One may of course ask how often the most probable derivation yields in fact the same parse as the computation of the most probable parse, but this can only be answered by actual experiments in section 5. Not surprisingly, predictions based on the most probable parse turn out to be more accurate than predictions based on the parse generated by the most probable derivation.

Estimating the most probable parse by Monte Carlo search

We will now deal with the question as to whether there exists a polynomial time *approximation procedure* that estimates the most probable parse with an error that can be made arbitrarily small. We have seen that a *select-best* search, as accomplished by Viterbi, can be used for finding the most probable derivation in STSG but not for finding the most probable parse. If we apply instead of a *select-best* search, a *'select-random'* search, we can generate a random derivation - provided that the random choices are based on the actual probabilities of the subderivations. By iteratively generating a large number of random derivations we can estimate the most probable parse as the parse which results most often from these random derivations (since the probability of a parse is the probability that any of its derivations occurs). The most probable parse can be estimated as accurately as desired by making the number of random samples as large as desired. According to the Law of Large Numbers, the most often generated parse converges to the most probable parse. Methods that estimate the probability of an event by taking random samples are known as Monte Carlo methods (Hammersley & Handscomb, 1964).[4]

The selection of a random derivation can be accomplished in a bottom-up fashion analogous to Viterbi. Instead of selecting the most probable subderivation at each node-sharing in the chart, a random subderivation is selected at each node-sharing (that is, a subderivation that has n times as large a probability as another subderivation should also have n times as large a chance to be chosen as this other subderivation). Once arrived at the S-node, the random derivation of the whole sentence can be retrieved by tracing back the choices made at each node-sharing. It trivially follows that

[4]Note that Monte Carlo estimation of the most probable parse is more reliable than the estimation of the most probable parse by generating the n most probable derivations by Viterbi, since it might be that the most probable parse is exclusively generated by many low probability derivations. The Monte Carlo method is guaranteed to converge to the most probable parse.

the sample probability of a derivation is equal to the probability of that derivation, since the probability of sampling a sequence of subderivations that make up a derivation is equal to the product of the probabilities of sampling the subderivations. We may of course postpone sampling until the S-node, such that we sample directly from the distribution of all S-derivations. But this would take exponential time, since there may be exponentially many derivations for the whole sentence. By sampling bottom-up at every node where ambiguity appears, the maximum number of different subderivations at each node-sharing is bounded to a constant (the total number of rules of that node), and therefore the time complexity of generating a random derivation of an input sentence is equal to the time complexity of finding the most probable derivation, $O(n^3)$. This is exemplified by the following algorithm.

Algorithm 1:
Sampling a random derivation from a derivation forest
Given: a derivation forest of a sentence of n words, consisting of labeled entries (i, j) that span the words between the ith and the jth position of the sentence. Every entry is labeled with linked elementary trees, together with their probabilities, that constitute subderivations of the underlying subsentence. Sampling a derivation from the chart consists of choosing at every labeled entry (bottom-up, breadth-first) at random a subderivation of each root-node:

```
for  k := 1 to n do
     for  i := 0 to n-k do
          for  chart-entry (i,i+k) do
               for each root-node X do
               select at random a subderivation of root-node X;
               eliminate the other subderivations
```

Let $\{(e_1, p_1), (e_2, p_2), ..., (e_{,} p_n)\}$ be a probability distribution of events $e_1, e_2, \ldots, e_n$; an event e_i is said to be *randomly selected* iff its chance of being selected is equal to p_i. In order to allow for 'simple sampling' (Cochran, 1963), where every event has equal chance of being selected, one must convert a probability distribution into a sample space for which holds that the frequency of occurrence r_i of each event e_i is a positive integer equal to $n \cdot p_i$, where n is the size of the sample space.

We now have an algorithm that selects a random derivation from a derivation forest. Converting this derivation into a parse tree gives a first estimation for the most probable parse. Since one random sample is not a reliable estimate, we need to sample a large number of random derivations and select the parse which results most often from these random derivations. However, we want to have an exact criterion for deciding at what number of samples N the most frequently generated parse is a reliable estimate for the most probable parse.

First, we need to have sufficiently small standard errors in the relative frequencies of the parses. We therefore demand that the number of samples N be made sufficiently large in order to make the standard errors sufficiently small (often 0.05 in sampling experiments). The variance of a parse with probability p_i is equal to $p_i(1 - p_i)/N$. Since $0 < p_i \leq 1$, the variance is always smaller or equal to $1/(4N)$. Thus, for a standard error σ (which is the square-root of the variance) holds that $\sigma \leq 1/(2\sqrt{N})$. This allows us to calculate a lower bound for N given an upper bound for σ, by $N \geq 1/(4\sigma^2)$. For instance, in order to obtain a standard error of 0.05, N must be at least 100.

A small standard error in the relative frequency of the estimated most probable parse does not guarantee that we have a reliable estimate for the actual most probable parse. For instance, there may be different parses in the top of the sampling distribution that are almost equally likely. We are thus interested in the probability that the most frequently generated parse is not equal to the most probable parse. The upper bound for this probability is given by $\Sigma_{i \neq 0}(1 - (\sqrt(p_0) - \sqrt(p_i))^2)^N$, where p_0 is the probability of the most probable parse and where p_i are the probabilities of the different parses i; N is the number of Monte Carlo iterations.[5] We will call this upper bound probability the *most probable parse error,* or simply *mpp error.* We cannot derive beforehand a lower bound for N as we did for the standard error, but we can estimate the mpp error by replacing p_i by the observed relative frequencies of the parses. Secondly we want to make the mpp error sufficiently small, for instance 0.05, by increasing N. This is not possible if the most probable parse is not unique, and N must be large if there is an i with p_i near to p_0.

Notice that it is not enough to have a small mpp error. We also need sufficiently small standard errors for the estimated parse probabilities. This is exemplified by the following algorithm.

Algorithm 2: *Estimation of the most probable parse (mpp)*
Given: a derivation forest of a sentence, and thresholds for the standard error and the mpp error:

[5]The formula is a special case of the problem of estimating the most frequent type in a population by means of sequential sampling (cf. Hammersley & Handscomb, 1964; Deming, 1966). I am indebted to Chris Klaassen for pointing this out to me.

```
repeat  until standard error and mpp error are smaller than threshold:
        sample random derivation from derivation forest (algorithm 1);
        store parse generated by sampled derivation;
        mpp := parse with maximal frequency;
        calculate standard error of mpp and mpp error.
```

There is an important question as to how long the estimation of the most probable parse may take. Is there a tractable upper bound on the number of samples N that have to be taken before the standard error and the mpp error are sufficiently small? The answer is yes: from the expressions for the standard error and the mpp error given above, it follows that the worst error in the mpp is quadratic in time cost. Therefore, the worst case time complexity of achieving an error ε is $O(\varepsilon^{-2})$. In practice, this means that in order to reduce ε by a factor of k, the number of samples N needs to be increased k^2-fold.

What is the worst case time complexity of parsing and disambiguation together? That is, given an STSG and an input sentence, what is the maximal time cost of finding the most probable parse of a sentence? If we use a chart parser, the creation of a derivation forest for a sentence of n words takes $O(n^3)$ time. Taking also into account the size G of an STSG (defined as the sum of the lengths of the yields of all its elementary trees), a derivation forest can be created in $O(Gn^3)$ time (cf. Graham, Harrison & Ruzzo, 1980). The time complexity of disambiguation is both proportional to the cost of sampling a derivation, i.e. n^3, and to the cost of achieving a maximal error by means of iteration, which is ε^{-2}. This means that the time complexity of disambiguation is given by $O(n^3\varepsilon^{-2})$. The *total* time complexity of parsing and disambiguation is equal to $O(Gn^3) + O(n^3\varepsilon^{-2}) = O((G+\varepsilon^{-2})n^3)$. Thus, there exists a tractable procedure that estimates the most probable parse of an input sentence. This procedure is linear in the grammar size, quadratic in the error probability, and cubic in the sentence length. Questions concerning the actual time performance of parsing and disambiguation will be dealt with when we discuss the experiments in section 5.

Notice that although Monte Carlo disambiguation can estimate the most probable parse of a sentence in polynomial time, it is not in the class of polynomial time decidable algorithms P. The Monte Carlo algorithm cannot *decide* in polynomial time what is the most probable parse; it can only make the error probability of the estimated most probable parse arbitrarily small. As such, the Monte Carlo algorithm is a probabilistic algorithm belonging to the class of Bounded error Probabilistic Polynomial time (BPP)

algorithms (cf. Balcazar et al., 1988). *BPP*-problems are usually characterized as follows: it may take exponential time to solve them exactly, but there exists an iterative estimation algorithm with an error that becomes arbitrarily small in polynomial time.

We hypothesize that Monte Carlo disambiguation is also relevant for other stochastic language models. It turns out that all stochastic extensions of CFGs that are richer than SCFG, need exponential algorithms for finding a most probable parse tree (cf. Carroll & Briscoe, 1992; Black et al., 1993; Magerman & Weir, 1992; Schabes and Waters, 1993). To our knowledge, it has never been studied whether there exist *BPP*-algorithms for these models. Alhough it is beyond the scope of our research, we conjecture that there exists a Monte Carlo algorithm for computing the most probable tree in stochastic tree-adjoining grammar.

5. EXPERIMENTS WITH DOP

To test DOP, we used a manually corrected version of the Air Travel Information System (ATIS) corpus (Hemphill et al., 1990) annotated in the Pennsylvania Treebank (Marcus, 1991). The following figure shows a random tree from the corpus. (For the annotation guidelines see Santorini, 1990, 1991.)

```
((SBARQ
  (WHNP WDT/What
        NNS/flights)
  (SQ   VBP/do
        (NP PP/you)
        (VP VB/have
          (PP (PP IN/from
                  (NP NP/San NP/Francisco))
              (PP TO/to
                  (NP NP/Dallas))))))
?)
```

Figure 12. Random tree from the ATIS corpus

The 750 trees from the ATIS corpus were stripped of their words in order to achieve a set of parse trees of part-of-speech sequences.[6] The part-of-speech tags were then marked in order to distinguish them from syntactic categories that bear the same name. For figure 12 this yields the following parse tree for the p-o-s string `"WDT NNS VBP PP VB IN NP NP TO NP"`.

[6]For the parsing of word strings with DOP, we refer to (Bod, 1995).

```
((SBARQ
  (WHNP @WDT
        @NNS)
  (SQ   @VBP
        (NP @PP)
        (VP @VB
          (PP (PP @IN
                  (NP @NP @NP))
              (PP @TO
                  (NP @NP))))))
?)
```

Figure 13. Tree of figure 12 without the words

We used the 'blind testing method', dividing the corpus at random into a 90% training set and a 10% test set. The 675 trees from the training set were converted into subtrees together with their substitution probabilities, yielding roughly $4 \cdot 10^5$ different subtrees. The 75 part-of-speech sequences from the test set served as input sentences that were parsed and disambiguated using the subtrees from the training set. To measure the accuracy of the system, we used the notion of *parse accuracy* (also known as *exact match accuracy*), defined as the percentage of the test strings for which the most probable parse is identical to the parse in the test set.

5.1. ACCURACY AS A FUNCTION OF SUBTREE DEPTH

It is one of the most essential features of DOP, that arbitrarily large subtrees are taken into consideration to estimate the probability of a parse. In order to test the usefulness of this feature, we performed different experiments constraining the *depth* of the subtrees. The depth of a tree is defined as the length of its longest path. Table 2 shows the results of seven experiments for different maximum depths of the training set subtrees.[7]

The parse accuracy is rounded off to the nearest integer. CPU time refers to average CPU time per string of parsing and disambiguation together (at an error-probability threshold of 0.05) employed by a Sun Sparc 2.
The table shows a dramatic increase in parse accuracy when enlarging the maximum depth of the subtrees from 1 to 2. (Note that for depth one, DOP is equivalent to a stochastic context-free grammar.) The accuracy keeps increasing, at a slower rate, when the depth is enlarged further. The highest accuracy is obtained by using *all* subtrees from the training set: 72 out of the 75 sentences from the test set are parsed and disambiguated

[7]Notice that if the depth of subtrees is constrained, their relative frequencies and thus their substitution probabilities change.

depth of subtrees	parse accuracy	CPU time (hours)
1	52 %	.04
≤ 2	87 %	.21
≤ 3	92 %	.72
≤ 4	93 %	1.6
≤ 5	93 %	1.9
≤ 6	95 %	2.2
unbounded	96 %	3.5

TABLE 2. Parse accuracies of DOP for different maximum subtree depths.

correctly. Thus, the accuracy increases if larger subtrees are used, though the CPU time increases considerably as well.

It may be relevant to mention that the *parse coverage* was 99%. This means that for 99% of the test strings the appropriate parse was in the derivation forest generated by the system. As we have already mentioned in section 1, the main problem of natural language systems is not the generation of the set of possible parses, but the selection of the appropriate parse from the possible parses. Above results show that the most probable parse in DOP is a very good estimation of the appropriate parse.

It may also be interesting to mention that the parse accuracy on *unedited* ATIS trees only reached 64%. This is because the original ATIS annotations (1991 release) contain many errors and inconsistencies. However, the *bracketing accuracy* obtained by using the unedited trees remained relatively high: 94.1%.

5.2. MOST PROBABLE DERIVATION VERSUS MOST PROBABLE TREE

Another very important feature of DOP is that the probability of a tree is computed as the sum of the probabilities of all different derivations of that tree. Although the most probable parse tree of a sentence is not necessarily generated by the most probable derivation of that sentence, there is a question as to how often these two coincide. In order to study this, we also calculated the parse accuracy from the trees generated by the most probable derivations. Table 3 shows the parse accuracy based on the most probable derivation against the parse accuracy based on the most probable parse, for the 75 test set strings from the ATIS corpus, using different maximum depths for the corpus subtrees.

The table shows that the two parse accuracies are equal if the depth of the

depth of copus-subtrees	parse accuracy	
	most probable derivation	most probable parse
1	52 %	52 %
≤ 2	47 %	87 %
≤ 3	49 %	92 %
≤ 4	57 %	93 %
≤ 5	60 %	93 %
≤ 6	65 %	95 %
unbounded	65 %	96 %

TABLE 3. Parse accuracy based on most probable derivation and most probable parse.

subtrees is constrained to 1. This is not surprising, as for depth 1, DOP is equivalent to SCFG where every parse is generated by exactly one (leftmost) derivation. What is remarkable, is, that the parse accuracy based on the most probable derivation decreases if the depth of the subtrees is enlarged to 2. If the depth is enlarged further, the accuracy increases again. The highest accuracy by employing the most probable derivation is obtained by using all subtrees from the corpus (65%), but remains far behind the highest parse accuracy based on the most probable parse (96%).

From this table we conclude that predictions based on the most probable parse are much more accurate than predictions based on the parse generated by the most probable derivation. In other words, if we want to predict the appropriate analysis of a string, we should not maximize the probability of the *process* of achieving that analysis but the probability of the *result* of that process.

5.3. THE SIGNIFICANCE OF ONCE-OCCURRING SUBTREES

There is an important question as to whether we need all subtrees for accurately predicting the appropriate parse of a string, or whether it is possible to eliminate subtrees on statistical grounds, by throwing away very infrequent ones. In order to study this question, we start off with a test result. Consider the test sentence *Arrange the flight code of the flight from Denver to Dallas Worth in descending order*, whose appropriate parse according to the test set is displayed in figure 14.

The corresponding p-o-s sequence of this sentence is the test string "VB DT NN NN IN DT NN IN NP TO NP NP IN VBG NN". At subtree-depth 2, the structure of figure 15 was estimated as the most probable parse for this

```
(S (NP *
   (VP VB/Arrange
       (NP (NP DT/the NN/flight NN/code)
           (PP IN/of
               (NP (NP DT/the NN/flight)
                   (PP (PP IN/from
                           (NP NP/Denver))
                       (PP TO/to
                           (NP NP/Dallas NL/Worth))))))
       (PP IN/in
           (NP (VP VBG/descending)
               NN/order))))
```

Figure 14. Appropriate parse according to the test set.

string (where for reasons of readability the words are added to the p-o-s tags).

```
(S (NP *
   (VP VB/Arrange
       (NP (NP DT/the NN/flight NN/code)
       (PP IN/of
           (NP (NP DT/the NN/flight)
               (PP (PP IN/from
                       (NP NP/Denver))
                   (PP TO/to
                       (NP NP/Dallas NL/Worth))))))
               (PP IN/in
                   (NP (VP VBG/descending)
                       NN/order))))
```

Figure 15. Most probable parse for subtree-depth ≤ 2

In this parse tree, we note that the prepositional phrase *in descending order* is incorrectly attached to the NP *the flight* instead of to the verb *arrange*. This wrong attachment may be explained by the high relative frequencies of the subtrees of depth 2, shown in figure 16 (that appear in structures of sentences like *Show me the transportation from SFO to downtown San Francisco in August*, where the PP *in August* is attached to the NP *the transportation*, and not to the verb *show*).

Only if the maximum depth was enlarged to 4, subtrees like the following could be used, which led to the generation of the appropriate parse tree.

```
NP NP              NP NP
   PP                 PP PP
   PP IN                 PP
      NP              PP IN
                         NP
```

Figure 16. Subtrees of depth 2

```
VP VB
   VP VP
      PP
   PP IN
      NP VP VBG
         NN
```

Figure 17. Subtree of depth 4

It is interesting to note that this subtree occurs only once in the training set. Nevertheless, it appears to induce the correct disambiguation of the test string. This seems to contradict the fact that probabilities based on sparse data are not reliable. Since many large subtrees are once-occurring events *(hapaxes)*, there seems to be a preference in DOP for an occurrence-based approach if enough context is provided: large subtrees, even if they occur once, tend to contribute to the generation of the appropriate parse, since they provide much contextual information. Although these subtrees have very low substitution probabilities, they tend to induce the most probable parse because fewer subtrees are needed to construct a parse.

Additional experiments confirmed this hypothesis. Throwing away all hapaxes yielded an accuracy of 92%, which is a decrease of 4%. Distinguishing between small and large hapaxes, showed that the accuracy was not affected by eliminating the hapaxes of depth 1 (however, as an advantage, the Monte Carlo convergence seemed to be slightly faster). Eliminating hapaxes larger than depth 1, decreased the accuracy.

Instead of eliminating subtrees on statistical grounds, one may also employ other elimination criteria. In (Sima'an, 1995), it is shown that by using maximally lexicalized corpus-subtrees, allowing not more than two nonterminals in the yields, the parse accuracy is unaffected while the efficiency is improved considerably (due to a reduction of the number of subtrees). Another optimization technique proposes to use only corpus-subtrees rooted with either an S or an NP (Sekine and Grishman, 1995). Though fast run times on the Wall Street Journal corpus are reported, it is not yet known whether this technique affects the parse accuracy.

6. CONCLUSIONS

Although the Viterbi algorithm provides a tool to derive in cubic time the most probable derivation generated by a stochastic context-free grammar, this algorithm is not applicable to stochastic language models that allow a parse tree to be generated by different derivations (like DOP or SLTAG), since the most probable derivation does not necessarily produce the most probable tree.

We showed that, by applying Monte Carlo techniques, the most probable parse tree can be estimated as accurately as desired, making its error arbitrarily small in polynomial time. We suggested that Monte Carlo parsing may also provide for other stochastic language models an interesting alternative to Viterbi. However, Monte Carlo seems especially apt to stochastic parsing with huge amounts of redundant data, where one parse tree is generated by exponentially many (different) derivations.

We tested DOP on a set of hand-parsed strings from the ATIS corpus. It turned out that parse accuracy improved if larger subtrees were used. We showed that predictions based on the most probable parse are much more accurate than predictions based on the parse generated by the most probable derivation. Finally, it turned out that the parse accuracy decreased if once-occurring subtrees were eliminated, while the elimination of unlexicalized subtrees does not harm the parse accuracy.

References

Balcazar, J., Diaz, J. & Gabarro, J. (1988). *Structural Complexity*, Springer Verlag, Berlin.

Black, E., Garside, R. & Leech, G. (1993). *Statistically-Driven Computer Grammars of English: The IBM/Lancaster Approach*, Rodopi: Amsterdam-Atlanta.

Bod, R. (1992). A Computational Model of Language Performance: Data Oriented Parsing, *Proc. COLING'92*, Nantes.

Bod, R. (1993). Using an Annotated Corpus as a Stochastic Grammar, *Proc. EACL'93*, Utrecht.

Bod, R. (1995). *Enriching Linguistics with Statistics: Performance Models of Natural Language*, ILLC Dissertation Series 1995-14, University of Amsterdam, Academische Pers, Amsterdam.

Carroll, J. & Briscoe, T. (1992). Probabilistic Normalization and Unpacking of Packed Parse Forests for Unification-based Grammars, *Working Notes Probabilistic Approaches to Natural Language*, AAAI Fall Symposium Series, Cambridge, Ma.

Cochran, W. (1963). *Sampling Techniques*, Wiley & Sons, New York (2nd edition).

Deming, W. (1966). *Some Theory of Sampling*, Dover Publications, New York.

Fujisaki, T. Jelinek, F., Cocke, J., Black, E. & Nishino, T. (1989). A Probabilistic Method for Sentence Disambiguation, *Proc. 1st Int. Workshop on Parsing Technologies*,

Pittsburgh.

Graham, S., Harrison, M. & Ruzzo, W. (1980). An improved context-free recognizer, *ACM Transactions on Programming Languages and Systems, 2(3): 415-462.*

Hammersley, J.M. and Handscomb, D.C. (1964). *Monte Carlo Methods*, Chapman and Hall, London.

Hemphill, C.T., Godfrey, J.J. & Doddington, G.R. (1990). The ATIS spoken language systems pilot corpus. *Proc. DARPA Speech and Natural Language Workshop, Hidden Valley*, Morgan Kaufmann.

Jelinek, F.,Lafferty, J.D. & Mercer, R.L. (1990). Basic Methods of Probabilistic Context Free Grammars, *Technical Report IBM RC 16374 (72684)*, Yorktown Heights.

Kay, M. (1980). Algorithmic Schemata and Data Structures in Syntactic Processing. *Report CSL-80-12*, Xerox PARC, Palo Alto, Ca.

Magerman, D. & Marcus, M. (1991). Pearl: A Probabilistic Chart Parser, *Proc. EACL'91*, Berlin.

Magerman, D. & Weir, C.(1992). Efficiency, Robustness and Accuracy in Picky Chart Parsing, *Proc. ACL'92*, Newark, Delaware.

Marcus, M. (1991). Very Large Annotated Database of American English. *DARPA Speech and Natural Language Workshop, Pacific Grove,* Morgan Kaufmann.

Pereira, F. & Schabes, Y. (1992). Inside-Outside Reestimation from Partially Bracketed Corpora, *Proc. ACL'92,* Newark.

Resnik, P. (1992). Probabilistic Tree-Adjoining Grammar as a Framework for Statistical Natural Language Processing, *Proc. COLING'92,* Nantes.

Santorini, B. (1990). *Part-of-Speech Tagging Guidelines for the Penn Treebank Project,* Dept. of Computer and Information Science, Univ. of Pennsylvania, Philadelphia.

Santorini, B. (1991). *Bracketing Guidelines for the Penn Treebank Project,* Dept. of Computer and Information Science, University of Pennsylvania, Philadelphia.

Scha, R. (1990). Language Theory and Language Technology; Competence and Performance (in Dutch), in Q.A.M. de Kort & G.L.J. Leerdam (eds.), *Computertoepassingen in de Neerlandistiek,* Almere: Landelijke Vereniging van Neerlandici.

Schabes, Y. (1992). Stochastic Lexicalized Tree-Adjoining Grammars, *Proc. COLING'92,* Nantes.

Schabes, Y., Roth, M. & Osborne, R. (1993). Parsing the Wall Street Journal with the Inside-Outside Algorithm, *Proc. EACL'93,* Utrecht.

Schabes, Y. & Waters, R. (1993). Stochastic Lexicalized Context Free Grammars. In H.C. Bunt & M.Tomita (eds.), *this volume.*

Sekine, S. & Grishman, R. (1995). A Corpus-based Probabilistic Grammar with Only Two Non-terminals, *Proc. 4th Int. Workshop on Parsing Technologies,* Prague.

Sima'an, K., Bod, R., Krauwer, S., & Scha, R. (1994). Efficient Disambiguation by means of Stochastic Tree Substitution Grammars, *Proc. Int. Conf. on New Methods in Language Processing,* UMIST, Manchester.

Sima'an, K. (1995). An optimized algorithm for Data Oriented Parsing, *Proc. Int. Conf. on Recent Advances in Natural Language Processing,* Tzigov Chark, Bulgaria.

Suppes, P. (1970). Probabilistic Grammars for Natural Languages, *Synthese 22.*

Viterbi, A. (1967). Error bounds for convolutional codes and an asymptotically optimum decoding algorithm, *IEEE Trans. Information Theory, IT-13, 260-269.*

Winograd, T. (1983). *Language as a Cognitive Process.* Volume I: Syntax. Reading, Mass.

15. STOCHASTIC LEXICALIZED TREE-INSERTION GRAMMAR

YVES SCHABES AND RICHARD C. WATERS
Mitsubishi Electric Research Laboratories
Cambridge, Massachusetts

Abstract.
Stochastic lexicalized tree-insertion grammar (SLTIG) is an attractive compromise between the parsing efficiency of stochastic context-free grammar (SCFG) and the lexical sensitivity of stochastic lexicalized tree adjoining grammar (SLTAG). SLTIG is a restricted form of SLTAG that can only generate context-free languages and can be parsed in cubic time. However, SLTIG retains the lexical sensitivity of SLTAG and is therefore a much better basis for capturing distributional information about words than SCFG.

1. MOTIVATION

The application of stochastic techniques to syntax modeling has recently regained popularity. Most of the work in this area has tended to emphasize one or the other of the following two goals. The first goal is to capture as much distributional information about words as possible. The second goal is to capture as many of the hierarchical constraints inherent in natural languages as possible. Unfortunately, these two goals have been more or less incompatible to date.

Early stochastic proposals such as Markov Models, N-gram models (Jelinek, 1990; Shannon, 1951) and Hidden Markov Models (Rabiner, 1989) are very effective at capturing simple distributional information about adjacent words. However, they cannot capture long range distributional information nor the hierarchical constraints inherent in natural languages.

Stochastic context-free grammar (SCFG) (Booth, 1969; Jelinek *et al.*, 1990; Lari and Young, 1990) extends context-free grammar (CFG) by associating each rule with a probability that controls its use. Each rule is

H. Bunt and M. Tomita (eds.), Recent Advances in Parsing Technology, 281–294.

associated with a single probability that is the same for all the sites where the rule can be applied.

SCFG captures hierarchical information just as well as CFG; however, it does not do a good job of capturing distributional information about words. There are at least two reasons for this. First, many rules do not contain any words and therefore the associated probabilities do not have any direct link to words. Second, distributional phenomena that involve the application of two or more rules do not have a direct link to any of the stochastic parameters of SCFG, because the probabilities apply only to single rules.

It has been observed in practice that SCFG performs worse than non-hierarchical approaches. This has lead many researchers to believe that simple distributional information about adjacent words is the most important single source of information. In the absence of a formalism that adequately combines this information with other kinds of information, the emphasis in research has been on simple non-hierarchical statistical models of words, such as word N-gram models.

Recently, it has been suggested that stochastic lexicalized tree-adjoining grammar (SLTAG) (Resnik, 1992; Schabes, 1992) may be able to capture both distributional and hierarchical information. An SLTAG grammar consists of a set of trees each of which contains one or more lexical items. These elementary trees can be viewed as the elementary clauses (including their transformational variants) in which the lexical items participate. The elementary trees are combined by substitution and adjunction. Each possible way of combining two trees is associated with a probability.

Since it is based on tree-adjoining grammar (TAG), SLTAG can capture some kinds of hierarchical information that cannot be captured by SCFG. However, the key point of comparison between SLTAG and SCFG is that since SLTAG is lexicalized and uses separate probabilities governing each possible combination of trees, each probability is directly linked to a pair of words. This makes it possible to represent a great deal of distributional information about words.

Unfortunately, the statistical algorithms for SLTAG (Schabes, 1992) require much more computational resources than the ones for SCFG. For instance, the algorithms for estimating the stochastic parameters and determining the probability of a string require in the worst case $O(n^6)$-time for SLTAG (Schabes, 1992) but only $O(n^3)$-time for SCFG (Jelinek *et al.*, 1990).

Stochastic lexicalized tree-insertion grammar (SLTIG) is a restricted form of SLTAG that retains most of the advantages of SLTAG without requiring any greater computational resources than SCFG. SLTIG restricts the elementary trees that are possible and the way adjunction can be performed. These restrictions limit SLTIG to producing only context-free languages and allow SLTIG to be parsed in $O(n^3)$-time in the worst case. However, SLTIG retains most of the key features of SLTAG enumerated above. In particular, the probabilities in SLTIG are directly linked to pairs of words.

SLTIG is a stochastic extension of lexicalized tree-insertion grammar (LTIG) (Schabes and Waters, 1993a; Schabes and Waters, 1993b). The following sections introduce LTIG, define the stochastic extension to SLTIG, present an algorithm that can determine the probability of a string generated by an SLTIG in $O(n^3)$-time, and discuss the algorithms needed to train the parameters of an SLTIG.

2. LTIG

Lexicalized tree-insertion grammar (LTIG) (Schabes and Waters, 1993a; Schabes and Waters, 1993b) is a tree generating system that is a restricted form of lexicalized tree-adjoining grammar (LTAG) (Joshi and Schabes, 1991). The grammar consists of two sets of trees: initial trees, which are combined by substitution and auxiliary trees, which are combined by adjunction. An LTIG is lexicalized because every initial and auxiliary tree is required to contain a terminal symbol on its frontier.

Definition 1 An *LTIG* is a five-tuple (Σ, NT, I, A, S), where Σ is a set of terminal symbols, NT is a set of non-terminal symbols, I and A are finite sets of finite trees labeled by terminal and non-terminal symbols, and S is a distinguished non-terminal start symbol. The set $I \cup A$ is referred to as the elementary trees.

The interior nodes in each elementary tree are labeled by non-terminal symbols. The nodes on the frontier of each elementary tree are labeled with terminal symbols, non-terminal symbols, and the empty string (ε). At least one frontier node is labeled with a terminal symbol. With the possible exception of one (see below), the non-terminal symbols on the frontier are marked for substitution. (By convention, substitutability is indicated in diagrams by using a down arrow ($\downarrow$).)

The difference between auxiliary trees and initial trees is that each auxiliary tree has exactly one non-terminal frontier node that is marked as the foot. The foot must have the same label as the root. (By convention, the foot of an auxiliary tree is indicated in diagrams by using an asterisk ($*$).) The path from the root of an auxiliary tree to the foot is called the *spine*.

Auxiliary trees in which every non-empty frontier node is to the left of the foot are called *left* auxiliary trees. Similarly, auxiliary trees in which

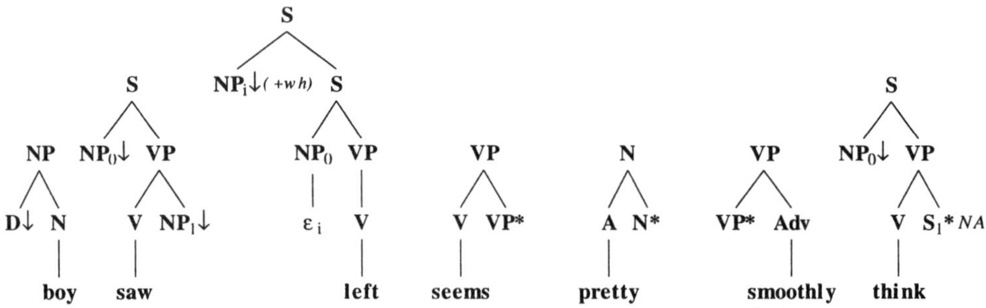

Figure 1. Example LTIG trees.

every non-empty frontier node is to the right of the foot are called *right* auxiliary trees. Other auxiliary trees are called *wrapping* auxiliary trees.[1]

Crucially, LTIG does not allow wrapping auxiliary trees. It does not allow elementary wrapping auxiliary trees, and it does not allow the adjunction of two auxiliary trees, if the result would be a wrapping auxiliary tree.

LTIG does not allow adjunction to apply to foot nodes or nodes marked for substitution. LTIG allows the adjunction of a left auxiliary tree and a right auxiliary tree on the same node. However, LTIG does not allow the adjunction of either two left or two right auxiliary trees on the same node.

Figure 1 shows seven elementary trees that might appear in an LTIG for English. The trees containing 'boy', 'saw', and 'left' are initial trees. The remainder are auxiliary trees.

An LTIG derivation must start with an initial tree rooted in S. After that, the tree can be repeatedly extended using substitution and adjunction. A derivation is complete when every frontier node is labeled with a terminal symbol.

As illustrated in Figure 2a, substitution replaces a node marked for substitution with a copy of an initial tree.

Adjunction inserts a copy of an auxiliary tree T into another tree at an interior node η that has the same label as the root (and therefore foot) of T. In particular, η is replaced by a copy of T and the foot of the copy of T is replaced by the subtree rooted at η. The adjunction of a left auxiliary tree is referred to as *left adjunction* (see Figure 2b). The adjunction of a right auxiliary tree is referred to as *right adjunction* (see Figure 2c).

LTIG's prohibition on wrapping auxiliary trees can be rephrased solely in terms of elementary trees. To start with, there must be no elementary wrapping auxiliary trees. In addition, an elementary left (right) auxiliary

[1] In (Schabes and Waters, 1993b) these three kinds of auxiliary trees are referred to differently as right recursive, left recursive, and centrally recursive, respectively.

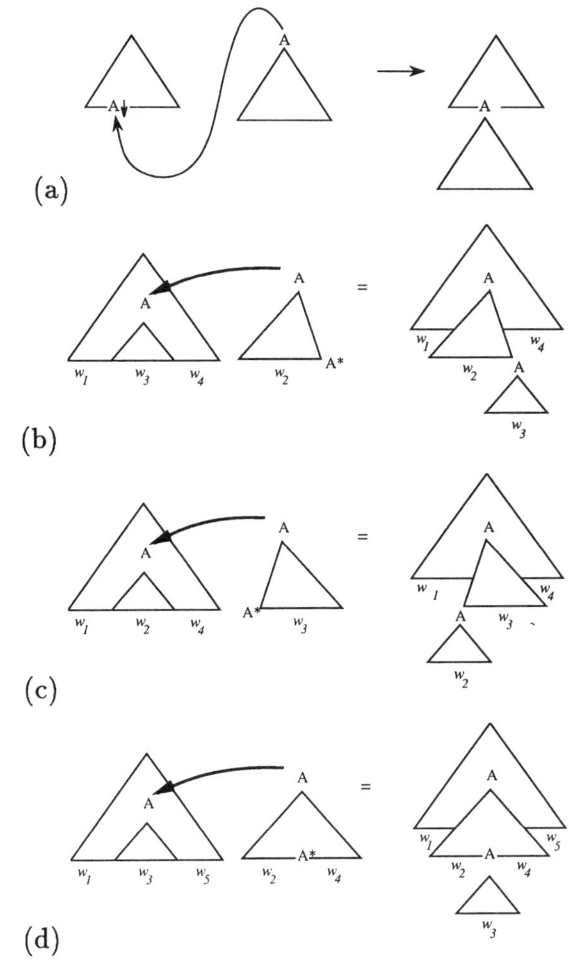

Figure 2. Tree combination: (a) substitution, (b) left adjunction, (c) right adjunction, and (d) wrapping adjunction, which is not allowed by SLTIG.

tree cannot be adjoined on any node that is on the spine of an elementary right (left) auxiliary tree. Further, no adjunction whatever is permitted on a node η that is to the right (left) of the spine of an elementary left (right) auxiliary tree T. (Note that for T to be a left (right) auxiliary tree, every frontier node subsumed by η must be labeled with ε.)

Tree adjoining grammar formalisms typically forbid adjunction on foot nodes and substitution nodes. In addition, they typically forbid multiple adjunctions on a node. However, in the case of LTIG, it is convenient to relax this latter restriction slightly by allowing right and left adjunction on a node, but at most once each. (Due to the other restrictions placed on LTIG, this relaxation increases the trees that can be generated without increasing the ambiguity of derivations.)

2.1. COMPARISONS

The only important difference between LTIG and LTAG is that LTAG allows both elementary and derived wrapping auxiliary trees. The importance of this is that wrapping adjunction (see Figure 2d) encodes string wrapping and is therefore context sensitive in nature. In contrast, left and right adjunction (see Figures 2b & 2c) merely support string concatenation. As a result, while LTAG is context sensitive in nature, LTIG is limited to generating only context-free languages.

To see that LTIG can only generate context-free languages, consider that any LTIG G can be converted into a CFG generating the same strings in two steps as follows. First, G is converted into a tree substitution grammar (TSG) G' that generates the same strings. Then, this TSG is converted into a CFG G''.

A TSG is the same as an LTIG (or LTAG) except that there cannot be any auxiliary trees. To create G' first make every initial tree of G be an initial tree of G'. Next, make every auxiliary tree T of G be an initial tree of G'. When doing this, relabel the foot of T with ε (turning T into an initial tree). In addition, let A be the label of the root of T. If T is a left auxiliary tree, rename the root to A_L; otherwise rename it to A_R.

To complete the creation of G' alter every node η in every initial tree in G' as follows: Let A be the label of η. If left adjunction is possible at η, add a new first child of η labeled A_L, mark it for substitution, and add a tree corresponding to $A_L \rightarrow \varepsilon$ if one does not already exist. Right adjunction is handled analogously by adding a new last child of η labeled A_R and insuring the existance of a tree corresponding to $A_R \rightarrow \varepsilon$.

The TSG G' generates the same strings as G, because all cases of adjunction have been changed into equivalent substitutions. Note that the transformation would not work if LTIG allowed wrapping auxiliary trees. The TSG G' can be converted into a CFG G'' by flattening each tree in G' into a context-free rule that expands the root of the tree into the frontier in one step.

Although the string sets generated by LTIG are the same as those generated by CFG, LTIG is capable of generating more complex sets of trees than CFG. In particular, it is interesting to look at the path sets of the trees generated. (The path set of a grammar is the set of all paths from root to frontier in the trees generated by the grammar. The path set is a set of strings over $\Sigma \cup NT \cup \{\varepsilon\}$.)

The path sets for CFG (and TSG) are regular languages (Thatcher, 1971). In contrast, just as for LTAG and TAG, the path sets for LTIG are context-free languages. To see this, consider that adjunction makes it possible to embed a sequence of nodes (the spine of the auxiliary tree) in place of a node on a path. Therefore, from the perspective of the path set, auxiliary trees are analogous to context-free productions.

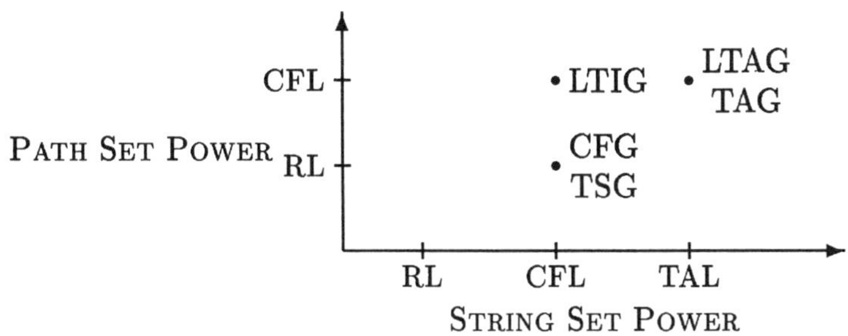

Figure 3. The tree and string complexity of LTIG and several other formalisms

Figure 3 summarizes the relationship between LTIG and several other grammar formalisms. The horizontal axis shows the complexity of strings that can be generated by the formalisms, i.e., regular languages (RL), context-free languages (CFL), and tree adjoining languages (TAL). The vertical axis shows the complexity of the path sets that can be generated.

CFG (and TSG) create context-free languages, but the path sets they create are regular languages. LTAG and TAG generate tree adjoining languages and have path sets that are context-free languages. LTIG is intermediate in nature. It can only generate context-free languages, but has path sets that are also context-free languages.

2.2. LTIG LEXICALIZES CFG

As shown in (Schabes and Waters, 1993a; Schabes and Waters, 1993b) LTIG lexicalizes CFG without changing the trees derived. Further, a constructive procedure exists for converting any CFG G into an equivalent LTIG G'.

The fact that LTIG lexicalizes CFG is significant, because every other method for lexicalizing CFGs without changing the trees derived requires context-sensitive operations (Joshi and Schabes, 1991) and therefore dramatically increases worst case processing time.

As also shown in (Schabes and Waters, 1993a; Schabes and Waters, 1993b) (and in Section 4) LTIG can be parsed in the worst case just as quickly as CFG. Since LTIG is lexicalized, it is expected that it can be parsed much faster than CFG in the typical case.

3. STOCHASTIC LTIG

The definition of stochastic lexicalized tree-insertion grammar (SLTIG) is the same as the definition of LTIG except that probabilities are added that control the combination of trees by adjunction and substitution.

Definition 2 An *SLTIG* is an 11-tuple $(\Sigma, NT, I, A, S, P_I, P_S, P_L, P_{NL}, P_R, P_{NR})$, where (Σ, NT, I, A, S) is an LTIG and P_I, P_S, P_L, P_{NL}, P_R, and P_{NR} are statistical parameters as defined below.

For every root ρ of an initial tree, $P_I(\rho)$ is the probability that a derivation starts with the tree rooted at ρ. It is required that:

$$\sum_{\rho} P_I(\rho) = 1$$

Note that $P_I(\rho) \neq 0$ if and only if ρ is labeled S.

For every root ρ of an initial tree and every node η that is marked for substitution, $P_S(\rho, \eta)$ is the probability of substituting the tree rooted at ρ for η. For each η it is required that:

$$\sum_{\rho} P_S(\rho, \eta) = 1$$

For every node η in every elementary tree, $P_{NL}(\eta)$ is the probability that left adjunction will not occur on η. For every root ρ of a left auxiliary tree, $P_L(\rho, \eta)$ is the probability of adjoining the tree rooted at ρ on η. For each η it is required that:

$$P_{NL}(\eta) + \sum_{\rho} P_L(\rho, \eta) = 1$$

$P_{NL}(\eta) = 0$ if and only if left adjunction on η is obligatory.

The parameters $P_{NR}(\eta)$ and $P_R(\rho, \eta)$ control right adjunction in an exactly analogous way.

An SLTIG derivation is described by the initial tree it starts with, together with the sequence of substitution and adjunction operations that take place. The probability of a derivation is defined as the product of: the probability P_I of starting with the given tree, the probabilities P_S, P_L, and P_R of the operations that occurred, and the probabilities P_{NL} and P_{NR} of adjunction not occurring at the places where it did not occur.

The probability of a string is the sum of the probabilities of all the different ways of deriving it. A most *likely derivation* of a string is a derivation that has as large a probability as any other derivation for the string. The probability of a tree generated by an SLTIG for a string is the sum of the probabilities of every way of deriving the tree. (Unlike in SCFG, in SLTIG there can be more than one way to derive a given tree.) A most likely tree generated for a string is a tree whose probability is as large as any other tree generated for the string. (Note that a most likely derivation need not generate a most likely tree.)

4. PARSING SLTIG

Since SLTIG is a restricted case of SLTAG, the $O(n^6)$-time SLTAG parser (Schabes, 1992) can be used for parsing SLTIG. Further, it can be straightforwardly modified to require at most $O(n^4)$-time when applied to SLTIG. However, this does not take full advantage of the context-freeness of SLTIG.

This section demonstrates that SLTIG can be parsed in $O(n^3)$-time by exhibiting a CKY-style bottom-up algorithm for computing the probability assigned to a string by an SLTIG. This algorithm can be trivially modified to extract a most probable derivation of the given string. More efficient SLTIG processors can be based on the Earley style LTIG recognizer presented in (Schabes and Waters, 1993a).

4.1. TERMINOLOGY

Suppose that G is an SLTIG and that $a_1 \cdots a_n$ is an input string. Let η be a node in an elementary tree (identified by the name of the tree and the position of the node in the tree).

$\mathsf{Label}(\eta) \in \Sigma \cup NT \cup \varepsilon$ is the label of the node. We define the predicate $\mathsf{Initial}(\eta)$ to be true if and only if η is the root of an initial tree. $\mathsf{Parent}(\eta)$ is the node that is the parent of η or $\perp$ if η has no parent. $\mathsf{FirstChild}(\eta)$ is the node that is the leftmost child of η or $\perp$ if η has no children. sf Sibling(η) is the node that is the next child of the parent of η (in left to right order) or $\perp$ if there is no such node.

The predicate $\mathsf{Substitutable}(\rho, \eta)$ is true if and only if η is marked for substitution and ρ is the root of an initial tree that can be substituted for η. The predicate $\mathsf{Radjoin}(\rho, \eta)$ is true if and only if ρ is the root of an elementary right auxiliary tree that can adjoin on η. The predicate $\mathsf{Ladjoin}(\rho, \eta)$ is true if and only if ρ is the root of an elementary left auxiliary tree that can adjoin on η.

The concept of *covering* is critical to the bottom-up algorithm shown below. Informally speaking, a node η covers a string if and only if the string can be derived starting from η.

More precisely, for every node η in every elementary tree in G, let T' be a copy of the subtree of T that is rooted at η. Extend T' by adding a new root whose only child is the original root of T'. Label the new root of T' with a unique new symbol S'. If there is a node on the frontier of T'

that is marked as the foot, relabel this node with ε. This converts T' into an initial tree. Let G_η be an SLTIG that is identical to G except that T' is introduced as an additional initial tree and the start symbol of G_η is S'. The probabilities associated with the the interior nodes of T' are identical to those for the corresponding nodes in T. The probabilities for the root of T' are $P_S = P_L = P_R = 0$, $P_{NL} = P_{NR} = 1$, and crucially $P_I = 1$. $P_I = 0$ for the other initial trees.

The node η covers a string $a_1 \cdots a_n$ with probability p in G if and only if the probability of $a_1 \cdots a_n$ in G_η is p. The node η covers a string $a_1 \cdots a_n$ without left (right) adjunction with probability p in G if and only if the probability of $a_1 \cdots a_n$ in G_η is p without considering derivations where left (right) adjunction occurs on the original root of T'.

(Note that if η is a foot node, T' is an empty tree. The only string covered by η is the empty string; however, the empty string is covered with probability 1, because the empty string is the only string derived by G_η.)

4.2. A BOTTOM-UP ALGORITHM

We can assume without loss of generality that every node in $I \cup A$ has at most two children. (By adding new nodes, any SLTIG can be transformed into an equivalent SLTIG satisfying this condition. This transformation can be readily reversed after parsing has been completed.)

The algorithm stores triples of the form $[\eta, code, p]$ in an $n \times n$ array C. In a triple, *code* is a set over the universe L (for left adjunction) and R (for right adjunction). The fact that $[\eta, code, p] \in C[i,k]$ means that η accounts for the substring $a_{i+1} \cdots a_k$ with probability p. More precisely, for every node η in every elementary tree in G, the algorithm guarantees that when the computation concludes:

- $[\eta, \emptyset, p] \in C[i,k]$ if and only if η covers $a_{i+1} \cdots a_k$ with probability p without left or right adjunction.
- $[\eta, \{L\}, p] \in C[i,k]$ if and only if η covers $a_{i+1} \cdots a_k$ with probability p without right adjunction.
- $[\eta, \{R\}, p] \in C[i,k]$ if and only if η covers $a_{i+1} \cdots a_k$ with probability p without left adjunction.
- $[\eta, \{L,R\}, p] \in C[i,k]$ if and only if η covers $a_{i+1} \cdots a_k$ with probability p.

The process starts by placing each foot node and each frontier node that is labeled with the empty string in every cell $C[i,i]$ with probability one. This signifies that they each cover the empty string at all positions. The initialization also puts each terminal node η in every cell $C[i,i+1]$ where η is labeled a_{i+1} with probability one. The algorithm then considers all possible ways of combining matched substrings into longer matched substrings—it fills the upper diagonal portion of the array $C[i, k]$ $(0 \leq i \leq k \leq n)$ for increasing values of $k - i$.

Two observations are central to the efficiency of this process. Since every auxiliary tree (elementary and derived) in SLTIG is either a left or right auxiliary tree, the substring matched by a tree is always a contiguous string. Further, when matched substrings are combined, the algorithm only has to consider adjacent substrings. (In SLTAG, a tree with a foot can match a pair of strings that are not contiguous—one left of the foot and one right of the foot.)

There are three situations where combination of matched substrings is possible: sibling concatenation, left concatenation, and right concatenation.

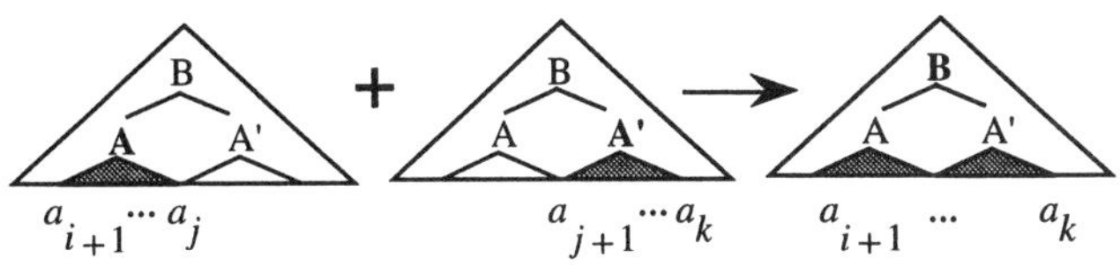

Figure 4. Sibling concatenation.

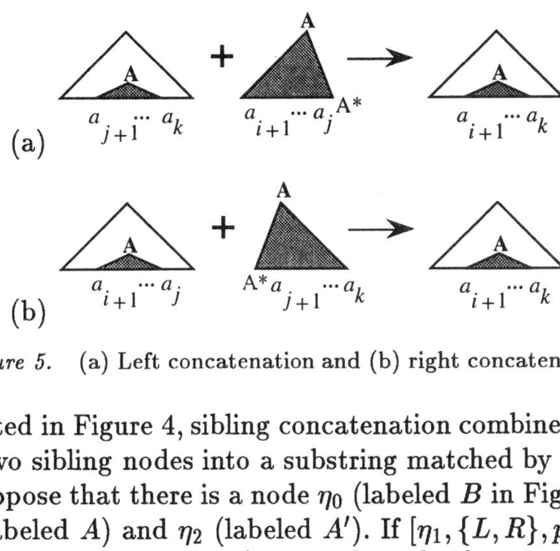

Figure 5. (a) Left concatenation and (b) right concatenation.

As illustrated in Figure 4, sibling concatenation combines the substrings matched by two sibling nodes into a substring matched by their parent. In particular, suppose that there is a node η_0 (labeled B in Figure 4) with two children η_1 (labeled A) and η_2 (labeled A'). If $[\eta_1, \{L, R\}, p_1] \in C[i, j]$ and $[\eta_2, \{L, R\}, p_2] \in C[j, k]$ then $[\eta_0, \emptyset, p_1 \times p_2] \in C[i, k]$.

Left concatenation (see Figure 5a) combines the substring matched by a left auxiliary tree with the substring matched by a node the auxiliary tree can adjoin on. Right concatenation (see Figure 5b) is analogous.

The algorithm (see Figure 6) is written in two parts: a main procedure Probability$(a_1 \cdots a_n)$ and a subprocedure Add$(\eta, code, i, k)$, which adds the triple $[\eta, code, p]$ into $C[i, k]$.

The main procedure repeatedly scans the array C, building up longer and longer matched substrings until it determines all the S-rooted derived

```
Procedure Probability(a_1 ··· a_n)
 begin
  for i = 0 to n
   for all foot nodes φ in A, Add(φ, ∅, i, i, 1)
   for all frontier nodes η in A ∪ I where Label(η) = ε, Add(η, ∅, i, i, 1)
  for i = 0 to n − 1
   for all frontier nodes η in A ∪ I where Label(η) = a_{i+1}, Add(η, ∅, i, i + 1, 1)
  for d = 0 to n
   for i = 0 to n − d
    set k = i + d
    for j = i to k
     for all nodes η in G
      if [η, {L, R}, p_1] ∈ C[i, j] and [Sibling(η), {L, R}, p_2] ∈ C[j, k]
       then Add(Parent(η), ∅, i, k, p_1 × p_2)
     for all nodes ρ and η in G where Ladjoinable(ρ, η)
      if [ρ, {L, R}, p_1] ∈ C[i, j] and [η, code, p_2] ∈ C[j, k] and L ∉ code
       then Add(η, L ∪ code, i, k, p_1 × p_2 × P_L(ρ, η))
     for all nodes ρ and η in G where Radjoinable(ρ, η)
      if [η, code, p_1] ∈ C[i, j] and R ∉ code and [ρ, {L, R}, p_2] ∈ C[j, k]
       then Add(η, R ∪ code, i, k, p_1 × p_2 × P_R(ρ, η))
  p = 0
  for all nodes ρ in G where IsInitialRoot(ρ) and Label(ρ) = S
   if [ρ, {L, R}, p_0] ∈ C[0, n] then p = p + p_0 × P_I(ρ)
  return p
 end
Procedure Add(η, code, i, k, p)
 begin
  if [η, code, p'] ∈ C[i, k] for some p' then update [η, code, p'] in C[i, k] to [η, code, p' + p]
  else C[i, k] := C[i, k] ∪ [η, code, p]
  if code = {L, R} then
   if FirstChild(Parent(η)) = η and Sibling(η) = ⊥ then Add(> Parent(η), ∅, i, k, p)
   for each node φ such that Substitutable(η, φ), Add(φ, ∅, i, k, p × P_S(η, φ))
  if L ∉ code then Add(η, L ∪ code, i, k, p × P_NL(η))
  if R ∉ code then Add(η, R ∪ code, i, k, p × P_NR(η))
 end
```

Figure 6. A procedure for computing the probability of a string given an SLTIG.

trees that match the input. The purpose of the codes ($\{L, R\}$ etc.) is to insure that left and right adjunction can each be applied at most once on a node. The procedure could easily be modified to account for other constraints on the way derivation should proceed, such as those suggested for LTAGs (Schabes and Shieber, 1992).

The procedure Add enters a triple $[\eta, code, p]$ into $C[i, k]$. If some other triple $[\eta, code, p']$ is already present in $C[i, k]$, then the probability p' is updated to $p' + p$ to reflect the fact that an additional derivation of $a_{i+1} \cdots a_k$ has been found. Otherwise, a new triple $[\eta, code, p]$ is added to $C[i, k]$.

The procedure Add also propagates information from one triple to another in situations where the length of the matched string is not increased—i.e., when a node is the only child of its parent, when substitution occurs, and when adjunction is not performed.

The $O(n^3)$ complexity of the algorithm follows from the three nested induction loops on d, i and j. (Although the procedure Add is defined recursively, the number of pairs added to C is bounded by a constant that is independent of sentence length.)

The algorithm does not depend on the fact that SLTIG is lexicalized—it would work equally well if were not lexicalized. If the sum $p'+p$ on the third line of the Add procedure is changed to $\max(p', p)$ the algorithm computes the probability of a most probable derivation. By keeping a record of every attempt to enter a triple into a cell of the array C, one can extend the algorithm so that derivations and therefore the trees they generate can be rapidly recovered.

5. TRAINING AN SLTIG

In the general case, the training algorithm for SCFG (Lari and Young, 1990) requires $O(n^3)$-time for each sentence of length n. A training algorithm for SLTIG can be constructed that achieves these same worst case bounds.

To start with, since SLTIG is a restricted case of stochastic lexicalized tree-adjoining grammar (SLTAG), the $O(n^6)$-time inside-outside reestimation algorithm for SLTAG (Schabes, 1992) can be used for estimating the parameters of an SLTIG given a training corpus. Straightforward modifications lead to an $O(n^4)$-time algorithm for training an SLTIG. However, this alone does not achieve the full potential of SLTIG.

The same basic construction that underlies the algorithm in the last section can be used as the basis for an $O(n^3)$ inside-outside training algorithm for SLTIG. As in the last section, the key reason for this is that computations involving SLTIG only require the consideration of contiguous strings.

It should be noted that in the special case of a fully bracketed training corpus, the parameters of an SCFG can be estimated in linear time (Pereira and Schabes, 1992; Schabes *et al.*, 1993). It is an open question whether this can be done for SLTIG. However, it should be straightforward to design an $O(n^2)$-time training algorithm for SLTIG given a fully bracketed corpus.

6. CONCLUSION

The preceding sections present stochastic lexicalized tree-insertion grammar (SLTIG). SLTIG combines the processing speed of SCFG with the much greater ability of SLTAG to capture distributional information about words. As such, SLTIG has the potential of being a very useful tool for natural language processing tasks where statistical assessment/prediction is required.

References

Booth, T. (1969) Probabilistic representation of formal languages. In *Tenth Annual IEEE Symposium on Switching and Automata Theory*, October 1969.

Jelinek, F. (1990) Self-organized language modeling for speech recognition. In Alex Waibel and Kai-Fu Lee, editors, *Readings in speech recognition.* Morgan Kaufmann, San Mateo, California, 1990.

Jelinek, F., Lafferty, J. D. and Mercer, R. L. (1990) Basic methods of probabilistic context free grammars. Technical Report RC 16374 (72684), IBM, Yorktown Heights, NY.

Joshi, A. K. and Schabes, Y. (1991) Tree-adjoining grammars and lexicalized grammars. In Maurice Nivat and Andreas Podelski, editors, *Tree Automata and Languages.* Elsevier Science, 1992.

Lari, K. and Young, S. J. (1990) The estimation of stochastic context-free grammars using the Inside-Outside algorithm. *Computer Speech and Language*, 4:35–56.

Pereira, F. and Schabes, Y. (1992) Inside-outside reestimation from partially bracketed corpora. In 20th *Meeting of the Association for Computational Linguistics*, Newark, Delaware.

Rabiner, L. R. (1989) A tutorial on hidden Markov models and selected applications in speech recognition. *Proceedings of the IEEE*, 77(2):257–285, February 1989.

Resnik, P. (1992) Probabilistic tree-adjoining grammars as a framework for statistical natural language processing. In *Proceedings of the* 14th *International Conference on Computational Linguistics.*

Schabes, Y. (1992) Stochastic lexicalized tree-adjoining grammars. In *Proceedings of the* 14th *International Conference on Computational Linguistics.*

Schabes, Y. Roth, M. and Osborne, R. (1993) Parsing the Wall Street Journal with the inside-outside algorithm. In *Sixth Conference of the European Chapter of the Association for Computational Linguistics*, Utrecht, the Netherlands.

Schabes, Y. and Shieber, S. (1992) An alternative conception of tree-adjoining derivation. In 20th *Meeting of the Association for Computational Linguistics.*

Schabes, Y. and Waters, R. C. (1993a) Lexicalized Context-Free Grammar: A Cubic-Time Parsable Formalism that Strongly Lexicalizes Context-Free Grammar, Technical Report 93-04, Mitsubishi Electric Research Labs.

Schabes, Y. and Waters, R. C. (1993b) Lexicalized context-free grammars. In 21st *Meeting of the Association for Computational Linguistics*, 121–129.

Schabes, Y. and Waters, R. C. (1994) Tree-insertion grammar: a cubic-time parsable formalism that strongly lexicalizes context-free grammar. Technical Report 94-13, Mitsubishi Electric Research Labs. To appear in *Computational Linguistics.*

Shannon, C. E. (1951) Prediction and entropy of printed english. *The Bell System Technical Journal*, 30:50–64.

Thatcher, J. W. (1971) Characterizing derivations trees of context free grammars through a generalization of finite automata theory. *Journal of Computer and System Sciences*, 5:365–396.

16. THE INTERPLAY OF SYNTACTIC AND SEMANTIC NODE LABELS IN PARSING

DAVID D. MCDONALD
Department of Computer Science
Brandeis University

Abstract.
In this chapter we present several extensions to the theory of semantic grammars. These extensions make semantic grammars linguistically disciplined and more systematic to develop while retaining the strength that comes from linking the categories used by the parser with the semantic categories of the domain model. We describe how the domain-specific labels on the productions of a semantic grammar can be complemented by labels from the standard syntactic vocabulary, and how these syntactic labels can extend the capacity of the grammar by providing default interpretations of standard constructions. We also describe how to systematically instantiate the semantic grammar rules for relational object types in the domain model by assigning them to families of phrase structure trees in a Tree Adjoining Grammar. These techniques are fully implemented and run as part of our "Sparser" natural language understanding system. Examples are taken from newspaper texts.

1. STATE OF THE ART DEMANDS

A cutting-edge natural language understanding system in the 1990s must be able to handle real texts — newspaper stories, encyclopedia articles, and the like — that are written by people for other people to read. Parsing the artificial and simplistic "John hit Peter" sentences that linguists devise to test their grammatical theories is no longer enough. The best test corpus today will be downloaded from a daily online service on the day of the test.

Today's systems must not only provide a structural, syntactic analysis of these texts, but they must also understand the information that they

H. Bunt and M. Tomita (eds.), Recent Advances in Parsing Technology, 295–323.

contain. In practice this means that they must relate some designated portion of the semantic content indicated by the text's wording to some fixed database schema. This is the task defined by the ARPA-sponsored Message Understanding Conferences (see, e.g., ARPA 1992, 1994), and it constitutes a standard that parsing systems today must meet.

This task poses two problems. The first is the problem of developing semantic models of the target subject domains. Grammar, per se, is not a significant problem since many syntactic grammars of considerable size and sophistication have already been developed. Instead, the rate-limiting step in advancing how much machines can understand from a text is the size and thoroughness of the semantic models that they use to make sense of the information it contains. A syntactic analysis by itself, no matter how thorough, is of little use when the point is to extract information from a text and relate it to information one already has.

The second problem follows from the fact that we are now dealing with real texts. Unlike an artificial corpus, a corpus of real articles will not be restricted to a single topic. Even in an otherwise very narrow corpus, off-topic texts segments may appear at any level: full sentences, appositives, even within minimal noun phrases. Thus while a system may have an extensive and effective model of the primary topic, the interjection of these wide-ranging secondary topics can confound the syntax-driven parsing techniques that were standard only ten years ago, and have led to the introduction of new techniques often referred to as 'partial parsing'.

2. PARTIAL PARSING

Partial parsers adapt to the limitations on their knowledge of the text by lowering their goals. Instead of insisting on a complete parse of every sentence in the text, a partial parser will limit its analysis to just minimal phrases (simplex clauses, isolated NPs, PPs, etc.). Later, a separate process with semantic knowledge of the text's domain analyzes this 'forest' of minimal constituents and makes the difficult decisions about attachment and scope in order to arrive at the text's meaning. (See, e.g., de Marken 1990, Ayuso et al. 1992, Hobbs et al. 1992.)

Part of the missing knowledge is the meaning and part of speech of unknown words and also any syntactic constructions that are outside of the competence of the grammar. The problem of new vocabulary is particularly ubiquitous once one begins to work with large corpora of real texts. Even narrow, single topic news columns — a text type that can be readily handled through sublanguage analysis — will constantly be introducing new people and locations or may incidentally refer to a piece of general news that is outside of their sublanguage. An example of this problem is shown below in an excerpt from the Wall Street Journal's "Who's News" column of February 14, 1991. The off-topic segment is shown in italics.

"Robert A. Beck, a 65-year-old former Prudential chairman *who originally bought the brokerage firm*, was named chief executive officer of Prudential Bache."

Proper names and off-topic interjections are substantive problems: the first because the set of possible names cannot be exhaustively listed, with the consequence that something other than the usual production-driven parsing algorithms must be used (see, e.g., McDonald 1993), and the second because the competence of effective language understanding systems today is invariably limited to only a few topics and the range of topics that may occur in real texts cannot be predicted in advance. Some gaps are inevitable.

Though it would not normally be seen as such, the larger part of the missing knowledge that motivates the use of partial parsers is meaning. Standard parsers, and virtually all of today's partial parsers, operate on syntactic knowledge alone, with consideration of meaning postponed to a follow-on process of 'semantic interpretation'. Even for known vocabulary these parsers only draw on knowledge of parts of speech in combination with a grammar of syntactically characterized rewrite rules or their equivalent. This is not a problem in a deliberately limited domain since the amount of structural or lexical ambiguity that may be encountered is limited and can be handled with reasonable efficiency by clever encodings or carefully staged semantic interpretation. (See respectively Tomita 1986 and Alshawi et al. 1992.) But while these techniques are effective when dealing with question answering tasks where the queries are short and the vocabulary limited, they are hopeless when faced with long, open-ended discursive texts.[1] Partial parsing is the present solution to this problem, since it postpones the difficult problems to domain-specific, semantically-driven processes where the selectional restrictions on the combination of the words and phrases are taken into account and only those compositions that make semantic sense in the task domain are allowed.

Faced with the text just above, a typical syntactic partial parser would return the sequence of constituents given below. It is clear how difficult the task of arriving at single analysis of this sentence would be with only syntactic knowledge to guide the system when we look at the text in this way — as a sequence of phrasal categories without any semantic information,

[1] As an example of how extensive pure structural ambiguity can be, consider that in an experiment in the early 1980s with a very broad-coverage syntactic parser that was developed to handle a corpus of business- oriented questions (Martin, Church & Patil 1981), we recovered eight hundred and four syntactically correct analyses of a single twenty seven word topic sentence from the New York Times. This was the result of the interaction of a conjunction and several ambiguous attachment points in what was a completely normal sentence that people understood perfectly with no effort.

like the following.[2]

```
<np , det adjp np wh vg np , vg np prep np .>
```

3. SEMANTIC GRAMMARS

It is not necessary to postpone consideration of meaning until after the parser is finished constructing its structural description of the text. Semantic information, especially the constraints due to selectional restrictions, can be directly integrated with the parsing process through the use of semantic grammars.

As a description of the space of possible configurations of constituents and grammatical relations in a natural language, a 'semantic' grammar is simply an otherwise normal grammar (e.g. a system of rewrite rules) where the nonterminals are taken from a semantic rather than a syntactic vocabulary. In Sparser's semantic grammar, for example, the example sentence would have the following analysis when viewed at the same granularity as the syntactically labeled analysis of it that we just saw. (The unknown words not included in Sparser's grammar for this sublanguage are given as "xxx" plus any recoverable grammatically significant suffix.)

```
< person , ‘‘a’’ age title ‘‘who’’ xxx-ly xxx company ,
  name-to-position title ‘‘of’’ company .>
```

Like the earlier syntactic analysis, this is a representation of a forest of labeled constituents. Unlike that analysis, however, it is a now trivial matter to define a grammar over this semantic vocabulary where the sentence has only one analysis (modulo the gap due to the unknown words). The selectional restrictions implicit in the choice of label names will restrict the legal combinations of phrases to just those that are sensible in this domain.[3]

Notice also that this version of the sentential form includes several words directly, without any covering preterminal part of speech label. All of the content words in this semantic grammar are immediately rewritten with one or more semantic labels. Function words are left alone until they combine

[2] This analysis assumes the use of a proper name analyzer. The category "vg", standing for "verb group", indicates a phrase consisting of the main verb and any auxiliaries or adverbs. Notice also that the punctuation of the original text has deliberately been retained since it provides excellent cues to the presence of appositives and sentential modifiers.

[3] Standard rule applications take this example to the sentential form: person ..., job-event person. Then Sparser's standard search rule for spanning appositives will take the sentence to a single constituent labeled 'job-event'.

with an adjacent phrase. In this respect Sparser uses a 'lexicalized' grammar in the sense of Schabes et al. 1988.

Our experience in writing semantic grammars[4] indicates that one can reasonably expect to be able to develop a label set and accompanying grammar where the question of whether any pair of adjacent constituents should compose can be answered deterministically without ambiguity. This makes it possible for the parser to quickly arrive at unique analyses through consideration of the selectional restrictions implicitly built into the rewrite rules of the grammar.

In addition, the use of semantic grammars provides an elegant means of ignoring the inevitable gaps in the grammar's coverage in a robust way. A standard grammar using syntactic labels will have an analysis of every word in the text, with the result that the parser will be able to come up with some syntactic analysis of the phrase structure of the gap which it will pass on for semantic interpretation just like any other phrase. (A part of speech assignment to the unknown words can be made through the use of a stochastic analyzer such as BBN's POST (Weischedel et al. 1993).) The only indication that there is a problem with the analysis of the gap will come later when the semantic interpretation component fails to find any assignable meaning for the unknown words or gets a selection restriction failure on an unanticipated phrasal combination.

By contrast, in a well designed semantic grammar no phrase will ever be formed if it does not also have a semantic interpretation. No effort will be wasted in trying to make sense of portions of the text that are not in the targeted sublanguage since the parser will leave those gaps unanalyzed and no interpretations will be initiated. The grammar will only provide an analysis if the semantic model will comprehend it.

Semantic grammars are the invention of Dick Burton, who used them as part of the Sophie system (Burton 1976; Burton & Brown 1975). Sophie was one of the very first intelligent computer-assisted instruction systems, and the semantic grammar was the basis of the natural language interface that students used to ask questions or to direct the system to carry out simple operations. Burton's semantic grammar was formalized as an augmented transition network. It built directly on the work of Woods 1970, but substituted a set of domain specific labels for the syntactic labels used

[4]Our original semantic grammar for the Who's News sublanguage comprised roughly two thousand context free and context sensitive rewrite rules. On a blind test over every Wall Street Journal article marked with the subject tag 'wnews' that occurred in the second half of February 1991, this grammar correctly recognized eighty percent of all of the incidents of 'job change' clauses that occurred. Of the recognized cases, eighty percent were correctly analyzed in all respects and only six percent were actual mistakes. The other fourteen percent were due to leaving some field of the result tuple empty.

in the Lunar system. Other notable systems in the literature that used semantic grammar include Ladder (Hendrix et al. 1978) and Planes (Waltz et al. 1976).

While semantic grammars have the advantage of easy, almost commonsense definition and extremely low run-time ambiguity, historically they have suffered from ad-hoc design and inability to appreciate linguistic generalizations, and have required considerable effort to port to other domains. This has led to their general disfavor in most of the computational linguistics community. This quote from James Allen's textbook is typical: "...semantic grammars have proven useful for the rapid development of parsers in limited application domains. The down side, however, is that they do not port well to new domains and cannot handle applications in broad domains. Generally a new domain will require a completely new semantic grammar, whereas most of a syntactic grammar for one domain will apply to another domain." (Allen 1995 pg. 334).

Part of the problem has simply been poor design on the part of the people who write semantic grammars. The other part has been the lack of any systematic way to project the semantic grammar for a domain from a linguistically principled general grammar or any ability to capture generalizations — standard interpretations — that will be present in every domain. These last problems are the subject of the rest of this chapter.

An example of the poor grammar design that makes the extension from one domain to the next virtually impossible can also be found in Allen (pg. 333). In constructing an example semantic grammar for the airlines flight reservations domain, he writes these two rules (Allen's glosses):

flight-dest	->	"to" city-np	*to Chicago*
city-np	->	city-mod city-cnp city-mod-arg	*nearest city to Dallas*

Already we can see a problem since in this grammar for just one sublanguage the phrase *to Chicago* is ambiguous. It is both a flight-destination and a city-modifying-argument. Obviously neither of these labelings would be meaningful in any other domain — they may not even reflect a correct bracketing (cp. *According to Dallas mayor John Doe, ...*) — and consequently a completely new grammar will indeed be needed.

The design flaw is in the choice of labels (non-terminal categories). Allen's labels do not record what the constituents are, rather they record the interpretation that this phrase is to have in each of the two contexts where it has been observed. It is the function-orientation of the choice of labels that makes this grammar and the others like it so difficult to extend. By encoding the function that the phrase is going to play in its larger context directly into the name of the label, the grammar is certain to be unable to "handle applications in broad domains" for the simple reason that these functions are narrow and domain specific. The chance of other domains requiring the same, type-specific functional roles is small indeed.

On the other hand, our analysis of *to Dallas* will remain valid in virtually every domain if we adopt a function-neutral style of semantic labeling, for example by just encoding the identity of the preposition and type of its complement, as in the following rule.[5]

to-city -> "to" city

The function of a constituent with this sort of neutral labeling is established case by case by the rewrite rules that use it. In that context the realization of the function could take place as part of the rule's semantic interpretation, or it could involve the application of a context sensitive rewrite rule.

One conceivable difficulty that this domain-independent style of grammar design could pose is that without functionally-oriented labels one can no longer read out the meaning of the text directly from the parse tree, a common practice in the simple systems used as interfaces to expert systems. (For a current example from the CL community, see Miller et al. 1994.) However, that practice is a mistake in any substantial application. Like any single-level, purely surface-oriented treatment of meaning it misses generalizations that factor out information structure from propositional content (i.e. the facts that transformations were developed to account for in the 1950s). In addition, leaving the semantics as just a tree structured description misses the enormous value that is gained by adopting a conventional, denotational semantics. In particular, we want to link the referents of the individuals mentioned in the texts to the long-term representations that they may have in the knowledge-based system that will be assimilating the information the parser extracts from the texts. The *Dallas* in the text should surely be identified with the one represented in the system's database.

Ensuring that referring expressions are linked to their appropriate denotations in the system's internal model of the world has been one of the principle design goals in Sparser's development. Moreover, these denotations do not exist in a vacuum. Before the parsing of a text begins, the model already contains objects representing well-known people, companies, places, etc., and, in its target applications, we would expect Sparser's model to also

[5] Of course in some domains "Dallas" is not a city. It could, for example, be the name of one of the American major league football teams or the name of a person. In the style of grammar writing we have adopted for Sparser, these would also form literally-labeled prepositional phrases with "to" such as, e.g., 'to-team' and 'to-person'. The ambiguity of the word "Dallas" would thus be propagated up through the pp, and in our experience would virtually always then be cashed out by the selectional constraints in operation when that pp was composed with its neighbor constituent(s).

contain objects representing earlier events, expectations, reports from other news sources, and so on. Sparser is intended to be used in a context of ongoing news events and extensive background knowledge, where the correct identification of an individual in the text with its counterpart in the model (if there is one) is essential.

To this end, and as part of coping with the problem of incomplete knowledge and gaps in the understanding of a text, the bulk of Sparser's semantic grammar is assembled as a side-effect of defining the types and individuals that populate its domain model. The mechanisms used for this are also the means by which the semantic grammar is ensured of being linguistically principled, i.e. a projection of the well-formed syntactic structures in Sparser's Tree Adjoining Grammar (TAG). We take these up in the next section.

4. PARSING TO OBJECTS

The idea that a word or phrase should 'refer' to an object in the world is fundamental to semantic theory. The modern, cognitive science version of this idea is that the mapping is actually from the linguistic term to a representation or model of the object in a person's mind, or to a database and KR system when the interlocutor is a machine (see, e.g., Woods 1975). Looking in the other direction, we can observe that the machine (computer program) will not be able to understand (represent, make sense of) a linguistic term for which it does not already have a representation in its model.[6]

Given this, Sparser's output — the result of a parse — is in effect the updates that are made to the domain model: the set of individuals and concepts that are accessed or constructed in the course of its analysis of the text.[7] A conventional parse tree (a populated chart) is also assembled, but epistemologically it is a means to an end rather than an end in itself.

[6]Of course this is only true barring the use of analogy or creative imagination, which are far beyond the scope of the current work. It does assume the ability to assemble new individuals (and in a restricted way also new concepts) by combining existing individuals in predefined ways and allowing the instantiation of new individuals given their names or descriptions.

[7]It is proper to talk about the model-level objects as produced directly by the parsing process since, as we will see, every rewrite rule is accompanied by a semantic interpretation function (or a direct reference to an object in the model) that executes at the moment the rule completes. The projection to the model is immediate, monotonic, and incremental as the parser scans words and applies rewrite rules bottom up in a single left to right pass through the text. Never is there any wait for larger constituents to be accumulated before the semantic interpretation of the daughter constituents is carried out. This does lead to some interesting problems in the formulation of the semantics because of the need for first class representations of incomplete information; some possible solutions are discussed in McDonald 1994c.

In any event, since Sparser is designed to analyze texts of arbitrary length rather than single sentences (often tens of thousands of words), the chart is consumed and recycled in the course of any extended analysis, while the domain model increases monotonically.

The best way to illustrate how Sparser establishes the direct connections between model-level objects and linguistic devices is through an example. We will start with a simple case. Consider the kind of model that we would have for the airline reservations domain. In an object-oriented treatment it would have types for airlines, flights, service classes, times of day and so on, and part of what would be entailed in setting up the initial model would be defining instances of those types — individuals — to represent particular airlines, flights, etc. To define the city of Dallas, Texas we could, for example, use a functional form like this:

```
(define-city ''Dallas'' :state Texas)
```

What we do in Sparser is extend such forms so that in addition to creating the object that is to represent the city, they create a rewrite rule based on the provided spelling form. They then associate the object that they created for the city with the rule as the rule's semantic interpretation or 'referent'. In Sparser's notation that rule is shown just below.

```
(define-context-free-rule  city  (''Dallas'')
   :form  proper-noun
   :referent  #<city Dallas> )
```

The object representing Dallas the city is given in angle brackets using the Common Lisp convention for printing typed objects. Words are denoted by strings given between double quotes. Semantic labels, or 'categories', are denoted by unadorned symbols. 'Define-context-free-rule' is the function that constructs a Sparser rewrite rule object from its arguments. The first argument is the left-hand side of the rule (the parent); the second argument is the right-hand side (the immediate constituents); the keywords ':form' and ':referent' establish the object just following them as their respective arguments to the function.

For a larger example, one that will lead to the creation of a dozen rewrite rules and illustrate the use of TAGs, we can now turn to a relational semantic category (an event type) from our model of the Who's News domain. In our analysis of this domain every verb is assumed to denote a category of event. When the verb is combined with its arguments and a temporal anchor, the result is an event individual. Consider the following text, which we will take examples from throughout the rest of the chapter. It was taken from the Wall Street Journal on June 14, 1990. Its size and syntactic style are the norm for articles in the Who's News column.

"Belmoral Mines Ltd. (Toronto) — J. Gordon Strasser, acting president and chief executive officer of this gold mining company, was confirmed in the posts, succeeding Kenneth Dalton, who retired as chairman and chief executive, and Clive Brown, who retired as president. Messrs. Dalton and Brown remain directors. A new chairman wasn't named."

From this text, Sparser presently extracts eight tuples that record the four fields person, title, company, and event or state. That is one for each verb and appositive, individuating the events by person rather than position so that, e.g., the second to last sentence is understood as two states rather than one.[8]

Our definition of the event-type 'confirm-in-position' is shown in figure 1. The representation language is called KRISP, and has been described in McDonald 1994b. KRISP is a cousin of Krypton in the Kl-One family, with special features that make it well suited as a source representation for language generation, and efficient data storage and indexing features that suit it to language comprehension.

The first several fields of confirm-in-position are what you would expect in a modern frame language. The category's position in the taxonomic hierarchy is given by its 'specializes' field. Its 'binds' field lists the participants that are specific to this event-type. An individual instance has additional participants like time and place by inheriting from the category 'event'. The participants' value-restrictions are indicated by the 'v/r' flag. For confirm-in-position the agent that causes a confirmation can be either a company or its board of directors; the participant who gets confirmed is a person; and that person is confirmed to some position. We will use these same categories as the labels for the corresponding constituents in the semantic grammar, where they will take on the force of selectional restrictions.

The 'instantiates' field indicates which category an instantiating individual should be indexed under in the discourse history; thus for purposes of searching the discourse history, a confirm-in-position event is taken to be equivalent to any other job-event, e.g. elect, appoint, resign, etc. The 'index' field specifies how individuals are stored. The 'saturation' field indicates that those three participants must be known before an individual of this type is fully individuated.

As we have said, every definition of a domain type in the model is to be accompanied by a specification of the rewrite rules that are to be con-

[8]We are still undecided as to what to record for the last sentence with its 'non-event'. That sentence is interesting syntactically, however, as it illustrates the case of a verb that takes three arguments in its active form, promotes the second when passivized (the person getting the position), and will even allow the promotion of its third argument (the title) when it is negated.

```
(define-category confirm-in-position
  :instantiates  job-event
  :specializes   get-position
  :binds ((agent (:v/r :or board-of-directors company))
          (person (:v/r person))
          (position (:v/r position)))
  :index (:temporary :list)
  :saturation (agent person position)
  :realization
    (:tree-family transitive/passive
     :mapping ((agent . agent)
               (patient . person)
               (s . job-event)
               (np-subject . (board-of-directors company))
               (vp . job-event\agent)
               (vg . :main-verb)
               (np/object . person)
     :main-verb ''confirm''
     :additional-rules
        ((:adjunct (job-event  (job-event in-position)
                      :head left-edge
                      :binds (position right-edge)))
         (:adjunct (job-event  (job-event as-position)
                      :head left-edge
                      :binds (position right-edge))) )))
```

Figure 1. The domain-specific model-level type 'confirm-in-position'

structed, so that instances of that type can be recognized when they occur in a text. This is done in the 'realization' field of the category definition.

The realization field must supply the word(s) that have that domain category as one of their senses, and it must supply the syntactic subcategorization frame that the word takes and the correspondences between the participants in the relation and the subcategorized arguments. With few exceptions, the needed subcategorization frames are common to a great many words, and consequently can be schematized and shared (e.g. transitive verb, intransitive, noun taking quantification of number, noun holding a position in a sequence, etc.). This can be captured through the use of Lexicalized Tree Adjoining Grammars (Joshi 1985; Schabes, Abeillé & Joshi 1988).

The extended domain of locality defined by a TAG allows the configurational and grammatical relations of all of a lexical head's arguments to be given at once, which is important here since the semantic relationship of each argument to its governing relation must be specified in the schema, and it is easier to do this if all of the participants of the relation can be paired with their syntactic counterparts in one statement. The schemas we adopt are a notational variant on the TAG Tree Families of Abeillé 1988, which give all of the transformational variations of a subcategorization frame in one structure. The particulars are described just below in the next section.

The tree family used with the relational category confirm-in-position is 'transitive/passive' as indicated by the ":tree-family" field within the category definition's realization field. The 'main-verb' field (vs. 'head-noun' or 'adjective, etc. in other cases) indicates that the word "confirm" should be used as the lexical head of the tree family. Its morphological variants are calculated automatically, though for irregulars the special cases would be given explicitly here.

The 'mapping' field in the realization indicates the correspondences between the participants of the category and the substitution positions in the tree family. We will take it up in a moment when we walk through the instantiation of part of the semantic grammar that the definition of the category (domain type) confirm-in-position will produce. First, however, we will describe the tree families themselves.

5. DEFINING PARSING RULES SCHEMATICALLY

The purpose of a TAG tree family in the Sparser system is to define a set of substitution schemata through which the grammatical constituent patterns of the language — defined syntactically in the TAG — are to be projected onto the components of the type definitions in the semantic model to form a set of rewrite rules in the semantic grammar.

The effect of this projection is as though we had taken a conventional syntactic grammar and performed two multiplications. The first takes the preterminal categories and multiplies them across the lexical choices and type definitions of the domain model. For every preterminal category in the syntactic grammar, say 'verb', there is now a set of semantic categories: one for every relational type defined in the domain model that can be realized as a verb, e.g. 'confirm-in-position', and there is variation on the corresponding unary rewrite rule for every spelling form in the verb's conjugation; see figure 3. The second multiplication takes the rules that compose syntactic nonterminal or preterminal categories and multiplies them across the sets of selectional restrictions on the participants defined by the relational types. An example of this is shown in the same figure.

The resulting semantic grammar is dramatically larger than the origi-

```
(define-exploded-tree-family  transitive/passive
  :binding-parameters ( agent patient )
  :labels ( s vp vg np-subject np-object )
  :cases
    ((:subject (s  (np-subject vp)
               :head right-edge
               :binds (agent left-edge))
     (:direct-object (vp  (vg np-object)
               :head left-edge
               :binds (patient right-edge)))
     (:passive (s  (np-object vg+passive)
               :head right-edge
               :binds (patient left-edge)))
     (:pos-nominalization (s  (np-object+
                               pos vg+nominalization)
               :head right-edge
               :binds (patient left-edge)))
     (:of-nominalization (s  (vg+nominalization of+np-object)
               :head left-edge
               :binds (patient right-edge)))))
```

Figure 2. TAG schema for rule creation

nal syntactic grammar, but it shows a equally dramatic increase in runtime efficiency. The efficiency comes from the semantic grammar's minimal ambiguity, and from its immediate and incremental connection to the semantic interpretation, which, after all, is the ultimate purpose of the grammar in the first place, namely to define the mapping between form and meaning.

In this section we will look at the TAG tree family for 'transitive/passive' that is used as the schema for the event type 'confirm-in-position' and similar domain types that are realized with transitive verbs that can passivize. This tree family is shown in figure 2.

Like every other structure in the Sparser system, the tree family is defined using a Lisp form based on a structure-defining function (here "define-exploded-tree-family") and a set of argument fields indicated by keywords. Here the 'cases' field holds five syntactic rewrite rules with their semantic interpretations. The rules are given in schematic form using substitution variables defined in the 'binding-parameters' and 'labels' fields of the definition (e.g. agent, patient, s, vp, vg, etc.).

The term at the beginning of each case (e.g. :subject) is just an indicator used by the grammar writer to help organize the cases. The parenthesized expression following the indicator is the rule proper. Left and righthand sides are indicated in the obvious way. The :head and :binds keywords following the syntactic part of the rule give its semantic interpretation. They indicate which of the two constituents on the righthand side is the head of the phrase and the semantic role that the other constituent fills. As Sparser is based on a chart, the constituents are referred to as 'edges', hence the terms 'left-edge' and 'right-edge' to indicate the constituents in a binary rule.[9]

The substitution variables of the tree family are divided into two sets. The variables in the binding-parameters field will correspond to the participant roles of the type definitions. They are used in the semantic interpretations. The variables in the labels field will correspond to the categories used as value-restrictions in the type definitions. They are used to specify the rewrite rules' non-terminal categories. They also designate the 'form labels' that are to accompany the corresponding semantic labels in the semantic grammar as discussed in section seven.

A full discussion of the relationship between this use of TAGs as substitution schemas and the other treatments of TAGs appears in McDonald 1994a. But we can mention that we independently have an extensive TAG grammar, organized as tree families, that we have been using in our work on language generation for many years. Here what we have done (by hand at the moment) is take those trees and decompose each of them into their layers of context-free rules, avoiding duplicates since many trees have identical sentential forms at some layer such as S -> NP VP.

The connectedness that characterizes the levels of immediate constituents in a TAG tree is obviously not present in these 'exploded' tree families. But it is reconstituted when the schema is applied to a domain type to assemble the rewrite rules of the semantic grammar. The tree families use standard labels like VP to indicate which constituent in the context-free production will lie on the headline of the tree that the schema as a whole implicitly defines. Since such labels appear in every syntactically described clause, they do not, per se, provide any of the 'glue' that would indicate that we are dealing with connected trees rather than a random set of immediate constituents. However, during the application of the schema to a type definition, these labels are replaced with unique, semantically characterized labels like confirm-in-position+passive. These unique labels then create a connection within the instantiated set of context free rules similar to the quasi-nodes of Vijay Shankar (1993).

[9] At runtime all of Sparser's rewrite rules are unary or binary. Rules with more than two terms on their righthand sides are converted to Chomsky Normal Form, using a dotted-rule convention to provide names for the intermediate non-terminal labels created in the process.

Let us look in detail at how one of the tree family's cases, the initial one specifying S -> NP-subject VP, is interpreted for confirm-in-position. This case uses four substitution variables: s, np-subject, vp, and agent. (This NP is annotated as the subject to distinguish it among the substitution variables from the other NP in the schema, the direct object.) To see how these variables are to be instantiated, we look to the 'mapping' that is given in the definition of confirm in position (figure 1). This mapping is a set of pairs associating the names of value restrictions or participants in the relation with the corresponding variables of the tree family. Some generalizations are also recorded in this mapping, as with the category assigned to the 'vp' variable: 'job-event\agent. It reflects the observation that all of the transitive 'get-position' event types in this domain map their active subjects to the same relationship in the semantics of the event; hence they all use the same category for VPs.

Examining the mapping specification for confirm-in-position we see we have to make two rules for this case because the subject np can take either of two values. The lefthand side of the both rules is made by substituting the category 'job-event' for the variable S in the tree family. We make the righthand side of one of the two rules by substituting the category 'board-of-directors' for the variable 'np-subject' and substituting 'job-event\agent' for 'vp'; the other rule gets 'company' substituted for its np-subject.

As described in more detail in section seven, the two rewrite rules must have a 'syntactic-form category', which will be the 'form label' on the edge created when the rules complete. This is taken from the substitution variable specified for the lefthand side of the case in the schema, 'S', which is now interpreted as a syntactic category. The rules must also have a 'referent' (semantic interpretation function). They get this from the corresponding part of the case in the schema. Reading out from the mapping, the participant role 'person' is substituted for the symbol 'agent', indicating that the referent of the left daughter of the completed edge is to be bound to the agent role of the confirm-in-position individual that will be found as the referent of the right daughter of the edge. (An example of the parsing process is described in detail in section six.)

In the case of confirm-in-position, the realization field in its definition indicates that there are two additional cases beyond the ones given in the tree family. They identify how the category's 'position' role is filled, namely with either of two different adjunct prepositional phrases, one using "*in*", the other "*as*". (They are analyzed as attaching to the sentence rather than the verb phrase for compatibility with the way nominalizations are treated.) This local augmentation of the set of tree families is convenient for specifying the often idiosyncratic way that individual verbs can subcategorize for optional complements.

```
(1)  job-event  ->  board-of-directors  job-event\agent
(2)  job-event  ->  company  job-event\agent
(3)  job-event  ->  job-event  in-position
(4)  job-event  ->  job-event  as-position
(5)  job-event  ->  person  confirm-in-position+passive
(6)  job-event  ->  person+pos  confirm-in-position+
                    nominalization
(7)  job-event  ->  confirm-in-position+nominalization
                    of-person
(8)  job-event\agent      ->  confirm-in-position  person
(9)  confirm-in-position ->  ``confirm''
(10) confirm-in-position ->  ``confirms''
(11) confirm-in-position ->  ``confirmed''
(12) confirm-in-position ->  ``confirming''
(13) confirm-in-position+nominalization  ->  ``confirmation''
```

Figure 3. Semantically labeled rules

Once the syntactic schemas defined by the cases in tree family and in the realization field have finished their application to the definition of the domain category denoting the domain type 'confirm-in-position', a total of thirteen rewrite rules have been added to the semantic grammar as listed in figure 3.

To summarize the framework so far, the Sparser system uses a grammar of rewrite rules that have semantic categories as their primary labels, a so-called semantic grammar. This semantic description of the phrase structure of the text is supplemented by a syntactic description that will trigger a body of domain-independent 'form' rewrite rules in occasions where the intended semantic interpretation is the same across domains. Each rewrite rule has an accompanying semantic interpretation function that will find or construct its denotation in Sparser's model when the rule completes. The semantic grammar rules and the set of model-level relational types and individuals are created at the same time by definitions that recruit the value restrictions on the participants of the relations to supply the semantic labels on the grammar's rules. There, they implicitly serve the role of selectional restrictions to ensure that the rules will not complete unless their constituents will make sense to the world model. The set of rules created by a type definition is determined by instantiating the TAG tree family(s) corresponding to the subcategorization frame(s) of the word or words that can realize the type in a text.

One of the decisions made in writing this particular grammar is worth

```
#<phrase-structure-rule psr11
  :lefthand-side  #<category confirm-in-position>
  :righthand-side  ( #<word ''confirmed''> )
  :syntactic-form  #<category verb+ed>
  :referent  #<category confirm-in-position> >
```

Figure 4. Rewrite rule 11

some notice. we have made a generalization about the semantic interpretations of a whole semantic class of verbs by deciding to specify the VP label in this mapping as 'job-event\agent' rather than, say, 'confirm-in- position-VP' (which would be as specific as we would be able to be). By choosing the more general category (which should be read as in a categorial grammar: look to compose with an agent to the left of this constituent and label the new edge 'job-event'), we are saying that all the verbs in this family (or rather the model-level denotations of the verbs) make the same interpretation of their subject NP, i.e. they all map it to their equivalent of the agent role. This points out that linguistic generalizations can be made in the semantic realm as well as the syntactic, and that by using a semantic grammar we are able to express them directly.

6. A PARSING EXAMPLE

We can see this set of semantic grammar rules in action by looking at how Sparser goes about parsing parts of the sentence "*J. Gordon Strasser, acting president and chief executive officer of this gold mining company, was confirmed in the posts*". The analysis at work views content words (nouns, verbs, adjectives) as denoting categories of individuals. The denotation of "*confirmed*" is the category (event type) whose definition we have just discussed: confirm-in-position. The denotation of the word "*company*" is the category used for individuals representing companies and similar enterprises; "*posts*" denotes the category for positions, specialized in this case to record that more than one title and/or company is involved; and so on.

The instantiation of a model-level object to represent this individual confirm-in-position event will begin when the word "*confirmed*" is scanned, firing rewrite rule 11 (figure 3). That rule has the internal representation shown in figure 4. The '#<>' notation indicates pointers to objects, where the first term in the brackets indicating the object's type and is typically followed by the symbol or string used to name it.

Note that the 'referent' given with the rule is already a pointer directly into Sparser's semantic model. It is available as part of the statement of

```
#<edge   e22 ;; a designator to use as the edge's name
   :starts-at #<position 18>
   :ends-at #<position 19>
   :category #<category confirm-in-position>
   :left-daughter #<word ''confirmed">
   :right-daughter :unary-rule ;; i.e. only the 'left'
                               ;; daughter matters
     :used-in nil ;; later points to the edge this is a
                  ;; daughter of
     :form #<category verb+ed>
     :referent  #<category confirm-in-position> >
```

Figure 5. An edge in the chart

the rule because, as we have described, the rule is created as a side-effect of defining the event-type. Notice also that the rule indicates the default syntactic label (category) that is to be given to the constituents that it forms, i.e. verb+ed. This additional label complements the primary semantic label given as the rule's lefthand side. This label too was assigned as part of the projection of the set of semantic rewrite rules from the combination of the event type's definition and the tree family it specified.

When completed, this rule creates a nonterminal node — an edge in Sparser's chart — as shown in figure 5. For purposes of illustration we have the example text start at chart position zero, which puts the word "*confirmed*" between chart positions 18 and 19.

The edge carries over the information given in rule 11. The category given as the 'lefthand-side' of the rule becomes the edge's 'category'. The category given as the 'syntactic-form' of the rule becomes the edge's 'form'. The first is the primary determinant of how the parse proceeds; the second is a default that will come into play only if the semantic label does not participate in any compositions with the neighbor edges.

The composition of a modifier onto a head may specialize the referent to one of its subcategories (as done with the plurality of "*posts*"). The composition of certain discourse anchors — tense for verbs or determiners for nouns — will pick out of the model or will construct an individual that instantiates the category of the phrase on the headline. This happens when "*was*" and "*confirmed*" are composed, where we will establish the 'confirm-in-position' individual. Because this is a general practice that applies to any combination of an event type and an instantiating anchor, it is done by a general 'rule of form', which we take up in the next section.

In the interest of space we will jump ahead in the parse to the point when the major constituents of the example have been formed so that we can concentrate on how the rules assembled for confirm-in-position are applied and how they take the new individual in the model — an instance of this event-type — and fill its participant roles with the individuals denoted by the argument constituents.

Below (figure 6) is a vertical presentation of the edges in the chart with the text they span, followed by a listing of the edges giving their semantic and syntactic labels and their denotations. A compact notation is used here for illustration purposes. The ids on the edges, e.g., 'e23', reflect the order in which the edges were formed. The numbers around the spanned texts are the chart positions.

At this point, Sparser will apply rule 5 to combine edges e20 and e23 and form edge e30. This new edge is a clause ('S') labeled 'job-event' spanning the text from position 1 to position 20. When that edge is formed, the denotations of its daughter edges are combined following the interpretation function given with the rule (shown schematically in figure 2. The result, the denotation of e30, is the same individual as denoted by e23, but now that individual is augmented by having its agent role bound to the person denoted by the subject edge e20.

```
  e20     1 J. Gordon Strasser ... of this gold mining
                                              company 18
  e23     18 was confirmed 20
  e29     20 in the posts 23

[e20: person, np, #<individual:person Strasser> ]

[e23: confirm-in-position+passive, vg, #<individual:confirm
                                          -in-position> ]

[e29: in-position, pp, #<individual:position:collective
                                           President ...> ]
```

Figure 6. Chart state and list of edges

The new edge (e30) is then combined with the pp-adjunct edge e29 using rule 3 with a similar result: the edge, e31, is formed as shown in figure 7. Its referent is again the same individual that was instantiated when the verb group edge was formed (i.e. the individual representing this instance of confirm-in-position). Now it gets its position role bound to the individual of type position denoted by e29.

```
#<edge  e31
  :starts-at #<position 1>
  :ends-at #<position 23>
  :category #<category job-event
  :left-daughter #<edge 30>
  :right-daughter #<edge 29>
  :used-in nil
  :form #<category S>
  :referent
    #<individual
      :type ( confirm-in-position past get-position
              job-event transition-event )
      :bindings ( #<binding person = #<individual:person
                                               Strasser>>
                  #<binding position =
                       #<individual:position:collective
                                   President ... >> )>>
```

Figure 7. Edge e31

The parse is now finished syntactically since we have recovered a grammatically complete unit, a sentence, and have consumed all of the text of this example. Semantically it is still incomplete, since the text did not explicitly mention the agent that did the confirming and so the event-type is not yet saturated. In this genre it is safe to infer that the agent is the board of directors of the company where the person now holds the position; in other Who's News articles this agent is explicit.

7. FORM RULES

The preponderance of the syntactic (surface form) rewrite rules in Sparser's grammar have semantic labels and are the result of the definition of a domain-specific type in the model. When the distinction must be made, we will refer to these as 'semantically characterized rules'. Sparser also has rewrite rules whose categories are taken from the regular syntactic vocabulary. We call these 'form rules' because they make reference to general aspects of surface form that are valid across all domains. Form rules are the subject of this section. We will look at an example of a form rule and the rationale behind its use, and then go through the 'check' algorithm that coordinates the selection of semantically characterized rules and form rules.

The purpose of a form rule is to capture a general fact about phrase formation in the language, one whose implications for the semantics of the resulting phrase — its denotation — is the same regardless of the domain. A form rule combines the word labeling one edge — call it the 'literal' — with the syntactic label, the 'form category', of an adjacent edge. That edge we can call the 'head' because it will always lie on the headline of the final tree. The literal will always be a specifier, an auxiliary, or a modifying adjunct or adverb.

The implementation of form rules makes them transparent to the semantically characterized rules of the grammar because the edge created by composing the literal and the head edges will have the same category as the head edge. Any semantically characterized rules that could apply to the head edge will apply to the new edge as though the literal had never been there. The reader may have already noticed that the set of rules in figure 3 was missing many cases needed to cover texts that can occur with that verb in its target sublanguage: "... *will be confirmed Wednesday in Seattle*", "... *has been confirmed*", etc. All such combinations — with time and place adjuncts, with complex verbal auxiliaries, etc. — are handled by form rules.

When the default interpretation needs to be overridden — as when a verb such as "*put*" subcategorizes specifically for a place — the grammar simply includes a semantically characterized rule for that combination. The parser looks for semantic rules in preference to form rules, as described in a moment.

The form rule that applies in the case of "*was confirmed*" is shown in figure 8. Notice that in this rule, the referent is not a direct pointer into the model as before but a schematic function. It takes the second of the two constituents, the 'right' edge — in this case edge-22 which denoting the category 'confirm-in-position — and looks in the model for one of its subtypes (specializations) that represents the event having occurred in the past. That specialized category then becomes the denotation of the new edge.

Informally speaking, this rule applies in the present example because the word "*was*" is adjacent to edge-22 and edge-22 has the form category 'verb+ed', and because there is no semantically characterized rule that combines "*was*" and edge-22's semantic category, 'confirm-in-position'. The new edge formed by the completion of the rule will have the label 'confirm-in-position+passive', as dictated by the form rule's "new- category" field. This is done in coordination with the tree family, 'transitive/passive' that defined the confirm-in-position event-type and made provisions for that composite label in the set of rules it created. (Had there been no new-category field in the rule, then by default the new edge would have taken the same label as the one on the head edge — confirm-in-position.)

```
#<form-rule  fpsr1
  :righthand-side  ( #<word ''was''> #<category verb+ed> )
  :new-category :passive
  :syntactic-form  #<category verb-group>
  :referent (:head :right-edge
             :subtype #<past> ) >
```

Figure 8. The applicable form rule for "*was confirmed*"

```
#<edge  e21
  :starts-at #<position 17>
  :ends-at #<position 18>
  :category #<word ''was''>
  :left-daughter #<word ''was''>
  :right-daughter :literal-in-a-rule
  :used-in #<edge 23>
  :form #<category verbal-auxiliary>
  :referent  nil >
```

Figure 9. The edge that spans the word "*was*"

The formal algorithm controlling this 'check' of the two edges will be presented in a moment, but first we should discuss some probably unusual aspects of the edge that spans the word "*was*", shown in (figure 9).

Note that the label on this edge (its 'category' field) is word rather than a category. There are two reasons for permitting this. The first is that allowing words as nonterminals permits an elegant treatment of abbreviations: One can simply rewrite the combination of the abbreviation and the period that follows it as the full, unabbreviated word, thereby avoiding any need to redundantly extend the grammar to include rules for the abbreviation and the full word both (e.g. "Company" -> "Co" "."). If an abbreviated spelling form has several expansions (such as "St."), then multiple edges will be put into the chart ("Street" and "Saint").

The second reason is to simplify the implementation of the parsing algorithm so that it needs to manipulate only a single data type when looking for rule applications, edges, rather than both edges and words. To this end, any word that is mentioned in a rewrite rule is covered with an edge when it is scanned, using the word as the edge's label. This policy also permits a simple way to discriminate between known and unknown words in the course of a parse. A known word (one with rules in the grammar) will always have one or more edges over it, if only a trivial edge labeled with that word. Unknown words will not have edges, leaving a gap among the preterminal edges of the chart which can be used to trigger heuristics for dealing with unknown words.

In describing the Check algorithm below we will not discuss the larger question of how the parsing algorithm determines when or whether two adjacent edges will be checked. Basically the parser operates bottom up and left to right, forming constituents from their heads outwards; however, overlaying that conventional traversal of the space of possible constituents is a moderately complex control structure that reduces the search to a deterministic algorithm. Every edge formed will be part of the final analysis and every edge will have a unique parent edge in the tree. The time complexity is linear on-line. For some of the particulars see McDonald 1992.

7.1. THE ALGORITHM THAT COORDINATES CHECKING FOR BOTH KINDS OF RULES

We can define Sparser's Check operation — its algorithm for seeing whether there is a rule in the grammar that combines two particular adjacent edges — as follows:

Consider two adjacent edges which we will call "Left" and "Right". Left ends at some position p in the chart, and Right begins at this same position p. Left is said to be earlier in the chart — closer to the beginning of the text — because it begins at some position p' such that p' is strictly less that p and because Right ends at some position p" such that p" is strictly greater than p. Positions are indexed numerically starting with zero before the first word of the text and increasing in the positive direction, one position between each word. The position at which an edge begins always has a lower numerical index than the position at which it ends; no edge can begin and end at the same position.

Only adjacent edges can be combined to form a new edge. The new edge will start at position p' and end at p". The possibility of two adjacent edges combining is function of their labels, where a label is either the word or category in the 'category' field of an edge, or one of a specially designated set of 'form categories' pointed to from the 'form' field of an edge. The form field may be empty.

The Check operation is based on a table compiled from the labels of the rules of the grammar. The table will associate the righthand sides of those rules, taken as ordered pairs of labels, with the rules themselves. (Once they have been compiled into Chomsky Normal Form, all of Sparser's rewrite rules are binary.) At runtime we use the table by forming an index from the labels of the adjacent constituents and looking the index up in the table to see if the pair of labels is one of the ones defined by the grammar. If it is, we return the rule located at that index in the table; if it is not, there will be no rule at that index and we return 'nil' indicating that the edges do not combine. We presently implement the table as a hash on the numerical index; it would lend itself to a hardware implementation as will be clear from its definition.

We form the table as follows. For each rule consider the two labels on its righthand side; call them LL and RL for the first and second (left and right) labels respectively. The rules are taken one at a time in some order and their labels are annotated as follows (the textual order of their definition in the files of the grammar suffices). We assign each label two unique numbers. One number stands for the label when it appears as the left label of a binary rule (LL); the second stands for when it appears as the right label of a rule (RL). If a label never appears on one of the sides we assign it nil for that component.

Numbers for RL labels are assigned starting at 1 and increasing by one with each successive RL up to some 'middle number' chosen to be well above the number of labels ever to appear in the grammar. Numbers for LL labels are assigned starting at that middle number plus one and adding that middle number to the prior LL index for each successive LL. The numbers are then stored with their labels for use during the Check operation.

Entries in the table are formed by adding the numbers for the two righthand side labels of each rule and assigning the rule to the table entry with that numerical index. This sum is guaranteed to be unique by the apt choice of the middle number that divides the two number sequences. It is chosen on the model of adding the two halves of a machine word on a computer. For a 32 bit word length we would select as the middle number 65,536 (two to the sixteenth), giving us a maximum of 64k labels. All of the LL labels will have zeros in their lower sixteen bits; all of the RL labels will have zeros in their upper sixteen bits; combining them with a logical AND will yield a new number unique to that combination of its two halves. Adding the two numbers in software has the same effect.

In checking whether two adjacent edges combine, we first check whether their two semantic labels combine; then only if those labels do not combine will we go further and check for the possible combination of one or the other of the semantic labels with the other constituent's form label. To facilitate this, the index assignment algorithm is complicated slightly: In iterating through the grammar's rules we distinguish between semantically characterized rules and form rules. Semantic combinations and form combinations are each given their own, unique indexes, and then two pairs of indexes are stored with each label; one pair for each direction in which a combination can be made. The first number in each pair is used for combinations with a semantic label, the second for combinations with a form label. The first numbers are established by iterating through the semantically characterized rules; the second by iterating through the form rules.

Given all this, the Check algorithm proper is the following. Given edges Left and Right as defined above, compute the index in the table of the combination's semantic labels (the 'category' fields of the two edges). For Left, retrieve the right-looking number that was assigned to it — the one it was given for the case when it appeared as the left of the two labels in a binary rule. Do the opposite for Right. Now add the two numbers, and use the sum as an index into the table. A rule will be returned if the two edges compose, and this rule is then used as the basis of the new edge spanning them. If that index into the table retrieves nil, indicating that no semantically characterized rule applies to that edge pair, then go on to check for combinations involving form rules. In the present example there will be no semantically characterized rule for "*was*" plus 'confirm-in-position', so we will move on to check form rules.

There will always be two possible form rules to check for: one combining the category field label of Left and the form field label of Right; the other combining the form label of Left and the category label of Right. Only one of these two pairs will have an index defined for it because of the requirement on form rules that one of the two labels on their righthand sides be either a literal word or a semantic category. We start by computing the table index for the first case (left semantic label, right form label), and only if that lookup into the table fails to return a rule do we try the second (left form label, right semantic label). If one or the other label fails to have a form option in its stored pair of index numbers, then that case is undefined. If neither succeeds, then the two adjacent edges do not compose.

This completes the description of Sparser's Check algorithm. It can be summarized as follows. Its purpose is to determine whether two adjacent edges can be composed to form a new edge. This is allowed in any of three cases: first if the semantic categories of the two edges match the righthand side of some rule in the grammar; failing that, if the semantic category of the first and the form category of the second correspond to some form rule in the grammar; and finally if there is a rule corresponding to the form category of the first and the semantic category of the second. The test is made by adding numbers that were assigned to the labels as the grammar rules were defined, and using that index as the key into a table that records which pairs correspond to rules.

The prohibition on having a form rule based on a pair of form labels is there to rule out the possibility of ever writing a conventional syntactic grammar in this formalism. We rule this out for two reasons. The first is that allowing 'pure' form rules would re-introduce to the grammar the massive structural ambiguities that syntactic grammars are prone to. The second is that doing so would miss the point of this grammar design, namely that the purpose of a grammar is to facilitate the mapping between form and meaning — between the edges formed over words or phrases and their denotations in the system's world model. We only allow form rules to be used when we are already constructing the projection to some individual in the model, i.e. when the combination is between an edge on the head line which will have a denotation and one of its complements or adjuncts.

We have presented the Check algorithm in this much detail because we have seldom seen the rule-lookup algorithms of other parsers described and feel that this kind of information should be added to the literature. In the present case, the very high efficiency of this constant-time lookup operation is important because of the very large number of rewrite rules in the grammar. A lookup algorithm that was sensitive to the size of the grammar (or for that matter the presence of any 'order of the size of the grammar' operation within the parser) would strongly penalize the use a semantic grammar. Optimizing algorithms for speed is important even with today's processors because of the ever growing volume of text that must be processed.[10]

8. CONCLUDING REMARKS

Two substantive complaints have been made against semantic grammars in the literature (see, e.g. Wallace 1984). One is that they cannot be easily extended as one moves from one domain to the next while a thorough syntactic grammar can be taken over unchanged. This observation misses a crucial point, however, namely the purpose of a grammar is to guide semantic interpretation. It is not an end in itself. Understanding a text means finding the correspondence between the structural analysis provided by the syntax and the entities known to the world model of the application system that is going to use the information. It is indisputable that the world model of the first domain that one works with will have to be extended when one moves to the next. The next domain will involve new kinds of objects and new types of relations, and these will have to be added to the model if texts in the new domain are to be understood. There is no other possibility. The fact that the syntactic grammar might not change is besides the point because it is not the whole story.

[10]One day of the Wall Street Journal averages about half a megabyte. It is available online at about six o'clock in the morning. We will want the results of our information extractions and their pragmatic analyses on the desks of clients when they come in three hours later, and the Journal is only one of a vast number of online text-based information services that might be important. Sparser processes the sublanguage-rich portions of a text at about 100 words a second (Macintosh Quadra 900, 68040, 40 mhz); off-topic portions run at about 200 words/sec.

By using a semantic grammar, and by having it constructed directly from the world model as is done with Sparser, we will able to keep the grammar in step with the extensions to the model. In particular, since each domain type must have a realization field we will be continually reminded as we work on the model that we need to determine the words and syntactic constructions that are used to talk about the new concepts.

The second substantive complaint is that semantic grammars are incapable of capturing linguistic generalizations. As a result, one cannot take advantage of these uniformities when writing the grammar and may be tempted to write rules that would be unreasonable from a linguistic perspective and so likely to be brittle in practice. This is the more legitimate of the two complaints, but it is also specifically what the present system was designed to address.

By keeping the grammarian (domain modeler) from writing semantic grammar rules directly except in the most idiosyncratic cases (e.g. for dates written as "3/31/93"), and forcing them instead to work from some well-crafted syntactic schemas, we have imposed a discipline on the grammar, forcing it to fit our conception of properly analyzed linguistic structure as captured in the schemas. At the same time, we have reduced the effort required to prepare the grammar, since it is markedly easier to adapt the realization fields of a set of similar domain-type definitions than to individually write out all the rewrite rules.

We have been using semantic grammars in the Sparser system since its inception in 1990. Form rules were introduced after the experience of writing its first major grammar, and had a significant amplifying effect since they allowed whole sets of generic constructions to be instantiated simultaneously just by adding the appropriate syntactic labels. The use of realization fields on model-level definitions and the development of the 'exploded tree families' used as schemas is comparatively recent, and we are only now redoing the original grammar for the Who's News domain in those terms. The proof of the pudding, as it were, will come as the models and grammars for new domains are added. If the effort to make these extensions is dramatically smaller than when the original grammars were developed by hand, then we will judge the design a pragmatic success. If a large set of tree families, especially for noun phrases, can be developed that handles the construction-types that we see in the business texts we work with, then we will have gotten a long way towards solving the problem of extending grammars to new domains.

References

Abeillé, A. (1988) *A French Tree Adjoining Grammar*. Technical Report, Dept. of Computer & Information Science, Univ. of Pennsylvania.

Advanced Research Projects Agency (1992) *Proceedings: Fourth Message Understanding Conference*. San Mateo, CA: Morgan Kaufmann.

Advanced Research Projects Agency ("ARPA") (1994) *Proceedings: Human Language Technology Workshop*. San Mateo, CA: Morgan Kaufmann.

Allen, J (1995) *Natural Language Understanding (second edition)*, Redwood City, California: Benjamin/Cummings.

Alshawi, H. (ed.) (1992) *The Core Language Engine*. Cambridge: MIT Press.

Ayuso, D., S. Boisen, H. Fox, H. Gish, R. Ingria and R. Weischedel (1992) *Description of the Plum System as Used for MUC-4*. In: Arpa 1992, 169 – 176.

Burton, R. (1976) *Semantic Grammar: An Engineering Technique for Constructing Natural Language Understanding Systems*. Report No. 3453, Bolt Beranek and Newman Inc., Cambridge, MA.

______ and J. S. Brown (1975) "Multiple Representations of Knowledge for Tutorial Reasoning", In: Bobrow & Colins (eds.) *Representation and Understanding*. New York: Academic Press.

Hendrix, G., E. Sacerdoti, D. Sagalowicz, and J. Slocum (1978) "Developing a natural language interface to complex data" ACM TODS. 3(2), 105 – 147.

Hobbs, J.R., D. Appelt, M. Tyson, J. Bear and D. Israel (1992) *Description of the Fastus System Used for MUC-4*. In: Arpa 1992, 268 – 275.

Joshi, A.K. (1985) "How much context- sensitivity is required to provide reasonable structural descriptions: tree adjoining grammars". In: Dowty, D.R., L. Kartutunen, A.M. Zwicky (eds) *Natural Language Processing*. Cambridge, U.K.: Cambridge University Press.

Kittredge, R. and J. Lehrberger (1982) *Sublanguage: Studies of Language in Restricted Semantic domains*. Berlin: de Gruyter.

de Marken, C.G. (1990) *A Large-Scale Parser for Unrestricted Text*. Dissertation. Dept. of Electrical Engineering and Computer Science, MIT.

Martin, W., K.W. Church and R.S. Patil (1981) *Preliminary Analysis of a Breadth-First Parsing Algorithm*. Technical Report 261. Laboratory for Computer Science, MIT.

McDonald, D. (1992) "An Efficient Chart- based Algorithm for Partial-Parsing of Unrestricted Texts". In: *Proc. of the 3d Conference on Applied Natural Language Processing*, 193 – 200.

______ (1993) "Internal and External Evidence in the Identification and Semantic Categorization of Proper Names". In: *Proceedings of the SigLex Workshop on Acquisition of Lexical Knowledge from Text*, 32 – 43.

______ (1994a) "Reversible NLP by Linking the Grammar to the Knowledge Base". In Strzalkowski, T. (ed), *Reversible Grammar in Natural Language Processing*. Dordrecht and Boston: Kluwer, 257 – 291.

______ (1994b) "KRISP: a representation for the semantic interpretation of real texts." *Mind and Machines* 4, 56 – 73.

______ (1994c) "Simplifying Analyses by Fitting the Semantic Representation Closely to

Language". In: Working Notes, AAAI Fall Symposium on Knowledge Representation for Natural Language Processing in Implemented Systems, 90 – 96.

Miller, Scott, R. Bobrow, R. Ingria and R. Schwartz () "Hidden Understanding Models of Natural Language". In: *Proc. of the 32nd Annual Meeting of the ACL*, New Mexico State University, 25 – 32.

Riesbeck, C. and C.E. Martin (1985) *Direct Memory Access Parsing*. Technical Report DCS/RR 354. Depart. of Computer Science, AI Group. Yale University.

Schabes, Y., A. Abeillé and A.K. Joshi (1988) "Parsing Strategies with 'Lexicalized' Grammars: Application to Tree Adjoining Grammars". In: *Proc. of Coling-88*, Budapest, Hungary.

Tomita, M. (1986) *Efficient Parsing for Natural Language*. Dordrecht and Boston: Kluwer.

Vijay-Shanker, K. (1993) "Using Descriptions of Trees in a Tree Adjoining Grammar". *Computational Linguistics*. 18(4), 481 – 517.

Wallace, M. (1984) *Communicating with databases in natural language*. Chichester, U.K.: Ellis Horwood.

Waltz, D., T. Finin, F. Green, B. Goodman and G. Hadden (1976) *The PLANES system: Natural language access to a large database*. Report T-34. Dept. of Computer Science, University of Illinois.

Weischedel, R., M. Meteer, R. Schwartz, L. Ramshaw and J. Palmucci (1993) "Coping with Ambiguity and Unknown Words through Probabilistic Models". In: *Computational Linguistics* (19)2. 359 – 382.

Woods, W.A. (1970) "Transition network grammars for natural language analysis". In: *Communications of the Association for Computing Machinery*. (13)10. 591-606.

Woods, W.A. (1975) "What's in a Link: Foundations for Semantic Networks". In Bobrow & Collins (eds) *Representation and Understanding*. New York: Academic Press, 35 – 82.

17. INTEGRATION OF MORPHOLOGICAL AND SYNTACTIC ANALYSIS BASED ON GLR PARSING

HOZUMI TANAKA, TAKENOBU TOKUNAGA
AND MICHIO AIZAWA
Department of Computer Science
Tokyo Institute of Technology

Abstract.
Morphological analysis of Japanese is very different from that of English, because no spaces are placed between words. This is also the case in many Asian languages such as Korean, Chinese, Thai and so forth. In the Indo-European family, some languages such as German have the same phenomenon in forming nominal compounds. Processing such languages requires the identification of the word boundaries in the first place. This process is often called *segmentation*. Segmentation is a very important process, since the wrong segmentation causes fatal errors in later stages such as syntactic, semantic and contextual analysis. However, correct segmentation is not always possible with morphological information only. Syntactic, semantic and contextual information are also necessary to resolve the ambiguities in segmentation. This chapter proposes a method to integrate the morphological and syntactic analysis based on the LR parsing algorithm. An LR table derived from grammar rules is modified on the basis of connectabilities between adjacent words. The modified LR table reflects both the morphological and syntactic constraints. Using the LR table and the generalized LR parsing algorithm, efficient morphological and syntactic analysis is posssible.

1. INTRODUCTION

Morphological analysis of Japanese is very different from that of English, because no spaces are placed between words. This is also the case in many Asian languages such as Korean, Chinese, Thai and so forth. In the Indo-

H. Bunt and M. Tomita (eds.), Recent Advances in Parsing Technology, 325–342.

European family, some languages such as German have the same phenomenon in forming nominal compounds. Processing such languages requires the identification of the word boundaries in the first place. This process is often called *segmentation*. Segmentation is one of the most important tasks of morphological analysis for these languages, since the wrong segmentation causes fatal errors in later stages such as syntactic, semantic and contextual analysis. Correct segmentation is not always possible with morphological information only. Syntactic, semantic and contextual information are also necessary to resolve the ambiguities in segmentation.

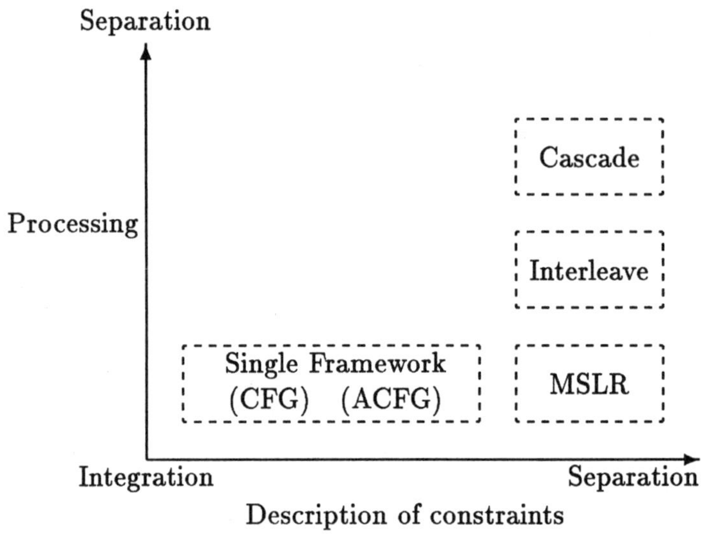

Figure 1 Relation of approaches

Over the past decades a number of studies have been made on the morphological and syntactic analysis of Japanese. From the viewpoint of two kinds of integration, description of constraints and processing, they would be classified into the following three approaches. The relation of these approaches is illustrated in Figure 1.

Cascade:
Separate the morphological and syntactic analysis and execute them in a cascade manner. The morphological and syntactic constraints are represented separately.

Interleave:
Separate the morphological and syntactic analysis and execute them in an interleaving manner. The morphological and syntactic constraints are represented separately.

Single Framework:
Represent both the morphological and syntactic constraints in a sin-

gle framework such as context free grammars (CFGs) and make no distinction between the two analyses.

Representing the morphological and syntactic constraints separately as in the first two approaches, Cascade and Interleave, makes maintaining and extending the constraints easier. This is an advantage of these approaches. Many natural language processing systems have used these two approaches. For example, Mine *et al.* proposed a method to represent the morphological constraints in regular grammar and the syntactic constraints in CFG, and interleave the morphological and syntactic analysis (Mine *et al.*, 1991). Most other systems use a connection matrix instead of regular grammar (Miyazaki, 1984; Sugimura, 1988). The main drawbacks of these approaches may be summarized as follows:

- It may require two different algorithms for each analysis.
- It must retain all ambiguities from the morphological analysis until the syntactic analysis begins. This wastes memory space and computing time.

On the other hand, from a viewpoint of processing, it is preferable to integrate the morphological and syntactic analysis into a single framework, since some syntactic constraints are useful for morphological analysis and vice versa. The last approach fulfills this requirement. There have been several attempts to develop CFGs that covers both the morphological and syntactic constraints (Kita, 1992; Sano *et al.*, 1992). However, it is empirically difficult to describe both constraints by using only CFG. In order to have CFG rules include morphological constraints, nonterminal symbols have to bear the morphological attributes which are used for checking connectabilities between morphemes. In other words, nonterminals should be more precisely subcategorized. This increases the number of nonterminals and thus that of grammar rules.

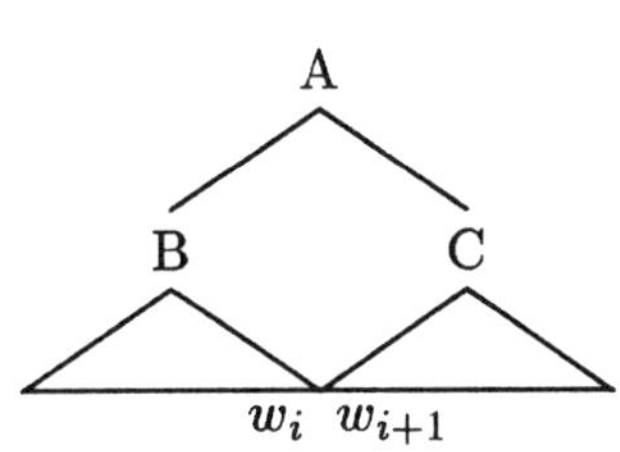

Figure 2 Connectability check by CFG

Using augmented context free grammar (ACFG) instead of CFG may remedy this problem. However, this may cause the delay of connectability checking. For example, in Figure 2, in order to check the connectability between adjacent words, w_i and w_{i+1}, the morphological attributes of each word should be propagated up to their mother nodes B and C, and the check is delayed until the application of the rule A → B C.

By using connection matrices for morphological analysis as in the Cascade/Interleave approaches, connectability checks between adjacent words is performed very easily. Therefore, it is desirable to represent the morphological and syntactic constraints separately as in Cascade/Interleave, and to integrate the execution of both analyses into a single process as in Single Framework approaches. Our method has captured these advantages by representing the morphological constraints in connection matrices and the syntactic constraints in CFGs, and compiling both constraints into an LR table (Aho *et al.*, 1986). The already existing efficient LR parsing algorithms would be used with minor modifications, enabling us to utilize both the morphological and syntactic constraints at the same time. Our approach, called MSLR (Morpho-Syntactic LR), locates at the right bottom of the map in Figure 1, which is the most preferable position.

In the next section, we first give a brief introduction to Japanese morphological analysis using an example sentence. In section 3, we describe the method of generating an LR table from a connection matrix and CFG rules, then in section 4 we explain the parsing algorithm. Our algorithm is essentially the same as Tomita's generalized LR parsing algorithm (Tomita, 1986). The only difference is that the input is not a sequence of preterminals, but a sequence of characters.

2. MORPHOLOGICAL ANALYSIS OF JAPANESE

A simple Japanese sentence consists of a sequence of postpositional phrases (PPs) followed by a predicate. The PP consists of a noun phrase (NP) followed by a postposition which indicates the case role of the NP. The predicate consists of a verb or an adjective, optionally followed by a sequence of auxiliary verbs (Morioka, 1987)).

We illustrate the Japanese morphological analysis with an example sentence "[ka] [o] [ru] [ni] [a] [i] [ma] [su] (meet Kaoru)[1]." We use a simple Japanese dictionary shown in Figure 3, and a connection matrix shown in Figure 4 which gives us the connectabilities between adjacent morphological categories (mcat). For example in Figure 4, the symbol "o" at the intersection of row 2 (p_1) and column 3 (vs_k) indicates that the morphological category vs_k can immediately follow the morphological category p_1.

[1]Each box corresponds to a Japanese character. We use such an ugly representation since no Japanese font is available.

entry	cat	mcat	meaning
ka o	n	n_1	face
ka o ru	n	n_1	person's name
ni	p	p_1	(dative)
a	vs	vs_k	open
i	ve	ve_k^2	(connect to verb)
i	ve	ve_k^{2i}	(connect to verb)
ku	ve	ve_k^3	(connect to nominal)
a	vs	vs_w	meet
i	ve	ve_w^2	(connect to verb)
tu	ve	ve_w^{2t}	(connect to verb)
ku	ve	ve_w^3	(connect to nominal)
ka o	vs	vs_r	smell sweet
ri	vs	ve_r^2	(connect to verb)
tu	ve	ve_r^{2t}	(connect to verb)
ru	ve	ve_r^3	(connect to nominal)
ma su	ax	ax_1	(polite form)
ta	ax	ax_2	(past form)

n	noun
p	case marker
vs	verb stem
ve	verb ending
ax	auxiliary verb

Figure 3 Example of a Japanese dictionary

RIGHT

LEFT	n_1	p_1	vs_k	vs_r	vs_w	ve_k^2	ve_k^{2i}	ve_k^3	ve_w^2	ve_w^{2t}	ve_w^3	ve_r^2	ve_r^{2t}	ve_r^3	ax_1	ax_2	$
n_1		o															
p_1	o		o	o	o												
vs_k						o	o	o									
vs_w									o	o	o						
vs_r												o	o	o			
ve_k^2															o		
ve_k^{2i}																o	
ve_k^3	o																o
ve_w^2															o		
ve_w^{2t}																o	
ve_w^3	o																o
ve_r^2															o		
ve_r^{2t}																o	
ve_r^3	o																o
ax_1																	o
ax_2																	o

Figure 4 Example of a connection matrix

Using only the dictionary, we would obtain the following twelve candidate segmentations for the sentence.

	ka o	ru	ni	a	i	ma su
(1)	n_1	ve_r^3	p_1	vs_k	ve_k^{2i}	ax_1
(2)	n_1	ve_r^3	p_1	vs_k	ve_w^2	ax_1
(3)	n_1	ve_r^3	p_1	vs_w	ve_k^{2i}	ax_1
(4)	n_1	ve_r^3	p_1	vs_w	ve_w^2	ax_1
(5)	vs_r	ve_r^3	p_1	vs_k	ve_k^{2i}	ax_1
(6)	vs_r	ve_r^3	p_1	vs_k	ve_w^2	ax_1
(7)	vs_r	ve_r^3	p_1	vs_w	ve_k^{2i}	ax_1
(8)	vs_r	ve_r^3	p_1	vs_w	ve_w^2	ax_1

	ka o ru	ni	a	i	ma su
(9)	n_1	p_1	vs_k	ve_k^{2i}	ax_1
(10)	n_1	p_1	vs_k	ve_w^2	ax_1
(11)	n_1	p_1	vs_w	ve_k^{2i}	ax_1
(12)	n_1	p_1	vs_w	ve_w^2	ax_1

By also referring to the connection matrix, we would be able to filter out illegal segmentations. From the examples above, we find that (1)–(4) violate the connectability between "ka o (n_1)" and "ru (ve_r^3)", and that (5)–(8) violate the connectability between " ru (ve_r^3)" and "ni (p_1)." Also, (9) and (11) violate the connectability between "i (ve_k^{2i})" and "ma su (ax_1)", and (11) violates the connectability between "a (vs_w)" and "i (ve_k^{2i})." Thus, by eliminating the illegal candidates we obtain the morphologically correct candidate (12). A long input sentence generally gives ambiguities which need to be resolved in later stages using syntactic, semantic and contextual information.

3. GENERATING AN LR TABLE

Connection matrices and CFG rules have been used for morphological analysis and syntactic analysis, respectively, by most Japanese processing systems. Because CFG rules were mainly used for syntactic analysis and connection matrices for morphological analysis, they have been developed independently of each other.

In this section, we propose a method to integrate morphological and syntactic constraints in the framework of LR parsing algorithms, and thus capturing the advantages of the Cascade/Interleave and Single Framework approaches described in section 1.

In order to combine connection matrices and CFG rules, the first step we have to take is to extend the CFG rules by relating the syntactic categories in the CFG rules with the morphological categories in a connection matrix. This is realized by adding CFG rules called morphological rules each of which is a unit production rule with a syntactic category in the left-hand side and a morphological category in the right-hand side.

s → v	(1)	v → vs ve	(4)
s → v ax	(2)	pp → n p	(5)
s → pp s	(3)		

Figure 5 Example of a CFG for Japanese

n → n_1	(6)	ve → ve_w^2	(14)
p → p_1	(7)	ve → ve_w^{2t}	(15)
vs → vs_k	(8)	ve → ve_w^3	(16)
vs → vs_w	(9)	ve → ve_r^2	(17)
vs → vs_r	(10)	ve → ve_r^{2t}	(18)
ve → ve_k^2	(11)	ve → ve_r^3	(19)
ve → ve_k^{2i}	(12)	ax → ax_1	(20)
ve → ve_k^3	(13)	ax → ax_2	(21)

Figure 6 Morphological rules derived from the dictionary in Figure 3

Let us take the example CFG rules shown in Figure 5. From the dictionary shown in Figure 3, we would extract a set of new CFG rules as shown in Figure 6, which are simply added to the CFG rules in Figure 5 to get an extended set of rules.

ACTION

state	n_1	vs_k	vs_w	vs_r	ax_1	ax_2	ve_k^2	ve_k^{2i}	ve_k^3	ve_w^2	ve_w^{2t}	ve_w^3	ve_r^2	ve_r^{2t}	ve_r^3	p_1	$
0	s6	s7	s8	s9													
1																	acc
2					s11	s12											r1
3	s6	s7	s8	s9													
4							s15	s16	s17	s18	s19	s20	s21	s22	s23		
5																s25	
6																r6	
7							r8	r8	r8	$\boxed{\texttt{r8}}$	$\boxed{\texttt{r8}}$	$\boxed{\texttt{r8}}$	$\boxed{\texttt{r8}}$	$\boxed{\texttt{r8}}$	$\boxed{\texttt{r8}}$		
8							$\boxed{\texttt{r9}}$	$\boxed{\texttt{r9}}$	$\boxed{\texttt{r9}}$	r9	r9	r9	$\boxed{\texttt{r9}}$	$\boxed{\texttt{r9}}$	$\boxed{\texttt{r9}}$		
9							$\boxed{\texttt{r10}}$	$\boxed{\texttt{r10}}$	$\boxed{\texttt{r10}}$	$\boxed{\texttt{r10}}$	$\boxed{\texttt{r10}}$	$\boxed{\texttt{r10}}$	r10	r10	r10		
10																	r2
11																	r20
12																	r21
13																	r3
14					r4	r4											r4
15					r11	$\boxed{\texttt{r11}}$											$\boxed{\texttt{r11}}$
16					$\boxed{\texttt{r12}}$	r12											$\boxed{\texttt{r12}}$
17					$\boxed{\texttt{r13}}$	$\boxed{\texttt{r13}}$											r13
18					r14	$\boxed{\texttt{r14}}$											$\boxed{\texttt{r14}}$
19					$\boxed{\texttt{r15}}$	r15											$\boxed{\texttt{r15}}$
20					$\boxed{\texttt{r16}}$	$\boxed{\texttt{r16}}$											r16
21					r17	$\boxed{\texttt{r17}}$											$\boxed{\texttt{r17}}$
22					$\boxed{\texttt{r18}}$	r18											$\boxed{\texttt{r18}}$
23					$\boxed{\texttt{r19}}$	$\boxed{\texttt{r19}}$											r19
24	r5	r5	r5	r5													
25	r7	r7	r7	r7													

GOTO

state	s	v	pp	vs	n	ax	ve	p
0	1	2	3	4	5			
1								
2						10		
3	13	2	3	4	5			
4							14	
5								24

Figure 7 LR table generated from rules (1)–(21)

We would generate an LR table as shown in Figure 7 from the extended CFG rules (1) through (21) from Figures 5 and 6. Note that the extended CFG rules do not include any information about connectability represented in the connection matrix in Figure 4. For example, rules (4), (10) and (14) allow the structure "[v [vs vs_r],[ve [ve_w^2]]]" which violates the connectability between vs_r and ve_w^2 with respect to Figure 4.

The second step is to introduce the constraints on connectability into the LR table by deleting illegal reduce actions. This is carried out by modifying the LR table with the procedure shown in Figure 8.

Deleting reduce actions by applying the above procedure prohibits the application of morphological rules which violates the connectability between two adjacent words, namely the current scanned word and its look-ahead word. Note that given an LR table and a connection matrix, this procedure can be performed automatically without human intervention.

```
For each reduce action A with a morphological rule in the LR table {
    if (Not Connect(RHS(Rule(A)), LA(A)) {
        delete A from the entry;
    }
}
where each function is defined as follows:
Rule : action → rule;
    returns a rule used by the reduce action.
LA : action → symbol;
    returns a look-ahead symbols of the action.
Connect : symbol × symbol → {T, F};
    returns true or false
according to the connectability of the two symbols.
RHS : rule → symbol;
    returns the rightmost symbol of the rule.
```

Figure 8 Procedure to modify an LR table

It is possible to incorporate this procedure into the LR table generation process, but it is better to keep them separate. Since this procedure is applicable to any type of LR table, separating this process from LR table generation enables us to use the already existing LR table generation program.

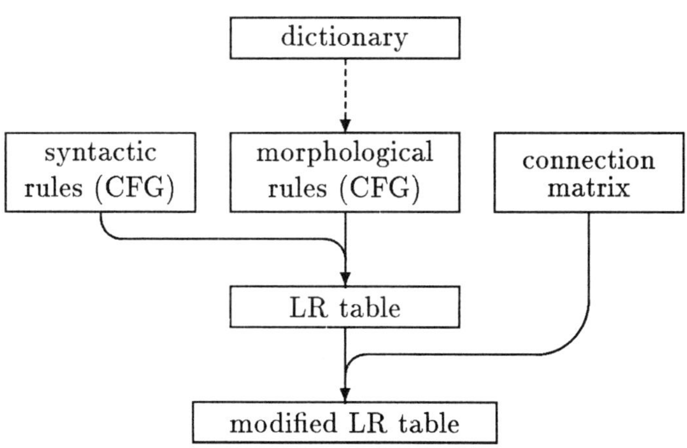

Figure 9 Outline of generating a modified LR table

For example, in Figure 7, the reduce action r8 in state 7 and column ve_r^3 is deleted, since the connection between vs_k, the RHS of rule (8), and ve_r^3, the look-ahead symbol, is prohibited according to the connection matrix in Figure 4. Similarly, reduce action r8 in state 7 and column ve_w^2 will be deleted, and so forth. The reduce actions which should be deleted is indivcted in Figure 7. Figure 9 gives an overview of the generation of a modified LR table.

Generally speaking, the order of the size of the LR table is exponential in the number of grammar rules. Including the morphological rules in the syntactic rules can cause an increase in the number of states in the LR table, thereby exponentially increasing the size of the overall LR table in the worst case. In our method, however, the increase of the number of states is equal to that of the morphological rules introduced. Suppose we add a morphological rule $X \rightarrow x$ to the grammar. Only the items of the form $[A \rightarrow \alpha \cdot X\beta]$ would produce a single new item $[X \rightarrow \cdot x]$ from which only a single new state $\{[X \rightarrow x \cdot]\}$ would be created. Thus the increase of the number of states is equal to that of the morphological rules introduced, and the size of the LR table will not grow exponentially.

4. ALGORITHM

The GLR parsing algorithm with the modified LR table is essentially the same as Tomita's generalized LR parsing algorithm. The only difference is that Tomita's algorithm assumes a sequence of preterminals as input, while our algorithm assumes a sequence of characters. Thus the dictionary reference process needs to be slightly modified. Figure 10 outlines our parsing algorithm.

```
initialize stack
for CS = 0 ... N {
  for each stack top node in stage CS {
    Look-aheads = lookup-dictionary(CS);
    for each look ahead preterminal LA in Look-aheads {
      do reduce while "reduce" is applicable;
      if "shift" is applicable {
        do shift creating a new node in stage (CS + length(LA));
      }
      if "acc" { accept }
      if no action { reject }
    }
  }
}
```

Figure 10 Outline of the parsing algorithm

In Figure 10 the stage number (CS) indicates how many characters have been processed. The procedure begins at stage 0 and ends at stage N, the character length of an input sentence. In stage 0, the stack is initialized and only the node with state 0 exists (step (1)). In the outermost loop (2)–(14), each stack top in the current stage is selected and processed. In step (4), the dictionary is consulted and look-ahead symbols are obtained. An important point here is that look-ahead symbols may have different character lengths. A new node is introduced by a shift action at step (8) and is placed into a stage which is ahead of the current stage by the length of the look-ahead word.

5. A WORKED EXAMPLE

The following example illustrates the algorithm in Figure 10. The input sentence is "ka o ru ni a i ma su $ " (meet Kaoru). We assign position numbers between adjacent characters.

ka	o	ru	ni	a	i	ma	su	$

0 1 2 3 4 5 6 7 8 9

In the following trace, the numbers in circles denote state numbers, and the numbers in squares denote the subtree number. The symbols enclosed by curly brackets denote a look-ahead symbol followed by the next applicable action, separated by a slash (/). The stage numbers are shown below the stacks.

Stage: 0

Dictionary reference:

[n_1, "ka o "] at 0–2

[vs_r, "ka o "] at 0–2

[n_1, "ka o ru "] at 0–3

We find three look-ahead symbols, n_1, vs_r, and n_1 by consulting the dictionary in Figure 3. A shift action is applied for each of them according to the LR table in Figure 7.

$$\textcircled{0} \left\{ \begin{array}{l} n_1/\mathtt{s6} \\ vs_r/\mathtt{s9} \\ n_1/\mathtt{s6} \end{array} \right\}$$

└0┘

After the shift actions, three new nodes are created at stage 2 or stage 3 depending on the length of look-ahead words. At the same time subtrees [1]–[3] are constructed. The current stage is updated from 0 to 2, since there is no node in stage 1. The look-ahead symbols are unknown at this moment.

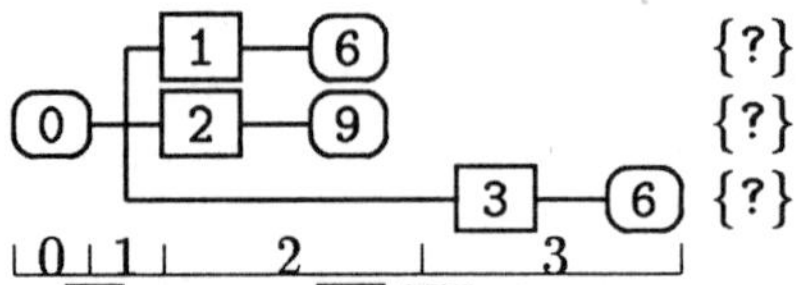

[1] : [n_1, "[ka] [o] "]

[2] : [vs_r, "[ka] [o] "]

[3] : [n_1, "[ka] [o] [ru] "]

Stage: 2

Dictionary reference:

[ve_r^3, "[ru] "] at 2–3

Dictionary reference gives one look-ahead symbol from position 2. Since the current stage number is 2, only the first two stack tops are concerned at this stage. No action is taken of the first stack, because the LR table has no action in the entry for state 6 and a look ahead symbol ve_r^3. As a result, the first stack is rejected. The reduce action (`r10`) is taken for the second stack.

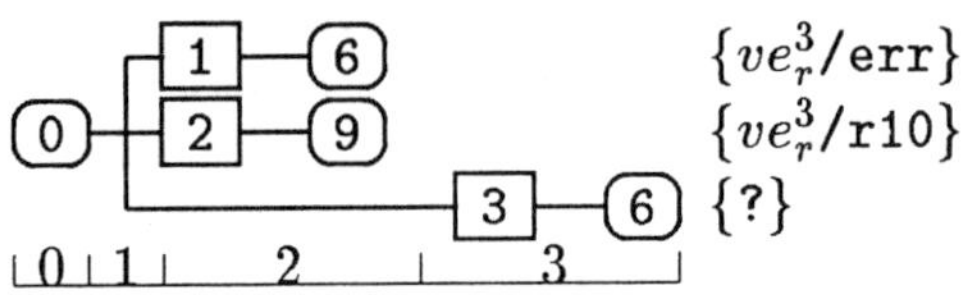

After `r10`, a shift action (`s23`) is carried out for the first stack.

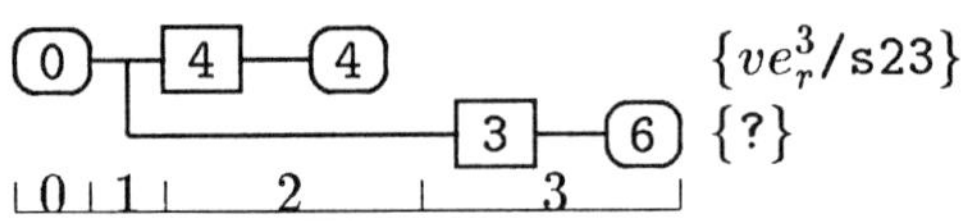

[4] : [vs, [2]]

After `s23`, we would proceed to stage 3.

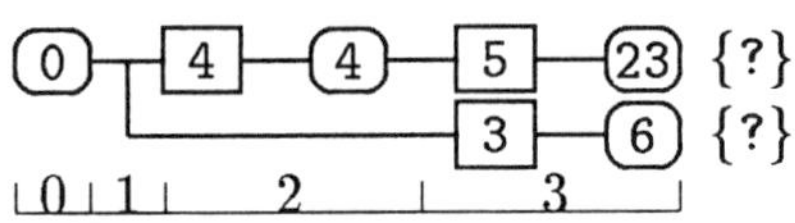

[5] : [ve_r^3, "[ru] "]

Stage: 3

Dictionary reference:

[p_1, "[ni] "] at 3–4

We obtain symbol p_1 by consulting the dictionary. Because the first stack can take no more action, it is rejected. The reduce action (`r6`) is then applied to the second stack.

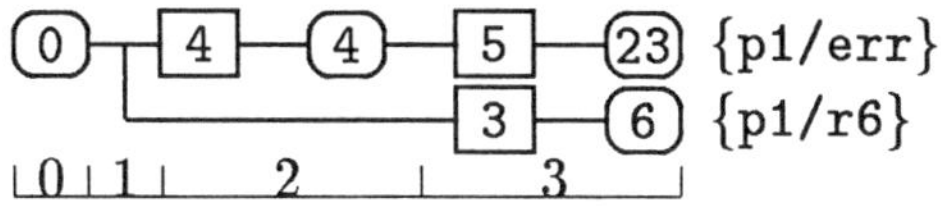

The shift action (s25) is applied to the following stack.

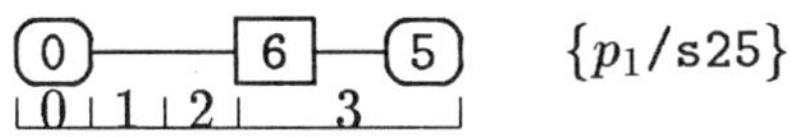

6 : [n, 3]

After the shift action (s25), new nodes are created in stage 4.

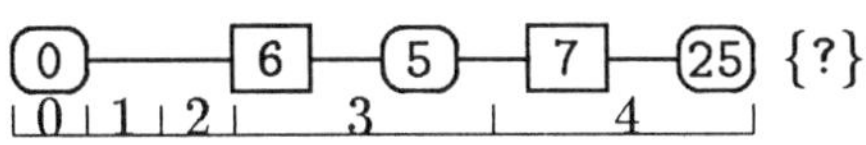

7 : [p_1, "ni "]

Stage: 4

Dictionary reference:

[vs_k, "a "] at 4–5

[vs_w, "a "] at 4–5

Dictionary reference provides two look-ahead symbols for the next word.

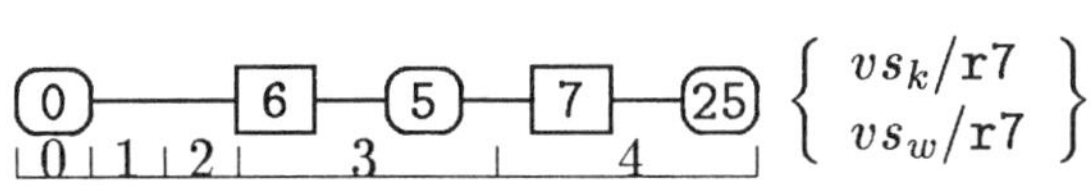

After the two reduce actions (r7), we get two nodes with the same state 24, and they would be merged. This is possible because these two reduce actions give the same structure as well. If the structures were different, we would not be able to merge the stacks. We will see such a case later in stage 5.

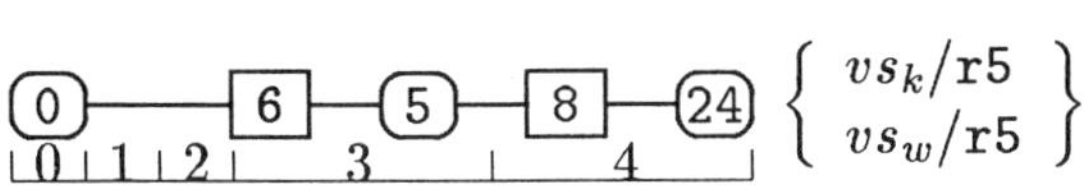

8 : [p, 7]

The process in stage 4 continues as follows.

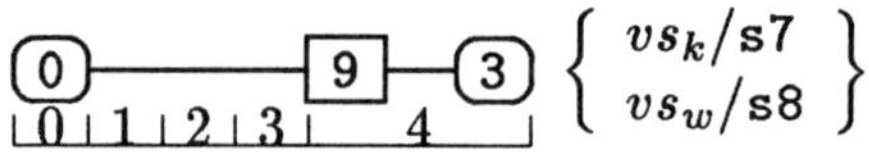

9 : [pp, 6, 8]

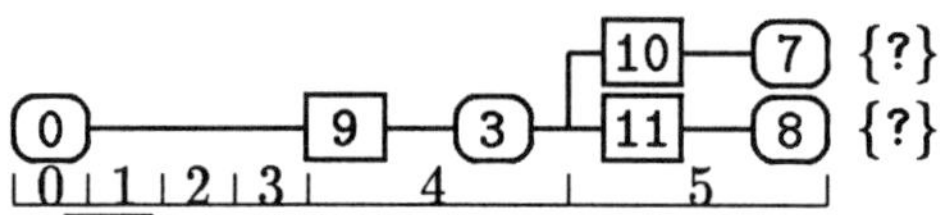

10 : [vs_k, "a "]

11 : [vs_w, "a "]

Stage: 5

Dictionary reference:

[ve_k^{2i}, "i "] at 5–6

[ve_w^2, "i "] at 5–6

We have two look-ahead symbols for each stack top. The reduce actions (r8 and r9) are performed.

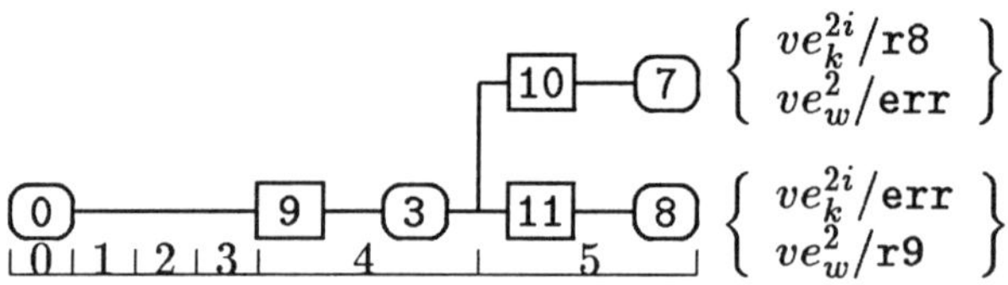

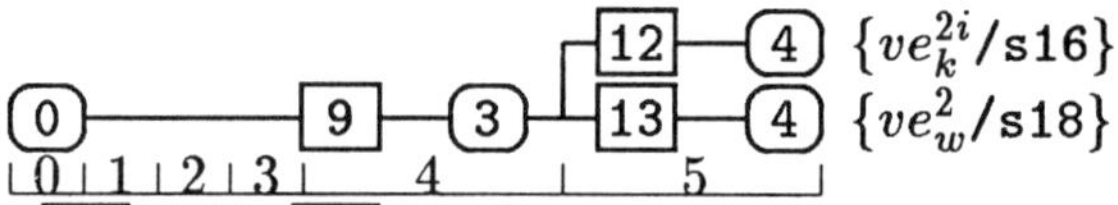

12 : [vs, 10]

13 : [vs, 11]

Note that we are not able to merge the stack tops even with the same state 4 since the structures of 12 and 13 are different. If two stack tops are merged here and then different shift actions (s16 and s18) are carried out, we might have invalid combinations of structures such as (12, 15) and (13, 14).

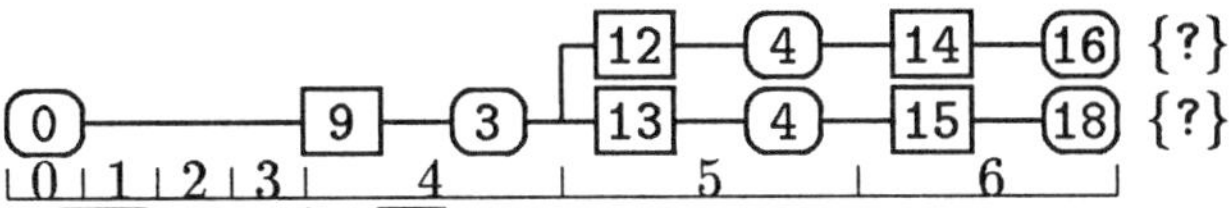

14 : [ve_k^{2i}, "i"]

15 : [ve_w^2, "i"]

After the shift actions (s16 and s18), we proceed to stage 6.

Stage: 6

Dictionary reference:

[ax_1, "ma su"] at 6–8

The process in stage 6 proceeds as follows.

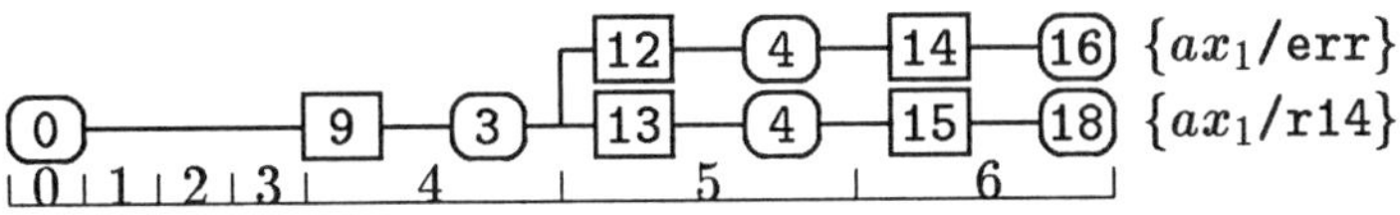

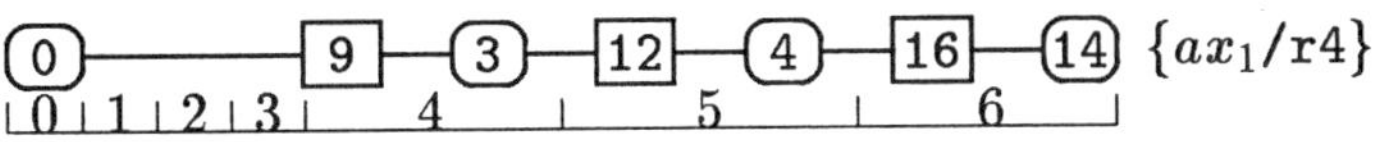

16 : [ve, 15]

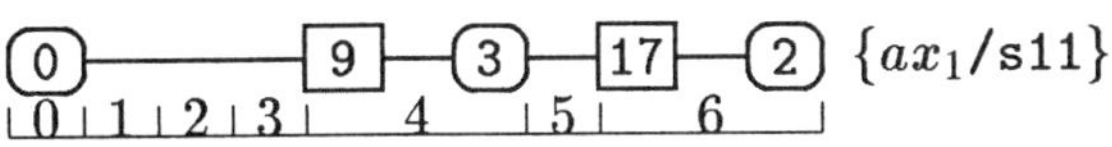

17 : [v, 12, 16]

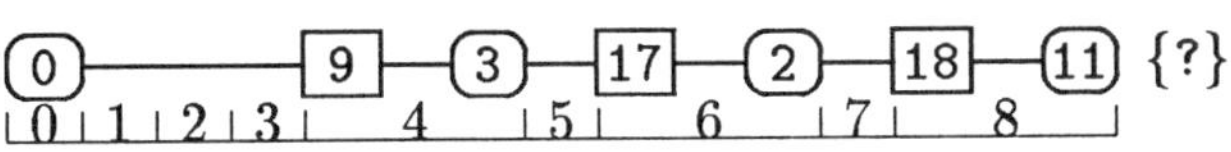

18 : [ax_1, "ma su"]

Stage: 8

Dictionary reference:

"$" at 8–9

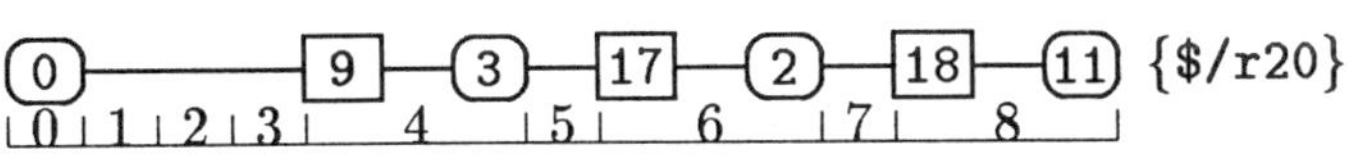

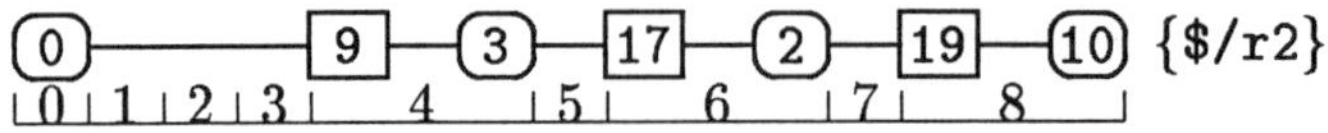

19 : [ax, 18]

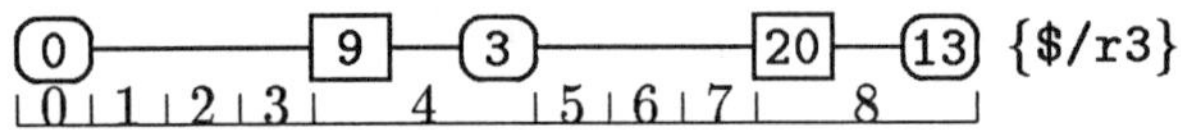

20 : [s, 17, 19]

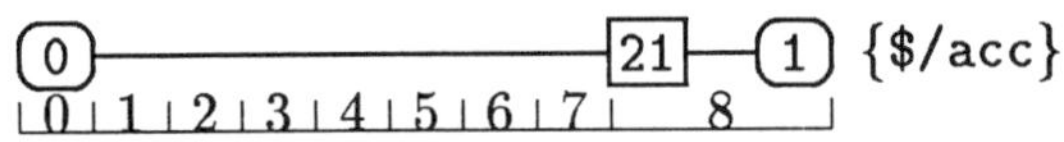

21 : [s, 9, 20]

The input sentence is automatically segmented and accepted, giving a final parse result 21 as shown in Figure 11.

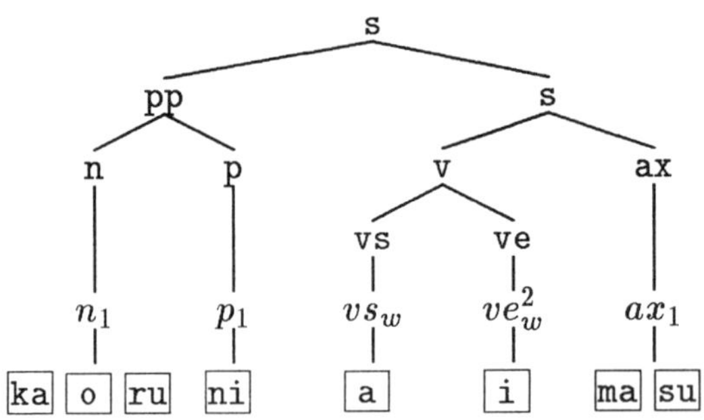

Figure 11 An analysis of "ka o ru ni a i ma su"

6. CONCLUSION

We have proposed a method for integrated morphological and syntactic parsing, representing morphological constraints in connection matrices and syntactic constraints in CFGs, and compiling both kinds of constraints into an LR table. The compiled LR table enables us to make use of the already existing, efficient generalized LR parsing algorithms through which integration of both morphological and syntactic analysis is obtained.

The advantages of our approach may be summarized as follows:

- Morphological and syntactic constraints are represented separately, which makes it easier to maintain and extend them.

- The morphological and syntactic constraints are compiled into a uniform representation, an LR table. We can use the already existing efficient algorithms for generalized LR parsing for the analysis.
- Both the morphological and syntactic constraints can be used at the same time during the analysis.

We have implemented the proposed method using the EDR dictionary with 300,000 words (EDR, 1993) from which 437 morphological rules are derived. This means only 437 new states are introduced to the LR table and this does not cause an explosion in the size of the LR table. The method proposed in this chapter is also applicable to integrate phonological and syntactic analysis, see (Tanaka *et al.*, 1994).

As the size of the CFG grows, generating a LR table consumes much time to create dotted items, and many of them will be deleted by using connectability constraints. Li et al. have developed an LR table generation algorithm which can avoid generating unnecessary items during the table generation and thus can save much space and time (Li et al., 1995).

Deleting an action may cause deleting another action. We call such propagation of deleting actions *'constraint propagation'*. Through constraint propagation, it is possible to reduce the size of an LR table drastically; this is detailed in (Tanaka *et al.*, 1994).

References

Aho, A., Ravi, S., Ullman, J. (1986). *Compilers: Principles, Techniques, and Tools.* Addision Wesley.

EDR (1993). *EDR Dictionary Manual.* Japan Electronic Dictionary Research Institute.

Kita, K. (1992). *A Study on Language Modeling for Speech Recognition.* Ph.D. thesis, Waseda University.

Li, H., Suresh, K. G. and Tanaka, H. (1995). Incorporation of Connection Constraints into Generation Process of Allophone-base LR Table. In *Proc. of 50th Annual Convention IPS Japan*, 463–464.

Mine, T., Taniguchi, R., and Amamiya, M. (1991). Coordinated Morphological and Syntactic Analysis of Japanese Language. In *Proceedings of IJCAI'91*, 1012–1017.

Miyazaki, M. (1984). An Automatic Segmentation Method for Compound Words using Dependency Analysis. *Transactions of Information Processing Society of Japan*, *25*(6), 970–979.

Morioka, K. (1987). *Formation of a Vocabulary.* Meizi-syoin (in Japanese).

Sano, H. and Fukumoto, F. (1992). On a Grammar Formalism, Knowledge Bases and Tools for Natural Language Processing in Logic Programming. In *Proceedings of FGCS'92.*

Sugimura, R., Akasaka, K., Kubo, Y. and Matsumoto, Y. (1988). Logic Based Lexical Analyzer LAX. In *Logic Programming '88.* Springer-Verlag.

Tanaka, H., Li, H. and Tokunaga, T. (1994). Incorporation of Phoneme-Context-Dependence in LR Table through Constraint Propagation Method. In *Proceedings of the Integration of Natural Language and Speech Processing,* 15–22.

Tomita, M. (1986). *Efficient Parsing for Natural Languages.* Kluwer, Boston/Dordrecht.

18. STRUCTURAL DISAMBIGUATION IN JAPANESE BY CASE STRUCTURE EVALUATION BASED ON EXAMPLES IN A CASE FRAME DICTIONARY

SADAO KUROHASHI AND MAKOTO NAGAO
Department of Electronics and Communication
Kyoto University

Abstract.

A case structure expression is one of the most important forms to represent the meaning of a sentence. Case structure analysis is usually performed by consulting case frame information in verb dictionaries and by selecting a proper case frame for an input sentence. Both word sense ambiguity and structural ambiguity present difficulties for this analysis. A conventional method for solving these problems is to use the method of selectional restriction, but this method has a drawback in the semantic marker (SM) system — the trade-off between descriptive power and construction cost.

This chapter describes a method of case structure analysis of Japanese sentences which overcomes the drawback in the SM system, concentrating on structural disambiguation. This method selects a proper case frame for an input using a measure of the similarity between the input and typical example sentences of each case frame. When there are two or more possible readings for an input because of structural ambiguity, the best reading will be selected by using such a similarity measure for each possible reading.

1. INTRODUCTION

Representing a sentence with a case structure is a basic form for dealing with its meaning. Therefore, transforming a sentence into a case structure expression is one of the most important techniques in natural language processing, and it is needed for machine translation, knowledge acquisition

H. Bunt and M. Tomita (eds.), Recent Advances in Parsing Technology, 343–358.

in which various expressions with the same content must be converted into the same representation, and so on.

Case structure analysis is usually performed by consulting case frame information in verb dictionaries. The dictionary describes what kind of cases each verb has and what kinds of noun can fill a case slot with what kind of case marker (in Japanese, postpositions (POs) function as case markers). Both word sense ambiguity and structural ambiguity present difficulties for this analysis.

A conventional method for solving these problems is the use of selectional restrictions (Katz and Fodor, 1963), where the category of the nouns which can fill a case slot is specified by means of semantic markers (SMs), such as *human*, *animate*, *action*, and so on. However, this method has the following weaknesses.

- An SM system with tens of SMs is too coarse to distinguish every case frame for a verb, which is the case with most electronic dictionaries and systems at present, such as LDOCE (Longman, 1978), the Mu system (Nagao et al., 1985), IPAL (IPA, 1987), and most commercial machine translation systems.
- On the other hand, it is quite expensive and time consuming to prepare a detailed SM system which has sufficient descriptive power to discriminate every usage of each verb, and which may require thousands of SMs (Ikehara et al., 1991). A further difficulty is to improve the SM system when needed.

In order to overcome the drawbacks in the SM method — the trade-off between descriptive power and construction cost, we have developed a method of case structure analysis of Japanese sentences based on examples in a case frame dictionary. We published some parts of our analysis system already elsewhere (Kurohashi and Nagao, 1994; Nagao, 1992). This chapter concentrates on the structural disambiguation in Japanese complex sentences through the case structure analysis process.

This method uses a case frame dictionary that has some typical example sentences for every case frame. When an input is a simple sentence without structural ambiguity concerning case components, a proper case frame is selected for the verb in the input sentence by matching the input sentence with the examples in the case frame dictionary. When an input is a complex sentence, the nouns cannot always be linked uniquely to the verbs in the sentence by case assignment. The important point is that the best matching score, which is utilized for selecting a proper case frame for a verb in a sentence, can be considered as the score for the case structure of the verb and its case components. The best reading (the correct reading or the most plausible reading) of a complex sentence is the one where all verbs in the sentence govern appropriate case components and their case structures have high scores. Therefore, the best reading of a sentence can be selected by checking all the possible case structures of all the verbs and by evaluating every possible reading according to the sum of the scores for the case structures in it. When the input is a compound sentence, we can detect the scopes of coordinate structures beforehand, so that we can limit the number of possible readings sufficiently that we can evaluate all of them.

From the viewpoint of example-based methods, there are several research activities concerned with resolving structural ambiguity (Inagaki et al., 1988; Nagao, 1990). Our method has the following characteristics in contrast with these.

- While other methods match an input sentence with examples basically in blocks of two words in a governor/dependent relation, our method matches them in blocks of a case structure. We can say in general that the wider range of components a method checks, the more reliable it becomes.
- Others use texts from their target domain as the main knowledge base. Limiting the text domain may be possible and useful, but it makes it very difficult to cover general domains. On the other hand, we use examples in the case frame dictionary, which can cover wider domains according to entries of the dictionary. Because in compiling a dictionary, lexicographers consult example sentences in which an entry word is used, it is a reasonable assumption that we can use examples in a dictionary in the computer analysis of natural language sentences.

2. SELECTING A PROPER CASE FRAME

2.1. JAPANESE ELECTRONIC DICTIONARIES

In this chapter, we use the basic verb dictionary which was constructed by the Information-technology Promotion Agency, Japan (hereafter, this dictionary is referred to as IPAL) (IPA, 1987). In IPAL, 861 basic verbs are entries, and each entry has sub-entries according to the differences in meaning and syntax. Case frame information is given at each sub-entry. The sub-entries total up to 3379 so that the average number of sub-entries and thus the average number of case frames for a verb is 3.9. As shown in Table 1, case frame information consists of the meaning of a verb, its case markers, SMs, examples and correspondences to deep cases for each case slot. SMs restrict the category of the nouns that can fill the case slots. IPAL uses 19 different SMs which have the tree structure shown in Figure 1 below. However, our method does not use this SM system because of its coarseness. We use a thesaurus dictionary, 'Bunrui Goi Hyou' (abbreviated

HAIRU			
Sub-entry 1			
Meaning : Enter from the outside to the inside.			
Case markers	*SMs*	*Examples*	*Deep cases*
N1-GA	[HUM/ORG/ANI/PRO]	he, party, cat, ship	agent
N2-KARA*	[LOC]	window, rear-gate	locational source
N3-NI/E	[LOC]	classroom, kitchen, port	locational goal / directional
Sub-entry 2			
Meaning: Added to food or drink.			
Case markers	*SMs*	*Examples*	*Deep cases*
N1-NI	[PRO]	coffee, cake	non-locational goal
N2-GA	[CON]	sugar, milk, cheese, poison	object
Sub-entry 3			
Meaning: Be reflected.			
Case markers	*SMs*	*Examples*	*Deep cases*
N1-NI	[PRO/ABS]	work, report, proposal	non-locational locative
N2-GA	[MEN]	thought, opinion, arbitrariness	object

A Case component marked with '*' is optional.

TABLE 1. Examples of case frames for HAIRU in IPAL.

as BGH) (NLRI, 1964) for calculating the similarity values between words. BGH has a tree with a six-layer abstraction hierarchy and more than 60,000 words are assigned to the leaves of the thesaurus tree.

2.2. CASE STRUCTURE ANALYSIS BY CASE FRAMES

Case structure analysis is usually performed by consulting case frames in a dictionary. Because the correspondence of each case component to a deep case is listed in the case frame, we can get deep cases for case components when we find a proper case frame for an input sentence and the correspondence of case components in the sentence to those in the case frame. In other words, case structure analysis is regarded as a selection of a proper case frame for an input sentence.

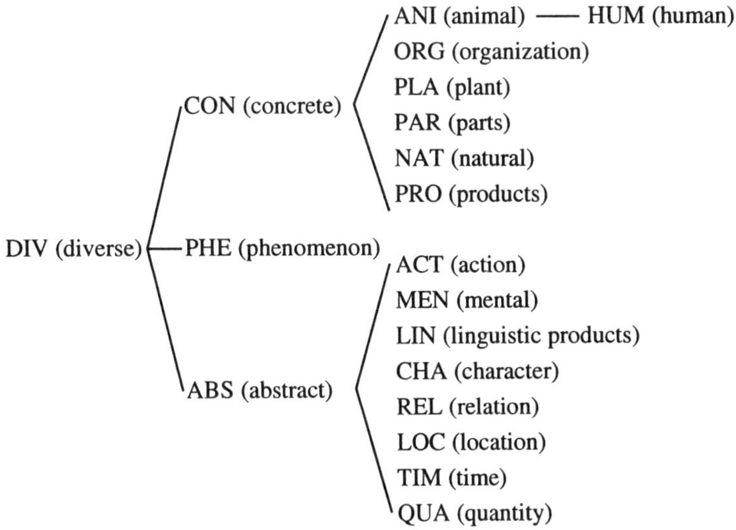

Figure 1. The set of SMs in IPAL.

2.3. SELECTING A PROPER CASE FRAME

A conventional method for selecting a proper case frame is using selectional restriction by SMs. However, the SM system with tens of SMs, such as IPAL, is too coarse to select a proper case frame for an input sentence. For instance, in selecting a proper case frame for the example sentence (ES1):

kisha-GA	ton'neru-NI	hairu.
(train)	(tunnel)	(enter)
[PRO]	[LOC/PRO]	

from the frames in Table 1, while sub-entry 3 can be removed by comparing the SM [PRO(product)] of *kisha*KISHA(train) with the SM [MEN(mental)] of case slot 'N2-GA', the incorrect case frame, sub-entry 2, is selected together with the correct case frame, sub-entry 1. On the other hand, it is quite expensive and time consuming to prepare a detailed SM system which has enough descriptive power to discriminate every usage of each verb.

In order to overcome this drawback of the SM method, we have developed a method for case structure analysis of Japanese sentences based on examples in a case frame dictionary. In brief, this method selects the case frame whose example is the most similar to the input sentence. Because ES1 above is much more similar to examples of sub-entry 1, "(he, party, cat, ship)-GA (classroom, kitchen, port)-NI", than to examples of sub-entry 2, "(coffee, cake)-NI (sugar, milk, cheese, poison)-GA", the correct case frame, sub-entry 1, can be selected.

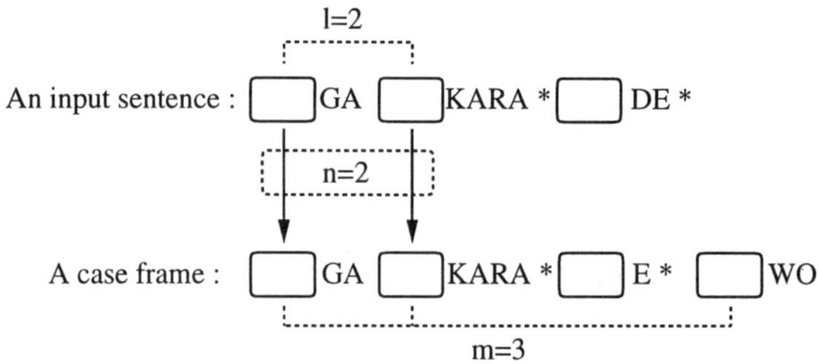

(* is attached to optional components)

The similarity score between an input sentence and examples of a case frame is calculated by the following algorithm. The algorithm assumes that case components depending on a verb are already known, as in the case of processing a simple sentence.

1. Matching case components.
   First, the case components of the input sentence and those of a case frame are matched by the equality of POs. A noun modified by a clause sometimes becomes a case component for the verb of the modifying clause. In this case, the modified noun can correspond to case slots followed by the postpositions 'GA', 'WO', 'NI' or 'DE'.
2. Calculating the score of a matching case component.
   A score of matching case components is defined as the greatest similarity value between a noun of the input sentence and example nouns assigned to a case slot in the case frame dictionary. The similarity value (SV) between two nouns is given according to the most specific common layer (CL) between them in BGH, as follows:[1]

[1]This way of correlating the most specific common layer (CL) with the similarity value has the following basis ($sv(i)$ means the similarity value between two nouns whose CL is layer i).

(a) Since the first layer of BGH consists of four classes: nouns, verbs, adjectives and the others, sharing the first layer of two nouns does not indicate that they are similar. Therefore, we let $sv(1)$ '0'.

(b) The greater the CL between two nouns is, the more similar they are. Furthermore, by studying BGH, we concluded that sharing the general layer (except the first layer) has more effect on the similarity between two nouns than sharing the specific layer. For this reason, $sv(i)$ is designed to simulate a convex and monotone increasing function.

CL	0	1	2	3	4	5	6	exact match
SV	0	0	5	7	8	9	10	11

3. Calculating the score of a matching pattern.
   It is assumed that *the matching pattern* between an input sentence and a case frame is given as follows:

   n : the number of matching components.

   l : the number of matching or obligatory case components in the input sentence. Case components followed by 'GA', 'WO', 'NI', 'E' or 'YORI', are regarded as obligatory case components.

   m : the number of matching or obligatory case slots in the case frame. Obligatory case slots are specified in IPAL.

   total_score : the sum of the scores of matching case components.

   The simplest way is to regard the *total_score* as the score of this matching pattern. However, we need to take more factors into consideration. We give the following score to this matching pattern:

$$\begin{cases} \text{if } l > n & 0 \\ \text{otherwise} & \textit{total\_score} \times \left(\frac{1}{n}\right)^{1/2} \times \left(\frac{n}{m}\right)^{1/2} \end{cases}$$

   We let the score '0' when l is greater than n, because the obligatory case components cannot remain unmatched in the sentence for its proper case frame. We include $(n/m)^{1/2}$ in the above formula in order to give priority to case frames with the higher ratio of matching case components to the total number of case components. We also include $(1/n)^{1/2}$ because it is preferable not only that there are many matching components but also that the scores of matching components are big. The exponents of $(n/m)^{1/2}$ and $(1/n)^{1/2}$ were determined empirically.

Matching calculation is performed for all the matching patterns between the input sentence and all case frames, and then the case frame whose matching pattern has the greatest score is selected as the final result.

The experiment of comparing the example based method with the SM method in IPAL, and the discussion of the validity of the example based method, have been reported in (Nagao, 1992).

3. STRUCTURAL DISAMBIGUATION USING CASE STRUCTURE SCORE

3.1. OUTLINE OF THE METHOD

In the preceding section we described a method of analyzing the case structure for an input sentence when case components depending on a verb are

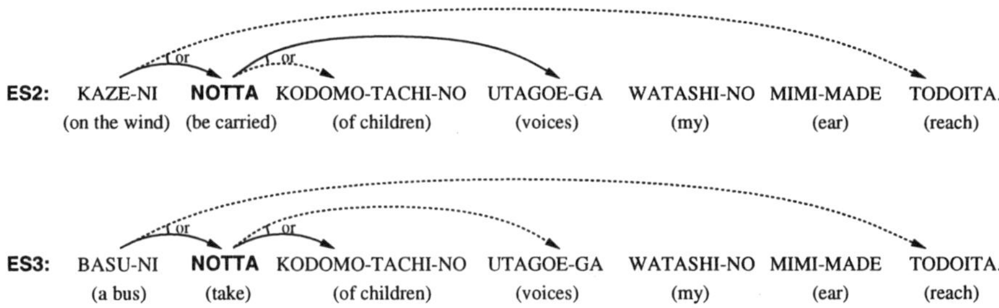

Figure 2. Need for a global disambiguation.

already known, as in the case of a simple sentence. This section introduces a way of extending the method to process complex or compound sentences.

The structure of Japanese sentences is best explained by "kakari-uke", which is essentially the governor/dependent relation between *bunsetsus*. A bunsetsu is the smallest meaningful block consisting of an independent word (nouns, verbs, adjectives, etc.) and accompanying words (POs, auxiliary verbs, etc.). A bunsetsu depends on, that is, modifies another bunsetsu to its right (not necessarily the adjacent bunsetsu). Sometimes a bunsetsu can depend on two or more bunsetsus, which creates structural ambiguity and makes case structure analysis hard. Other work concerning structural disambiguation (Inagaki et al., 1988; Nagao, 1990) solves this problem locally, that is, they try to determine the governor of each bunsetsu independently. However, in order to improve the precision of analyzing sentences, the ambiguity of the governor of a bunsetsu must be processed simultaneously with the ambiguity of the governors of other bunsetsus and with the word sense ambiguity. The ambiguity in the example sentences ES1 and ES2 in Figure 2 makes this problem clear. In ES2, the meaning of the verb 'NOTTA' is 'be carried (on the wind)', and 'NOTTA(be carried)' depends on 'UTAGOE-GA(voices)'; whereas, in ES3 which differs from ES2 only in the first word, the meaning of the same verb 'NOTTA' is 'take (a bus)', and the verb depends on 'KODOMO-TACHI-NO(of children)'. This means that whether 'NOTTA' depends on 'KODOMO-TACHI-NO(of children)' or 'UTAGOE-GA(voices)' can not be determined independently of the structural ambiguity of other case components of the verb 'NOTTA' and its word sense ambiguity.

For such a global disambiguation, we can use the best matching score which is utilized for selecting a proper case frame for each verb. The best matching score between an input sentence and a typical example for the usage of a verb can be considered as *the appropriateness* (score) for the case structure of the verb and its case components. When there are two or more readings (dependency structures) for a sentence because of structural

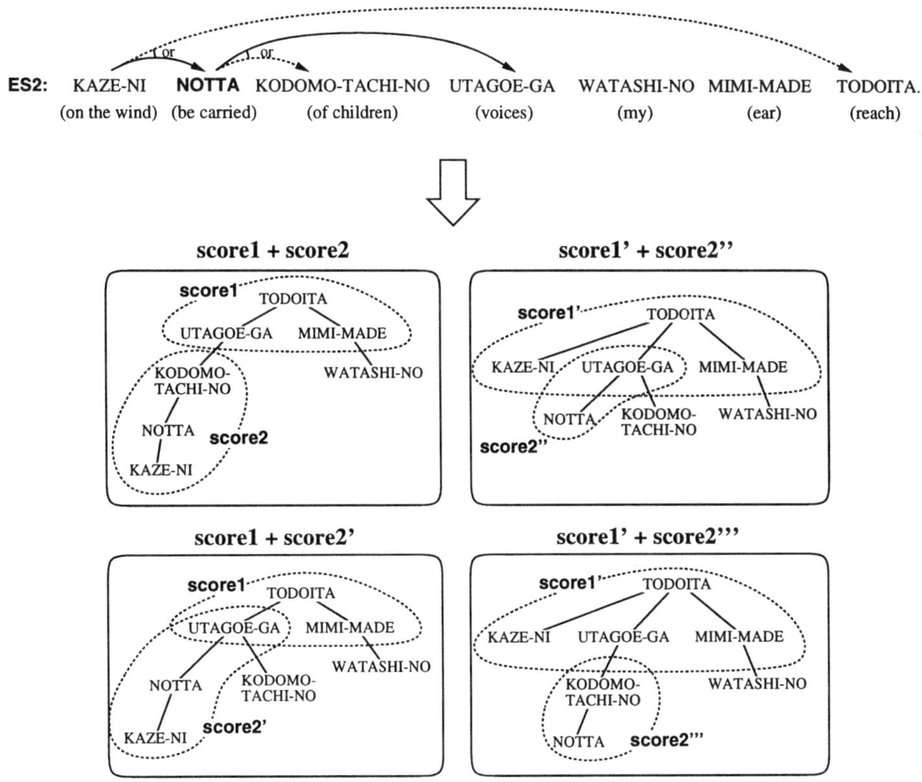

Figure 3. Outline of the method.

ambiguity, the best reading is the one where all verbs in the sentence govern appropriate case components and their case structures have high scores. This means that the best reading of a sentence can be selected by evaluating the sum of the scores for the case structures of all verbs in a sentence (Figure 3).

In order to evaluate all the possible readings, it is necessary to expand all the structural ambiguity for a sentence. However, before entering this analysis stage, we determine the scope of coordinate structures in the sentence using another method (Kurohashi and Nagao, 1994) to avoid the combinatorial explosion problem. The main reason that a sentence becomes long, particularly in Japanese, is that two or more matters are expressed in a sentence, that is, a sentence has coordinate structures. Therefore, by detecting the scopes of coordinate structures beforehand, the number of possible readings is limited sufficiently that we can evaluate all of them.

We will explain this method in detail in the following subsections.

1.	**Key bunsetsu of coordinate structure (KB)**	Bunsetsu which indicates the existence of a coordinate structure, such as "...SHI", and "...TO". This type is treated as depending on the last bunsetsu in the coordinate structure.
2.	**PB depending on PB**	PB in a kind of subordinate structure, such as "...SURE-BA (if ...V)", "...SITA-NODE (because ...V)".
3.	**NB depending on PB**	Case components, such as "...GA", "...WO".
4.	**PB depending on NB**	PB in a clausal modifier, such as "...SITA (which ...=V)". A governor of this type of a bunsetsu may become a case component for the bunsetsu.
5.	**NB depending on NB**	NB, such as "A-NO" in the noun phrase "A-NO B".

TABLE 2. Dependent types.

3.2. CALCULATION OF THE POSSIBLE DEPENDENCY MATRIX (PDM)

For evaluating each possible dependency structure, we first get all the possible governor/dependent relations between two bunsetsus. These relations are expressed in the form of a triangular matrix $A = (a_{ij})$ (Figure 4), called possible dependency matrix (PDM), whose diagonal element a_{ii} is the i-th bunsetsu (hereafter expressed as B_i) in a sentence and whose element a_{ij} (i < j) expresses whether B_i can depend on B_j ('1' means yes).

As a governor, each bunsetsu is classified into one of two types according to parts of speech; nominal bunsetsu (abbreviated as NB) and predicative bunsetsu (abbreviated as PB). As a dependent, each bunsetsu is classified into one of five types in Table 2 according to its PO or conjugation.

The way of determining an element a_{ij} is rather simple. The value of element a_{ij} is set to '1' when B_i is type 2 or type 3 (which can depend on PB) and B_j is a PB, or when B_i is type 4 or type 5 (which can depend on NB) and B_j is a NB.

3.3. MASKING THE PDM BY THE SCOPE OF THE COORDINATE STRUCTURE

When an input sentence contains a key bunsetsu of coordinate structure (abbreviated as KB) which indicates the existence of a coordinate structure, we determine its scope by the method in which the two most similar series

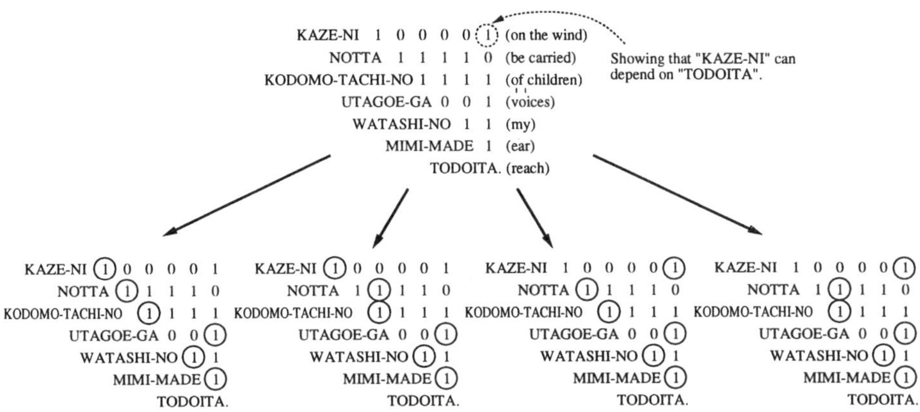

Figure 4. Making the possible dependency structures by consulting the PDM (ES2).

of bunsetsus on the left and right side of the KB are detected and are regarded as the scope of the coordinate structure concerning the KB (see (Kurohashi and Nagao, 1994) for details).

After detecting the scopes of coordinate structures in a sentence, the following two operations are performed on the PDM (Figure 5).

– *Setting the governor of a KB*: A KB is treated as depending on the last bunsetsu of a coordinate structure. When B_i is a KB and B_j is the last bunsetsu of its scope, the value of the PDM element a_{ij} is adjusted to '1'.
– *Masking the PDM*: Because the prior and the posterior parts of a coordinate structure have their own consistent structures and meanings, they are parsed independently into dependency structures. Therefore, the bunsetsu in a coordinate structure does not depend on or become governor of any bunsetsu outside its scope, except the last bunsetsu of the coordinate structure which has governor/dependent relations to bunsetsus outside its scope. In order to express these characteristics, the value of the PDM elements on the upper and right side of a coordinate structure are set to '0'.

As a result of this process, the number of possible dependency structures of a sentence can be reduced drastically.

3.4. MAKING THE POSSIBLE DEPENDENCY STRUCTURES

Next, we expand the ambiguities of the case components of an input sentence and make the possible dependency structures by consulting the PDM. Because governor/dependent relations do not cross each other in Japanese, the *no-cross condition* can be set as follows: when B_i depends on B_j, B_k

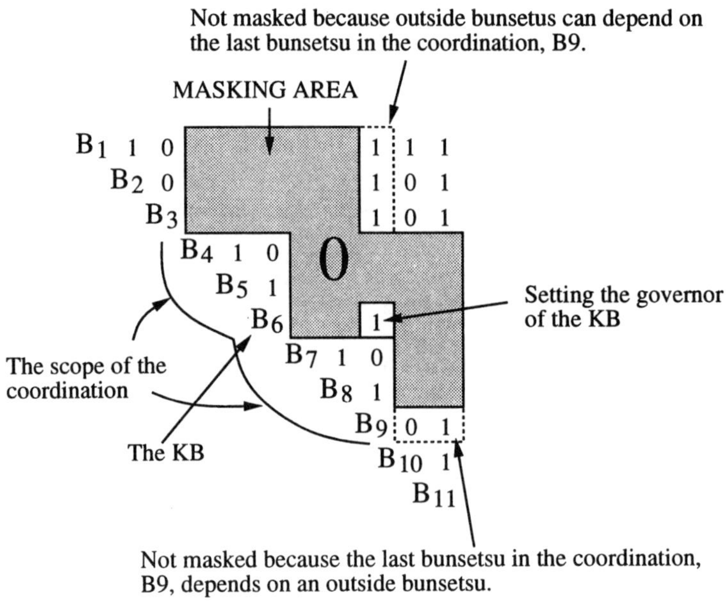

Figure 5. Masking the PDM.

(k < i) cannot depend on bunsetsus from B_{i+1} to B_{j-1}. For the following explanation, we define *a dependency set* of a bunsetsu as a set consisting of bunsetsus on which the bunsetsu can depend. This set is fixed dynamically by the PDM and the no-cross condition.

The governor is determined for each bunsetsu from right to left. When a bunsetsu concerning a case component (type 3 or type 4 in Table 2) has the possibility of depending on two or more bunsetsus (that is, its dependency set consists of two or more bunsetsus), two or more partial dependency structures are made according to the type of its governor, and the structures on the left side of each partial structure are analyzed. On the other hand, when a bunsetsu, not concerning case components (type 2 or type 5), can depend on two or more bunsetsus, its governor is determined uniquely to be the nearest bunsetsu in its dependency set, because a bunsetsu usually depends on the nearest bunsetsu in Japanese (of course, this heuristic rule sometimes makes a mistake. We will deal with this problem in future work).

In the case of ES2 in Figure 4 above, because 'NOTTA (be carried)' can depend on either 'KODOMO-TACHI-NO (of children)' or 'UTAGOE-GA (voices)' and 'KAZE-NI (on the wind)' can depend on either 'NOTTA (be carried)' or 'TODOITA (reach)', four possible dependency structures are created.

3.5. EVALUATION OF POSSIBLE DEPENDENCY STRUCTURES

Case frame selection is performed for all verbs in each possible dependency structure which is made in the above-mentioned processes. Of all possible dependency structures, we select the structure which has the maximum sum of the best matching scores for all verbs in the sentence. In the case of ES2, the correct structure, the second one from the left in Figure 4, is selected by this method, selecting proper case frames for the verbs 'NOTTA' and 'TODOITA' (the sub-entry whose meaning is "be carried" is selected correctly for 'NOTTA').

If there are two or more structures which have the maximum score, the structure which is most similar to the *default dependency structure* is selected. Here, a default dependency structure is that in which each bunsetsu depends on its nearest bunsetsu in its dependency set.

Our method	MT systems	Type3	Type4	Total
○	○ ×	56	12	68
○	× ×	23	15	38
×	○ ○	5	0	5
×	○ ×	6	0	6
○	○ ○	104	6	110
×	× ×	2	4	6

TABLE 3. Comparison between our method and commercial MT systems.

4. EXPERIMENT

We report an experiment which illustrates the effectiveness of this method for resolving structural ambiguity. The validity of the initial step in this method, which limits the number of possible readings by detecting coordinate structures, has already been reported in (Kurohashi and Nagao, 1994). The remaining problem is the ambiguity in a complex sentence. Therefore, in this chapter, we show an experiment of analyzing complex sentences.

We had a language-trained person compose a set of about 450 complex test sentences each of which includes one or more clausal modifier. Then we analyzed these test sentences with our method and evaluated the analysis results from the viewpoint of structural disambiguation for the following sentence types.

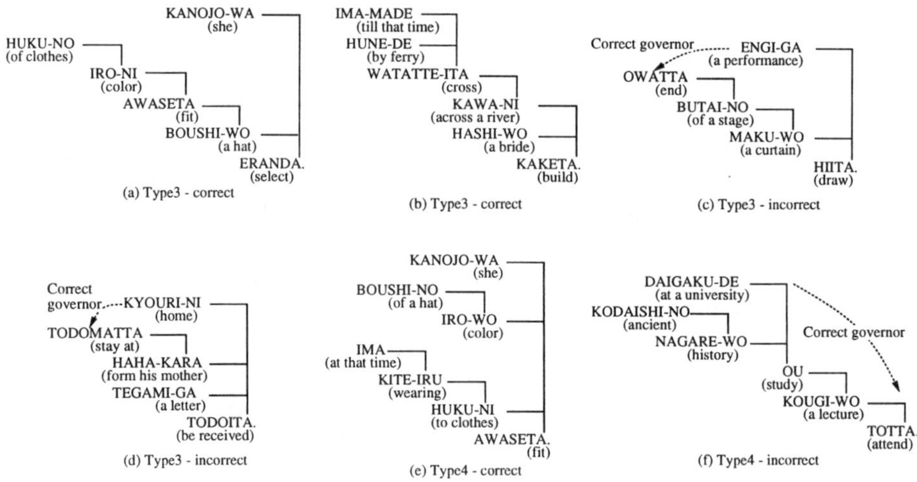

Figure 6. Examples of detecting dependency structures.

	Our method			MT system I			MT system II		
	○	×	Sr*	○	×	Sr*	○	×	Sr*
Type 1	219	0	100%	-	-	-	-	-	-
Type 2	12	0	100%	-	-	-	-	-	-
Type 3	183	13	93%	133	63	68%	147	49	75%
Type 4	33	4	89%	12	25	32%	12	25	32%
Type 3 and 4	216	17	93%	145	88	62%	159	74	68%

*Sr : Success ratio

TABLE 4. Results of experiments.

Type 1 A sentence which has no structural ambiguity concerning case components.

Type 2 A sentence which has two or more correct dependency structures. That is, it contains intrinsic ambiguity which cannot be solved without contextual information.

Type 3 A sentence which has two or more possible dependency structures and whose correct dependency structure is its default dependency structure.

Type 4 A sentence which has two or more possible dependency structures and whose correct dependency structure is not its default dependency structure.

The left part of Table 4 shows the results. This table shows that the success ratio of getting a correct dependency structure by this method is very high. Examples of correct and incorrect analysis are shown in Figure 6. The reasons of incorrect analysis are listed below.

- Inadequacy of the case frame dictionary IPAL regarding surface cases, distinction between obligatory case and optional case, and category specification for case slots (which means oversight of examples).
- Inadequacy of the thesaurus dictionary BGH. This problem is closely related to the method for correlating the level of most specific common layer with their similarity value. Generally speaking, BGH is not reliable enough to calculate an accurate similarity value between words.
- Insufficiency of examples in the case frame dictionary. Some case slots have only one or two examples. This problem can be solved simply by adding the wrongly analyzed sentences as new examples of their proper case frames.

In order to see how well these test sentences are analyzed by conventional SM methods, we translated test sentences of type 3 and 4, which have structural ambiguity, by two commercial machine translation (MT) systems. The commèrcial MT systems have a lot of heuristic rules, but they are thought to be based on tens or hundreds of SMs. We evaluated their outputs based on whether the syntactic analysis of Japanese sentences is correct or not (in the right part of Table 4). Furthermore, we compared the analysis results of our method with those of commercial MT systems (Table 3). We can see that the disambiguation of complex sentences is fairly difficult for conventional SM methods and that our example-based method is significantly better at structural disambiguation than conventional SM methods. The most powerful heuristic rule for analyzing Japanese sentences is to let each bunsetsu depend on its nearest governor. By this heuristic rule, it is not so difficult even for conventional methods to analyze sentences of type 3, because their correct dependency structures are their default dependency structures. However, in order to analyze sentences of type 4 correctly, there must be other means which can constrain the powerful heuristic rule, and checking coarse SMs is not powerful enough. This is the reason why conventional methods cannot analyze sentences of type 4 well. Our method, by contrast, is powerful enough to analyze such sentences.

5. CONCLUSIONS

We have proposed a method that detects case structure not only for simple sentences, but also for complex sentences. In this method, word sense ambiguity for verbs and structural ambiguity are resolved simultaneously. The basis of this method is the process of selecting a proper case frame for the input sentence by matching it with example sentences in the case frame dictionary. We have reported experiments showing this method's superiority over the conventional, coarse-grained SM method.

The remaining problems are the following.

- The accuracy of the thesaurus employed, on which not only case structure analysis but also many other kinds of natural language processing depend. Research is required on the framework of a thesaurus where various aspects of the relations of words are handled, and also on methods for automatic construction of such a thesaurus.
- The separate determination of the scopes of coordinate structures and the subsequent determination of the case structure of a sentence. It is desirable that the coordinate structure and the case structure of a sentence are evaluated by one integrated process. In order to do this while avoiding a combinatorial explosion of ambiguities, we need to devise a data structure and a search method for handling these problems together, or need to devise a method for judging dynamically which information is the most reliable.

References

Katz, J. and Fodor, J. (1963) The Structure of a Semantic Theory. *Language*, 39, 170-210.

Kurohashi, S. and Nagao, M. (1994) A Syntactic Analysis Method of Long Japanese Sentences based on the Detection of Conjunctive Structures. *Computational Linguistics* 20(4), 507–534.

Ikehara, S. et al. (1991) Semantic Analysis Dictionaries for Machine Translation. *Information Processing Society of Japan SIG Notes*, NL–84–13 (in Japanese).

Inagaki, H. et al. (1988) Modification Analysis using Semantic Pattern. *Information Processing Society of Japan SIG Notes*, NL–67–5 (in Japanese).

IPA (Information-technology Promotion Agency), Japan (1987) *IPA Lexicon of the Japanese Language for Computers IPAL (Basic Verbs)* (in Japanese).

Longman Group Ltd. (1987) *Longman Dictionary of Contemporary English.*

Nagao, M. et al. (1985) The Japanese Government Project for Machine Translation. *Computational Linguistics* 11(2–3), 91–110.

Nagao, K. (1990) Dependency Analyzer : A Knowledge-Based Approach to Structural Disambiguation. *Proc. 13th Int. Conference on Computational Linguistics.* Helsinki.

Nagao, M. (1992) Some Rationales and Methodologies for Example-based Approach. *Proc. Int. Workshop on Future Generation Natural Language Processing*, Manchester.

NLRI (National Language Research Institute) (1964) *Word List by Semantic Principles.* Syuei Syuppan (in Japanese).

19. FLOWGRAPH PARSING

RUDI LUTZ
School of Cognitive and Computing Sciences
University of Sussex

Abstract.
Many applications make use of diagrams to represent complex objects. In such applications it is often necessary to recognise how some diagram has been pieced together from other diagrams. Examples are electrical circuit analysis, and program understanding in the plan calculus (Rich, 1981). In these applications the recognition process can be formalised as flowgraph parsing, where a flowgraph is a special case of a plex (Feder, 1971). Nodes in a flowgraph are connected to each other via intermediate points known as tie-points. Lutz (1986, 1989) generalised chart parsing of context-free string languages (Thompson and Ritchie, 1984) to context-free flowgraph languages, enabling bottom-up and top-down recognition of flowgraphs. However, there are various features of the plan calculus that complicate this - in particular attributes, structure sharing, and relationships between tie-points. This chapter will present a chart parsing algorithm for analysing graphs with all these features, suitable for both program understanding and digital circuit analysis. For a *fixed* grammar, this algorithm runs in time polynomial in the number of tie-points in the input graph.

1. INTRODUCTION AND MOTIVATION

Many applications make use of diagrams to represent complex objects, and we often need to recognise how some diagram has been constructed. Examples are electrical circuit analysis, and program understanding in the plan calculus (Rich, 1981), in which programs are represented by data- and control- flow graphs, and stereotypical programming techniques and algorithms (plans) are represented similarly. Understanding how a program has been built up then amounts to treating plans as forming a grammar,

H. Bunt and M. Tomita (eds.), Recent Advances in Parsing Technology, 359–383.

and the understanding process as parsing. Ignoring control flow connections enables us to formalise this as flowgraph parsing. Nodes in a flowgraph consist of labelled boxes with distinguished input and output attaching points (ports), and input ports are connected to output ports via intermediate points known as tie-points, with the restriction that a port is only ever connected to a single tie-point, although fan-out and fan-in is allowed at tie-points. Lutz (1986, 1989) generalised chart parsing of context-free string languages (Thompson and Ritchie, 1984) to context-free flowgraph languages, enabling bottom-up and top-down recognition of flowgraphs. However, there are features of the plan calculus that complicate this:

1. Attributes — control flows in the plan calculus are treated as attributes of the grammar which are propagated during parsing.
2. Data Plans and Overlays — Some plans in the plan calculus allow the introduction of new tie-points not in the input graph. These tie-points either represent aggregate data structures corresponding to collections of other tie-points, or represent a more abstract view of some tie-point (e.g. viewing a list as implementing a set), and act as inputs or outputs of "higher-level" operations. Dealing with this involves using a second chart storing information about data objects.
3. Structure Sharing — when one component feeds one or more of its outputs to more than one other component (fan-out). In this situation the source component can be viewed as playing more than one role in the structure, and could have been duplicated so that separate copies of the component were responsible for each of these roles. This leads to no change in functionality, although there may be a loss in efficiency as measured by the number of components (digital circuits), or computational effort and code size (plan calculus).

This chapter will present a parsing algorithm for analysing graphs with these features, noting that we *permit* structure sharing, but do *not enforce* it. For a *fixed* grammar, this algorithm runs in time polynomial in the number of tie-points in the input graph. We will begin by discussing simple flowgraphs, and then progressively deal with the above features.

2. NOTATION AND DEFINITIONS

Flowgraphs and *flow grammars* are special cases of plex languages and plex grammars (Feder, 1971). A *plex* consists of labelled nodes having an arbitrary number, n, of distinct *attaching points*, used to join nodes together. Such a node is called an n-attaching point entity (NAPE). Attaching points of NAPEs do not connect directly, but via intermediate points known as tie-points. A single tie-point may connect two or more attaching points. If the direction of the connections is important then the plex is said to be directed. Many types of graph structure (e.g. webs (Pfaltz and Rosenfeld, 1969); (Rosenfeld and Milgram, 1972), directed graphs, and strings) are special cases of directed plexes. We will consider the special case of directed plexes in which each NAPE's attaching points (from now on called *ports*) are subdivided into two mutually exclusive groups, known as *input ports* (restricted to only have incoming connections) and *output ports* (restricted to only have outgoing connections). We further restrict ourselves to the case in which each port of a NAPE is only connected to a single tiepoint. This type of plex will be called a *flowgraph* and is a generalisation of Brotsky's (1984) use of the term. See Figure 1(top) for a simple example. A production in a string grammar specifies how one string may be replaced

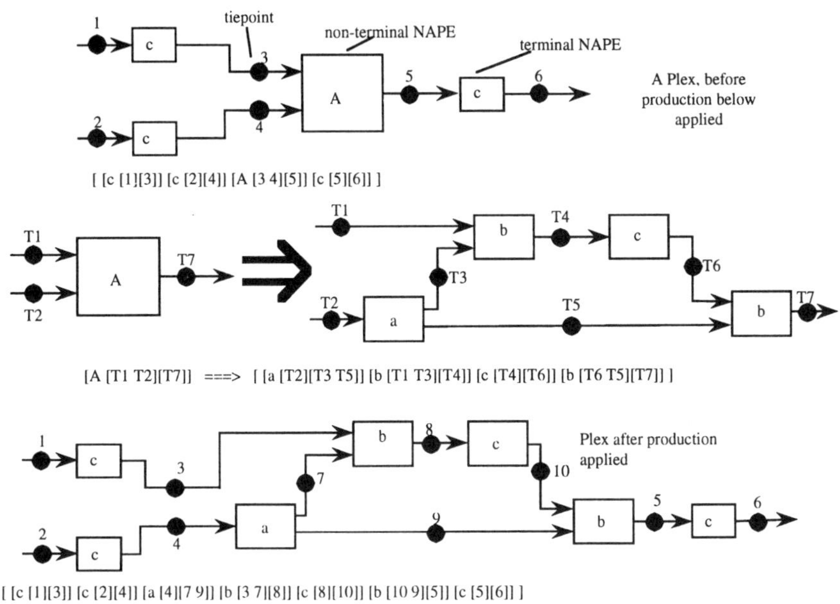

Figure 1. Simple Flowgraph and Rules

by another. However, with flowgraph grammars we encounter a difficulty (due to their 2-dimensional nature) not apparent in the string case. In the string case a production

$$A \Longrightarrow aXYb$$

applied to a string

$$\ldots dAe \ldots \text{(say)}$$

results in the string

$$\ldots daXYbe \ldots$$

and the question of how the replacement string is embedded in the host string never arises because there is a single obvious choice i.e. whatever is to the left of A in the original string is to the left of the replacing string, and similarly on the right. With flowgraphs we no longer have this simple ordering on the NAPEs and embedding becomes much more complicated. Most of the discussion of this is in the web and graph grammar literature (e.g. Pfaltz and Rosenfeld(1969); Rosenfeld and Milgram(1972)), but most of it also applies to flowgraphs. Our approach is to specify with each production which tie-points on the left correspond to which tie-points on the right and then connect everything connecting to one of these left hand tie-points (from the surrounding subgraph) to its corresponding right-hand tie-point.

We define a flowgraph grammar to be a 4-tuple (N,T,P,S) where:

N is a finite non-empty set of NAPEs known as nonterminals.
T is a finite non-empty set of NAPEs known as terminals.
P is a finite set of productions.
S is a special member of N known as the initial, or start, NAPE

where the intersection of N and T is empty.

If we arbitrarily order the input and output ports of a NAPE then each NAPE in a flowgraph can be represented as a triple

(NAPE-label, input list, output list)

where NAPE-label is the label on the NAPE, and input list is a list in which the ith entry is the tie-point to which the ith input port is connected. Similarly the output list specifies to which tie-point each of the output ports is connected. Using this convention a flowgraph G can be represented as a set G^c (the component set) of such triples.

With the above conventions the productions in a flowgraph grammar have the general form

$$AL_iL_o \Longrightarrow CR_iR_o$$

where

A is known as the left-side structure, represented as a component set
C is known as the right-side structure, represented as a component set
L_i is the left-side input tie-point list
R_i is the right-side input tie-point list
L_o is the left-side output tie-point list, and
R_o is the right-side output tie-point list.

L_i and R_i must be of the same length, as must L_o and R_o , and specify how an instance of the right-side structure is to be embedded into a structure W containing an instance of the left-side structure which is being rewritten according to the production. We define the *arity* of the left side of the rule to be the ordered pair $(|L_i|, |L_o|)$ and the arity of the right side of the rule to be the ordered pair $(|R_i|, |R_o|)$. So this requirement simply states that the left- and right-side arities must be the same. The rewriting and embedding is done as follows:

The instance of the left-side structure is removed from W and replaced by an instance of the right-side structure. Now, for each tie-point X in L_i any previous connections from NAPEs in W to X are replaced by connections from the same attaching points of the same NAPEs to the corresponding tie-point in R_i . The same is done for tie-points in L_o and R_o. One can eliminate the need for explicit storing of R_i and R_o by using the same variable names on the left and right hand sides of the production to denote corresponding tie-points.

Just as in the string case, by considering restrictions on X and Y in a production of the form:

$$X \Longrightarrow Y$$

one can arrive at the notions of context-sensitive, context-free, and regular grammars (Ehrig, 1979). In particular, restricting the productions to have a single NAPE in their left-side structure gives us a context-free flowgraph grammar, and we will restrict ourselves to these from now on. In this case we no longer need to store L_i and L_o since the input and output lists of the single triple on the left of the production already specify this information. See Figure 1 for an example of the notation and of rewriting process.

3. CHART PARSING OF CONTEXT-FREE FLOWGRAPHS

In a chart parser, assertions about what has been found by the parser are kept in a "database" known as the *chart*. Such assertions will be called *patches*, and are of two kinds — *complete* patches and *partial* patches. A complete patch asserts that a complete grammatical entity (corresponding to some terminal or non-terminal symbol of the grammar) has been found. Partial patches are assertions that part of some grammatical entity has been found, and about what needs to be found to complete it. One can think of a patch as being a closed loop drawn round some subgraph of the flowgraph, indicating that this subgraph corresponds to all or part of some grammatical entity. Regarding the right-side structures of rules as uninstantiated templates, then complete patches with non-terminal labels correspond to the occurrence of an instantiation of the right-side structure of some rule, thus forming an occurrence of the left-side structure of the rule. Partial patches correspond to partially instantiated instances of the right-side structure of some rule, and thus to partially recognised instances of the left-side structure. Each patch A contains the following information:

1. *label(A)* — the name (one of the terminal or non-terminal symbols) of the grammatical entity corresponding to the patch.
2. *inputs(A)* — a set of input tie-points for the patch.
3. *outputs(A)* — a set of output tie-points for the patch.
4. *components(A)* — a list of the patches involved in making up this patch.
5. *needed(A)* — what else needs to be found to complete the patch. For complete patches this will be empty, and for partial patches this will be a flowgraph structure, represented as a list of triples.

For a partial patch, the input and output tie-points (i.e. those by which the patch connects to the surrounding flowgraph) are each subdivided into two categories — the set of *active* tie-points where the patch still needs other components to attach to these tie-points, and the set of *inactive* tie-points which are those which would be inputs or outputs of the patch were it complete. A NAPE needed by a partial patch will be called *immediately needed* if any of its tie-points are active. The components entry of a patch lists (instantiated versions of) those NAPEs in the right-side structure of the rule which have been completely instantiated, and the needed entry lists uninstantiated (as yet) parts of the rule. Note that some of the *tie-points* in the *needed entry* may be instantiated. These are where the needed NAPEs connect to the ones already found. We will say that a partial patch A is *extendible* by a complete patch B (or that B *can extend* A) in the case where A immediately needs a patch of the same type as B and the instantiated tie-points in this needed patch do not conflict with any instantiations actually occurring in B. The essence of the chart parsing strategy can then be stated as follows:

> Every time a complete patch is added to the chart a search is made for any partial patches immediately needing a patch like the one just added. For each of these partial patches a *new* patch is made extending it by the complete one, and this new patch is then added to an agenda of patches to be processed at some appropriate time. Similarly, every time a partial patch is added to the chart a search is made for complete patches which can extend the partial patch just added, and if any are found new patches are made extending the partial one, and these are added to the agenda to be processed when appropriate.

Note that patches are only ever added to the chart. They are never removed, thus avoiding duplication of previous effort.

The basic operation of the algorithm is joining a complete patch to a partial patch to make a new enlarged patch. Figure 2 shows a partial patch being joined to a complete patch to make a new patch (the enclosing box). The resulting patch has the same items in its *components entry* as the original partial patch plus the complete patch. Its *needed entry* is equal to

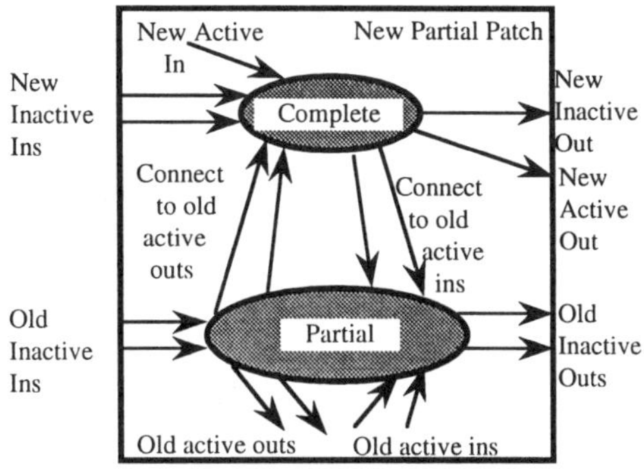

Figure 2. The Joining Operation

that of the original partial patch minus the needed patch corresponding to the complete patch. Note that the matching of a needed patch to an actual complete patch may introduce further instantiations of tie-points in the *needed entry* of the new patch. On connecting the two patches all the inactive tie-points of the partial patch remain inactive. Some of its active tie-points will correspond to tie-points of the complete patch (this is where the two patches actually join). Other active tie-points remain active in the new patch since it is still looking for other patches to attach to them. Of the complete patch's (input and output) tie-points some have already been mentioned i.e. those connecting directly to the partial patch. Others will become new inactive tie-points of the resulting patch since it will not be looking for anything to attach to them. However other (input and output) tie-points of the complete patch may now become active (viewed as belonging to the new patch) since it may now expect other patches to attach to them in order to complete itself. Provided all these distinctions are kept clear there is no great difficulty in implementing the joining operation. With this joining operation a limited type of structure sharing happens automatically. This is illustrated in Figure 3. If we wish to prevent this, then, when trying to extend a partial patch P by a complete patch C, the parser must check (recursively!) that none of the components of P have any sub-components in common with C, thus preventing structure sharing at any level. This check will be referred to as the *no-sharing check*.

The initialisation of the agenda will now be described. Initially a complete patch is added to the agenda for each of the terminal NAPEs in the original graph. If the algorithm is to run top-down then an additional step is needed in which partial patches with empty *components entries* are made for every rule in the grammar whose left-side structure is labelled by the start symbol of the grammar. Each such rule leads to several such empty

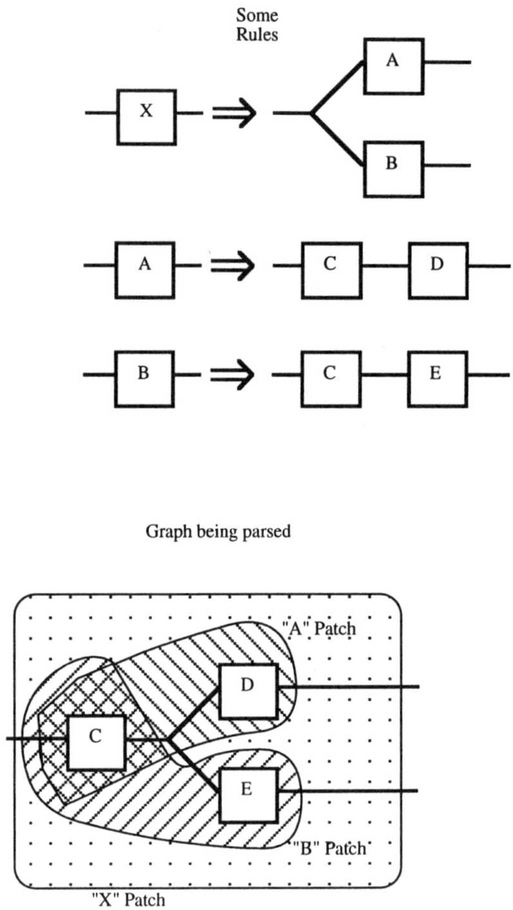

Figure 3. Occurrence of Structure Sharing Without No Sharing Check

patches, one for each permutation of the input tie- points of the input graph. The *inactive-inputs* and *active-outputs* entries for these patches are the permuted inputs. The *needed entry* is the right-side structure of the rule with appropriate instantiations of the tie points occurring in it. These patches are also added to the agenda. The complete algorithm is shown in Figure 4.

On termination the parsing is successful if the chart contains a complete patch for S whose *inputs* and *outputs* entries are the input and output tie-points of the input graph.

How can we organise the chart for efficient searching? The chart is divided into two parts, one for complete patches, and one for partial. The

```
initialise chart and agenda;
until the agenda is empty do
   pick a patch A from the agenda;
   unless A is already in the chart then
      add A to the chart;
      if A is complete then
         for each partial patch B in chart extendible by A do
            make a new patch extending B with A and put on agenda;
         endfor;
         if bottom-up then
            for each rule R in P such that rhs(R) has an input NAPE labelled by label(A) do
               for each such NAPE X in R do
                  make new empty patch B with label(B)=lhs(R) and
                     needed(B)=rhs(R) with instantiations dependent on match between X and A and
                     inputs(B)=inputs(A) and
                     active-outputs(B)=inputs(A);
                  add B to agenda;
               endfor;
            endfor;
         endif;
      else
         for each complete patch B in chart which can extend A do
            make a new patch extending A with B and put on agenda;
         endfor;
         if top-down then
            for each object C immediately needed by A do
               for each rule R in P with lhs(R)=label(C) do
                  make new empty patch B with label(B)=label(C) and
                     needed(B)=rhs(R) with instantiations dependent on match between C and lhs(R) and
                     inputs(B)=inputs(C) and
                     active-outputs(B)=inputs(C);
                  add B to agenda;
               endfor
            endfor
         endif
      endif
   endunless
enduntil;
```

Figure 4. The Chart Parsing Algorithm

part for complete patches is organised as two arrays, one for indexing each patch by its inputs, and one for indexing by its outputs. So each complete patch is entered several times into the chart, once for each of its inputs and outputs. For further efficiency each of the elements in these arrays is a hash table and the patches are actually entered into these hashed by their label. So the entries in the hash table are actually lists of patches with the same label which share a given input or output tie-point. This enables efficient retrieval of all patches with a particular label at a particular tie-point. The treatment of partial patches is slightly more complicated. For each of their immediately needed NAPEs partial patches are entered into their part of the chart indexed by the active inputs and outputs of the needed NAPE, and hashed by the labels of each of these NAPEs. This structure for the chart enables a complete patch to easily find partial patches immediately needing it, and enables partial patches to easily find complete patches that they immediately need.

A similar technique can be used to store the grammar rules in order to enable efficient retrieval of appropriate rules.

4. COMPLEXITY ANALYSIS

4.1. A POLYNOMIAL BOUND

In this section a relatively informal argument will be given to show that, for a *fixed grammar*, the algorithm runs in time polynomial in the number of tie-points T of the input graph (if the grammar is allowed to vary and is therefore regarded as part of the input to the parsing problem, then Wills(1992) has shown that the problem becomes NP-complete). We will not give a tight upper bound on the running time, but simply show that it is polynomial. Let:

G =number of NAPEs in the graph
T =number of tie-points in the graph
K =maximum number of inputs to a NAPE
M =maximum number of outputs from a NAPE
L =number of possible labels
R =number of rules in the grammar
Q =maximum number of NAPEs in the right-side structure of a rule
A =maximum possible number of active tie-points in a partial patch.

Note that K, M, L, R, Q, and A all depend on the grammar, and are independent of the input graph.

For the purposes of adding new patches to the chart, patches are only distinguished according to some of the information contained in them, rather than strict equality being necessary. Complete and partial patches will be dealt with separately.

Complete patches are distinguished which differ in at least one of their input tie-points, their output tie-points, or their label. The maximum number of inputs and outputs in a patch is determined by the grammar, as is the number of possible labels. So the number of possible complete patches in the chart is bounded above by the product of L and the number of possible ways of selecting at most K out of T tie-points, and the number of possible ways of choosing at most M out of T tie-points. This gives us $O(L \cdot T^{K+M})$ complete patches altogether. A similar argument shows that at a given set of K (input) tie-points, there are *at most* $O(T^M)$ complete patches with a given label.

Partial patches are distinguished which differ in at least one of their inactive input tie-points, their inactive output tie-points, their label, or in what they need in order to complete themselves (their *needed* entry). Now, a partial patch represents the partially recognised right side structure of a rule. The rule used determines the label, and there are at most 2^Q subsets of the (at most) Q NAPEs in the rule that could still be needed. Each such subset determines a set of (at most) A active tie-points for the patch. So there can be at most

$$O(R \cdot 2^Q \cdot T^A \cdot T^K \cdot T^M) = O(R \cdot 2^Q \cdot T^{A+K+M})$$

partial patches altogether. In fact there will be very much less than this, as this includes complete patches with nothing needed, and (more importantly) ignores completely any additional constraints implied by the connectivity of the graph.

Since the basic operation of the chart parsing algorithm involves extending partial patches by complete ones, we need to know, for a given partial patch, the largest number of complete patches that could possibly extend it. A partial patch can be extended at any of its (at most) A active tie-points, and any complete patch which could extend it must join at least one of these tie-points, and must share a label with at least one of the NAPEs immediately required by the partial patch. So there are *at most* $O(A \cdot Q \cdot T^{K+M-1})$ such complete patches. Similarly, given a complete patch, there are at most $O((K+M) \cdot R \cdot 2^Q \cdot T^{K+M+A-1})$ possible matching partial patches.

We can use these upper bounds to demonstrate that the algorithm terminates, and does so in polynomial time. Let N denote the number of iterations of the main loop of the algorithm while it is running, and let:

C_N =number of complete patches in the chart after iteration N
P_N =number of partial patches in the chart after iteration N
A_N =length of agenda after iteration N

Then in the top-down case we have:[1]

$$\begin{aligned} A_0 &= G + R_S P_G \\ C_0 &= 0 \\ P_0 &= 0 \end{aligned}$$

and

$$A_{N+1} \begin{cases} = A_N - 1 & \text{(patch already present in chart)} \\ \leq A_N - 1 + AQT^{K+M-1} + QR & \text{(partial not in chart)} \\ \leq A_N - 1 + (K+M)R2^QT^{K+M+A-1} & \text{(complete not in chart)} \end{cases}$$

$$C_{N+1} \begin{cases} = C_N & \text{(patch already present in chart)} \\ = C_N & \text{(partial not in chart)} \\ = C_N + 1 & \text{(complete not in chart)} \end{cases}$$

$$P_{N+1} \begin{cases} = P_N & \text{(patch already present in chart)} \\ = P_N + 1 & \text{(partial not in chart)} \\ = P_N & \text{(complete not in chart)} \end{cases}$$

[1] R_S is the number of rules for S (the start symbol); P_G is the number of permutations of inputs of graph.

In the bottom-up case we have

$$\begin{aligned} A_0 &= G \\ C_0 &= 0 \\ P_0 &= 0 \end{aligned}$$

and

$$A_{N+1} \begin{cases} = & A_N - 1 \quad \text{(patch already present in chart)} \\ \leq & A_N - 1 + AQT^{K+M-1} \quad \text{(partial not in chart)} \\ \leq & A_N - 1 + (K+M)R2^QT^{K+M+A-1} + QR \ \text{(complete not in char} \end{cases}$$

$$C_{N+1} \begin{cases} = & C_N \quad \text{(patch already present in chart)} \\ = & C_N \quad \text{(partial not in chart)} \\ = & C_N + 1 \quad \text{(complete not in chart)} \end{cases}$$

$$P_{N+1} \begin{cases} = & P_N \quad \text{(patch already present in chart)} \\ = & P_N + 1 \quad \text{(partial not in chart)} \\ = & P_N \quad \text{(complete not in chart)} \end{cases}$$

So, in both the bottom-up and top-down cases, C_N and P_N are monotonic functions of N. As discussed earlier both are bounded above. Therefore after some number of iterations they must both have reached their maximum value (normally *much less* than the crude estimates above). Once this happens all patches on the agenda must be already present in the chart and A_N decreases by one on each subsequent iteration until it reaches 0 (an empty agenda), and the algorithm terminates. Now on each iteration it can be seen that either:

1. both C_N and P_N remain constant (in which case A_N decreases), or
2. P_N increases by 1, and items are possibly added to the agenda, or
3. C_N increases by 1, and items are possibly added to the agenda.

From the above, at most $O(LT^{K+M})$ iterations involve adding a complete patch to the chart and add some items to the agenda, and at most $O(R2^QT^{A+K+M})$ iterations involve adding a partial patch to the chart and add some items to the agenda. All other iterations simply remove items from the agenda. So how many items get added to the agenda? This is given by:

(no. of items in initial agenda)
+(no. added for complete patches)
+(no. added for partial patches)

In the top down case this bounded by

$$\begin{aligned} A0 + O(LT^{K+M})O((K+M)R2^QT^{K+M+A-1}) \\ + O(R2^QT^{A+K+M})(O(AQT^{K+M-1})) + QR \end{aligned}$$

and in the bottom-up case this is bounded by

$$A0 + O(LT^{K+M})(O((K+M)R2^{Q}T^{K+M+A-1}) \\ + QR) + O(R2^{Q}T^{A+K+M})O(AQT^{K+M-1})$$

which are both clearly polynomial.

So, in both cases the number of items added to the agenda, which is the same as the number of iterations performed, is polynomially bounded. How much work is done on each of these iterations? The cost of seeing if a patch is already in the chart can be done in polynomial time. This is because (even with no clever indexing) there are at most a polynomial number of patches in the chart that need to be checked. If the no-sharing check is included then the cost of checking if one patch is extendible by another can be done in time at worst O(G) since both the partial and complete patches are each ultimately made up of at most G NAPEs (at lowest level), and checking for intersection of these two sets can be done in linear time. If the no-sharing check is omitted then the cost of checking if one patch is extendible by another can be done in constant time (since it depends on checking that the instantiated tie-points of the patches are compatible with each other, and the number of tie-points involved depends on the grammar), as can the cost of making a new patch. All the costs involved in checking rules etc. are purely a function of the grammar. So the total cost of the algorithm is easily seen to have an upper bound which is a polynomial function of T.

4.2. FINDING ALL PARSES

Athough the algorithm performs flowgraph *recognition* in polynomial time, it does not find *all parses* in polynomial time. This is because for some flowgraphs and some grammars there may well be an exponential number of parses (this is even true of Earley's algorithm operating on strings!). The algorithm will however find a parse if one exists. If an application requires all possible parses, then the algorithm is easily modified to compute a structure from which all parses can be easily computed after the parsing process has finished. This can be done by adding an extra field to each complete patch which is added to the chart. In this field a list will be stored of all other patches having the same label, inputs and outputs, but different subpatches to the patch which has been added. With this arrangement, after theparsing has finished, instead of a single parse tree we will have computed a parse forest. It can be regarded as an AND/OR tree as discussed in (Billot and Lang, 1989), and shares structure maximally between the separate parse trees represented in the forest.

5. DEALING WITH ATTRIBUTES

As stated earlier graphs and rules in the plan calculus also have a second type of connection between NAPEs - control flow arcs. These are handled as attributes of the graphs, where the attribute for a non-terminal NAPE is calculated from the attributes of its components. Details of this method of handling the control flows can be found in Wills(1986, 1990, 1992), and a generalisation can be found in Lutz(1992). For our purposes we will assume that each NAPE in the original graph is annotated with initial values for the attributes, and we will also assume that each rule has annotations describing how each attribute for the left-hand side of the rule is computed from the attributes of the NAPEs on its right-hand side. These annotations have the general form:

$$A_{lhs} = f_{Rule}(A_1, \ldots, A_k)$$

where A_{lhs} represents an attribute of the left hand side of the rule, f_{Rule} represents the rule specific computation, and $A_1, \ldots, A_k$ represent the attributes of the NAPEs on the right.

Computing the attributes is straightforward. Each patch is given an extra field for each of its attributes. When a *complete* patch (corresponding to some rule of the grammar) whose components have attributes $A_1, \ldots, A_k$, is added to the chart, $f_{Rule}(A1, \ldots, Ak)$ is computed, and stored in the appropriate field for the attribute in the patch. The initial patches receive their attribute values from the original graph.

6. DEALING WITH TIE-POINT RELATIONSHIPS

In order to capture implementation decisions, and data abstractions, the plan calculus contains what Rich(1981) calls data plans and data overlays. So far as the grammatical formalism is concerned, these can be viewed as allowing rules to express named functional relationships that hold between tie-points. To handle these our grammatical formalism is extended to allow annotations (following the keyword *where*) of the form:

$$t_i = F(t_{j_1}, \ldots, t_{j_k}) \quad \text{for } k \geq 1$$

where t_i represents either any of the tie-points occurring in the NAPEs of the rule, or an additional new tie-point, $t_{j_1}, \ldots, t_{j_k}$ represent any of the tie-points occurring in the NAPEs of the rule or any new tie-points mentioned on the left of other relationships in the rule (this must be non-recursive!), and F is the name of the functional relationship involved. The set of these will be referred to as the *tie-point relationships* of the rule.

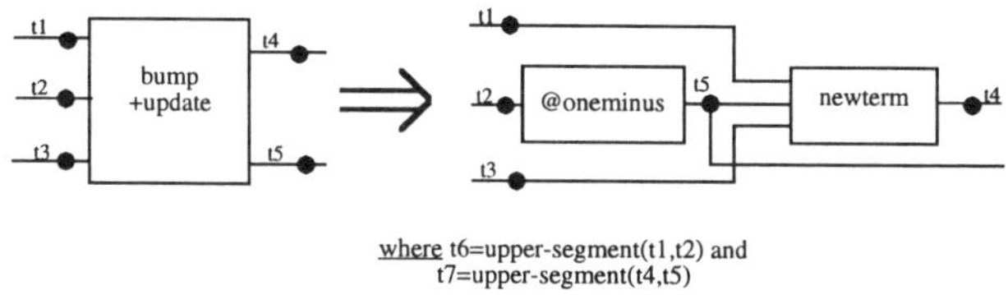

Figure 5. Bump+Update

We will only discuss the changes to deal with tie-point relationships for the parser running in bottom-up mode. Dealing with them in top-down mode is rather complicated and will not be described further in this chapter.

Consider the rules *bump+update* and *bump+update->push* (Figures 5 and 6), which cause problems for the algorithm. Flowgraph grammar rules as described earlier have the same arities for their left- and right-hand sides, and this is true for *bump+update*. However, the left-hand side of *bump+update->push* has arity (2,1), while the right hand side has arity (3,2). Furthermore, although the tie-point t3 occurs as input on both sides of the overlay, this is not true of t6 and any tie-point of the *bump+update* plan. It does not even correspond to the compound object (the *upper-segment*) represented by t1 and t2. It corresponds to the *upper-segment* viewed as a *list* (via a function *upper-segment->list*). To cope with these features the basic bottom-up chart parser presented earlier is modified as follows:

1. The rule format is modified to include the left-hand side inputs and outputs, since these may now be distinct from those on the right. Correspondingly, each patch now has two extra fields — *left-hand-ins*, and *left-hand-outs*, in addition to the two fields *inputs* and *outputs* (corresponding to inputs and outputs of the right hand side of the rule). Complete patches are stored in the chart indexed by their *left-*

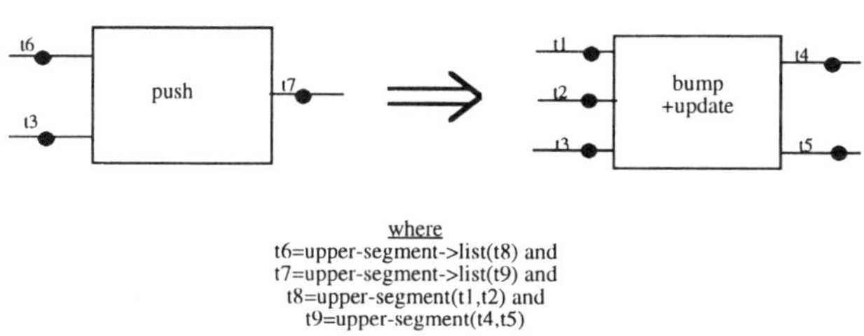

Figure 6. Bump+Update->push

hand-ins and *left-hand-outs*, rather than by their inputs and outputs as before. Partial patches are stored as before.

2. A second chart is added. This chart (the *tie-point chart*) stores the functional relationships between tie-points discovered during parsing. It contains entries with the form:

$$T = F(S_1, \ldots, S_k)$$

where T and $S_1, \ldots, S_k$ are known (i.e. instantiated) tie-points. This chart is organised similarly to the earlier (complete) chart, in that it is split into two parts, one used for storing relationships indexed by the left hand side tie-point (T) and by the relationship name (F), and the other used for storing the relationships indexed by the right-hand side tie-points $(S_1, \ldots, S_k)$, and by the relationship name.

3. Two new fields are added to each patch. These are:
   (a) *relations-needed* — When an empty patch is created this is initialised to the set of tie-point relationships of the rule involved in creating the patch.
   (b) *relations-found* — When an empty patch is created this is initialised to empty.

4. When a new patch is created, either by extending a partial patch, or by creating a new empty patch for some rule, any instantiations for the tie-point variables occurring in the patch are also propagated into the relations-needed entry. The following is then repeated until there is no change to the patch:
   (a) If some relationship in the relations-needed entry is fully instantiated (i.e. no tie-point *variables* occur on either its left or right hand sides) then it is moved from the relations-needed entry to relations-found.
   (b) If some relationship in the relations-needed entry has a fully instantiated right-hand side i.e. is of the form:

$$V = F(S_1, \ldots, S_k)$$

where V is a tie-point variable, and $S_1, \ldots, S_k$ are all known tie-points, then the tie-point chart is consulted to see if there is an entry of the form:

$$T = F(S_1, \ldots, S_k)$$

where T must be a known tie-point. If there is, then V is instantiated to T, and this instantiation is propagated throughout the patch (including its relations-needed entry). If not, then a *new* tie-point T is *created*, the assertion:

$$T = F(S_1, \ldots, S_k)$$

is added to the tie-point chart, V is instantiated to T, and this instantiation is propagated throughout the patch (including its relations-needed entry).

(c) If some relationship in the relations-needed entry has an instantiated left-hand side i.e. is of the form:

$$S = F(T_1, \ldots, T_k)$$

where S is a known tie-point, and $T_1, \ldots, T_k$ are *either* known tie-points *or* tie-point variables, then the tie-point chart is consulted to see if there is an entry of the form:

$$S = F(S_1, \ldots, S_k)$$

where $S_1, \ldots, S_k$ are all known tie-points. Matching $T_1, \ldots, T_k$ against $S_1, \ldots, S_k$ either succeeds, in which case any variables in $T_1, \ldots, T_k$ get instantiated, and these instantiations are propagated throughout the patch. If the match fails (because two *different* known tie- points are being matched against each other) then the whole patch is invalid, and is rejected (i.e. is not added to the chart).

5. A patch is only considered complete if *both* its needed entry *and* its relations-needed entry are empty. If they are, then the patch is added to the chart as normal. If not, then the patch is considered partial, and is stored in the chart indexed as before, but also indexed by the relationship names and instantiated tie-points of any immediately needed (in the obvious generalised sense of the term) relationships in the relations-needed entry.
6. When a relationship is added to the tie-point chart, the (patch) chart is consulted to see if there are any partial patches waiting for a tie-point relationship compatible with the one just added. If so, the patch is extended by the relationship, and added to the agenda.

Figure 7 illustrates this for the above rules.

Now consider rules like those in Figure 8, which includes a rule (for A) with a "straight-through" arc, and a graph like that in Figure 9. This can be recognised as forming an S, by the following sequence of events:

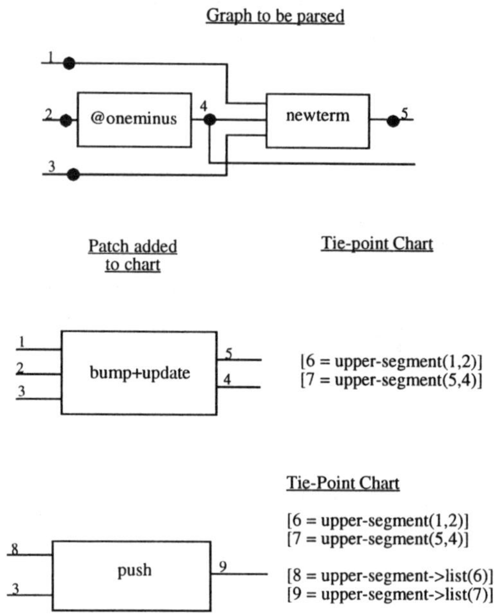

Figure 7. Use of Tie-point Chart

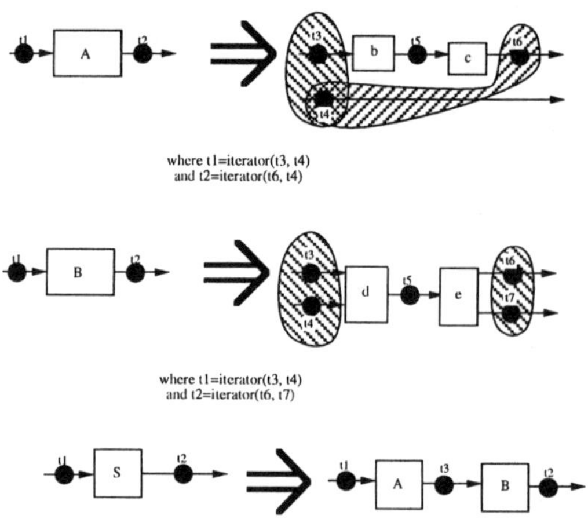

Figure 8. Some Rules (with a "straight-through" arc)

1. The NAPEs labelled b and c in Figure 9 are recognised as forming a partial A, which still has:

$$t1 = iterator(1, t4)$$

$$t2 = iterator(3, t4)$$

in its relations-needed entry.

2. The NAPEs labelled d and e in Figure 9 are recognised as forming a complete B, with input given by a em new tie-point 8, and output given by a *new* tie-point 9, satisfying:

$$8 = iterator(3, 4)$$

$$9 = iterator(6, 7)$$

These relationships are added to the tie-point chart.

3. When the relationship 8=*iterator*(3, 4) is added to the tie- point chart, the main chart is consulted to see if there are any partial patches immediately needing a relationship matching this one. The partial A discovered earlier is found, and on matching

$$8 = iterator(3, 4)$$

and

$$t2 = iterator(3, t4)$$

t4 gets instantiated to 4, and t2 gets instantiated to 8. The patch is therefore extended, and it now has only the single relationship:

$$t1 = iterator(1, 4)$$

in its relations-needed entry. This causes the creation of a new tie-point 10 to which t1 is instantiated, and an assertion:

$$10 = iterator(1, 4)$$

is added to the tie-point chart. As a result of all this we now have a complete A patch (with input 10 and output 8) which gets added to the chart. This causes the creation of an empty S patch (with input 10) immediately needing an A (with input 10) to be added to the chart.

4. This patch is extended first by the A patch, and then again by the B patch, giving us a complete S patch with input 10 and output 9, where:

$$10 = iterator(1, 4)$$

and

$$9 = iterator(6, 7)$$

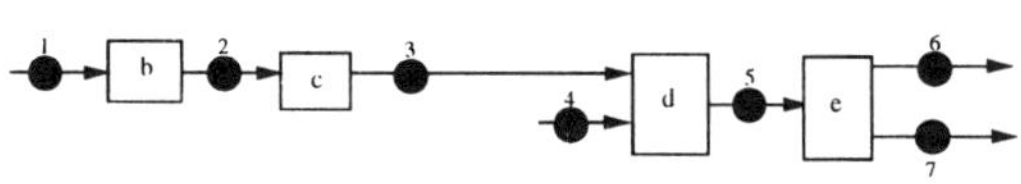

Figure 9. Graph to be Parsed by Rules of Figure 8

This illustrates very nicely the role of the second chart.

7. CHART PARSING OF STRUCTURE-SHARING FLOWGRAPHS

As stated earlier we are also interested in the case where structure sharing is allowed. However, for reasons discussed in Lutz(1992), we do not want to allow *any* two NAPEs sharing the same inputs to be collapsed, but only NAPEs with appropriate labels. To make this more precise we define a slightly more general notion:

A *restricted structure sharing flowgraph grammar* (RSSFG) is defined to be a 5-tuple (N, T, P, S, R) where N, T, P, S are the same as for ordinary context free flowgraph grammars, and $R \subseteq N \cup T$. R is the set of NAPEs for which collapsing is allowed. Such a grammar has an additional rewriting rule which will be described below. We define a relation *R-collapses* on the set of flowgraphs over $N \cup T$ by:

> G2 *R-collapses* G1 iff G1 and G2 are flowgraphs, and G1^c contains two triples of the form $T1 = (A, (t_1, \ldots, t_n), (x_1, \ldots, x_m))$ and $T2 = (A, (t_1, \ldots, t_n), (y_1, \ldots, y_m))$, where A $\in R$ and $G2^c$ can be obtained from $G1^c$ by removing these two triples and replacing them by a single triple of the form $T3 = (A, (t_1, \ldots, t_n), (z_1, \ldots, z_m))$ and then replacing all occurrences of $x_1, \ldots, x_m$ and $y_1, \ldots, y_m$ by $z_1, \ldots, z_m$ respectively throughout the remaining triples.
> In other words, G2 *R-collapses* G1 iff G1 contains two instances of some NAPE A (whose label is in R) which have the same inputs, and G2 is identical to G1 except that the two instances of A have been replaced by a single instance of A (with the same inputs) and all NAPES which originally connected to the outputs of one or other of the two instances of A now connect to the single instance (in G2). This amounts to identifying the two instances of A and their corresponding tie-points.

The reflexive, transitive, symmetric closure of *R-collapses* is then an equivalence relation (R-share-equivalence) on the set of flowgraphs, and we want any parsing algorithm which can recognise some graph G to also be able to recognise any flowgraphs R-share-equivalent to G. We also want the grammar to be able to generate not only the flowgraphs derivable directly from the grammar, but also all R-share-equivalent flowgraphs. This can be done if we allow at any point in the generation of a flowgraph the replacement of the graph so far generated (G1) by any graph G2 for which *either* G1 *R-collapses* G2 or G2 *R-collapses* G1. If $R = \emptyset$ then the grammar is an ordinary flowgraph grammar, and if $R = N \cup T$ then we get a (full) structure sharing flowgraph grammar as defined in Lutz(1989a).

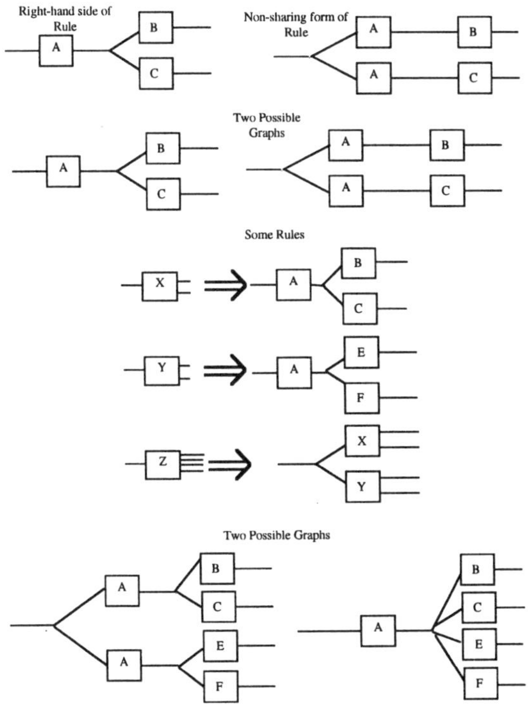

Figure 10. Structure Sharing and Collapsing Phenomena

Figure 10 illustrates several phenomena that can occur with RSSFGs, and which motivated the above definition.

To see how the parsing algorithm can be modified to cope with RS-SFGs it should first be noted that for any flowgraph G there is a *smallest* flowgraph G_{min} which is R-share-equivalent to G. Secondly, the right-side structure of any rule in an RSSFG can be replaced by any flowgraph R-share-equivalent to it without altering the generative capacity of the grammar. We therefore define a canonical form for an RSSFG in which each rule of the form:

$$A \Longrightarrow B$$

has been replaced by the rule:

$$A \Longrightarrow B_{min}$$

So the first change to the algorithm is to put the grammar into canonical form. The second change is to the action of adding a complete patch to the chart. Previously the only check that was done was to see if the patch was already in the chart. Now the algorithm must additionally check if the label of the patch is in R and if there is another patch in the chart with the same label and the same inputs. If so, the algorithm must collapse the new patch and the one already present into a single patch, by identifying the output tie-points of the two patches. Provided tie-points in the various triples making up the patches are represented as pointers to pointers to tie-points (rather than storing the tie-points directly in the triples) then simply changing the values of the second set of pointers will implement the identification universally throughout all patches in the chart. This can lead to "chains" of pointers which need to be fully dereferenced in order to actually access the tie-points themselves (this is similar to the way variables are handled in many implementations of Prolog). After collapsing an additional step is needed since there may be patches in the chart indexed by the tie-point which has been effectively removed by the identification. These patches must now be stored in the chart indexed by their new output tie-points. If the information that collapsing has been done is needed by an application the algorithm can make a note this fact either by annotating the tie- points involved or by an assertion held separately. Finally, the no-sharing check must be omitted.

If the grammar also has attributes, then we need to specify how to compute the attribute A_{res} of a NAPE resulting from collapsing two patches with attributes A_1 and A_2. This specification takes the form (for each attribute):

$$A_{res} = f_{collapse}(A_1, A_2)$$

where $f_{collapse}$ is a function which computes the value of the attribute for the new patch from the values for the two collapsed patches. Two NAPEs are only collapsed when an attempt is made to add a complete patch P_2 (with attribute A_2) to the chart, and there is already a patch P_1 (with attribute A_1) present in the chart with the same label and inputs. In this case P_1 is left in the chart (i.e. it is the output tie-points in P_2 which are identified with those in P_1). P_1 then has the value of its attribute set to $f_{collapse}(A_1, A_2)$. If this new value for its attribute is different from its previous value, then any complete patches in the chart which have P_1 as one of their components must also have their attributes recalculated, and any of these patches whose attributes change must also have their attributes recalculated, and so on recursively. To facilitate this, each complete patch P needs an extra field *partof* which holds a list of all complete patches of which P is a component. To maintain this field, whenever a complete patch P is added to the chart, P is added to the *partof* field of each of its component patches. The initial patches (corresponding to the original graph) all have this field initially set to empty.

8. CONCLUSIONS

This chapter has presented a polynomial time chart parsing algorithm for context-free flowgraph languages, capable of handling all the features of the plan calculus (Rich, 1981), and which is also applicable to digital circuit analysis. This algorithm forms the basis of the program understanding process described in Lutz(1989b, 1991, 1992).

Although there is a large literature on the generative abilities of various types of graph grammar formalisms (see e.g. Ehrig(1979); Feder(1971); Fu(1974); Gonzalez and Thomason(1978); Pfaltz and Rosenfeld(1969); Rosenfeld and Milgram(1972)), there is relatively little on parsing strategies, except for restricted classes of graph and web grammars (e.g. Della Vigna and Ghezzi(1978)). In its top-down strictly left-to-right form chart parsing of context-free string languages corresponds to Earley's algorithm (Earley, 1970), which was generalised by Brotsky(1984) to parsing flowgraphs of the kind described here, except that his algorithm could not cope with fan-out at tie-points, or with tie-point relationships. However the approach taken here can also run bottom-up, which is particularly useful in applications in which we want to recognise as much as possible even though full recognition may be impossible (because of errors in the graph, or because the grammar is necessarily incomplete). Wills(1986, 1990) modified Brotsky's algorithm to cope with fan-out, but her algorithm only runs in a pseudo-bottom-up fashion by starting it running top-down looking for every possible non-terminal at every possible place in the graph. More recently, Wills(1992) developed an algorithm heavily based on the chart parsing algorithm described here and in Lutz(1986, 1989), which is also capable of dealing with attributes and tie-point relationships. However her algorithm and graph representations make no mention of tie-points, but deal directly with the edges connecting NAPEs. This makes it harder to deal elegantly with the tie-point relationships.

More recently there have been several papers in the visual language literature which have adopted a chart parsing approach. In particular, Wittenburg *et al.*(1991) and Golin(1991) have developed bottom up parsers for 2-dimensional languages, while O'Gorman(1992), Costagliola *et al.*(1991), and Wittenburg(1992) have developed top-down parsers. This work is all similar in spirit to that presented here, although differences in representation, and application, make it very different in detail. Indeed this seems to be a general problem with work on 2-dimensional languages - there is no known general method suitable for conveniently representing all the different classes of language, and this leads to algorithms for one domain being very different from those in another. Of course, some kind of definite clause encoding could be used for all of these, but this is not always natural, and does not always lend itself to the development of efficient algorithms. In this connection it should be noted that the flowgraph languages discussed in this chapter can be encoded in the Datalog formalism (Abitoul and Vianu, 1988) for which it is known that parsing can be performed in polynomial time. However, a special-purpose algorithm like the one presented can be particularly efficient and adaptable (cf. the control of structure sharing).

A particular advantage of a chart parser is that it keeps a record of all partial patches. This is useful when we do not just wish to analyse how some graph has been generated, but also to make suggestions based on "near-miss" information about how to correct the graph. As such this algorithm is being used as the basis of an intelligent debugging system for Pascal programs (Lutz, 1992).

The algorithms described in this chapter have been implemented in Pop-11, running under the POPLOG^{TM} system.

References

Abitoul, S. and Vianu, V. (1988) Datalog Extensions for Database Updates and Queries. I.N.R.I.A. Technical Report No. 715.

Billot, S. and Lang, B. (1989) The structure of Shared Forests in Ambiguous Parsing". *Proceedings of 27th meeting of the Association for Computational Linguistics.*

Brotsky, D.C. (1984) An Algorithm for Parsing Flow Graphs. AI-TR-704, MIT Artificial Intelligence Laboratory.

Costagliola, G., Tomita, M., and Chang, S.-K. (1991) A Generalised Parser for 2-D Languages. *Proceedings of IEEE Workshop on Visual Languages* 98–104.

Della Vigna, P. and Ghezzi, C. (1978) Context Free Graph Grammars. *Information and Control* Vol. no. 37, 207–233.

Earley, J. (1970) An Efficient Context-Free Parsing Algorithm. *Communications of the ACM* Vol. no. 13, 94–102.

Ehrig, H. (1979) Introduction to the Algebraic Theory of Graph Grammars (A Survey). In: Claus, V., Ehrig, H., and Rozenberg,G. (eds) *Graph Grammars and their Application to Computer Science and Biology* Lecture Notes in Computer Science. Springer-Verlag.

Feder, J. (1971) Plex Languages. *Information Sciences* Vol. no. 3, 225–241.

Fu, K.S. (1974) *Syntactic Methods in Pattern Recognition.* New York: Academic Press.

Golin, E.J. (1991) Parsing Visual Languages with Picture Layout Grammars. *Journal of Visual Languages and Computing* Vol. no. 2, 371–393.

Gonzalez, R.C. and Thomason, M.G. (1978) *Syntactic Pattern Recognition: An Introduction.* Addison-Wesley.

Lutz, R.K. (1986) Diagram Parsing - A New Technique for Artificial Intelligence. CSRP-054. School of Cognitive and Computing Sciences, University of Sussex.

Lutz, R.K. (1989a) Chart Parsing of Flowgraphs. *Proceedings of 11th Joint International*

Conference on AI, Detroit, USA.

Lutz, R.K. (1989b) Debugging Pascal Programs Using a Flowgraph Chart Parser. *Proceedings of 2nd Scandinavian conference on AI*, Tampere, Finland.

Lutz, R.K. (1991) Plan Diagrams as the Basis for Understanding and Debugging Pascal Programs. In: Eisenstadt, M., Rajan, T., and Keane,M. (eds) *Novice Programming Environments* London: Lawrence Erlbaum Associates.

Lutz, R.K. (1992) *Towards an Intelligent Debugging System for Pascal Programs: On the Theory and Algorithms of Plan Recognition in Rich's Plan Calculus.* Ph.D. Thesis, The Open University, Milton Keynes, England.

O'Gorman, L. (1992) Image and Document Processing Techniques for the RightPages Electronic Library System. *Proceedings 11th IAPR International Conference on Pattern Recognition* Vol. no. 2, 260–263.

Pfaltz, J.L. and Rosenfeld, A. (1969) Web Grammars. *Proceedings of 1st International Joint Conference on AI*, 609–619.

Rich, C. (1981) Inspection Methods in Programming. AI-TR-604, MIT Artificial Intelligence Laboratory.

Rosenfeld, A. and Milgram, D.L. (1972) Web Automata and Web Grammars. In: Meltzer, B. and Michie, D. (eds): *Machine Intelligence 7*, Edinburgh University Press, 307–324.

Thompson, H. and Ritchie, G. (1984) Implementing Natural Language Parsers. In: O'Shea, T. and Eisenstadt, M. (eds) *Artificial Intelligence: Tools, Techniques, and Applications*, Harper and Row, 245–300

Wills, L.M. (1986) Automated Program Recognition. MSc Thesis. MIT Electrical Engineering and Computer Science.

Wills, L.M. (1990) Automated Program Recognition: A Feasibility Demonstration. *Artificial Intelligence* Vol. no. 45, 113–171.

Wills, L.M. (1992) Automated Program Recognition by Graph Parsing. Ph.D. Thesis. MIT, Boston, Mass.

Wittenburg, K. (1992) Earley-style Parsing for Relational Languages *Proceedings of IEEE Workshop on Visual Languages*, 192–199.

Wittenburg, K., Weitzman, L., and Talley, J. (1991) Unification-based Grammars and Tabular Parsing for Graphical Languages. *Journal of Visual Languages and Computing* Vol. no. 2, 347–370.

20. PREDICTIVE PARSING FOR UNORDERED RELATIONAL LANGUAGES

KENT WITTENBURG
Bellcore
Morristown, NJ

Abstract.
Among the proposals for multidimensional grammars is a family of constraint-based grammatical frameworks that includes Relational Grammars. In Relational Languages, expressions are formally defined as a set of relations whose tuples are taken from an indexed set of symbols. Both bottom-up parsing and Earley-style parsing algorithms have previously been proposed for different classes of Relational Languages. The Relational Language class for Earley style parsing in Wittenburg (1992a) requires that each relation be a partial order. However, in some real-world domains, the relations do not naturally conform to these restrictions. In this chapter I discuss motivations and methods for predictive, Earley-style parsing of multidimensional languages when the relations involved do not necessarily yield an ordering, e.g., when the relations are symmetric and/or nontransitive. The solution involves guaranteeing that a single initial start position for parsing can be associated with any member of the input set. The domains in which these issues are discussed involve incremental parsing in interfaces and off-line verification of multidimensional data.

1. INTRODUCTION

Relational Languages, those sets of expressions that are generable (or recognizable) by Relational Grammars, are characterized as relations on sets of symbols or, in practice, typed objects (Crimi et al., 1991; Golin and Reiss, 1990; Helm and Marriott, 1986, 1990; Wittenburg et al., 1991; Wittenburg, 1992a, 1992b, 1993). Sentential forms and elements of derivations are formally defined as sets of relations, each of which in turn is a set of ordered

H. Bunt and M. Tomita (eds.), Recent Advances in Parsing Technology, 385–407.

tuples, in the symbol (or object type) vocabulary set. This approach to grammar and language definition generalizes over many other proposals for multidimensional grammars in the literature since arrays, graphs, and specialized spatial data structures can easily be modeled as sets of relational tuples.

Relational Grammars are motivated by domains in which the sets of objects to be generated or analyzed can not comfortably be represented as strict linear orders of symbols. Examples include expressions in 2-D such as mathematics notation, flowcharts, or schematic diagrams; 2-D or 3-D graphical layouts and displays, perhaps with time or additional media as added dimensions; and n-dimensional data to be found in empirical data collections or various types of databases. One must generalize the data type of language expressions from, say, one-dimensional arrays (strings) to 2-, or perhaps n-dimensional arrays or, more generally, sets of relational tuples. Notions of replacement in derivations have to be generalized also, and, as attested by the literature on array and graph grammars (e.g., Ehrig et al., 1991), there are many variations on how to define grammar productions and the notion of replacement (called the embedding problem in the graph-grammar literature).

The Relational Language (RL) framework provides for an abstraction over the particular data structures used to hold the object sets being processed. The grammar productions make mention of the relations expected to hold in the data but there is flexibility in choosing exactly how the data is represented and stored as well as the implementation of how the relations are checked or queried. Such an approach accommodates many kinds of data representations, including array or graph structures, K-D trees, or even databases in which indexings may be precisely tuned for efficiency.

Various parsers have been previously proposed for different classes of Relational languages. Bottom-up algorithms (Golin, 1991; Wittenburg et al., 1991) are the most straightforward and general, although they they are not suited to all applications. More efficient deterministic techniques proposed for graph grammars by Flasinski (1988; 1989) have been adapted by Ferrucci et al. (1991) to their relational grammar framework, but the restrictions on relations and grammar productions make it unclear that the class of languages is widely useful. On the other hand, this algorithm has been shown to have a low polynomial bound on complexity. An Earley-style algorithm (Earley, 1970) has been proposed by Wittenburg (1992a) for a larger class of nondeterministic languages whose relations individually are partial orders.

The limitations of these previously proposed algorithms have become evident in two domains for Relational Grammars under investigation: on-line incremental parsing of visual language expressions (Wittenburg et al.,

1991; Weitzman and Wittenburg, 1993) and off-line verification of multi-dimensional data. While bottom-up parsing may be employed, there are reasons to consider predictive parsing techiques. In the case of incremental parsing of visual languages consisting of connected diagrams or geometric layouts, one might use predictive parsing to detect errors as soon as they occur or to offer incremental directives (e.g., the analogue of completion in command input) to drawing or palette selections. However, to use deterministic algorithms one must use grammars that are often not expressive enough for the constraints desired. In particular, no non left- or right-unique relations are allowed with the Flasinski approach and yet geometric layouts of objects of different sizes and shapes invariably include such relations. For example, in the following mathematical expression, all elements in the denominator stand below the horizontal line. The obvious definition of the *below* relation would then be non left-unique.

$$\frac{E_1}{E_2 + E_3}$$

The Earley-style algorithm of Wittenburg (1992a) is unsuited to incremental interface applications because more flexibility in a parser's scanning order is desired than is afforded by this algorithm. Unlike with one-dimensional text, it is not easy to anticipate in a two- or n-dimensional world exactly what orderings will seem most natural to users. It seems clear that for most diagramming languages, for example, interfaces that allow a good deal of flexibility in how users build up diagrams would be preferred over interfaces that insist that users build up diagrams in pre-specified orders that happen to conform, say, to temporal control relations that are reflected in the arcs of the diagrams. Further, many visual languages contain relations that may be symmetric or nontransitive, in which case the Wittenburg (1992a) algorithm is not usable. One set of examples arises with languages whose primitives are directed line segments. Relations between line segments such as head-to-head or tail-to-tail are symmetric, precluding the use of algorithms depending on the intrinsic ordering properties of the relations to direct scanning. Cycles are of course common in diagramming languages supporting control flow to represent control loops, so one may have trouble defining an order based on relations there as well.

In the case of off-line data verification and correction, the size of the input sets involved may preclude bottom-up parsing for efficiency reasons. The following scenario is an example of the problem. Suppose one is verifying that all the line segments that comprise the border of each region in a geospatial database in fact enclose that region and that any attributes of the data are in conformance. One approach is to define grammars that independently combine the line segments surrounding each region to yield a closed polygon of some form. But blind bottom-up parsing would take each and every line segment to be the start of the polygon constituent, rebuilding it many, many times over. In geographical data sets such as the U.S. Census Bureau's Tiger database, the number of line segments representing the border of a single state typically reaches into the thousands. It is not hard to see that such a redundant algorithm would be ill-advised. Not only is it inefficient, but the problem of error detection is, at least on the face of it, made more difficult than if the parsing enumeration were systematically ordered and based on systematic prediction.

The goal addressed in this work is to design a predictive, Earley-style algorithm for Relational Grammars without relying on the relations themselves to provide scanning orderings. Such an algorithm allows predictive parsing methods to be employed with higher-dimensional languages whose relational graphs contain cycles, i.e., one or more of the relations are not partial orders. To design such an algorithm requires solving the problem of finding a start element for the parser to begin its predict and scan operations. The Wittenburg (1992a) algorithm uses minimal elements of the relations to initialize the parser at possibly multiple starting positions. The goal here is to allow the parser to start with a single arbitrary member of the input set and still guarantee completeness.

The remainder of this chapter is structured as follows. First, a Relational Grammar subclass is defined that includes unordered languages. This definition is a refinement of a class of Relational Grammars first proposed in Wittenburg et al. (1991) and a superclass of Fringe Relational Grammars defined in Wittenburg (1992a). An Earley-style parsing algorithm and example trace are presented next. The conclusion includes remarks regarding the extensions to this work necessary to fully solve the problems of incremental, predictive parsing for higher-dimensional languages.

2. ATOMIC RELATIONAL GRAMMARS

While productions for string-based grammars implictly assume string adjacency as a relation among right-hand-side rule elements, Relational Grammar productions must explicitly state relations between elements.

Example 1.

Subtree → prim Row
    (below 2 1)
    (centered-in-x 1 2)

Example 1 shows a defining form for a rule fragment that states that a Subtree can expand to (or be reduced from) two objects of type prim and

Row, as long as they stand in the stated *below* and *centered-in-x* relations. The integers in the textual rule definition act as references to rule elements: the left-hand-side of a rule is conventionally referenced as 0; the one or more right-hand-side elements are referenced 1...n in the order in which they appear in the definition. A relational constraint such as *(below 2 1)* is to be interpreted as a requirement that the object matching rule element 2 (of type Row in this case) must stand in the *below* relation to the object matching rule element 1 (of type prim).

During parsing, relational constraints either have the effect of generating possible candidates for rule element matches or filtering candidate matches that have been proposed. We call the generating relations *expander* relations. They must be binary, and the parser will execute a query based on these relational expressions as it explores candidates to match rule elements. For example, the query *(below :? i)* would be executed when matching rule the rule in Example 1 in order to expand the match to the second right-hand-side element, assuming *i* is an index to the input matching the first right-hand-side element. On the other hand, one might want to include further relational constraints (of any arity). A parser would execute such constraints as predicates. In Example 1, *(centered-in-x 1 2)* would likely be executed as a predicate.

Figure 1 shows a graphical depiction of the rule in Example 1 in which composition is represented as spatial enclosure. Thus one sees that the Subtree object is composed of the prim and Row objects. The arrows represent the required spatial relations.

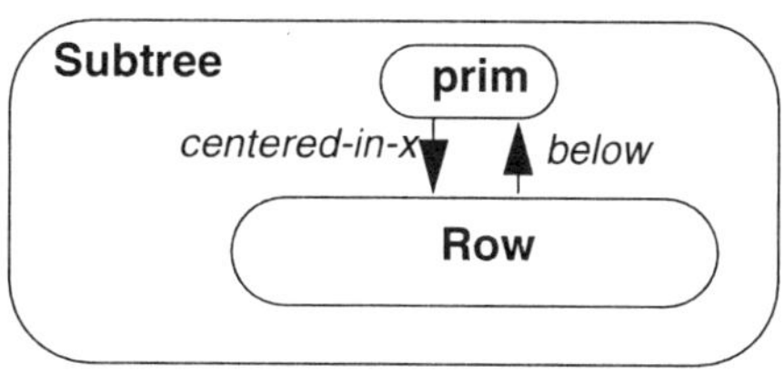

Figure 1. A simple layout rule

Despite our referencing convention, the right-hand-side elements of RG rules are unordered — what really matters are the relational constraints, which may only partially determine the order in which a parser matches the rule elements. However, our approach is to assume that a grammar compiling operation produces an expanded rule set that is ordered, given an initial set of rule definitions that may be unordered. This is because a parser is going to have to match rule elements in some order or other. In bottom-up parsing, it is possible to choose only a single ordering of the right-hand-side elements of each production. Wittenburg et al. (1991) discuss the constraints in choosing such an ordering. The following constraint, which we refer to as the connectedness constraint, must hold of an order for right-hand-side rule elements in RGs:

Restriction 1. For an ordering of rhs rule elements $D_1 \ldots D_n$, there must exist at least one expander constraint between each element D_j, $1 < j$, and an element D_i where $i < j$.

That is, considered as a graph with the expander relations as arcs and the rule elements as nodes, the right-hand-side of a rule must be connected and, when ordered, each element in turn must be connected to some other element earlier in the ordering. This requirement implies that this class of Relational Grammars can generate only connected relation graphs since, for every production, we assume that there is at least one ordering that meets this condition. Since the expander constraints are going to provide the parser with a query function that can find the candidates to combine with next at each step, this restriction ensures that an expander query can fire at each stage in the rule match. Once an ordering is found, a grammar compiler can place an expander or predicate expression with the first rule element in which all the arguments of the relational expression will be bound.[1]

A definition useful in subsequent sections on parsing follows:

Definition 1. We know, given Restriction 1, that for every ordered production, an expander constraint of the form $(rel\ x\ y)$ must exist for every ordered daughter at position $j > 1$ where either x or y will be grounded by matching a daughter at position j and either x or y (whichever doesn't satisfy this previous condition) is already grounded by a daughter at a position $i < j$. These arguments are defined as the to-be-bound argument and the already-bound argument, respectively, at position j.

A fundamental issue in Relational Grammar representation is whether to allow nonterminals to appear as direct arguments to relational constraints. The natural interpretation of a nonterminal in such a constraint is that it is a reference to the set of input objects in its derivational yield. Let us presume a grammar having the rule in Example 1 has other rules expanding the nonterminal category Row in such a way that a bottom-up parser can build up a horizontally aligned set of primitive objects. Consider the effect of executing the query *(below :? i)* assuming that i is a reference

[1] Ordering the constraints in a grammar compiling operation as discussed here obviates the need for residuation in unification operations, the basis for the unification extensions discussed in Wittenburg (1993).

to an input element matching the category prim. If this query is executed against the original input only, it will never find a Row object since the existence of such an object is an artifact of parsing. A solution to this problem requires dynamic updating of what we call an object store, which starts out as a collection of input objects. Composite objects are introduced as the parser finds them through rule matches. A grammar thus must define derived nonterminal objects in terms of terminal objects. For example, if input data is characterized as rectangular regions (which is reasonable for many graphical applications), then composites introduced through rule matches might be defined as the summation of the rectangular regions of the rule's daughters and added to the object store during parsing.

Including relational constraints directly on composites is reasonable when using bottom-up parsing, but it complicates the definition of Relational Grammars as generative systems since the composition-of relation must in principle be reversible. Further, significant problems are introduced for Earley-style parsing, or any other form of predictive parsing, as discussed in Wittenburg (1992a). The alternative is to write grammars that state relational constraints only on individuals in the input set and use feature percolation to pass up bindings of these individuals as attribute values in derivations. We will refer to this latter subclass of Relational Grammars as Atomic Relational Grammars (ARGs), noting that the most significant restriction is that the arguments of relational constraints must be atomic.

As an illustration, consider Example 2, the rule set of a flowchart grammar fragment. The start symbol for this grammar is Flowchart.

Example 2: Flowchart Grammar.

```
Flowchart:
    Flowchart → oval P-block oval
        (connects-to 1 (in 2))
        (connects-to (out 2) 3)
        (in 0) = 1
        (out 0) = 3
Conditional:
    P-block → diamond P-block circle
        (Y-connects-to 1 (in 2))
        (connects-to (out 2) 3)
        (N-connects-to 1 3)
        (in 0) = 1
        (out 0) = 3
Basic-p-block:
    P-block → rectangle
        (in 0) = 1
        (out 0) = 1
```

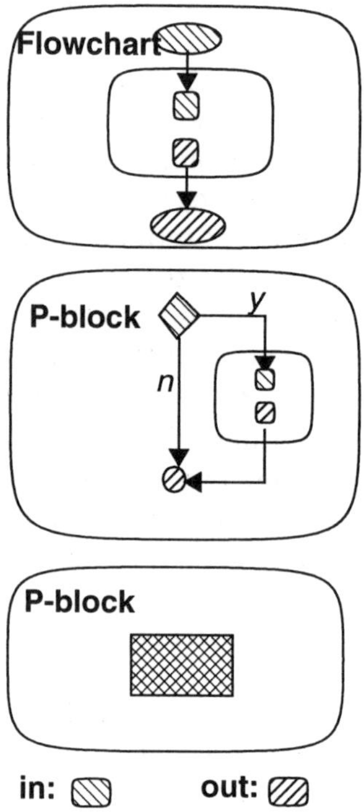

Figure 2. Graphical views of flowchart productions

A graphical depiction of each rule is shown in Figure 2. A visual indication that the relational constraints do not hold of composite sets directly is that the arcs (representing relations) cross the enclosing perimeters of nonterminal objects. All constraints in this example are relations on individual members of the input set. Consider, for example, the relational constraint *(connects-to 1 (in 2))* appearing in rule Flowchart. The first argument, *1* , is a direct reference to a terminal object with lexical type oval. The second argument, *(in 2)* , is an indirect reference to the value of the in attribute of an object of (nonterminal) type P-block. This attributed value will eventually be replaced by an index to a terminal object in a successful derivation.

Definition 2. We call the set of attributes *expander attributes* that appear in any of the arguments to expander relations in a grammar.

In Flowchart Grammar, *in* and *out* are both expander attributes. In fact, there are only expander attributes included in this example, but we make note that other attributes may be utilized in the full formalism.

To ensure that relational arguments eventually ground out, the rules must percolate references to individual members of the input as feature values from the right-hand-side of each rule to its left-hand-side. We use forms such as $(attr_x\ 0) = (attr_y\ i)$ to represent feature percolation. The are intended to be operationally equivalent to feature assignment functions in attribute grammars. Unlike general attribute passing, however, we assume equality as the only relation between values in feature percolation.[2]

We propose the following restriction for Atomic Relational Grammar productions, whose utility will become most evident when we consider the parsing algorithm later in this chapter:

Restriction 2. Each ARG production must percolate a value for every expander attribute used in the grammar.

In the grammar of Example 2 we can see that this condition is met since *in* and *out* are the only expander attributes used in the grammar and every production associates the value of each of these attributes in its left-hand-side with some value on its right-hand-side. An important link in this chain is in evidence in the rule Basic-p-block, where the values of features *in* and *out* are linked directly to terminal input, in this case, an individual input object of lexical category rectangle.

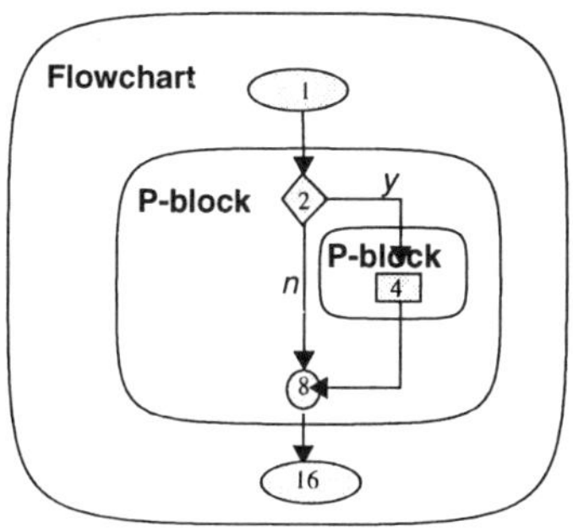

Figure 3. A derivation

A visual representation of a derivation is shown in Figure 3. The input set is indicated as filled shapes indexed by integers representing binary numbers. Relations between input elements are graphed as arcs. The visual convention in evidence here—dominance represented with nonterminal symbols labeling enclosing shapes—is an effective means of conveying the fact that, unlike the derivation trees of context-free string grammars, the equivalence class on derivations for these grammars is defined with trees whose daughter nodes are unordered.

[2]For attributes other than expander attributes, relationships between attribute values may involve function evaluation. See Wittenburg (1992b; 1993).

For the remainder of this chapter, we simplify the exposition by ignoring the role of any relational constraints and attributes other than expander relations (which are binary) and expander attributes. The expressions generable or recognizable by Relational Grammars are defined as follows.

Definition 3. An *indexed multidimensional multiset (indexed md-set)* $\mathcal{C}$ is an n-tuple $(I, R_1 \ldots R_n)$ such that $R_1 \ldots R_n$ are binary relations on the indexed multiset of symbols I.

An index here is a one-to-one and onto function from the set of integers to members of the multiset. In productions, the indexing will be based on string position in rule definitions; our implementations make use of indexing based on integers representing values in binary (to optimize set operations). We will sometimes ignore the indices in the exposition that follows when the reference to an individual occurrence of a symbol in the multiset is clear. Also, we will sometimes write an indexed md-set as the set of tuples $\{(r_i\ x_a\ x_b), (r_j\ x_c\ x_d) \ldots (r_n\ x_e\ x_f)\}$ where each r_i is a symbol indicating the relation in position i of $R_1 \ldots R_n$ and each $x_\alpha \in$ I.

Definition 4. An Atomic Relational Grammar (ARG) is a 6-tuple $\mathcal{G} = (N, \Sigma, S, R_e, \Gamma, P)$ where

1. N is a finite set of nonterminal symbols.
2. Σ is a finite set of terminal symbols, disjoint from N.
3. S is a distinguished symbol in N called the start symbol.
4. R_e is a finite set of relation symbols called the expander relation symbols.
5. Γ is a finite set of expander attribute symbols.
6. P is a finite set of productions of the form $A \rightarrow \alpha/\beta/F$, where

   $A \in N$;

   $\alpha \in (n \mid \sigma)^+$ where $n \in N, \sigma \in \Sigma$;

   β is a set of constraints of the form $(r_e x\ y)$ where $r_e \in R_e$ and x, y are either integers referencing a member of α or else an expression of the form $(\gamma\ i)$ where $\gamma \in \Gamma$ and i is an integer referencing a member of α. Further, at least one ordering of α meets Restriction 1;

   F is a set of feature assignment statements of the form $(\gamma\ \ 0) = x$ where $\gamma \in \Gamma$ and x is either an integer referencing a member of α or an expression of the form $(\gamma\ i)$ as above. Further, there must be exactly one feature assignment statement $(\gamma_i\ \ 0) = x$ for each $\gamma_i \in \Gamma$ (Restriction 2).

Definition 5. The immediately derives relation '$\Longrightarrow$' is defined over md-sets: Md-set $(I_1, R_1 \ldots R_n) \Longrightarrow (I_2, R_1{\prime} \ldots R_n{\prime})$ if there is production $p = A \rightarrow \alpha/\beta/F$ such that $A \in I_1$ and I_2 is equal to I_1 except for the replacement of a single occurrence of A with the elements of α and $R_1{\prime} \ldots R_n{\prime}$ is equal to $R_1 \ldots R_n$ except for the addition of relational tupes $(r_e\ x\ y)$ in β and the replacement of all arguments of relational tuples as directed by the substitutions in F.

Definition 6. Given a relational grammar $\mathcal{G} = (N, \Sigma, S, R_e, \Gamma, P)$, $(I_j, R_1 \ldots R_n)$ is a sentential form of $\mathcal{G}$ if there exists a derivation $(\{S\}, \emptyset) \Longrightarrow (I_i, R_1 \ldots R_n) \Longrightarrow \ldots \Longrightarrow (I_j, R_1{\prime} \ldots R_n{\prime})$ such that $I_j \subseteq \Sigma$ and all arguments of relational tuples $R_1{\prime} \ldots R_n{\prime}$ are indices to I_j.

Example 3. The derivation depicted in Figure 3 is: ({Flowchart}, $\emptyset$) $\Longrightarrow$
({oval$_1$, P-block$_1$, oval$_{16}$}, (connects oval$_1$ (in P-block$_1$)), (connects (out P-block$_1$) oval$_{16}$)) $\Longrightarrow$
({oval$_1$, diamond, P-block$_2$, circle, oval$_{16}$}, (connects oval$_1$ diamond), (y-connects diamond (in P-block$_2$)), (n-connects diamond circle), (connects (out P-block$_2$) oval$_{16}$)) $\Longrightarrow$
{(oval$_1$, diamond, rectangle, circle, oval$_{16}$}, (connects oval$_1$ diamond), (y-connects diamond rectangle), (n-connects diamond circle), (connects rectangle oval$_{16}$)).

3. PARSING PRELIMINARIES

The intuitive idea of the Earley parsing algorithm presented in Wittenburg (1992a), much of which will be carried over here, is as follows. The parser is initialized in Earley style with dotted productions expanding root symbols of the grammar at each of the minimal elements of the input. Extended predict, scan, and complete steps carry over from Earley's algorithm, so the parser will build up item sets through enumerations of the nodes of the input relation graph originating at the minimal nodes. Note that no matter where the parser starts in the input, a successful derivation starting from that position will have to visit all the nodes of the input graph at least once. The main goal in designing the algorithm was to minimize the number of enumerations while still ensuring completeness. When two or more enumeration sequences converge, the algorithm is able to detect when a prediction has been made before so that the same prediction (and all items that ensue) don't have to be re-created. In order to be able to absorb the products of a previous prediction into a converging enumeration sequence, a fourth step has to be added to Earley's predict, scan, and complete. It is called inverse-complete. Where complete is given an inactive state and asked to extend active states that end where the inactive state starts, inverse-complete is given an active state and tries to extend it with any inactive states that start where the active state ends.

As suggested in the concluding remarks of Wittenburg (1992a), there is still research to be done to minimize enumeration sequences further. One strategy is look for ways of reducing the number of requisite start points. While we address a different problem in the remainder of this chapter, the solution is relevant to this question since the parser need only initialize its search at a single position.

4. PRELIMINARIES TO A PARSER

Here we present the preliminaries necessary to define an Earley-style algorithm for Atomic Relational Grammars that can be initialized from any start element. As is discussed in the concluding remarks, the parsing algorithm solves only part of the problem for defining incremental, predictive parsing for Relational Grammars, but it is of interest in its own right. We begin with the following observations.

The existence of an Earley predictive state (an active state that covers no input) in a parse table implies that a derivation headed by the nonterminal on the left-hand-side of the dotted rule may "begin" at that positional index. A scanning action is valid, given some positional index, only if the terminal symbol at that position is a valid left-corner of a possible derivation subtree predicted to start at that index. For a parser to adquately predict top-down expansions of the grammar's root symbol from any position in the input and only that position, it follows that every element of any parsable input sets must be a possible left-corner of a valid derivation tree headed by the root symbol. As a condition on a grammar, this implies that for every nonterminal, there must be variants of any production expanding that nonterminal such that any member of its terminal yield can be ordered first in the production's right-hand-side.

Part of our proposal then is to require ordering variants of the right-hand-sides of every production so that every rhs-element appears first in at least one variant. It is not hard to see that such a mechanism carried through will satisfy the any-start requirement. Intuitively, if for any local subtree in a derivation admitted by the base grammar, there exists another derivation subtree reordered such that an arbitrary rhs-element appears first, then, by induction, any derivation tree can be transformed by a series of local reorderings such that an arbitrary terminal node appears as a left-corner in at least one (other) derivation tree.

Then there is the question of remaining ordering variations once a parser has chosen a start position. Note here that it is *not* a requirement that once the parser has chosen its first element, that the next choice for scanning may arbitrarily be any of the remaining input elements. A natural requisite for ordering variants once the algorithm has been initialized at a start position is to allow for any variations of input elements that are connected through some relation to the input already scanned. Such an approach would be consistent with the parsing algorithms discussed previously since queries formed from relational constraints could serve as the basis for expanding rule matches. To fully realize even this set of ordering variations would require extensions beyond the scope of the present chapter, however. Here we concentrate on the problem of an arbitrary starting point and choose to direct the parser to scan remaining input nondeterministically in orders (not necessarily all orders) consistent with the connectedness constraint just mentioned. A simple extension allows for all connected ordering variations within local rules.

In Wittenburg (1992a), the predict subroutine makes use of the function F-permute to find all candidate rules for prediction. This function maps from an expander attribute and a predicted nonterminal to rule variants appropriately ordered that can expand that nonterminal. Appropriately ordered here implies that the production can provide a possible percolation path such that, as the left-branch of an eventual derivation subtree bottoms out, terminal elements scanned at that position can ground the value of the expander attribute used in prediction. To get an intuitive grasp of this relationship of percolation paths and prediction, consider again the input in Figure 3 with the grammar in Example 2. Assume that an Earley-style parser has scanned the topmost oval, indexed as 1 in the figure. This would imply the existence of an item that incorporated an ordered, dotted variant of the rule Flowchart shown here.

```
Flow -> start . P-block end
    (connects-to 1 (in 2))
    (connects-to (out 2) 3)
    (in 0) = 1
    (out 0) = 3
```

Note now that the expander constraint (connects-to 1 (in 2)) is of relevance in predicting the next input to be scanned. Given just this item, only those input elements that are candidates to bind the in attribute of a P-block constituent need be considered. In particular, we need not consider ordering variants of P-block rules in which the initial right-hand-side element cannot serve to bind this attribute. These observations lead us to the following definition.

Definition 7. A triple $< N, \gamma, p >$, N a nonterminal category, γ an expander attribute, and p an ordered production of Atomic Relational Grammar $\mathcal{G}$ is in the starts-by-binding relation iff the left-hand-side category of $p = N$ and there exists a feature assignment statement of the form $(\gamma\ 0) = 1$ or $(\gamma\ 0) = (\delta\ 1)$ in P.

The starts-by-binding relation forms the basis for precompiling a Prediction Table. A rule variant in the table indexed by some nonterminal category X and some expander attribute γ implies that the production expands nonterminal X and that there is an assignment of the form $(\gamma\ 0) = \ldots 1 \ldots$ in the feature percolations of that production, i.e., the index of the first right-hand-side element grounds γ if it is a terminal or it carries an attribute whose value is linked to γ if it is a nonterminal.

The derivation of a table representing this relation is in two steps. We first generate rule ordering variants. Here we assume an algorithm that, for each production, forms one ordering variant per right-hand-side element such that the right-hand-side element is ordered first. Ordering the remaining elements is done arbitrarily subject to the connectedness condition in Restriction 1.[3] Step two generates a table representing the starts-by-binding relation in the grammar and, in addition, we include in the table the special "attribute" start, whose entry includes a set of rule variants such that for each production expanding that nonterminal category, there is at least one variant ordering each right-hand-side element first, regardless of feature percolations.

Example 4 shows the Atomic Relational Grammar appearing previously in Example 2 with the addition of named ordering variants for non-unary productions. The ordering variants are indicated, again, by integers referring to the positions of right-hand-side elements in the context- free backbone part of each rule.

Example 4: Extended Flowchart grammar.

```
Flowchart
    Flowchart -> oval P-block oval
    (connects-to 1 (in 2))
    (connects-to (out 2) 3)
    (in 0) = 1
    (out 0) = 3

    Ordering variants:
    flowchart-1 <1, 2, 3>
    flowchart-2 <3, 2, 1>
    flowchart-3 <2, 1, 3>

Conditional
    P-block -> diamond P-block circle
```

[3]If a scanning algorithm is desired that will allow for all orderings consistent with Restriction 1, then more variants can simply be produced here.

```
    (Y-connects-to 1 (in 2))
    (connects-to (out 2) 3)
    (N-connects-to 1 3)
    (in 0) = 1
    (out 0) = 3

    Ordering variants:
    conditional-1 <1, 2, 3>
    conditional-2 <3, 2, 1>
    conditional-3 <2, 1, 3>

Basic-p-block
    P-block -> rectangle
    (in 0) = 1
    (out 0) = 1
```

TABLE 1. Flowchart-grammar Prediction Table

Nonterm	**Expander Attribute**	**Production Variant**
Flow	in	flowchart-1
	out	flowchart-2
	start	flowchart-1 flowchart-2 flowchart-3
P-block	in	conditional-1 basic-p-block
	out	conditional-2 basic-p-block
	start	conditional-1 conditional-2 conditional-3 basic-p-block

Table 1 shows a Prediction Table for the grammar in Example 4. We assume the existence of a function starts-by-binding(N, γ) that for some Atomic Relational Grammar $\mathcal{G}$ returns the set of production variants in the Prediction Table at nonterminal N and attribute γ.

Definition 8. The first-attrs of an ordered production p in Atomic Relational Grammar $\mathcal{G}$ is $\{\delta \mid$ there exists an assignment statement $(\gamma\ 0) = (\delta\ 1)$ in $p\}$.

For example, the first-attrs of ordered production conditional-1 is the set $\{\}$. The first-attrs of ordered production basic-p-block is the set $\{$in out$\}$. The first-attrs of a production are those expander attributes associated with the first rhs element of a production that provide bindings for expander attributes in the left-hand-side. They are used in the recursive predict step of the Earley-style algorithm to follow.

5. EARLEY-STYLE RECOGNITION FOR ARGS

We now turn to an Earley-style algorithm for the full class of Atomic Relational Grammars in which the starting position is arbitrary. We will summarize the essential points here, and confine our attention to a recognition algorithm.

First we define the states, or items, used in a parse table given an indexed md-set $\mathcal{C}$. Inactive states are representative of completely matched rules and thus they include a category as well as the feature values assocated with the rule's left-hand-side.

Definition 9. Inactive states relative to an indexed md-set $\mathcal{C} = (I, R_1, .., R_n)$ are a triple $[cat, f, c]$ where *cat* is a nonterminal or terminal symbol, f is a vector of features (especially, the set of expander attributes), and c is an integer (a logical bit vector) representing a subset of I (the state's terminal yield, or *cover*).

Inactive states will be indexed in the parse table by the values of an expander attributes appearing in f (all of which must be indices to individual occurrences of input elements). Intuitively, we consider inactive states to begin as well as end at every terminal that is bound by an expander attribute. However, this parser doesn't make the distinction between beginning and ending so we need only a single indexing array.

We next turn to active states, which represent partially matched or unmatched rules. We assume the Earley algorithm convention of a set of dotted productions, with the dot representing a position in the ordered right-hand-side elements.

Definition 10. Active states are a triple $[p, i, (d_1 \ldots d_n)]$ where p is a production; i, the Earley positional dot, is an integer ranging from 1 to the length of the right-hand-side of p representing the next daughter to match; and $(d_1 \ldots d_n)$ is an ordered list of pointers to inactive states of daughters matched so far.

The cover, or terminal yield, of an active state is derivable from the covers of the inactive states that have already been matched.

Definition 11. The cover of an active state $[p, i, (d_1 \ldots d_n)]$ is defined to be the union of the covers of the inactive states $(d_1 \ldots d_n)$.

As with inactive states, active states are indexed by individual members of the input set I. The intuition is that active states are indexed by individuals in the input that are candidates to be used in the next advancement of that active state. For any daughters but the first, one can make use of the expander constraint at that positional dot to find such candidates. For active states that have not yet matched any daughters, their input indices are derived from higher predictions, initialized with the input element at the starting position.[4]

The following definition is useful in the recursive predict step of the Earley-style algorithm. It is necessary to pick out the expander attributes that can acquire bindings through matching the next daughter.

Definition 12. The to-be-bound-attrs of an active state $s = [p, i, (d_1, .., d_n)]$ are defined to be first-attrs(p) if $i = 1$, else $\{\gamma \mid \gamma$ is the attribute of the to-be-bound argument of the expander constraint at position $i\}$.

Agenda items are defined next.

Definition 10. An agenda item is a pair [state, keys] where state is an active or inactive state and keys is a set of state indices (to individuals in I of an md-set $\mathcal{C}$).

Agenda items represent states and their indices relative to some input. As in chart parsing, the agenda will hold a list of items to be potentially added to the parse table. There is flexibility in its management. Here we assume a FIFO queue.

Procedure 1. `Advance(a-state, i-state, a-index)`

Input: An active-state a-state $= [p, i, (d_1, \ldots d_n)]$, and an inactive-state i-state $= [\text{cat}, f, c]$.[5]

Output: A list of agenda items, possibly null, that are the result of advancing `a-state` with `i-state`.

[4]In the bottom-up algorithm of Wittenburg et al. (1991), active states were indexed by the already-bound argument. The change is necessary to make indexing of predictive states (which have no cover, and thus no bound argument) consistent with the indexing of other active states.

[5]A variant of this procedure must also accommodate input items directly in place of the inactive-state argument when called by the scan procedure. It is straightforward to form a (transient) inactive state from an input item.

Method:

Case 1: If i = length of rhs of p (new state will be inactive), then let c' = union-covers$((d_1 \ldots d_n), c)$ and let f' = percolate$(p, (d_1, .., d_n), c, f)$. Return an agenda item [i – state′ = [cat′, f', c'], keys] where cat′ = lhs of p and keys is the list of inactive state indices of i-state′.

Case 2: (New state will be active.) Let a-state′ = $[p, i+1, c' = (d_1, .., d_n, c)]$. Let e = expander-at-position$(p, i+1)$. Let q = query(expander, c', Q). If q is non-null, return an agenda item [a – state′, q].

The advance procedure is called by scan, complete, and inverse-complete, to be defined shortly. As we have pointed out, active states are indexed at an element in the terminal yield of any potential next daughters to be matched (rather than the last one to have been matched), so they will be added to the parse table only if some tuple in the required relation can be shown to exist in the input. This question is satisfied by a call of the form query(expander, c', Q). Here we assume that given an expander constraint and the daughters matched so far, a subroutine can dereference the arguments to the expander constraint, binding the already-bound one, and then execute a query that will return the members of the input that can bind the to-be-bound argument.

Algorithm 1. Membership in L(ARG)

Input: An Atomic Relational Grammar $\mathcal{G} = (N, \Sigma, S, R_e, \Gamma, P)$, an indexed multidimensional set $\mathcal{C} = (I, R_1 \ldots R_n)$, and a starting element q that is an arbitrary member of I.

Output: A parse table of state sets S_j.

Auxiliary data structures:

Agenda: a FIFO list of states to process, initially null.

Init-states: the set of starting predictive states, initialized as follows: For every p in starts-by-binding(S, start), add a state $[p, 1, \emptyset]$ to init-states. For every state $s = [p', 1, \emptyset]$ in init-states, if the rhs symbol x at rhs position 1 of p' is a nonterminal, then let init-states = union(init-states, starts-by-binding(x, start)).

Parse table: a hash table of state sets S_j, where j is an individual index in I.

Method: We initialize as follows:

- For every s in init-states, add an agenda item $[s, \{q\}]$ to the Agenda.

- Until Agenda is empty, do:
  - Remove one item = [state, keys] from Agenda.
  - For k in keys, if an equivalent state is not already at S_k, add state at S_k. Then do:

    Scanner: If state = $[p, i, (d_1 \ldots d_n)]$ at k is active and the rhs symbol x at position i of p is terminal, if the terminal symbol of input item = y at k matches x and k does not intersect cover(state), then add any item in advance(state, y, k) to Agenda.

    Predictor: If state = $[p, i, (d_1 \ldots d_n)]$ is active and the rhs symbol X at position i of p is a nonterminal, then for every attribute a in to-be-bound-attrs(state), for every production p' in starts-by-binding(X, a), add item [state$'$ = $[p', 1, \text{null}], k]$ to Agenda.

    Completer: If state = $[\text{cat}, f, c]$ is inactive, then for every a-state = $[p, i, (d_1 \ldots d_n)]$ in union$(S_k, \text{init} - \text{states})$, if cat matches the rhs symbol at position i of p, the intersection of c and cover(a-state) is null, and k satisfies the expander constraint at position i of p, then add any item in advance(a-state, state, k) to Agenda.

    Inverse-completer: If state $[p, i, (d_1 \ldots d_n)]$ is active, then for every i-state = $[cat, f, c']$ at S_k, if cat matches the symbol at position i of p, the intersection of cover(state) and c' is null, and k satisfies the expander constraint at position i of p, then add any item in advance(a-state, state, k) to Agenda.
- If there is an inactive state of the form $[X, f, u]$ in the parse table such that X = S and $u = I$, then succeed. Else fail.

6. PARSE TRACE

The following trace of a parsing run uses the grammar from Example 4 together with the input shown in Figure 3. This trace picks the rectangle, indexed as 4, as the start element. Each step of the trace represents a state added to the table and includes the following information:

- <dotted-rule> or <category / feature vector>,
- <cover>,
- <indices>, and
- <source>.

Active and predictive states show the rule-name and dotted production in the form [<rule-name>: <dotted-rule>]. Inactive state categories and feature vectors are shown as $\#S(\langle cat\rangle : \langle feat_1\rangle\langle feat_n\rangle\langle val_n\rangle)$. The <cover> is shown as an integer representing a logical bit vector. For example, 15 represents the logical bit vector 1111, which in turn is the union of items indexed with integers 1, 2, 4, and 8. <Indices> is a list of input covers by which the inactive or active state is indexed in the parse table. The <source> information explains which subroutine produced the state.

1. [flowchart-2: Flow -> . P-block start end], 0, (4), init.
2. [flowchart-3: Flow -> . end P-block start], 0, (4), init.
3. [flowchart-1: Flow -> . start P-block end], 0, (4), init.
4. [conditional-1: P-block -> . decision P-block junction], 0, (4), init.
5. [conditional-3: P-block -> . junction P-block decision], 0, (4), init.
6. [conditional-2: P-block -> . P-block decision junction], 0, (4), init.
7. [basic-p-block: P-block -> . procedure], 0, (4), init.
8. #S(P-block :in 4 :out 4), 4, (4), scan 7.
9. [conditional-2: P-block -> P-block . decision junction], 4, (2), complete 6 with 8.
10. [conditional-2: P-block -> P-block decision . junction], 6, (8), scan 9.
11. #S(P-block :in 2 :out 8), 14, (8 2), scan 10.
12. [flowchart-2: Flow -> P-block . start end], 14, (1), complete 1 with 11.
13. [flowchart-2: Flow -> P-block start . end], 15, (16), scan 12.
14. #S(Flow :in 1 :out 16), 31, (16 1), scan 13.

The careful reader may wonder why this trace does not include all states one might suppose would be generated by an Earley-style algorithm. For example, why does state 8 not combine through a complete operation with state 1? The answer is that although the initial conditions for such an advancement are met, there is no possible index for the resulting active state. Recall that active states are indexed by the candidates that are potentially able to match the next daughter, and in this case there are no such candidates.

7. CONCLUSION

The algorithm presented here is the first predictive, Earley-style algorithm that we know of for the full class of Atomic Relational Grammars. This class of grammars appears to be widely useful and is easily implemented through unification-based approaches; more specialized implementations closer in spirit to attribute grammars are also afforded. An attribute-style implementation has been done at Bellcore that is an extension to the code documented in Wittenburg (1992b), and it has been applied to problems described in the introduction.

Although the Earley-style algorithm presented here is of interest in its own right, there are remaining issues in exploring incremental, predictive parsing of visual language interfaces. To carry out the goal of providing an analogue of command completion in visual language interfaces requires at least two extensions beyond the work reported on here. First, more variations in scanning order are likely to be desired than what can be provided for here. Note that with the current algorithm, the ordering variants relative to a single global scanning order are restricted to local permutations within rules. What may be desired is the multidimensional analogue of predictive parsing of free-word-order languages that can scramble not only within grammatical constituents but also across constituents (subject to the connectness constraint). Further, algorithms more akin to island-based parsing (from a single island out) are likely to be preferable for interface parsing than an Earley-style algorithm. Note that by following all permitted scanning orders reachable from a given start position, the Earley-style algorithm expands multiple islands in parallel, each of which may cover only part of the input globally processed so far.

Finally, a few short remarks on related literature. In the theoretical graph grammar literature, there have been recent results suggesting a natural class for a useful and general class of graph grammars, namely, context-free hypergraph grammars of bounded degree (Englefreit, 1992). An interesting line of research would be to investigate the relationship between Atomic Relational Grammars and Hypergraph grammars. The role of features and percolation in Atomic Relational Grammars seems to be quite similar to hyperedges and hyperedge replacement in Hypergraph Grammars. Elsewhere in the graph grammar literature, an active chart parsing algorithm for flowgraphs has been proposed (Lutz, 1989; Wills 1990) that is related to the parsing algorithm discussed here and in Wittenburg et al. (1991). Again, the exact relationship between flowgraphs and Atomic Relational Languages is worthy of investigation.

The most closely related parsing algorithms from the visual language literature are to be found in Tomita (1990) and Costagliola and Chang (1991), both of which extend Earley-style parsing into multidimensional domains. Although there is commonality at the level of parsing subroutines, indexing methods differ substantively. These differences arise in part because of different assumptions regarding the nature of the language expressions handled by the grammar formalisms. Both these other proposals assume that the input is held in a grid of some kind with elements of equal size. Relations are defined accordingly. There are no such assumptions here. Costagliola and his collaborators have also been extending LR algorithms to a class of grammars called Positional Grammars (Costagliola et al., 1991; Costagliola 1993). As in the present chapter, Costagliola (1993) addresses the issue of ordering a parser from an arbitrary starting position. The question of whether LR techniques such as his can be extended to the more general class of Relational Languages will be clarified in future work.

Acknowledgements

This research was carried out in the Bellcore Computer Graphics and Interactive Media research group, directed at the time by Jim Hollan. Thanks to Steve Abney, Bernard Lang, David Weir, and Louis Weitzman for discussions related to the topic of this chapter.

References

Costagliola, G. (1993) (Pictorial) LR Parsing from an Arbitrary Starting Point. *Proc. IWPT-93, Third International Workshop on Parsing Technologies*, Tilburg, The Netherlands and Durbuy, Belgium, August 1993, 49–59.

Costagliola, G., and Chang, S.K. (1991) Parsing 2-D Languages with Positional Grammars. *Proc. IWPT-91, Second International Workshop on Parsing Technologies*, Pittsburgh, Pennsylvania, February 1991, 235–243.

Costagliola, G., Tomita, M., and Chang, S.K. (1991) A Generalized Parser for 2-D Languages.*Proc. IEEE Workshop on Visual Languages*, Kobe, Japan, October 1991, 98–104.

Crimi, C., Guercio, A., Nota, G., Pacini, G., Tortora, G., and Tucci, M. (1991) Relation Grammars and their Application to Multi-dimensional Languages. *Journal of Visual Languages and Computing*, Vol. 2 no. 4, 333–346.

Earley, J. (1970) An Efficient Context-Free Parsing Algorithm. *Communications of the ACM*, Vol. 13, 94–102.

Ehrig, H., Kreowski, J., Rozenberg, G. (eds.) (1991) *Graph Grammars and Their Application to Computer Science: 4th International Workshop*, Bremen, Germany, March 1990, Lecture Notes in Computer Science 532, Springer-Verlag.

Engelfreit, J. (1992) A Greibach Normal Form for Context-free Graph Grammars. In: W. Kuich (ed.): *Automata, Languages and Programming: 19th International Colloquium*, Wien, Austria, July 1991, Lecture Notes on Computer Science 623, Springer-Verlag, 138–149.

Ferrucci, F., Pacini, G., Tortora, G., Tucci, M., and Vitiello, G. (1991) Efficient Parsing of Multidimensional Structures. *Proc. IEEE Workshop on Visual Languages*, Kobe, Japan, October 1991, 104–110.

Flasinski, M. (1988) Parsing of edNLC-Graph Grammars for Scene Analysis. *Pattern*

Recognition, Vol. 21, 623–629.

Flasinski, M. (1989) Characteristics of edNLC-Graph Grammar for Syntactic Pattern Recognition. *Computer Vision, Graphics, and Image Processing*, Vol. 47, 1–21.

Golin, E. J. (1991) Parsing Visual Languages with Picture Layout Grammars. *Journal of Visual Languages and Computing*, Vol. 2, 371–393.

Golin, E.J., and Reiss, S.P. (1990) The Specification of Visual Language Syntax. *Journal of Visual Languages and Computing* Vol. 1, 141–157.

Lutz, R. (1989) Chart Parsing of Flowgraphs. *Proc. 11th International Joint Conference on Artificial Intelligence*, Los Altos, California, 116–121.

Helm, R., and Marriott, K. (1986) Declarative Graphics. *Proc. Third International Conference on Logic Programming*, Lecture Notes in Computer Science 225, Springer-Verlag, 513–527.

Helm, R., and Marriott, K. (1990) A Declarative Specification and Semantics for Visual Languages. *Journal of Visual Languages and Computing*, Vol. 2 no. 4, 311–331.

Tomita, M. (1990) The Generalized LR Parser/Compiler V8-4: A Software Package for Practical NL Projects. *Proc. COLING-90*, Volume 1, 59–63.

Tomita, M. (1991) Parsing 2-Dimensional Language. In: M. Tomita (ed.) *Current Issues in Parsing Technology*, Kluwer Academic Publishers, Dordrecht, 277–289.

Weitzman, L., and Wittenburg, K. (1993) Relational Grammars for Interactive Design. *Proc. 1993 IEEE/CS Symposium on Visual Languages*, Bergen, Norway, August 1993, 4–11.

Wills, L. (1990) Automated Program Recognition: A Feasibility Demonstration. *Artificial Intelligence*, Vol. 45, 113–171.

Wittenburg, K., Weitzman, L., and Talley, J. (1991) Unification-Based Grammars and Tabular Parsing for Graphical Languages. *Journal of Visual Languages and Computing*, Vol. 2 no. 4, 347–370.

Wittenburg, K. (1992a) Earley-style Parsing for Relational Grammars. *Proc. 1992 IEEE Workshop on Visual Languages*, Seattle, Washington, September 1992, 192–199.

Wittenburg, K. (1992b) The Relational Language System. Bellcore Technical Memorandum TM-ARH-022353, Morristown, New Jersey, USA.

Wittenburg, K. (1993) F-PATR: Functional Constraints for Unification-based Grammars. *Proc. 31st Annual Meeting of the Association for Computational Linguistics*, Columbus, Ohio, June 1993, 216–223.

INDEX

U

V

W

Y